RIOTS, POGROMS, JIHAD

RIOTS, POGROMS, JIHAD

Religious Violence in Indonesia

JOHN T. SIDEL

CORNELL UNIVERSITY PRESS

Ithaca and London

First published 2006 by Cornell University Press
First printing, Cornell Paperbacks, 2006

Printed in the United States of America

Library of Congress Cataloging-in-Publication Data

Sidel, John Thayer, 1966–
    Riots, pogroms, jihad : religious violence in Indonesia / John T. Sidel.
       p. cm.
    Includes bibliographical references and index.
    ISBN-13: 978-0-8014-4515-6 (cloth : alk. paper)
    ISBN-10: 0-8014-4515-9 (cloth : alk. paper)
    ISBN-13: 978-0-8014-7327-2 (pbk. : alk. paper)
    ISBN-10: 0-8014-7327-6 (pbk. : alk. paper)
    1. Indonesia—Religion. 2. Islam—Indonesia. 3. Violence—Religious aspects—Islam.
4. Terrorism—Religious aspects—Islam. 5. Terrorism—Indonesia. 6. Religion and politics—Indonesia. 7. Ethnic conflict—Indonesia. I. Title.
    BL2112.S56 2006
    363.3209598—dc22
                                                                                2006014486

Cornell University Press strives to use environmentally responsible suppliers and materials to the fullest extent possible in the publishing of its books. Such materials include vegetable-based, low-VOC inks and acid-free papers that are recycled, totally chlorine-free, or partly composed of nonwood fibers. For further information, visit our website at www.cornellpress.cornell.edu.

Cloth printing   10 9 8 7 6 5 4 3 2 1
Paperback printing   10 9 8 7 6 5 4 3 2 1

For my mother,
with affection, gratitude, and hope

Contents

Illustrations

Preface

Over the past decade, the study of religious violence has evolved into a veritable cottage industry. More than a field of academic research, religious violence is now a topic in which U.S. government agencies, international institutions such as the United Nations and the World Bank, and all manner of think tanks and foundations have developed an interest. Understanding religious violence has become not only an intellectual but a political imperative, with analysis geared toward the generation and modification of policies, funding programs, and other forms of intervention.

Indonesia exemplifies this trend. On the one hand, a vast and growing literature has emerged under the auspices of such institutions as the Asia Foundation, the Ford Foundation, the United Nations, and the World Bank to address problems of interreligious tension and conflict there. This literature has not only offered analytical frameworks for mapping and gridding observable patterns of local conflict and violence across the Indonesian archipelago but also promoted the implementation of policies and the allocation of resources to ease tensions and resolve conflicts in localities around the country. The establishment of statistical correlations between patterns of conflict and variation in levels of poverty or social capital has come to serve as the basis for decisions to fund programs for the promotion of economic development and to strengthen "civil society" and "governance" in various parts of Indonesia.

On the other hand, a similarly sizable body of writings has been produced by think tanks and other policy-oriented research outfits based in various Southeast Asian capitals and in key power centers such as Brussels, Canberra, London, and Washington, D.C., to address Islamist terrorism in

Indonesia. These writings have not only identified the groups responsible for terrorist bombings in Indonesia since 2002 but also documented links to Al-Qaeda and traced mobilization, recruitment, and internal transformation over the years. Through these writings, "terrorism experts" have helped government policymakers to prosecute—and, more important, to justify—the War on Terrorism in the region. The study of religious violence in Indonesia, as elsewhere, has become intimately bound up with the exercise of various forms of power.

Riots, Pogroms, Jihad suggests an alternative approach to the study of religious violence, both in the specific context of Indonesia and more broadly. This approach is rooted in a political, institutional, and intellectual tradition very different from the dominant strands of the "religious violence industry" identified above. Politically, the book takes as its premise a critical distance not only on the U.S.-led War on Terrorism but also on those avowedly secular, ecumenical, or religiously tolerant and disinterested institutions that claim to be promoting conflict resolution and multifaith religious coexistence and understanding. Much as critical scholars have shown how the "Holocaust industry" has worked to shape scholarship on European history and Middle Eastern politics to suit particular interests, so is this book intended to undermine the smug liberal notion of a "view from nowhere" in the study of religious violence in Indonesia and beyond. Against the prevailing tendency to pin the blame for religious violence in Indonesia—and elsewhere—on "intolerant," "extremist" Muslims, if not on "fundamentalist" Islam as a belief system, I have tried to show how both the structures and the agency of forces associated with Christianity, secularism, and ecumenicism have been in considerable measure responsible for the broad pattern of religious violence in Indonesia as well as many of its specific episodes.

Riots, Pogroms, Jihad takes a skeptical view of large-scale research projects linked to major funding bodies, government agencies, and other centers of state power. Insofar as this book is part of a broader collective enterprise, it is one staffed by independent scholars with proven commitment to the study of Indonesia (and specific localities therein) and by Indonesian researchers with persistent track records of promoting empowerment, democratization, and social transformation in a country that has long suffered from authoritarian rule and state violence against its citizens. The notes are thus filled with references to the countless anthropologists, human rights activists, and investigative journalists whose work has informed and inspired the writing.

This book's intellectual treatment of religious violence in Indonesia is rooted in the traditions of Southeast Asian studies scholarship and comparative historical sociology. "Religion" is understood here neither as a matter of individual belief nor as a "cultural system," as Clifford Geertz famously argued; rather it is regarded sociologically, as a field structured by its own institutions, authority relations, instilled dispositions (habitus), means of production and accumulation, and representation of symbolic or spiritual capital, as outlined by Pierre Bourdieu. Much as Peter van der Veer has suggested in his writings on the impact of British colonial rule on Hinduism, Islam, and Sikhism in India, I portray the religious field in Indonesia in the light of its specific historical formation dating back to Dutch colonial rule in the archipelago, and of both continuities and shifts in the place of religion in the public sphere and the relations between religious institutions and state power since independence. As I argue, the pattern of linkages between religious denominations, school networks, associational activities, and political parties described in the Netherlands as "pillarization" (*verzuiling*) has been transplanted to Indonesia and redubbed as one of diverse competing streams or currents (*aliran*) in the nation's political and social life. In short, I treat religion comparatively, historically, and sociologically.

From this perspective, the question of religious violence in Indonesia calls for comparative historical and sociological analysis. As my title signals, *Riots, Pogroms, Jihad* takes as its primary question the shifting pattern of religious violence in Indonesia: *riots* in provincial towns and cities in 1995–97, antiwitchcraft campaigns in Java and interreligious *pogroms* in Central Sulawesi and Maluku in 1998–2001, and paramilitary mobilization and terrorist bombings under the sign of "jihad" in 2000–2005. The essential puzzle concerns the shift from one form of religious violence to another, as seen in the varying locations, perpetrators, targets, processes of mobilization, forms of agency, and outcomes associated with each phase. My contribution, then, lies not in original research or analysis of any single specific episode of religious violence but in the provision of a framework for understanding the broad pattern of variation and change in religious violence.

This framework differs markedly from those already developed under the auspices of the "religious violence industry." In contrast with the actor-centered accounts of the "terrorism experts," the stress here is on the powerfully determining effects of historical and sociological context. Shifts within the religious field in Indonesia, and in the position of religion in the broader field of power relations, have prefigured corresponding shifts in the modalities of religious violence. In contrast with the methodological individualism of studies by economists and liberal-pluralist researchers, the sociological context emphasized here is the peculiar nexus of class relations in Indonesian society and the prominent but problematic role of religious institutions and authority relations within this nexus.

In structural terms, each phase of religious violence in Indonesia over the past ten years has been associated with one or more religious hierarchies and the problems that accompanied efforts to assert and maintain religious authority over, and identity among, one or another religious flock (*jemaah*). The provincial town riots of 1995–97, for example, accompanied the effort by elements within the All-Indonesian Association of Islamic Intellectuals (ICMI) to push new claims to represent Islam in Indonesia, and they reflected the tensions, contradictions, and limitations of this initiative. The antiwitchcraft campaigns of 1998–99 likewise came into view as the "traditionalist" Islamic association Nahdlatul Ulama (NU) faced new threats to its established position in areas of rural East and West Java. Similarly, the interreligious pogroms of 1999–2001 unfolded amid rising anxiety, instability, and uncertainty as to the boundaries of authority commanded by local Protestant organizations and their Muslim counterparts in the religiously divided provinces of Central Sulawesi and Maluku. Finally, the Islamist paramilitary mobilization of 2000–2001 and terrorist bombing campaign of 2002–5 were undertaken precisely as the Islamist networks identified with Al-Irsyad, Persatuan Islam, and Dewan Dakwah Islamiyah Indonesia (DDII) began to lose the positions of influence, access, and security within the national political class that they had so painstakingly attained in the 1990s. Each one of these religious hierarchies, it is worth noting, faced challenges and threats not only from external religious enemies but also from the internal tensions, contradictions, and limitations of their own religious authority and capacity to maintain religious identity among their respective *jemaah*. Thus the successive phases of violence emanating from under the broad umbrellas of these religious hierarchies worked—structurally, if not instrumentally—not only to effect an extrusion of internal problems onto religious "Others" but also to reassert the structures and boundaries of religious authority upon those claimed as the followers of their faith.

Riots, Pogroms, Jihad offers an explanation of the pattern of religious violence in Indonesia since 1995 that is self-evidently structuralist—and, in some ways, poststructuralist—in its underpinnings. The upshot is a predictable, and in some measure regrettable, tendency to skirt complex questions surrounding the lived experience—whether of perpetrators, victims, spectators, or other interested parties—within individual episodes of religious violence. This limitation reflects not so much my wholehearted commitment to the relentless gridding exercises of comparative politics, as a confession of my own diffidence and deficiencies in conducting research.

The challenge of credibly reconstructing one or another episode of violence through eyewitness accounts and other ethnographic materials is, if not insurmountable, then certainly beyond my intellectual and interpersonal skills. Yet the extent to which lived experience—and interpretation—of collective violence by individuals is shaped by relations of inequality and power points to the potential value of an analysis of the sociological, political, and discursive context in which it unfolds. To be sure, the difficulty of establishing—and investigating—plausibly relevant counterfactual cases limits the kinds of claims that can be made about the causal significance of context. Yet the tracing of the argument through all the shifting modalities of religious violence—timing, location, perpetrators, targets, mobilization processes, forms of agency, and outcomes—across a ten-year period reveals how powerfully and consistently the conditions identified as necessary—if not sufficient—have exerted a kind of structural determination.

To this end, *Riots, Pogroms, Jihad* draws heavily upon two kinds of sources. On the one hand, the book extensively cites, quotes, and otherwise credits dozens of anthropologists who have conducted ethnographic fieldwork in various parts of Indonesia over the last thirty years. Without the rich ethnographic literature contributed by anthropologists, our appreciation of Indonesian politics and society would be utterly impoverished, and our understanding of religious violence in the country would be dismal indeed. On the other hand, the book extensively cites, quotes, and otherwise credits dozens of Indonesian investigative journalists, human rights activists, and other researchers. This nonscholarly but often quasi-academic Indonesian-language literature constitutes another rich trove of research and writings indispensable for understanding Indonesia and unparalleled in quantity and quality elsewhere in Southeast Asia (to my best knowledge). More than my many months spent in Indonesia over a ten-year period and rather feeble efforts to conduct interviews and other independent inquiries into one or another episode of religious violence in the country, the empirical basis of this book is the work of these other scholars and researchers. In short, *Riots, Pogroms, Jihad* owes much to a broader tradition of independent intellectual production at odds with the commanding heights of the "religious violence industry." Thus although it advances specific arguments about religious violence, it has been written in support—and, in some measure, in celebration—of this independent tradition.

Since the process of researching and writing this book has a long and somewhat tortuous history, I feel obliged to acknowledge not only the debts to various helpful parties accumulated along the way but also the mounting sense of embarrassment that has accompanied the very gradual process of research, writing, and preparing for publication.

The origins of the book date to the mid-1980s, when I began studying the Indonesian language under the tutelage of the legendary linguist Rufus Hendon. My classmates then included such future luminaries as Jeff Hadler (double-majoring in Southeast Asian Studies and Stand-Up Comedy), Jeff Winters (then experimenting with interesting facial hair), and Paul Hutchcroft (my fellow Philippinist interloper). Prominent among our readings were articles selected from the Indonesian weekly magazine *Tempo,* of which I best recall several detailing the so-called Tanjung Priok Incident of September 1984. This incident began with allegations of inflammatory Friday sermons (*khotbah*) at a mosque in the Jakarta harbor area known as Tanjung Priok, defilement of the mosque by members of the security forces, a protest by local residents, and a violent response by the security forces which left dozens, if not hundreds, of casualties in its wake. The months that followed saw both a harsh government crackdown on Islamic activists in various parts of Indonesia and a wave of bombings around the archipelago attributed to shadowy Muslim "extremists."

Subsequent media coverage, trial documents, and investigations by human rights groups sparked my interest in the question of religious violence in Indonesia and shaped my approach to this question in the years to come. Even in the early *Tempo* articles, the image of popular mobilization by poor pious Muslims against a self-evidently secular and Christian-dominated authoritarian regime, and the conspiracy theories tracing government incitement, manipulation, and repression excited my adolescent Orientalist imagination. Thus to this day I remain grateful to Pak Hendon and my fellow classmates not only for my still rather bookish Bahasa *Tempo* but also for my early exposure to these aspects of Indonesian society and politics.

After many years of studying the Philippines, I revived my interest in Indonesia in the mid-1990s while teaching at the School of Oriental and African Studies (SOAS) in London. With research leave from SOAS and a generous research grant from the Committee for South East Asian Studies of the British Academy, I made exploratory trips to Indonesia and then spent the 1997–98 academic year in Surabaya, with occasional side trips to Jakarta. For this period of extended research and for my subsequent sojourns in Indonesia, I am grateful to all concerned. For the encouragement and support of my former colleagues at SOAS—especially Steve Heder, Steve Hopgood, and Julia Strauss, as well as Anne Booth, Ian Brown, Ulrich Kratz, Jonathan Pincus, and Bob Taylor—I am also deeply indebted.

My stay in Surabaya was made possible, productive, and enjoyable by hosts of various kinds. Wawan, Novi, Yufi, and Nia Radjamin took me into their home and shared with me the joys of family life. Hotman Siahaan helped me gain access to the *Surabaya Post* newspaper library, whose staff provided valuable assistance during my long months of reading local newspapers. Dede Oetomo, Pak Joko, Pak Oei, and Agus Sunyoto were all very generous with their time and, in very different ways, with their illuminating insights on Indonesian society and politics. Above all, the guidance, encouragement, and friendship of Arief Djati made all the difference. Many thanks to all these Arek Suroboyo.

Countless trips to Jakarta and elsewhere in Indonesia were also made possible by the kindness and hospitality of many friends. Benny Subianto is certainly at the top of this list, having shared countless contacts, documents, and bits of information, not to mention his own special store of jokes, anecdotes, insights, and expertise on the culinary delights of Jakarta. Other generous hosts and friends in Jakarta and Bandung over the years have included Daniel Ziv, Indraneel Datta, Fridia Sulungbudi, Sarah Maxim, Jeff Hadler, Kumi Sawada, Joshua Barker, and Hans Antlov. Many thanks to them all for their hospitality and friendship, and here in London to my pal Liston Siregar for the same.

The protracted process of writing this book was facilitated by many different parties to whom I also record my thanks. Various chapters were written in settings as diverse as Surabaya, Los Angeles, Ithaca, London, Oxford, and Penang. For a spring spent on research leave, I again thank SOAS, as well as the Center for Southeast Asian Studies at UCLA and the Southeast Asia Program at Cornell. Special thanks go to Barbara Gaerlan, Mark McGurl, Tony Reid, Geoffrey Robinson, and Michael Salman for hospitality in LA and to Eric Tagliacozzo and Kathy Lee, Jim Siegel, and Anne Berger for hospitality beyond the call of duty in Ithaca. The final burst of writing was assisted by a Research Readership from the British Academy (and by Ken Emond's assistance and encouragement along the way), and by nearly four relaxing months spent in Penang based at the Center for International Studies at Universiti Sains Malaysia. I thank Johan Savaranamuttu and Francis Loh for their hospitality during that period.

I was greatly assisted by critical feedback and encouragement from Indonesia specialists and other colleagues around the world. Jacques Bertrand, Martin van Bruinessen, Gerry van Klinken, Mike Laffan, and Ruth McVey deserve special thanks for their various forms of personal kindness, and for the formative influence they have had upon my work. Presentations at SOAS, LSE, Ohio State University, Humboldt University in Berlin, Cornell, Harvard, the University of California at Los Angeles, UNC Chapel Hill, University of Chicago, and USM in Penang provided occasions for fruitful exchange. I am grateful to all concerned for their constructive crit-

ical comments and suggestions. Special thanks go to Henk Schulte Nordholt for running a workshop at the KITLV in Leiden, the Netherlands, to
help me and Gerry van Klinken with our respective books. For incisive comments on the manuscript I especially thank Ben Anderson, Arief Djati,
Lotta Hedman, Henk Schulte Nordholt, Danilyn Rutherford, Rosanne
Rutten, Ratna Saptari, Gerry van Klinken, and Oskar Verkaaik.

The transition from manuscript to published volume was overseen from
afar by Roger Haydon, whose finely honed editorial skills and indulgent
e-mail manner have earned my lasting appreciation and gratitude. I also
thank the two anonymous readers chosen by Cornell University Press for
their thoughtful comments, pointed questions, and very helpful suggestions
for revision, which I hope I have at least partially addressed in this final version. Additional thanks go to Pat Sterling for the copy editing and to Dave
Prout for the indexing. Special thanks go to Pete Loud for the great maps,
and to both Steve Hopgood and Lotta Hedman for nudging me to contact
Roger at CUP in the first place.

Finally, I want to identify five people who played a special role in this
project. Four of them—Arief Djati, Jim Siegel, Lotta Hedman, and Matilda
Hedman Sidel—made it much, much more difficult to write the book. In
the lexicon of late twentieth-century Indonesian politics, this *kelompok tertentu* thus stands accused of playing the role not only of *instigator* and *provokator* but also of *makar* and *subversif*. For example, it is clearly Arief's
fault that I spent so much time in Surabaya goofing around with him and
even more time following up on his slyly perceptive advice. Weeks—nay,
months—were spent refining, qualifying, and documenting arguments that
he suggested were less than convincing, and otherwise covering up for my
ignorance and indolence. It is also obviously Jim's fault that I have written
such a self-evidently unoriginal book, clumsily derivative of his theoretical
approach in general and his insights on Indonesia in particular. Without
his encouragement and friendship, I would not be so haunted by an awareness of the evasive and hollow quality of my own method of inquiry and
analysis.

It is likewise patently Lotta's fault that my own attempts to treat the sociology and politics of religion in Indonesia read like a rehashed version of
her scholarship on other parts of Southeast Asia, rather than something I
came up with all by myself. More generally, if not for her, I might be able
to enjoy academic life as a fully monastic experience. And it is undoubtedly
not only Lotta's but also Matilda's fault that the whole process of writing
a book in the first place came to lose its original appeal. Against the company of these loves of my life, and against the bookstores, eateries, parks,
playgrounds, and swimming pools of London, Oxford, and Penang, the

book could simply not compete. With friends and family like this, writing the book has been a real struggle. I can forgive, but I can't forget.

And fifth, at the risk of revealing myself to be a middle-aged mamma's boy, I thank my mother, Nancy Jarmon Sidel, for her own special role in this book, not to mention her various visits to Indonesia, London, Oxford, and Penang over the past several years. Insofar as this book sheds light on questions of religious identity, authority, and faith, I have her to thank above all. On the one hand, she has imbued me and my brother Henry Sidel with an outsider's appreciation of the ways in which power and domination are inflected by religious institutions and sensibilities in the world today. On the other hand, she has inspired a sense of humility and wonder in the face of the sublime and terrible mysteries that mark our lives as creatures of both faith and doubt, whether religious, secular, or superstitious. Instead of filial piety or any other form of piousness, she has instilled something simultaneously more Spinozist, more skeptical, and more sentimental. For all this, and for so much more, I shall always be grateful.

JOHN T. SIDEL

London

RIOTS, POGROMS, JIHAD

1

Indonesia

From Ethnic Conflict to Islamic Terrorism?

In the final decade of the twentieth century, Indonesia distinguished itself as a nation of what have been described as "deadly ethnic riots" and seemed a classic case of ethnic conflict in the early post–Cold War era.[1] Beginning in Medan in 1994 and recurring in such provincial towns and cities as Pekalongan in 1995, Situbondo and Tasikmalaya in 1996, and Banjarmasin and Makassar in 1997, a certain pattern of disturbances (*kerusuhan*) seemed to crystallize in riot form. In episode after episode, crowds attacked, destroyed, and burned shops, supermarkets, department stores, goods, and other property owned by Chinese Indonesians; Catholic and Protestant churches and other houses of worship; and police stations and other government buildings. By early 1998 these so-called anti-Chinese disturbances (*kerusuhan anti-Cina*) had become a regular feature of the political landscape, with a familiar repertoire of commentary and investigation by government, military, civic, and religious figures played out after every incident of rioting.

With the onset in 1998 of the economic crisis, local newspapers were filled with stories of riot simulation exercises by expectant police and military units, and foreign journalists and cameramen parachuted into the country by the dozen in anticipation that a wave of riots would hit such cities as Surabaya, the capital of East Java. In the event, January and February 1998 witnessed a series of minor riots along the north coast of Java that targeted shops, supermarkets, and department stores owned by Chinese Indonesians. In May of that year, simultaneous rioting in Jakarta and such cities as Solo, Medan, and Palembang led to the destruction of hundreds of Chinese business establishments, the rape of dozens of Chinese

1

women, and the deaths of more than one thousand people in Jakarta alone. These riots brought the country to a virtual standstill and helped to precipitate the resignation of the longtime Indonesian leader, President Suharto.

The first three years of the post-Suharto era, moreover, saw a broad variety of forms of collective violence across the archipelago. So-called anti-Chinese riots occurred in the Central and West Javanese towns of Purworejo and Karawang in the months following the transfer of power in Jakarta. In villages in rural East Java, crowds attacked and killed suspected "sorcerers" (*dukun santet*) in an antiwitchcraft campaign lasting several months. In January 1999, moreover, mob killings in the religiously divided city of Ambon escalated into a broader pattern of communal violence, with armed groups of Christians and Muslims in villages scattered around Ambon and elsewhere in the province of Maluku engaging in sporadic attacks that left some 4,000 dead and countless others wounded, traumatized, and homeless over the next two years. Violence across the religious divide in the Central Sulawesi town of Poso during the same period produced similar results. Meanwhile, attacks by armed Dayak and Malay groups on Madurese communities in West Kalimantan in March 1999 and early 2001 (as well as earlier in 1996–97) and in localities in Central Kalimantan in February–March 2001 likewise claimed hundreds of lives and created thousands of internally displaced persons (IDPs).

Unfolding against the backdrop of the violent disintegration of Yugoslavia, the genocide in Rwanda, recurring communal violence in India, and a resurgence and proliferation of separatist struggles in civil wars in Africa, Asia, and Europe, these disparate events in Indonesia in the middle to late 1990s were often cited as part of a global trend, variously identified with such terms as "ethnic conflict," "ethnic cleansing," and "ethno-nationalist revivalism." Whether cast as results of uncertainties accompanying market-driven globalization[2] or the opportunities and imperatives created by a new wave of post–Cold War democratization,[3] this turn to nasty forms of "identity politics" had its roots in developments of a self-evidently global nature.[4] Through this lens, Indonesia appeared as merely one case among many, its riots and pogroms of a piece with those taking place, virtually simultaneously, elsewhere around the world.

In the wake of the September 11, 2001, attacks on the twin towers of the World Trade Center in New York City and on the Pentagon in Washington, D.C., however, the threat and practice of "ethnic conflict" rapidly receded from the academic, journalistic, and policy spotlight as the specter of "global Islamic terrorism" came into view, in Indonesia among a number of countries around the world. The involvement of armed paramilitary

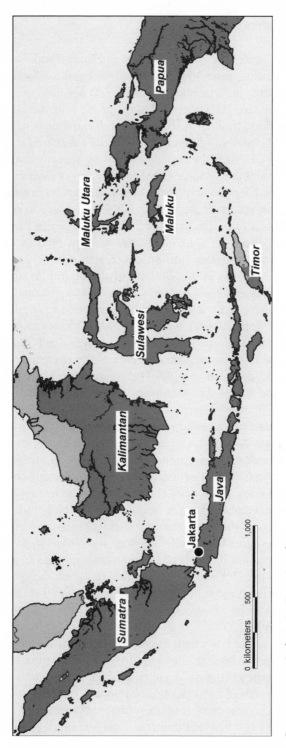

Contemporary Indonesia (Peter Loud)

groups such as Laskar Jihad in the conflicts in Maluku and Poso attracted considerable attention, generating a flurry of academic and journalistic reports as well as calls in Washington and Jakarta for their demobilization and detention. By late 2001 a crackdown against armed Islamist groups was well under way, leading to their virtual disbandment early the next year. But in 2002 a series of bombings led to the fingering of a previously unknown group, identified by the authorities as Jemaah Islamiyah. The bombing of a nightclub in Bali in October 2002, an explosion outside the Marriott Hotel in Jakarta in August 2003, a detonation outside the Australian Embassy in Jakarta in September 2004, and a second set of bombs in the tourist resorts of Bali in October 2005—as well as a handful of less spectacular detonations—claimed hundreds of lives, both of Indonesians and of tourists from Australia, Europe, and North America.

Along with the August 2000 bombing of the Philippine ambassador's residence in Jakarta and the Christmas Eve 2000 explosions at churches around the archipelago, these attacks were attributed to local agents and affiliates of the "global Islamic terrorist network" known as Al-Qaeda.[5] The arrest and trial of alleged Jemaah Islamiyah activists in Indonesia, and the detention and interrogation of members of the network elsewhere in the region, produced a steady trickle of information seen as confirming the picture of activists schooled in "Wahhabi," "Salafi," or "fundamentalist" Islam, trained in jihad in Afghanistan in the 1980s and 1990s, and connected through a secretive cell-like structure to like-minded Islamists elsewhere in Southeast Asia and, through key intermediaries, to Osama bin Laden and Al-Qaeda.[6] Defined either very narrowly as terrorists (i.e., as isolated, deviant individuals) or more broadly as representatives of Islam (or of movements and tendencies therein), the perpetrators are self-evidently involved in a global struggle, whether an essentially military conflict beween Al-Qaeda and the U.S. government and its allies, an ideological war between fundamentalist Islam and the forces of secularism, or a grandiose clash of civilizations pitting Muslims in general against the Christian world. Thus today, as in the 1990s in the era of ethnic conflict, the spotlighting of Islamic terrorism is fully in tune with developments elsewhere in the world, the Bali and Jakarta bombings often mentioned in the same breath as attacks on Western targets in Kenya, Morocco, Saudi Arabia, Turkey, and Yemen and on Western cities such as New York, Madrid, and London.

Needless to say, this tendency to see Indonesia simply through the prism of global trends carries its own dangers, problems, and limitations. After all, the Indonesia viewed through the global lens of either ethnic conflict or Islamic terrorism may appear at times somewhat grotesquely distorted to those whose bird's-eye view of the archipelago presents a picture of rather scattered, episodic, and occasional violence in the—largely peaceful—fourth most populous country in the world. Such a lens, moreover, also appears too wide-angled, as it were, to afford a close view of the modalities of violence: when, where, and how it occurs, with what targets, forms of mobilization, and consequences. Finally, the switch from the analytical lens or prism of ethnic conflict to that of Islamic terrorism remains an unexplained non sequitur of sorts, as if, by the 2010s, we should unblinkingly expect, say, "anarcho-syndicalism" as the next phase of Indonesia's experience of trends in global violence.

Thanks to the tireless efforts of Indonesian and foreign reporters, researchers, and scholars over some ten years, however, it is possible to see beyond these often distorted and hazy global lenses and to zoom in on the nuances and specificities of various episodes of violence in the archipelago. Despite considerable logistical difficulties and political restrictions, Indonesian newspapers and magazines have published countless articles reporting on—and in some cases investigating—the riots, pogroms, and bombings that have occurred since 1995. In the late 1990s, nongovernmental organizations (NGOs) such as the Institut Studi Arus Informasi (ISAI), or Institute for the Study of the Flow of Information, and Yayasan Lembaga Bantuan Hukum Indonesia (YLBHI), or Indonesian Legal Aid Society, published serious studies of various riots and conflicts, and the Indonesian government itself commissioned a few informative reports, most notably those on the May 1998 riots in Jakarta.[7] More recently, the Jakarta office of the International Crisis Group, headed by the highly respected Indonesia specialist Sidney Jones, has put out a series of in-depth reports on Jemaah Islamiyah, drawing on a wide range of sources to present a detailed and nuanced picture of this shadowy network.[8]

Meanwhile, a number of anthropologists have provided close examinations of successive episodes of violence in Indonesia, combining ethnographic fieldwork with political analysis in treatments of antiwitchcraft campaigns in East Java and communal conflict in West Kalimantan, Maluku, and Central Sulawesi.[9] Today, there is hardly a provincial town riot or a local conflict or a bombing in Indonesia that has not been covered in some depth by journalists, NGO researchers, or foreign scholars. The World Bank is now devoting millions of dollars to the study of violent conflicts around the Indonesian archipelago, with the United Nations Development Program (UNDP), United States Agency for International Development (USAID), and other international agencies also generously funding such work.

Yet for all the wealth of in-depth information and on-the-spot analysis they provide, these writings on violence in Indonesia since the early 1990s suffer some notable limitations. Just as the analytical prisms of "ethnic conflict" or "Islamic terrorism" have proved too hazy for close analysis of the specificities of violence in Indonesia, so has the zoom lens approach, adopted by country experts of various kinds, left unanswered important questions about the broader pattern of the events and developments that have unfolded over the subsequent decade. Like a set of snapshots taken in different places at different times, the accounts of individual riots and conflicts and bombings do not add up to a coherent picture of the drama as a whole. With the lens trained so closely not only on isolated incidents (a riot here, a bombing there) but also on specific individuals or sets of individuals (first victims, then perpetrators), there is little opportunity to step back to trace the processes through which violence has unfolded, to identify patterns of change in the forms which violence has assumed, or to situate the violence against a broader historical and sociological canvas. Nor is there the perspective from which one might pose comparative, and counterfactual, questions: why has violence assumed certain forms, involved certain kinds of agency and mobilization, occurred at certain times, in certain places, with certain targets and certain consequences—*but not others*? Why violence, rather than other forms of action? Why, for the most part, no violence at all?[10]

The importance of these questions—or perhaps just their obviousness—becomes clear if we consider certain curious and seemingly inexplicable shifts in the pattern of violence observed in Indonesia since the mid-1990s. The years 1995–97, for example, witnessed a series of riots in provincial towns and cities where buildings—business establishments, churches, temples, government offices—were attacked, damaged, looted, and often burned to the ground by crowds of people but where there were few if any attacks on people themselves and only occasional casualties. May 1998, by contrast, saw a more national riot in the Indonesian capital of Jakarta, and several other major cities as well, in which assaults on buildings were accompanied by an unprecedented set of gang rapes and large numbers of deaths.

The remaining months of 1998 passed without a return to or escalation of the earlier pattern of provincial town riots; instead, they brought the first hints of a new form of violence, one characterized by murderous collective attacks on individuals, ranging from crowd lynchings of suspected thieves in various parts of Java to gang warfare in neighborhoods of Jakarta to coordinated armed assaults on entire neighborhoods and villages. In 1999–2001, pogroms in West and Central Kalimantan, Maluku, and the Central Sulawesi town of Poso claimed hundreds, even thousands, of lives, while ethnic cleansing forced tens of thousands from their homes and communities in these disparate parts of the archipelago.

By late 2001, however, these pogroms too had apparently run their course and were replaced, as it were, by a new form of violence crystallizing under the sign of jihad. First apparent in the guise of armed paramilitary groups dispatched to Maluku and Poso in 2000–2001, this jihad soon assumed the form of bombings, beginning with explosions at the residence of the Philippine ambassador in Jakarta (August 2000) and at Christian churches around the Indonesian archipelago in December 2000, but then shifting to such Western targets as a tourists' nightclub on Bali (October 2002), a McDonald's outlet in Makassar (June 2003), an American hotel in Jakarta (August 2003), the Australian Embassy in Jakarta (September 2004), and tourist resorts in Bali (October 2005).

Thus, over the years since 1995 a shift in the forms of violence witnessed in Indonesia has been discernible, from *riots* (1995–1998) to *pogroms* (1999–2001) to *jihad* (2000–2004). As evident in its title, this broad shift in the forms of violence observed in Indonesia constitutes the focus of this book. Also evident in my book's title is the essential premise that much of this violence should be understood as *religious*. The term "religious violence" here refers to collective physical attacks on persons or property launched in avowed defense or promotion of religious beliefs, boundaries, institutions, traditions, or values, and behind religious symbols and slogans.

Such a definition is accompanied by at least four potential problems, all of which this book addresses. First of all, the definition may privilege acts of direct physical violence at the expense of more subtle but no less powerful forms of coercion and structural violence. Indeed, some theorists contend that an absence of religious conflict is a sure sign of repression on behalf of one or another faith. I take as my point of departure a contextualization of religious institutions within the broader matrix of class relations in the country. It is precisely the embeddedness of religion—not only religious institutions but religious identities as they are invoked by avowed representatives of the major faiths—within a set of shifting relations of class and state power in Indonesia that has made the mobilization of violence under the banner of religious faith so attractive in recent years.

Second, and more important, the notion of religious violence may be understood to suggest that certain forms or instances of violence can be attributed to certain religions or to religion in general. In either case, the implication is that such violence is solely, purely, religious in nature and that secular institutions and individuals—through their supposed differentiation from their religious counterparts, their putative neutrality, and their alleged tolerance—are commendably immune to this pathology.[11] This book, however, is intended to shed light—a rather harsh light, it might be added—not only on more subtle, structural forms of violence but also on the unacknowledged role of secularism and secular institutions and individuals in this violence, and the intertwined nature of the religious, the economic, and the political in Indonesia and elsewhere in the world.[12]

A third and perhaps related problem with the foregoing notion of religious violence might lie in the presumption as to what constitutes "religious" violence in the first place. After all, scholars have questioned the very notion of "religion" itself. The anthropologist Talal Asad, for example, has argued that "there cannot be a universal definition of religion, not only because its constituent elements and relationships are historically specific but because that definition is itself the historical product of discursive processes."[13] In Indonesia, moreover, the shift from riots to pogroms to jihad over a decade has seen concomitant variation in the religious nature of the violence itself. The riots of 1995–97, for example, all began with perceived slights to Islam and unfolded through mobilization by students from Islamic schools and attacks on non-Muslim houses of worship as well as business establishments and government buildings. The pogroms of 1998–2000, by contrast, all unfolded without incidents involving the institutions of religious worship and education; they claimed as their victims not clerics but entire communities of faith. Finally, the "terrorist" jihad since 2001 has apparently been waged by members of a secretive Islamist network (many of whom graduated from a certain set of Islamic schools) but has chosen targets that although symbolic of Western presence and power in Indonesia—embassies, tourist nightclubs, hotels—are decidedly secular in nature.

Violence, then, may be "religious" in very different senses: both the perpetrators and the targets may vary in the nature and extent of their religious identity. As many authors are keen to point out, moreover, one effect of violence waged under the sign of a given religious faith is to produce religious identities and boundaries, whether between bodies of belief or between bodies of believers, between two recognized religious faiths or between one recognized religion and something else—"heresy," "Godlessness," or "magic."[14] With these concerns in mind, it is precisely to undermine simplistic notions of religious violence, and to interrogate—and disaggregate—the varying forms assumed and effects produced by religious violence under different circumstances, that I have written this book.

The fourth and final problem with the definition of religious violence might appear to be its limited analytical value for examining the manifold forms of violence observed in Indonesia since the early 1990s.[15] Indeed, many localities have witnessed episodes of violence in connection with criminal activities and organizations, and with conflicts over labor, land,

and other scarce economic resources. The attacks by armed Dayak and Malay groups on Madurese communities in West and Central Kalimantan in 1996–97 and 1999–2000, moreover, certainly appear to be ethnic rather than religious in nature, and violent conflicts in the provinces of Aceh and Papua seem to stem from separatist struggles for independence. The definition offered above does indeed exclude these instances of collective—and state—violence, but, as argued in chapter 6, it helps to explain why religious violence in particular has been so pronounced in Indonesia, and to examine how it has compared—and in some senses competed—with other forms of disruptive popular mobilization in the country.

The prominence and prevalence of recent *religious* violence in Indonesia may in part be understood in light of the broader pattern of conflicts observed around the world since the end of the Cold War and of enduring problems with the place of religious faiths and institutions in the modern world. Indeed, as scholars have noted, one striking feature of most of the supposedly ethnic conflicts is their outbreak along a specifically religious divide.[16] Among earlier instances of ethnic cleansing, the (Christian) Armenian genocide and (Jewish) Holocaust are the most prominent examples; in the 1990s, Bosnia-Hertzogovina and Kosovo in the former Yugoslavia are obvious cases in point. As Michael Sells, a scholar of recent Bosnian history has argued:

> The word "ethnic" in "ethnic cleansing" is a euphemism. Bosnian Serbs, Croats, and Muslims all speak the same language, despite the fact that for political reasons they each call it now by a different name. They all trace their descent to tribes that migrated to the area around the sixth century and were Slavic in language and culture by the time they settled in the area. Those who have been singled out for persecution have fallen on the wrong side of a dividing line based solely on religious identity.[17]

Violent religious conflict, the anthropologist Jack Goody claims, is especially prominent for two reasons. The first is "the sheer penetrative depth and divisiveness of religion as an ideological system," in monotheistic faiths (as many other scholars have argued, "To believe in one God is to exclude the many").[18] Second, Goody notes, religious identities are inherently uncertain and open to doubt and contestation:

> Religious differences can also be erased by conversion, leaving other "primordial" features of an individual or community in place, yet replacing the ideology and institutions that otherwise define them. Might not this very possibility render the boundaries between religions particularly fraught,

making them an existential danger zone that calls for supreme defensive measures against any threat of corrosion or contamination—what we now often refer to as a fundamentalist reaction?[19]

As other scholars have noted, this sense of uncertainty and vulnerability is not simply a matter of external challenges to religious communities; it is, rather, inherent in the very nature of religious authority itself. Religion, conceived not as a disembodied system of belief but in terms of relationships of power ("the power to regulate, uphold, require, or adjust *correct* practices," Talal Asad has argued, "and to condemn, exclude, undermine, or replace *incorrect* ones"),[20] rests, according to Gregory Starrett, on "a peculiar form of property relation—a relation between people with regard to texts and intellectual technologies—that [is] potentially more fluid than other sorts of class relations."[21]

Perhaps the decade of religious violence in Indonesia observed here may also in part be understood in relation to the country's specific location within the early post–Cold War global order, as that order is seen in various fashionable conceptualizations by today's most influential theorists. Situated at the easternmost antipode of the Muslim world, Indonesia, is, for example, in the context of the so-called Clash of Civilizations, a "fault-line state" along "Islam's bloody borders."[22] Located at the periphery of the "world capitalist system, moreover, the predominantly Muslim Indonesian archipelago has been profoundly penetrated by and subordinated to the core capitalist economies of the—overwhelmingly non-Muslim and secular—North (i.e., Western Europe, North America, Japan).[23] Yet Indonesia's sheer size, its history of anticolonial revolution, and its claim to vast oil reserves arguably make the country a likely host for so-called anti-systemic movements.[24] Incorporated within the new economic circuitries of what has come to be known as the Information Age, the Indonesian version of "the network society" is thus said to provide fertile soil, as in other Muslim settings, for the growth of "anti-globalization movements" in the form of secretive Islamic terrorist networks linked to Al-Qaeda.[25] Increasingly open(ed) not only to financial but also to "televisual" globalization, Indonesia has also been subjected to the profoundly Christian globalized mediatization of religion which has been labeled "globalatinization." It thus may be a likely site for protests against this hegemony—which, writes Jacques Derrida, "is political, economic, and religious at once"—and for the appropriation and redirection of mediatic powers against "Christian teletechnological hegemony."[26] In short, in the wake of the Cold War, in the throes of globalization, the information age, and, by the late 1990s, a global economic crisis, and in the midst of a worldwide wave of attempted democratization, some kind of reaction under the banner of Islam is viewed from various quarters as highly likely in Indonesia. "The 'religious,'" argues Hent de Vries, "'returns' at the juncture at which the politics of a 'secular' modernity is recognized as being contingent upon the authority of a dominant religion, if not directly, at least by way of its renegotiation."[27]

Yet such broad-brush accounts offer little to illuminate the specific modalities of religious violence observed in Indonesia or to help examine the discernible but seemingly inexplicable shifts noted above in the forms, targets, processes of mobilization, and consequences of this violence in successive periods. For these tasks, an appreciation of the specific Indonesian historical and sociological context is necessary, as is an understanding of the place of religion in general and of the dominant faith of Islam in particular within this context. Scholars of Dutch history, after all, have had occasion to reflect on the peculiar ways in which religious identities and institutions were incorporated into the field of modern political and social life in the Netherlands, Indonesia's colonial master until the 1940s.[28] Students of Indonesian history, moreover, have examined the ways in which this Dutch pattern of so-called pillarization (*verzuiling*) along religious lines resurfaced in the colony in the form of *aliran* or currents likewise defined in large part along religious lines.[29] Scholars of other countries in the Muslim world, moreover, have pointed to the significance of broad changes in the realms of education and media for what the anthropologist Gregory Starrett has termed the "objectification" and "functionalization" of Islam.[30] By these terms, Starrett refers to "the growing consciousness on the part of Muslims that Islam is a coherent system of practices and beliefs, rather than merely an unexamined and unexaminable way of life," and the increasing opportunities to put Islam "consciously to work for various types of social and political projects."[31] Finally, Starrett and other scholars of Muslim societies have shown how such sociological shifts have combined with political changes to promote new forms of political mobilization and activism—both violent and nonviolent—under the banner of "Islam."[32]

Informed and inspired by such scholars, this book proceeds to explain the shifting modalities of religious violence in Indonesia as reflecting sociological and political changes that variously enabled and constrained the possibilities for articulating, representing, mobilizing, and promoting Islam. As argued in chapter 2, the place of Islam in Indonesian society has in no small measure been determined by the distinctive nexus of class relations in the archipelago, by the peculiar and highly ambiguous position of the political class vis-à-vis the business and working classes in the country, and by the intimate but inherently unstable connection between religion, education, and admission into this political class. As elaborated in chapter 3, moreover, the processes of capitalist development unfolding in Indonesia under the long years of the Suharto regime (1966–98) gave rise to internal transformations and tensions within the country's social classes, including the political class occupying state power, and shifts within and between the competing streams or currents defined along religious educational lines. These changes spelled new possibilities for representing Islam in Indonesian society and for making claims on its behalf.

As spelled out in chapters 4–7 the expectations, uncertainties, and anxieties accompanying these shifts help to explain the emergence, subsidence, and transformation of successive forms of religious violence. chapter 4 argues, for example, that the riots targeting ethnic Chinese Indonesians' property and non-Muslim houses of worship in provincial towns and cities in 1995–97 occurred against the backdrop of increasingly assertive claims on public space and state power under the banner of Islam, as well as rising concerns and frustrations with the constraints imposed on these claims. As suggested in chapter 5, moreover, the rioting that led to gang rapes of dozens of ethnic Chinese women, hundreds of casualties, and the destruction of thousands of Chinese shops and business establishments in the national capital of Jakarta came at a moment when avowed representatives of Islam were poised to seize power at the national level. As elaborated in chapter 6, by contrast, the antiwitchcraft campaigns and interreligious pogroms that claimed the lives of hundreds, indeed thousands, of people in 1999–2001 unfolded precisely as the very basis of claims to represent Muslims shifted with the unraveling of authoritarian rule, the onset of competitive elections, and the loss of state power by forces most insistent on the promotion of Islam. Finally, as concluded in chapter 7, the shift from large-scale collective violence to paramilitary and terrorist activity, and from domestic to international targets, from 2001 onward coincided with the (re)entrenchment of secular and Christian forces in the seats of state power in Jakarta. Thus variation observed in the modalities of religious violence—the timing, location, targets, mobilization processes, and forms of agency associated with their occurrence—over the decade under consideration must be understood in terms of the problems with the place of Islam in Indonesian society.

This gridding of the structural coordinates of religious violence is firmly rooted in the tradition of comparative historical sociology, but it also rests on a particular conception of the phenomenology and psychology of religious violence. In contrast with most actor-centered accounts of various forms of violence in Indonesia and other countries around the world, this book is based on the assumption that perpetrators of religious violence are best understood neither as rational actors pursuing narrowly self-interested goals,[33] nor as committed believers in seamlessly coherent belief systems,[34] nor as sufferers of particular emotional or mental states, whether Roger D. Petersen's "fear, hatred, or resentment"[35] or running amok.[36] Instead of positing that religious violence is best understood as perpetrated by identifiable individuals or groups with stable religious identities, interests, beliefs, and values, this book includes among the very puzzles to be addressed the often elusive and ever shifting agents associated with successive forms of religious violence in Indonesia, from mobs and their instigators in the riots of 1995–98 to entire local communities—and the politicians, gangsters, and religious activists egging them on—in the pogroms of 1999–2001, to the narrow network of terrorists said to be responsible for the bombings of 2002–3.

This book takes as its underlying premise a notion—long argued by scholars in philosophy, psychology, and social theory, and articulated most clearly and forcefully in the Indonesian context by the anthropologist James Siegel—of the inherently incomplete, unstable, and interactive nature of what we call "identity," religious or otherwise.[37] After all, at the core of any identity is always a constitutive sense of lack, of inadequacy, or of a "theft" that can be imputed to an Other who deprives "us" of the full enjoyment of those material, discursive, and social practices which, we imagine, (would) allow "us" to be fully "ourselves."[38] Thus what is disavowed is the essentially split nature of subjectivity, the inherent fissure and internal antagonism within—each of—"us," the disavowed Egyptian within the Jew of Freud's *Moses and Monotheism*.[39]

In this light, instances of religious violence can no longer be understood to reflect the strength and intensity of religious identities held by individuals and groups as they promote their ideas and pursue their interests. Religious violence, instead, erupts amid heightened states of uncertainty and anxiety as to religious identities and their boundaries, and attendant efforts toward the (re)definition of the self and the (re)articulation of claims of authority. The literary theorist René Girard, for example, moving from Freud's suggestive but tentative remarks on the "narcissism of minor differences,"[40] famously argued: "It is not the differences but the loss of them that gives rise to violence."[41] The sociologist Charles Tilly has drawn a similar conclusion in his survey of collective violence in modern history: "Violence generally increases and becomes more salient in situations of rising uncertainty across the boundary. It increases because people respond to threats against weighty social arrangements they have built on such boundaries—arrangements such as exploitation of others, property rights, in-group marriage, and power over local government."[42] And the anthropologist Arjun Appadurai writes of the link between uncertainty and "ethnocidal" violence:

> The forms of such uncertainty are various. One kind of uncertainty is a direct reflection of census concerns: how many persons of this or that sort really exist in a given territory? Or, in the context of rapid migration or refugee movement, how many of "them" are there now among "us"? Another kind of uncertainty is about what some of these megaidentities really mean: what are the normative characteristics of what the Constitution defines as a member of an OBC (Other Backward Caste) in India? A further uncertainty is about whether a particular person really is what they claim or appear to be or to have historically been. Finally, these various forms of uncertainty create intolerable anxiety about the relationship of many individuals to state-provided goods—ranging from housing and health to safety and sanitation—since these entitlements are frequently directly tied to who "you" are and thus to who "they" are. Each kind of uncertainty gains increasing force whenever there are large-scale movements of persons, when new rewards or risks attach to large-scale ethnic identities, or when existing networks of social knowledge are eroded by rumour, terror, or social movement. Where one or more of these forms of social uncertainty come into play, violence can create a macabre form of certainty and can become a brutal technique (or folk discovery-procedure) about "them" and, therefore, about "us."[43]

In such contexts of uncertainty, the redefinition of the self and the reassertion of boundaries and claims of authority are achieved not only through violent opposition to an antagonistic Other but through recognition in the—imagined—gaze of a broader audience and within a larger symbolic order.[44] Religious violence is thus by definition performative[45] and representational, in both senses of the term.[46] For example, Islamic terrorist groups, Werner Schiffauer has noted,

> represent Islam both in the sense that they conjure up a certain picture of it, and inasmuch as they claim to speak for Muslims—thus representing the Islamic community in the political sense. The success or failure of their representative work in this field depends on the extent to which they succeed in gathering around them a community that recognizes itself in the image and feels represented by it. Because this arena is not simply viewed (by being subjected to analysis and comparison, for example), but instead is represented in the light of the press, it constitutes a process of reflection: the amusing feature here—as with every glance in the mirror—is identity formation. If you can see how your own representative is perceived by third

parties (and hence how you are), and are thus able to compare how the representative of the others affects third parties (and hence how others themselves do), you are able to ascertain your own identity. From this it also becomes clear why the third parties (that is, the stage of press publicity) are needed: they stand for "objectivity" in the sense that they are neutral in the battle for representation in the Islamic field.[47]

Religious violence, then, must be understood not only as actions taken by individuals or groups but also in terms of (anticipated) responses by audiences and thus as broader discursive and social formations in which religion has a prominent—and problematic—role. Religious violence must thus be understood not simply in view of its destructive consequences but also in light of its productive effects.[48]

The link between uncertainty and anxiety over identity, on the one hand, and violence, on the other, is evident in the kinds of political, sociological, and discursive contexts associated with riots, pogroms, and terrorism around the world, as noted in several important studies. Paul Brass, for example, has situated communal violence in India in the 1990s against the backdrop of "the rise of intercaste conflict" and the threat of electoral mobilization by coalitions of (Hindu) "backward" castes with low castes and Muslims.[49] In this context, Brass shows how "Hindu-Muslim riots are a product of actions designed to consolidate one community or the other or both at the local, regional, and national levels into a cohesive political bloc."[50] Meanwhile, Michel Wieviorka's research on the use of terrorist violence by Basque and Palestinian nationalists and German and Italian left-wing radicals has revealed a similar pattern. "*The organized practice of indiscriminate and irredeemable violence,*" he argues, "*is not a faltering movement's last best hope or final act of desperation but rather a substitute for a movement which has either become imaginary or has fallen out of sync with the hopes pinned on it.*"[51] He concludes:

> In its purest—and most extreme—manifestations, terrorism always betrays the disintegration of some collective action. Wherever the social, national, or communal consciousness is strong, and wherever a social or any other kind of movement is capable of being formed, there can be no place for terrorist spinoffs. These appear, and take shape—and become rationales of action rather than mere situational combat strategies—through the disintegration of a collective consciousness, or in the collapse, breakdown, or failure of a social, national, or communist movement.[52]

Likewise the writings of Olivier Roy and Gilles Kepel depict the rise of transnational jihadist networks such as Al-Qaeda at the turn of the twenty-first century as a response to the co-optation, defeat, or disintegration of various Islamist movements in the 1990s and, more broadly, the "deterritorialization" of Islam and the consequent weakening of this religion's social authority.[53] "Radical militant jihadists," Roy notes, "fight at the frontier [of the Muslim world] to protect a centre where they have no place. They fight not to protect a territory but to re-create a community. They are besieged in a fortress they do not inhabit."[54] Overall, these studies suggest that religious violence should be understood as reflecting not the strength and solidity of religious faiths, identities, and solidarities but their perceived fragility and vulnerability in the face of competing—religious and nonreligious—forms of consciousness, association, and mobilization.

Illuminated in this perspective, the specific modalities of religious violence in Indonesia since 1995 are recast in a new light in these chapters. The precise timing, location, targets, and forms of violence in Indonesia since the mid-1990s are understood to reflect the particular nature of both anxieties as to the threats to religious identities and aspirations as to the reconstitution of religious identities through confrontation with and effacement of these threats. Thus the changes in the forms assumed by religious violence are shown to reflect the emergence of new kinds of threats to religious identities as well as the shifting circumstances within which such identities could be reconstituted and reasserted.

This approach undergirds the analysis I offer of religious violence in Indonesia. In my treatment of its successive phases and forms, the actions, experiences, and self-understandings of the elusive agents involved in the promotion and perpetration of this violence are thus understood in terms neither of religious ideas nor of rational interests behind those ideas. Instead, the changing forms of violence observed in Indonesia are shown to correspond to evolving *fantasies* about religious identities, about threats to these identities, and about possibilities for the—imagined—recuperation and restoration of these identities. Such fantasies are not fantasies in the sense of departures from the matrix of social relations in the Indonesia of the past decade. They are fantasies in the sense of understandings of this matrix of social relations and of the place of religion(s) within it, "schemas" that offer roles to be played in defense and promotion of religious institutions and identities, most notably those associated with Islam.[55] Such fantasies are, as Freud noted, "protective structures, sublimations of the facts, embellishments of them, and at the same time serve for self-exoneration."[56] By occluding the inherent internal fissures and antagonisms at the heart of (in this case, Muslim) "identity," these fantasies construct a schema around which to organize the recuperation of that stolen—Islamic—essence of which Indonesian Muslims have been deprived by Others, whether Christian, Jewish, secular, or syncretist.[57] Insofar as these fantasies have been variously constrained and enabled by the context in which they have emerged and unfolded, an analysis of the location of religious institutions and identities—and of Islam in particular—within the matrix of social relations in Indonesia is in order. It is this historical and sociological analysis that constitutes the focus of the following two chapters.

2

Situating "Islam" in Indonesia

The Matrix of Class Relations

The "religious" nature of the diverse forms of violence witnessed in Indonesia in recent years cannot be divined simply through an exploration of Islamic beliefs, practices, and institutions in this predominantly Muslim archipelago, or with reference to confessional diversity and differences among Muslims or between Muslims and Christians. Instead, the complex pattern of religious violence in Indonesia must be understood with reference to the location of religious identities and institutions within the country's peculiar matrix of class relations, which can be traced back to the era of Dutch colonial rule. Here "class" is understood not only in terms of *difference* in relation to the means—economic, cultural, social, and symbolic—of production and capital accumulation but also as the basis of relationships that have been worked out historically through a process of mutual (self-) definition. As E. P. Thompson argued nearly forty years ago, class is

> something which in fact happens (and can be shown to have happened) in human relationships. More than this the notion of class entails the notion of historical relationships. Like any other relationship, it is a fluency which evades analysis if we attempt to stop it dead at any given moment and anatomise its structure. The finest-meshed sociological net cannot give us a pure specimen of class, any more than it can give us one of deference or love. The relationship must always be embodied in real people and in a real context. Moreover, we cannot have two distinct classes, each with an independent being, and then bring them into relationship with each other. We cannot have love without lovers, nor deference without squires and labourers. And class happens when some men, as a result of common ex-

18

periences (inherited or shared), feel and articulate the identity of their interests as between themselves, and as against other men whose interests are different from (and usually opposed to) theirs.[1]

Although this configuration of class relations has in no small measure been shaped by the Dutch colonial state in the Netherlands East Indies and its successors in an independent Indonesia, it is also the product of an interactive and ongoing process of class identity construction and recognition. The Indonesian pattern has assumed a distinctive form, one in which questions and "fantasies" of representation have loomed particularly large, and in which religion—and Islam in particular—has occupied an especially prominent but problematic place. It is a pattern traceable from the formation of new social classes in the Dutch colonial era through various permutations in class relations during the Soekarno era (1950–65) and the first decades of Suharto's "New Order" regime (1966–98). Stressing the distinctive ambiguity, instability, and dynamism inherent in the nexus of class relations in Indonesia and situating religious identities and institutions within this nexus provide a crucial backdrop to the changes in class relations in the Suharto era and the subsequent development of religious violence.

"Capitalism with a Chinese Face": A Pariah Business Class

First and most famously, the pattern of class relations in Indonesia has been distinguished by the decisively problematic status and political weakness of its overwhelmingly ethnic Chinese capitalist class, a legacy of Dutch colonial policies. As elsewhere in Southeast Asia, trade between ports in the Indonesian archipelago and the Celestial Kingdom dates back many centuries. Long before the arrival of Europeans, merchants from the southern coast of China not only traded but also settled in ports along the northern coast (*pasisir*) of Java and in coastal communities of the Moluccas, Sulawesi, Sumatra, and Borneo. By the fourteenth century these immigrant men and the locally born (*peranakan*) offspring of their unions with indigenous women had established permanent settlements. As the Dutch East India Company (Verenigde Oost-Indische Compagnie [VOC]) began to dominate and intensify long-distance trade in the seventeenth and eighteenth centuries in the archipelago, these merchants played pioneering roles in the incipient commercialization and monetization of the economy. In the nineteenth century, moreover, an unprecedented wave of migration—most notably of Hokkien, Cantonese, Hakka, and Teochiu speakers from the provinces of Fujian and Guangdong—brought hundreds of thousands of new men from southern China to the Netherlands East Indies and other parts of Southeast Asia.[2] The complex of "push" and "pull" factors for this massive wave of migration, it is clear, derived essentially from the differential extent of incorporation of the two zones into the world capitalist economy at this historical juncture and the consequently earlier onset of "primitive accumulation" (to use Karl Marx's term) in China.[3]

In this mid-nineteenth-century Southeast Asian context of relatively sparse population, predominantly subsistence-oriented agriculture, and considerably limited domestic capital formation, immigrants from the south coast of China were far better placed—and more forcibly compelled—than their local counterparts to assume leading roles in the intertwined processes of agricultural commercialization and urban growth, to become wage laborers, compradors, and revenue farmers for the colonial states in the region. This early exposure to and immersion in the urban cash nexus— rather than any genetically or culturally inherited disposition—prefigured the rise of immigrant Chinese and their offspring, in the course of the twentieth century, to a position of preeminence and predominance in capitalist development and industrial growth in Southeast Asia. As Maurice Freedman's study of the so-called overseas Chinese in the region concluded: "the will and ability of Chinese to work hard could not have been the sufficient cause of their progress in the amassing of riches. They accumulated wealth because, in comparison with the people among whom they came to live, they were highly sophisticated in the handling of money. At the outset they knew not only how to work themselves but also how to make their money work."[4]

Crystallization: Dutch Colonial Rule

Against this common backdrop of Chinese immigration and involvement in the spread of capitalism throughout Southeast Asia, state policies in the Dutch colonial era shaped the crystallization of a distinctive capitalist class formation. Before the establishment of VOC rule, immigrants from the southern coast of China had assimilated easily into Javanese society and into communities elsewhere in the Indonesian archipelago, as seen in their involvement in the process of Islamization in the fifteenth and sixteenth centuries, and their intermarriage and incorporation into the ranks of the indigenous aristocracy during the same period.[5] Like so-called Baba Chinese in Malaya, Chinese *mestizos* in the Philippines, and Sino-Thai *lukjin* in Siam, generation after generation of locally born (*peranakan*) children of immigrant Chinese men and native women assumed many of the cultural, linguistic, and religious trappings of the societies in which they were raised.

Yet with the evolution of Dutch rule on Java, a new pattern of segregation and ghettoization emerged in the eighteenth century. Not only was Chinese entry into the ranks of the Javanese aristocracy barred by the Dutch, but a set of separate residency requirements, legal codes, and administrative practices were imposed by the VOC on the Chinese population on Java. This segregation of Chinese communities and their subordination to a Dutch-appointed *Kapitan Cina,* which worked to enhance Dutch claims to manpower and tax revenues at the expense of the Javanese aristocracy, began to harden ethnic boundaries and to create obstacles to movement across them.[6] Moreover, G. William Skinner's argument that the gradual subordination of the Javanese principalities to Dutch colonial authorities reduced the attractiveness of assimilation, by delinking it from upward social mobility, is supported by evidence suggesting

(1) that the complete assimilation of the descendants of Chinese immigrants into Javanese society—and especially into the elite strata—was not uncommon prior to the mid-eighteenth century; (2) that Peranakan communities were first stabilized in north coast towns only after these towns had been isolated from the royal courts and their local rulers humbled, subjected, or deposed by the Dutch; (3) that rates of Chinese assimilation into the Javanese elite steadily declined for Java as a whole during the eighteenth and nineteenth centuries; and (4) that at any given point in time during those two centuries assimilation rates tended to be lower in the areas of Java directly administered by the Dutch than in the indirectly ruled principalities of central Java, where the traditional Javanese elite retained considerable prestige and formal power.[7]

These trends toward segregation accelerated and deepened with the intensification of colonial rule and capitalist penetration in the Netherlands East Indies in the nineteenth and early twentieth centuries. Beginning with the brief but important British interregnum on Java (1811–16) during the Napoleonic interlude, the colonial authorities removed residual control over trade routes, markets, and other sources of taxation from the Javanese aristocracy and auctioned off these and other new revenue farms to the highest bidders, invariably members of the local Chinese merchant community.[8] The new opportunities for tax farming and commercial penetration of the Javanese hinterland "attracted large numbers of newly arrived Chinese immigrants to the princely states, most of whom had no knowledge of local conditions and were barely conversant in vulgar, 'market' (*pasar*) Malay, let alone Javanese."⁹ With the establishment of the Cultivation System (*Cultuurstelsel*) on Java in 1830, moreover, James Rush writes that the Dutch colonial regime introduced new rules "confining the Chinese to designated neighborhoods and severely restricting their movement throughout the island by requiring them to possess short-term travel passes."¹⁰ Yet, at the same time, the Dutch granted exemptions to Chinese revenue farmers and their employees to facilitate the operations of the (most notably opium) farms that were crucial to colonial state revenues.

The consequences of this policy were twofold. On the one hand, instead of assimilation (as in Siam and the Spanish Philippines during this period), the nineteenth century saw the emergence of a separate community in which not only new immigrants but the locally born offspring of mixed immigrant and indigenous parentage were all designated as Chinese and, their cultural and linguistic creolization aside, kept in urban ghettos apart from the "native" population. On the other hand, through the opium and other revenue farms, vast Chinese commercial networks evolved over the course of the nineteenth century, with Chinese capital pioneering not only the collection of taxes but the introduction of commodities, the extension of credit, and the expansion of commerce deep into the rural hinterlands of the archipelago. By the 1870s, as James Rush, a leading historian of this period, has noted:

> where the economy was concerned, the Chinese were ubiquitous and essential. Sooner or later everyone doing business in Java had to do business with a Chinese—from the Dutch planter needing wagons and tools to the Javanese villager with fruits and eggs to sell. So dependent were Europeans and other urbanites on Chinese-provided goods and services that daily life itself . . . was impossible without them. Moreover, except for a few schoolmasters, Java's Chinese men—and an untold number of the peranakans and indigenous women to whom they were married or related—were almost all active in the money economy.
>
> From top to bottom, commerce marked the Chinese. They were shippers, warehousemen, and labor contractors; builders and repairmen; and suppliers of *all things* to town and country. They were tinsmiths, leather tanners, and furniture makers. They bought and sold real estate, worked timber concessions, and speculated in the plantation economy. They organized the manufacture of batik and tobacco products. The Chinese brought the products of village farmers to market—rice, sugar, indigo, cotton, pepper, coconuts, cacao, and soybeans, fruits, ducks, chickens, and eggs. They milled rice, tapioca, cotton and sugar; processed *kapok* [a type of tree] and copra and castor oil; and manufactured *tahu* [tofu] and soy sauce. And, aside from their own wares, they supplied indigenous vendors

with goods like gambir, salt, *trasi,* [shrimp paste] and cooking oil for the village trade. As opium farmers, they brought opium to everyone; as, for instance, "water buffalo farmers," they took in fees for slaughtering animals and, on the side, did a brisk business in hides. Those Chinese who acted as officials were not only merchants but Java's biggest and richest entrepreneurs.

Chinese merchants, shopkeepers, and petty traders were also often the first source for loans and credit and certainly the last. Most of Java's day-to-day banking was in their hands. Most of this activity occurred within the Chinese community, but Dutch and *priyayi* [Javanese aristocratic] officials also borrowed heavily from them: loans were provided on easy terms in return for privileges and favors. In the rural economy, Chinese loans to village farmers and petty hawkers fueled the trade of village commodities for store-bought things: threads and yarns, knives, scissors, mirrors. These debts compromised the Dutch: they bent the *priyayi* to Chinese interest; and they bound the peasant to the Chinese peddler (and his patrons elsewhere), who offered cash and goods on credit secured by the upcoming harvest.[11]

Even with the demise of the Cultivation System in the 1870s and the abolition of the opium farm system in the 1890s, this pattern not only survived but deepened in the final decades of Dutch colonial rule. The establishment of a directly state-run "Opium Regie" and the phasing-out of other revenue farms at the turn of the century worked to undermine—and in many cases to bankrupt—the sprawling commercial empires of the great *peranakan* families. But these shifts in state policies coincided with a new wave of immigration from China, with women and non-Hokkien speakers arriving in large numbers for the very first time. Such "re-Sinifying" trends combined with nationalist agitation and dynastic decline in China to produce demands for new freedoms and privileges, such as the European legal status that the Dutch had granted to Japanese residents of the Indies in 1899. By the turn of the century the Chinese association Tiong Hoa Hwee Koan (THHK) was established, and in a few short years THHK schools were in operation in a number of cities and towns in Java and Sumatra. At the same time, Chinese chambers of commerce were set up in major commercial centers. The Dutch colonial authorities, alarmed by the rise of Chinese nationalism in the Indies, responded with important concessions, effectively dismantling the system of restrictions on Chinese residence and travel and founding Dutch Chinese schools (*Hollandsch-Chineesche scholen*) even before the collapse of the reigning Ch'ing dynasty in 1912 and the subsequent establishment of a Chinese republic.[12]

The remaining three decades of Dutch rule thus saw alternative poles of attraction—Chinese nationalism and Western liberalism—for the Chinese population in the era of the Ethical Policy and the expansion of modern education, neither of which led toward assimilation with the broad mass of the population. At the same time as Chinese *mestizos* were becoming "Filipinos" in the Philippines and *lukjin* were becoming "Thais" in Siam, their creolized counterparts in the Netherlands East Indies remained decidedly "Chinese." Meanwhile, with the effective removal of restrictions on Chinese travel and residence in the archipelago, a new wave of foreign-born (*totok*) Chinese merchants more closely tied—through recent migration, marriage, language, and schooling—to China came to occupy the same set of commercial roles once occupied by the vast networks of the old opium-farm-based *peranakan* dynasties.[13] Insofar as these *totok* and their children became absorbed and acculturated into their new surroundings, the path of assimilation followed the footsteps of the their *peranakan* fellow-"Chinese" into modern education and the professional classes. As Dutch rule drew to a close in the 1940s, the Chinese were thus firmly stereotyped as one of Edna Bonacich's "middleman minorities"[14] and segregated in a classic example of what John Furnivall described as a "plural society":

> It is in the strictest sense a medley, for they mix but do not combine. Each group holds by its own religion, its own culture and language, its own ideas and ways. As individuals they meet, but only in the market-place, in buying and selling. There is a plural society, with different sections of the community living side by side, but separately, within the same political unit. Even in the economic sphere there is a division of labour along racial lines. Natives, Chinese, Indians and Europeans all have different functions, and within each major group subsections have particular occupations. There is, as it were, a caste system, but without the religious basis that incorporates caste in social life in India.[15]

Early Postcolonial Permutations

The pattern of class formation under Dutch colonial rule left a number of important legacies in postindependence Indonesia. Most obviously, since independence at the end of 1949, state policies have reflected and reproduced the problematic and vulnerable position of a putatively alien, pariah capitalist class in postcolonial Indonesia. Although locally born residents of Chinese ancestry were offered Indonesian citizenship at the time of independence, foreign-born Chinese were designated as aliens, and in practice the absence of documentary proof of Indonesian citizenship in the 1950s meant that there was "no way for a person who had a Chinese name to prove he was not an alien, a serious drawback, because in business and travel they frequently had to show proof of citizenship," explains Mary Somers.[16] Indeed, the early postindependence Soekarno era saw the establishment of myriad restrictions on Chinese business in the name of economic nationalism, as the national government, writes William Skinner, "used its controls over credit facilities, import and manufacturing licenses, wholesale rights, and foreign exchange to favor not just Indonesian citizens but *asli* ('indigenous') Indonesians."[17] In addition to restrictions on further Chinese immigration, controls on Chinese schools and media outlets, and taxes and other regulations imposed on "aliens," even Indonesian citizens of Chinese descent were prohibited from owning land, rice mills, and other key economic resources.[18] In 1959, moreover, a new government regulation banning retail trade by aliens in rural areas, although inconsistently enforced, led to the exodus of 100,000 residents of Chinese origin from Indonesia in subsequent months.[19] Overall, instead of embracing ethnic Chinese capitalists as a domestic bourgeoisie deserving of national state protection and promotion, the early postindependence state viewed them as compradores for or elements of foreign capital and treated them accordingly.[20]

Under the conservative Suharto regime inaugurated in the mid-1960s, moreover, a full-fledged reversion to the double-edged policies of the Dutch colonial era was effected. On the one hand, ghettoization and discrimination were promoted in the social and cultural realm. Playing on fears and resentments drummed up in the anti-Communist pogroms of 1965–66, the Suharto regime exaggerated and demonized ethnic Chinese links to Beijing and imposed draconian constraints on the cultural life of the ethnic Chinese community as a whole. In the name of national integration, displays of Chinese cultural, linguistic, and religious distinctiveness were restricted, even as discriminatory policies impeded access to state employment for Indonesians of Chinese ancestry.[21] New government relations forcing all Indonesians to declare their religious faith, expanding religious instruction in schools, and banning interfaith marriages worked to harden religious identities and boundaries, thus further distancing the overwhelmingly non-Muslim Chinese from the broad mass of the Indonesian population.

On the other hand, in the realm of private capital accumulation, the Suharto regime relied heavily on Chinese pariah entrepreneurs to oil the rusty cogs of the state machinery and the domestic market, much as the Dutch colonial administration had done in the nineteenth century. Economic liberalization in the late 1960s and an oil boom in the 1970s created unprecedented opportunities for capital accumulation under a state-led program of (mostly import-substitution) industrialization, with old patterns of army "parallel financing" and business partnerships with Chinese cronies persisting at the local level and now extrapolated to the national arena as well. In the first two decades of the New Order, such men as Liem Sioe Liong and Bob Hasan, Chinese business partners of Suharto since the 1950s, began to construct vast, diversified economic empires through state bank loans, monopoly franchise concessions, and other special government facilities.[22] Additional well-connected Chinese *konglomerat* similarly emerged and thrived through partnerships with key military commands and subcontracting deals with state enterprises.[23] The New Order's pattern of centralized and insulated state power prefiguring a pattern of "market corruption" based on monetary transactions—rather than enduring webs of influence—between private businessmen and government officials.[24] In the 1980s and early 1990s, moreover, as economic growth accelerated under an export-oriented industrialization strategy, Chinese *konglomerat lokal* emerged in cities and towns scattered throughout the archipelago and engaged in a broad variety of business activities facilitated by collusive relationships with local military and civil officials.[25] Yet their steady advancement was confined to capital accumulation in only the narrowest sense: New Order policies discriminating against the Chinese impeded their ascendancy within the military hierarchy, the bureaucracy, and other circuitries of state power.

The continued designation and stereotyping of Chinese Indonesians as a putatively foreign, pariah capitalist class has held important consequences for class relations in Indonesia more broadly. First and foremost was the equation of "Chinese" with money in the eyes of many Indonesians.[26] As the sociolinguist Dede Oetomo noted about his hometown in East Java in the 1980s, "When most Javanese and other non-Chinese in a place like Pasuruan think about the Chinese, almost invariably the first thing that comes up in their mind is money."[27] This association of "Chinese" with money—and more important, perhaps, money with "Chinese"—was especially significant insofar as it rendered the operations of the capitalist economy essentially foreign and unassimilable to Indonesian society. The political scientist Yoon Hwan Shin noted in the early 1990s:

> Since independence, the concept of private capitalism has had negative connotations in Indonesia. Because the Indonesian usage of the term capitalism often accompanies such modifiers as free fight after Sukarno [Soekarno] used it that way, many Indonesian elites exploited the term politically and implanted connotations of inherent chaos, unfairness, and selfishness in it. Their suspicion of capitalism was frequently expressed in creative but unsubstantiated conceptual forms. During Parliamentary

Democracy, there was Assatism; Sukarno popularized communalistic Marhaenism; now under the New Order, much ink has been spilled to debate the Pancasila Economic System (Sistem Perekenomian Pancasila). These expressions, despite the different emphases and nuances among them, share at least one connotation: a hatred of a social stratum that the indigenous society lacks and that was and is occupied by the former colonizers and their collaborators. An economic system that leaves or helps them go their way was believed to undermine the well-being of the indigenous population.[28]

This widely shared ambivalence, skepticism, and hostility toward unbridled *kapitalisme* found in Indonesian society created strongly felt absences, antagonisms, and opportunities. As suggested most clearly by their real or perceived awkwardness, obliviousness, and impropriety in the context of the Javanese linguistic hierarchy, the—allegedly exclusionary, arrogant— Chinese came to occupy an uneasy, ambiguous, outsider position in Indonesian society.[29] Thus, unlike their assimilated counterparts in the Philippines and Thailand in the 1980s and early 1990s, for example, the predominantly Chinese business class in Indonesia was singularly ill suited and disinclined to assert itself politically, to assume the leadership of the struggle for democratization, or to anticipate the enhancement and entrenchment of its interests under conditions of democracy. In contrast with Philippine and Thai democratization, (see chapter 5), Chinese capital in Indonesia was conspicuous only by its absence during the mobilization against Suharto in 1998. And in the competitive elections of 1999, Chinese businessmen were relegated to minor supporting (financial)—rather than starring (political)—roles.[30]

Meanwhile, since petty capitalist middlemen roles had been allocated almost exclusively to Chinese immigrants and their offspring in the Dutch colonial "plural society," the indigenous aristocracies of the archipelago (most notably on Java) were fossilized and gradually bureaucratized, rather than reoriented and transformed in the direction of private capital accumulation. The result, enduring "traditional" residues of distaste and distrust vis-à-vis mercantile roles and monetized market relations among many Indonesians, has been reported by ethnographers as recently as the early 1990s.[31] Given the obstacles placed in the path of native entrepreneurs by the Dutch colonial regime, the advantages of early immersion in the urban cash nexus, and the accumulated experience, informal networks, and capital enjoyed by immigrant Chinese capitalists,[32] latecomer challenges by alternative Indonesian elites—whether dressed up as Communism, Nationalism, or Islam—would always, by definition, be *political* projects heavily dependent on control over the Indonesian state.[33] Whether waged in the name of the Proletariat, the *Rakyat* [the People] or the *Ummat* [Islamic community], such struggles from the 1920s through the 1990s would always rest on a strong assumption—or perhaps an abiding projection—of the latent possibility of popular radicalism inherent in the broad mass of the Indonesian population.

"The Hidden Force": The Popular Classes

Of all the countries in Southeast Asia (with the partial exception of central and northern Vietnam), Indonesia is distinguished by indigenous working classes whose real and imagined horizontal solidarities, collective identities, and capacities for popular mobilization have far exceeded those of their counterparts elsewhere in the region. Indonesia's peasants, workers, and unemployed urban poor folk have long been viewed—if not always by themselves, then by significant others—as enmeshed within class, community, and cultural collectivities rather than as atomized individuals. This distinctive—latent or active—strength of Indonesia's subaltern classes can be traced to the peculiar pattern of insertion of the peasantry into the world capitalist system under Dutch colonial rule, especially as it crystallized in the course of the nineteenth century.

Crystallization: Dutch Colonial Rule

More than that of any other colony in Southeast Asia, the administration of the Netherlands East Indies depended heavily on the strengthening of village institutions, understood by Dutch officials to have enjoyed considerable traditional depth and strength and consequently relied upon, reinforced, and reinvented as the bases for political control and economic extraction vis-à-vis the peasantry.[34] Thus Dutch officials often referred to villages, whether on Java, Sumatra, or in the Moluccas (today's Maluku) as "village republics" (*dorpsrepublieken*) and congratulated themselves on their efforts to weaken and eliminate the myriad intermediary figures—both native and Chinese—whom they viewed as "meddling" in village affairs.[35] Over the course of the late nineteenth and early twentieth centuries, moreover, Dutch colonial scholars of "customary" or *adat* law, most notably those coming out of the *adatrecht* school in Leiden, began to systematize *adat* law and to reify *adat* institutions so that, as Carol Warren explains, through the "invention of tradition" a *desa adat,* or customary village, emerged as a supposedly "autonomous, corporate village commu-

nity—the ideal-type *dorpsrepubliek.*[36] Revisionist scholars have concluded that "the village as a corporate, autonomous, and territorially defined unit was in a certain sense a creation of intensified colonial rule in the
early nineteenth century."[37]

The strength of community boundaries created by Dutch administrative
policies was further enhanced by colonial reliance on the village as the essential unit for economic extraction, most notably in the clove monopoly
in the Moluccas and under the Cultivation System of forced extractions of
sugar, coffee, and other cash crops in Java. Although some precolonial villages had strongly established patterns of communal land tenure and labor-
sharing schemes,[38] colonial-era villages in the Netherlands Indies more
widely and insistently relied on communal cultivation of various export
crops and the rotation and apportionment of land and labor at the village
level.[39] Significantly, too, the colonial regime erected formidable barriers
to the alienation of land to nonvillagers and left considerable landholding
in the realm of village control—whether in the form of communal lands or
the salary lands (*tanah bengkok*) awarded to village officials.[40] By the early
twentieth century in the *Vorstenlanden* (principalities) of Yogyakarta and
Surakarta on Java, for example, Takashi Shiraishi points out,

> usufruct rights in village communal land were distributed to the villagers,
> while dominion over the land belonged to the ruler and ownership rights
> to the village. Village communal land was parceled out in plots, each of
> which was approximately half a *bau,* and the usufruct right was given to
> a villager. The villager who was given the usufruct right in half a *bau* of
> arable land and was also given a housing plot was called *kuli kenceng.* . . .
> As long as village communal land was available, all the male household
> heads capable of performing obligations to the village and the state were
> accorded the hereditary status of *kuli kenceng,* which as a rule was inher-
> ited by the eldest son.[41]

Aside from land tenure, membership in the village entailed certain obligations, most notably participation in corvée labor and in local policing.
"First, the *kuli kenceng* was obliged to perform labor for the village, maintaining village roads, ditches, bridges, and graveyards, and in *ronda* (night
watch). Second, he had to perform corvée labor for the state in the maintenance of public roads, irrigation canals, and dams. And third, he had to
pay the land tax for his half a *bau* of rice land and his housing plot," writes
Victor Magagna. In short, if the essential dimensions of community
strength are "the mechanisms of authoritative control and jurisdiction of
membership, the channels of discursive focus that establish a folklore of

place, and the forms of economic cooperation that underpin membership claims to local subsistence," then certainly Dutch policies created strong notions of community when compared with colonial-era villages elsewhere in Southeast Asia.[42] Small wonder that beyond Sinicized Annam and Tonkin, only village Java has been designated by anthropologists—hyperbolically—as characterized by "closed corporate communities."[43]

Under Dutch colonial rule the processes of early proletarianization and urbanization also unfolded under distinctly communitarian auspices. Nowhere was this more true than in Java, where the state-run Cultivation System of the mid-nineteenth century forced the peasantry into a complex web of relations of production unparalleled in their intensity in Southeast Asia at the time. The Cultivation System awarded collective ownership of land to villages and assigned villagers collective responsibility for payment of land taxes (*landrente*). Robert Cribb points out that these obligations, as well as restrictions on mobility, tied Javanese peasants to their villages, which "were reorganized both to emphasize the uniform obligation of all village members and to facilitate supervision."[44] Thus, as Clifford Geertz has noted: "The Javanese cane worker remained a peasant at the same time that he became a coolie, persisted as a community-oriented household farmer at the same time that he became an industrial wage laborer. He had one foot in the rice terrace, and the other in the mill."[45] After the passage of the Agrarian Law of 1870, and with the dawning of the Ethical Policy in the early 1900s, this pattern was preserved through contracts between Javanese villages and European estates. Geertz continues:

> Not only did the estate have to adapt to the village through the land-lease system and various other "native-protection" devices forced on it by an "ethical" colonial government, but, even more comprehensively, the village had to adapt to the estate. The mode of its adaptation was again involutional. The basic pattern of village life was maintained, and in some ways even strengthened, and the adjustment to the impingements of high capitalism effected through the complication of established institutions and practices. In land tenure, in crop regime, in work organization, and in less directly economic aspects of social structure as well, the village . . . faced the problems posed by a rising population, increased monetization, greater dependence on the market, mass labor organization, more intimate contact with bureaucratic government, and the like, not by a dissolution of the traditional pattern into an individualistic "rural proletarian" anomie, nor yet by a metamorphosis of it into a modern commercial farming community. Rather . . . it maintained the over-all outlines of that pattern while driving the elements of which it was composed to ever-higher degrees

of ornate elaboration and Gothic intricacy. Unable either to stabilize the equilibrated wet-rice system it had autochthonously achieved before 1830, or yet to achieve a modern form on, say, the Japanese model, the twentieth-century lowland Javanese village—a great sprawling community of desperately marginal agriculturalists, petty traders, and day laborers—can perhaps only be referred to, rather lamely, as "post-traditional."[46]

Meanwhile, as the expanding urban centers of Batavia, Bandung, Medan, Makassar, Semarang, and Surabaya began to attract large numbers of migrants from their rural hinterlands, Dutch colonial policies of administration, policing, and surveillance promoted the emergence of well-defined urban neighborhoods. Just as Chinese residents were confined to designated urban areas as late as the early twentieth century, so were urban residents of indigenous origin subordinated to the logic of a finely meshed administrative grid, with Dutch policing complemented by neighborhood (*kampung*) night-watch patrols (*ronda*), as in village Java.[47] During the brief period of Japanese occupation (1942–45) during World War II, moreover, a system of neighborhood associations based on the Tonari Gumi model used in Japan was formalized and made compulsory in all urban centers.[48] This pattern of local policing in urban areas was revived and intensified in the postindependence era, with *ronda*, RT/RW, and police-trained civilian neighborhood security guards (*hansip*) making up what the New Order state termed a "security environment system" (*siskamling* or *sistem keamanan lingkungan*).[49] In rural areas, likewise, with minor modifications, the Dutch system of village administration was imposed or reimposed throughout Indonesia: elected village headmen (on eight-year rather than lifelong terms), large patches of communal land allocated to villages, (plus salary land for village headmen), and agricultural cooperatives, development subsidies, and other state programs—health care, literacy, cleanliness, culture—organized at the village level.[50]

Early Postcolonial Permutations

The intensity of local administration, policing, and surveillance on the part of the postcolonial state reflected in part a response to the perceived density of community identities, activities, and associational forms in Indonesian society, which under the New Order were recognized, reified, and reinvented as "culture" and "tradition." Picking up where Dutch colonial scholars in Leiden's *adatrecht* school left off in the 1930s, U.S.-trained Indonesian anthropologists operating under the Parsonian modernization/political development paradigm of the 1950s and early 1960s described In-

donesian villages as "social systems" that stressed not only customary law
(*adat*) but community practices of reciprocity and mutual aid (*gotong-roy-
ong*) and rule by consensus (*musyawarah*).[51] In Java, for example, anthropologists lavished considerable attention on the communal feasting rituals
(*slametan*) accompanying all life-cycle rituals as well as other important
occasions,[52] and in some cases described Javanese villages as "closed corporate peasant communities."[53] Robert Jay's important ethnographic account of Central Java in the early postindependence era noted:

> The various relationships of reciprocity and dependence spread out from
> an individual household like a closely woven net. Yet the mesh does not
> simply become wider and wider and more lightly woven in passing from
> the center outward, although it is in this way that the villagers conceive of
> their individual, local ties. There are instead more or less sharply defined
> locales within which the villagers exchange more frequently with each
> other than any of them do with households outside of the locale. *These
> units, which may be called "neighborhoods," have turned out to be highly
> solidary politically, and as factionalism has spread and intensified in rural
> Modjokuto, cutting across dukuhan and even village communities, only
> the local neighborhood has remained unfractured.*[54]

In the Moluccas, villages were depicted as "discrete *adat* communities,"[55]
while on Bali scholarly focus centered on the "compound of social structures, each based on a different principle of social affiliation," which characterized villages there.[56]

Ironically, national-level Indonesian politicians drew on such conceptions of traditional community to justify new forms of authoritarian rule:
Soekarno, the country's first president, dissolved the elected parliament in
1960 and installed in its stead an appointed Gotong Royong Parliament.
His successor, Suharto, made use of a largely appointed supraparliamentary body, the Majelis Permusyawaratan Rakyat (MPR) or People's Consultative Assembly, which convened on a quintennial basis to rubber-stamp
his "reelection."[57] Under Suharto's New Order, moreover, the creation of
a centralized, bureaucratic, authoritarian state entailed the standardization
of communities as "essentially uniform replicas of a generic village," especially after the passage of the Village Act of 1979.[58] Thus in Java, for example, according to John Pemberton, "within the New Order's intensely
cultural discourse, all villages [were] imagined to contain, willy-nilly, ex-
plicitly ritual events aimed toward the same general end: the preservation
of a broader inheritance—of 'Java.'"[59]

Yet even those anthropologists amply suspicious of the reinvention and redeployment of village tradition under the Suharto regime remained impressed by the density of community activities, identities, and forms of association. In Java as late as the early 1990s, Pemberton noted, "village practices abound both in kind and in number and disclose a complexity that, in many respects, far exceeds that of the more routinely celebrated domestic events."[60] In Ambon and elsewhere in Maluku, scholars highlighted the importance of *pela gandong,* pacts forged between village communities, in the settlement of local disputes.[61] Meanwhile, on Bali, ethnographic research traced the importance of "intersecting but semi-autonomous corporate units of a special purpose character" in everyday village life. As catalogued by Carol Warren:

> The *banjar* is the civic community; the *subak* (agricultural associations) organize irrigation and other aspects of farming which require common coordination; the *dadia* or *soroh* is a kin-group based on descent through the male line; *pemaksan* (temple support groups) are responsible for the maintenance of village shrines and the organization of much of local ritual beyond the life cycle and ancestral ceremonies of family and kin-groups; and *seka* include clubs and voluntary work-groups formed to do just about everything else. *Banjar, pemaksan,* and *seka* usually draw their memberships from within the *desa,* while *subak* and *dadia* memberships frequently cross-cut it. The result is a complicated, nevertheless highly structured, arrangement of overlapping but non-coordinate corporate groups, a pattern Clifford Geertz termed "pluralistic collectivism."[62]

Overall, this persistent understanding of peasants—and their urban poor and proletarian counterparts—as essentially "pre-organized"[63] inflected class relations in Indonesia with a strong sense of both danger and possibility. On the one hand, Dutch colonial officials, Chinese businessmen, and others seen—or seeing themselves—as outsiders and intruders have feared popular (and violent) sanctions at the hands of the "dangerous" classes. After all, as James Siegel has shown, the Indonesian village or urban neighborhood (*kampung*) community has been built on the threat and practice of violence. From its inception, community policing, as embodied in the *ronda,* has defined the boundaries of community membership, and on both Java and Bali countless acts of "local justice" (*main hakim sendiri*) such as (fatal) crowd beatings and lynchings of accused witches and thieves were recorded throughout the twentieth century.[64] Meanwhile, on Ambon and elsewhere in Maluku, the *pela gandong* long served as the basis not only for the settlement of disputes between villages but also for the forging of alliances between some villages in wars against other villages.[65] Thus, as suggested by the title of Louis Couperus's celebrated novel of late nineteenth-century Java, Dutch officials sensed the power of a "Hidden Force" beneath the calm veneer of colonial *rust en orde* (tranquillity and order) in the Netherlands East Indies.[66] As Benedict Anderson has noted, "any reading of Dutch colonial literature astounds one with its obsessive concern with menaces to order."[67]

The successors to the Dutch have been haunted by similar fears in post-independence Indonesia. The "*Revolusi*" (1945–49), after all, was accompanied by a number of local social revolutions in Java and elsewhere in the archipelago; and in the highly mobilized mass politics of the Soekarno era the pattern of local strike actions, demonstrations, and unilateral land seizures (*aksi sepihak*) in various parts of the country far exceeded even the agenda of the Partai Komunis Indonesia (PKI).[68] Even under the highly authoritarian and repressive Suharto regime, Indonesia was unmatched in Southeast Asia as a country in which crowds of ordinary people—football hooligans, opposition party campaign convoys, wildcat striking workers, villagers, and urban residents fighting evictions or environmental problems—took action. Small wonder that urban, middle-class Indonesians have been haunted by a much stronger sense of class fear than their counterparts elsewhere in the region. Pemberton noted in the early 1990s that "although glosses like the 'people' (*rakyat*), 'little people' (*wong cilik*), or simply 'villagers' (*wong desa*) are recalled to keep the inhabitants of rural Java in place, behind such constructs looms the threat of their dissolution. Part of an urbanite's fear of becoming disoriented in rural travels lies precisely in the fantasized possibility of coming face-to-face with a crowd of villagers who might mistake him for a thief and, no questions asked, take action."[69]

On the other hand, since at least the late colonial era, this Hidden Force has been viewed more positively, as something to be appropriated, invoked, and deployed for the acquisition of political power. Perhaps the earliest realization of such a possibility on a significant scale was the Sarekat Islam in the 1910s and 1920s, which grew into the Netherlands East Indies' first mass social movement *pergerakan* in part by drawing on urban *ronda* as well as established practices of village protest and work stoppages.[70] Through rallies and other mass actions, the leaders of this new movement—and journalists in the new Indonesian-language newspapers of the era—came to believe that they spoke for "Islam," "the proletariat," or "the people." The potential of popular radicalism resurfaced in the mid-1940s, thanks largely to the unparalleled mobilization of Indonesian youth in paramilitary organizations during the Japanese occupation period.[71] Thus the immediate aftermath of World War II witnessed neither a carefully stage-managed pattern of decolonization (as in British Malaya or the American-ruled Philippines) nor a guerrilla war led by a tightly centralized Leninist organization (as in Vietnam) but instead a form of popular struggle for independence notable for its loosely structured wave of local mobilizational efforts, often verging on or spilling over into local "social revolutions."[72] The enduring traces of this pattern were abundantly evident in the populist, mobilizational politics of the Soekarno era, and especially in the ill-fated PKI, whose cadres and affiliated front organizations constituted the largest Communist Party outside the Soviet bloc and the People's Republic of China (PRC) in the late 1950s and early 1960s. As suggested by Soekarno's claim to be the "extension of the tongue of the people" (*penyambung lidah rakyat*), the politicians of this period strongly imagined and repeatedly invoked the notion of a mobilized—or mobilizable—national community, variously construed as the *Ummat,* the *Rakyat,* or the Proletariat.[73] The perceived power of the Hidden Force, in short, gave rise to diverse fantasies about the potential consequences of popular mobilization under various banners.

With the ouster of Soekarno and the crystallization of a conservative authoritarian regime under Suharto in the mid-1960s, the performative, constitutive invocation of "the people" was replaced by that of "PKI," the abbreviation for the Indonesian Communist Party or its members, which, against the backdrop of the military-directed pogroms that killed hundreds of thousands and left many others in prison, functioned as a performative but, through disarticulation, literally as a death sentence. As James Siegel has noted, "Words of disarticulation fill[ed] in the place left vacant by *rakyat* and 'revolution,' aiming to reverse the effects of that word. But the force that generated *rakyat* continue[d]."[74] Although the profoundly demobilizational and repressive thrust of the Suharto regime's policies recast most forms of popular expression and participation as "criminal" or "subversive" threats to "security" (*keamanan*) and "development" (*pembangunan*), the displaced but never fully dissolved Hidden Force of popular radicalism persistently haunted the New Order. Surfacing time and again in countless land seizures, strikes, and other episodes (*peristiwa*) of disruptive mass mobilization, and in raucous campaign rallies for the Partai Persatuan Pembangunan (PPP), or United Development Party, in the 1970s and 1980s and Partai Demokrasi Indonesia (PDI) in the 1990s,[75] the spectral power of the *Rakyat* was clearly on the rise as Indonesia entered the final years of the Suharto era. Thus, over the course of the twentieth century the problematic and "alien" status of the predominantly Chinese capitalist class in Indonesia combined with the latent powers and imagined possibilities of this Hidden Force to help create space for the emergence, entrenchment, and evolution of a national political class.

Aliran: Education, Religion, and the Political Class

The historically determined unsuitability of the putatively alien capitalist class to rule for itself in Indonesia has left control of the state—in large part by default—in the hands of a separate political class whose power has rested on its claims to state power. The recruitment and reproduction of this political class through institutions of learning has assigned education—and religion—an especially important role in mediating and reproducing social and political relations of inequality and domination in the country. As with Indonesia's problematically Chinese business class and its distinctly "dangerous" popular classes, the formation of the political class owed much to the peculiarities of Dutch rule in the archipelago from the seventeenth century to the 1940s. Its origins in the nexus of state power—rather than in economic relations of production—prefigured a highly complex and unstable pattern of internal differentiation and change, from the onset of independence in late 1949 to the late Suharto era in the 1990s. It is within the pattern of formation and transformation of this political class that the peculiar position of religious institutions and authority in Indonesia must be situated.

Crystallization: Dutch Colonial Rule

Over the course of the long colonial era, Dutch reliance on the indigenous aristocracies of the archipelago—most notably the Javanese *priyayi*—shifted from loose tributary relations with ruling dynasties to direct incorporation into a bureaucracy in which entry and ascendancy depended on criteria increasingly requiring modern educational qualifications rather than merely familial connections.[76] Thus the final century of colonial rule saw the expansion not only of the native bureaucracy but also of the modern school system, out of which many leaders of the Indonesian nationalist movement eventually emerged. For both the Dutch colonial regime in the era of the Ethical Policy and the Indonesian nationalist movement in its infancy, education and modernization came to rival, if never fully replace, tradition as the basis for the claim to rule over the archipelago.

In addition, the Dutch colonial era saw the crystallization of a pattern in which modern religious identities and educational networks were established and intertwined. In various localities around the Netherlands East Indies, residual Catholic influences from the early Portuguese era (especially in the eastern islands) and much later Protestant missionary efforts under Dutch (or occasionally English or German) auspices created small pockets of Christian identity centered on missionary schools of various denominations and affiliations.[77] Such schools not only introduced these converts to the Bible and to a distinctly modern notion (a "Great Tradition") of religious faith and identity but also served as transmission belts for the recruitment of colonial civil servants, soldiers, teachers, and other professionals. The small but privileged minority of Indonesian Christians was destined to be markedly overrepresented in the ranks of the bureaucracy, the army, the universities, and the urban middle class.[78]

Thus the connection between religious identity, education, and access to state power was established in a pattern strikingly reminiscent of the pillarization (*verzuiling*) of Dutch society back in the metropole as early as the late nineteenth century.[79] As scholars have noted, Protestant and Catholic "pillars" of Dutch society created dense webs of educational and associational activity divided along religious lines.[80] "These deep religious cleavages," relates Albert Schrauwers, resulted in the development of separate religious school systems, religious political parties, and a host of religiously oriented service agencies such as housing developments, unions, newspapers, radio stations, and hospitals, which elsewhere in the West were sponsored by a secular state. Earlier in this century, typical pillarized Dutch working-class citizens would, for example, rent a house in a Protestant church-sponsored housing development, send their children to a church-sponsored school, read Protestant newspapers, and vote for the Anti-Revolutionary Party (the Orthodox Calvinist party)."[81]

Against this backdrop, and in the context of broader changes far beyond the Indonesian archipelago, the last half-century of Dutch colonial rule also saw the efforts of self-consciously "modernist" Muslims—drawn largely from the small indigenous mercantile class—to create their own network of modern educational institutions, most notably under the associational rubric of Muhammadiyah, an organization founded in 1912. Inspired by the ideas and aspirations of Islamic modernism and reformism circulating since the late nineteenth century in centers of Muslim learning in the Middle East, Muhammadiyah established a network of modern schools known as *madrasah*, which were intended to combine new forms of religious instruction with the kind of Western-style schooling that had given Christians such advantages in the Netherlands East Indies.[82]

By contrast and in reaction to Muhammadiyah, the formation of the Nahdlatul Ulama (NU) in 1926 signified the defense of the long-established system of rural Islamic boarding schools on Java and elsewhere in the archipelago. In these *pesantren* (or *pondok, surau,* or *dayah,* as they are sometimes known outside Java), the method of learning grew out of a largely oral tradition of scholasticism in which religious scholars called *ulama* or *kyai* led instruction in the vocalization and interpretation of the Qur'an and other key Islamic texts in classical Arabic.[83] The *kyai* in the *pesantren* milieu came to enjoy what is often described as charismatic authority; the activities involved in their multiplicity of roles ranged from scholastic inspiration to economic patronage, political brokership, martial arts instruction, and spiritual guidance and healing. As Martin van Bruinessen, an authority on the *pesantren,* has noted: "The *pesantren* tradition is pervaded by a highly devotional and mystical attitude. Supererogatory prayers and the recital of litanies (*dhikr, wird, ratib*) complement the canonical obligations. Many *kyai* are moreover affiliated with a mystical order (*tariqa*) and teach their followers its specific devotions and mystical exercises. Visits to the graves of local saints and great *kyai* are an essential part of the annual cycle; most Javanese *pesantren* hold annual celebrations on the anniversaries of the deaths of their founding *kyai.*"[84] Advanced pupils (*santri*) in the *pesantren* studied for years under the tutelage of a single *kyai,* often spending additional years in other *pesantren* in the archipelago linked to that of their *kyai* through dense webs of mentorship, influence, and intermarriage, and sometimes making the Hajj and circulating through Islamic schools in the Middle East.[85]

The *pesantren* network was thus not a set of educational institutions from which students graduated and launched themselves into broader orbit in the world at large but rather a milieu within which *santri* remained immersed, circulated, and accumulated cultural, intellectual, and social capital. Even though the style and substance of instruction in the *pesantren* changed over the course of the twentieth century in response to the forces and exigencies of modernization, these schools retained more distance from the modern school system and all that it implied (e.g., access to the modern state) than did the *madrasah.*[86]

Scholars have shown that these different school networks provided the sociological basis for the formation of the Indonesian nationalist elite during the struggle for independence and the early postindependence period. Whether in the Indies or in the Netherlands itself, Dutch schooling, while designed to reshape the children of the local aristocracies into colonial bureaucrats, also helped to produce the bilingual intelligentsia from which such prominent figures as Soekarno, Hatta, and Sjahrir emerged.[87] Protestant and Catholic missionary schools, though often imparting a strong sense of identification with the Netherlands among their graduates, contributed significantly to the growth of literacy and the circulation of thousands of Ambonese soldiers, bureaucrats, teachers, and missionaries—and Minahasan policemen, company clerks, plantation overseers, and mine foremen—throughout the archipelago that would become Indonesia.[88] More important, perhaps, Islamic schools of various stripes broadened the social consciousness and sociological connectedness of hundreds of thousands or, indeed, millions of Indonesians.[89] As noted in Siegel's study of Aceh, for example, the Islamic *ulama* and their students in the *pesantren* and *madrasah* had a special place in society:

> Only they were born into a sphere of life—the village—which they had to leave in order to achieve their status. Chieftains, sultans, and peasants were all, in theory, born to their places. *Ulama,* however, had to leave the village, where relationships were governed by kinship, in order to unite as Muslims in the religious schools. The experience of two radically different kinds of life made them stress the qualities common to all men regardless of social identifications. They saw their own life in the religious schools as a manifestation of common human nature. . . .
>
> The experience of two radically different cultural worlds, which were not linked by the normal expectations of the life cycle, led the *ulama* to stress that man's nature could be the basis of unity between men even when sociological distinctions separated them. In the absence of cultural bonds between men, the *ulama* formulated ideas out of their own experience which could tie men together. Islamic ideas provided an idiom by which unity despite social distinction could be expressed.[90]

Thus, as scholars have shown, during the *Revolusi* in 1945–49, these schools combined with the mass paramilitary schooling that had been offered by the Japanese occupational authorities in 1943–45 to provide diverse—and competing—sources of recruitment for nationalist mobilization. against the Dutch. Brought together from villages and provinces around the archipelago, the *pemuda* (youth) who championed the independence struggle forged solidarities among themselves—and made claims to represent Indonesia and Indonesians more broadly—based on their shared experiences of schooling and school-based socialization.[91] Yet, as suggested by the proclamation of an Islamic State of Indonesia (Negara Islam Indonesia) by Islamist elements among the revolutionaries in August 1949 and the persistence of armed struggle for an Abode of Islam (Darul Islam) through the 1950s and into the early 1960s in West Java, pockets of Central Java, South Kalimantan, South Sulawesi, and Aceh, the postindependence history of Indonesia would be scarred by conflict and violence among rival currents or streams (*aliran*) in the country's religious and social life.

Early Postcolonial Permutations

In the early years of the independent republic, the embryonic Indonesian national state constituted itself through *aliran* now reconfigured as political parties. Under Soekarno, as is well known, the broad patterns of political party cohesion and conflict in Indonesian society corresponded to major *aliran* that were rooted in different sets of educational institutions and experiences. As in Dutch *verzuiling,* the Indonesian *aliran* pattern linked all the major political parties—the Partai Nasionalis Indonesia (PNI), the Partai Komunis Indonesia (PKI), Masjumi (the modernist Islamic party), and Nahdlatul Ulama (NU)—to distinct educational and associational networks. "With one or another of these parties as nucleus," writes Geertz, "an *aliran* was a cluster of nationalist organizations—women's clubs, youth groups, boy scouts, charitable societies, cooperatives, lending societies, private schools, athletic clubs, religious organizations, labor and peasant unions, art groups, trade organizations—sharing a similar ideological direction or standpoint and loyalty to the same all-Indonesia leadership. There was a PNI peasant organization, a PKI peasant organization, a Masjumi peasant organization, and an NU peasant organization; there were PNI, PKI, Masjumi, and NU boy scouts, and so on: even the kindergartens divided up this way."[92]

Thus the two political parties identified as representing the interests and aspirations of most devout Muslims were both designated as *santri*—a term that not only refers to students in traditional Islamic boarding schools (*pesantren*) in particular but also connotes Islamic piety in general. The cleavage between the two parties, and between them and the other major parties, corresponded to their respective networks of religious schools: *pesantren* in the case of Nahdlatul Ulama, and modernist *madrasah* in the case of Masjumi. The leadership of the PNI, by contrast, owed its cohesion to networks and solidarities forged through the secular schools organized by the Dutch colonial regime to educate civil servants and native aristocrats, even while the PKI counted among its cadres many graduates of the experimental nationalist Taman Siswa schools and, more important, depended on a vast constituency of uneducated and illiterate peasants and workers who could be schooled through the PKI's own apparatus of popular education.[93] Of course, the leaders of these Big Four parties also relied heavily on opportunistic alliances and political machine mobilization, as in other democracies. But the abiding interparty cleavages in society at large and the fluctuating coalitions within and between party leaderships were markedly shaped by educational affiliations. "More than anything else," noted Joel Rocamora, "it was education that formed the basis of the elite status of Indonesia's nationalist politicians as a whole."[94]

Whereas the political parties thus worked to mediate—and to facilitate—the recruitment of a political class through the penetration and capture of the porous early postcolonial state in the Soekarno era, educational institutions and religious networks served as more direct transmission belts for the socialization and reproduction of the new political class that emerged under Suharto's New Order. Given the military predominance in most branches of government and the absence of competitive multiparty elections, the competition between *aliran* based in different educational institutions and identities became channeled and confined within the nation's military academies and universities, highly secularized institutions that fed directly into the core circuitries of the New Order state: the military officer corps, the ministries, and national and regional assemblies. Yet as Indonesia entered the final decade of the twentieth century, the pattern of enduring, evolving, and ever shifting contestation among rival networks (*jaringan*)—defined by educational and religious experiences and identities within the circuitries of the state—combined with ongoing changes in society to spell continuing, deepening uncertainty and instability within and beyond this political class.

Conclusion

In short, Dutch colonial rule left Indonesia with a pattern of class relations unique in Southeast Asia, one within which religious institutions and authority figured both prominently and problematically. Unlike the Philippines and Thailand, where assimilation of Chinese immigrants facilitated the rise of a properly indigenous business class capable of ruling for itself, the segregation and stigmatization of *peranakan* and *totok* Chinese alike precluded the political hegemony of Indonesia's overwhelmingly ethnic Chinese bourgeoisie. Instead, the pariah and putatively foreign status of the country's established business class impeded the localization and legitimation of capitalism among the broad mass of the population, even as it impelled aspiring indigenous elites to seek power and wealth not through private capital accumulation but instead through the articulation of claims to state power. Hence the weakness of business support for democracy in

Indonesia on the one hand, and on the other the popularity of variously Communist, Islamist, and Nationalist schemes for heavy state intervention in the economy.

Meanwhile, unlike British colonial Malaya, where the Malay peasantry was preserved and "protected" while Chinese and Indian immigrants dominated the ranks of the colonial proletariat, Dutch policies in the Netherlands East Indies prefigured the early formation of a much more threatening indigenous Indonesian working class. More than anywhere else in Southeast Asia, the peasantry of the Indonesian archipelago was drawn into production for the world capitalist economy under administrative structures that reified, reinvented, and reinforced collective identities. More than anywhere else in Southeast Asia, the pattern of anticolonial struggle in Indonesia—from the campaigns of the Sarekat Islam of the 1910s to the *Revolusi* of the late 1940s—involved widespread popular mobilization. Small wonder that by the early 1960s Indonesia boasted the single largest Communist Party in the world outside the Soviet Union and China, and that even after the anti-Communist pogroms of 1965–66 the national elite has remained haunted by considerable fear of a mobilized underclass.

Finally, unlike either the competitive parliamentary democracies or the one-party regimes found elsewhere in Southeast Asia, Indonesia has inherited from the Dutch a distinctive pattern of rule by a political class defined—and divided—by educational background and achievement. Given the obvious unsuitability of the "alien Chinese" business class as rulers of an independent Indonesia and the evident capacity of "the People" for popular mobilization, claims to state power have by necessity been made on the basis of something broader—and newer—than narrow patron-client relations or neotraditionalism. Instead, since the emergence of the Indonesian nationalist movement in the early decades of the twentieth century, the recruitment and reproduction of the country's political class have been channeled through institutions of education. Hence the pattern of so-called *aliran* politics, whether under conditions of multiparty competition in the Soekarno era or via the university belt in Suharto's New Order regime.

Overall, the pattern of class relations in Indonesia has thus been characterized by considerable ambiguity, tension, and dynamism. In a country without a properly domestic business class, whose working classes preorganized to meet the intrusions and exactions of the market, capitalist development would remain a self-consciously political and inherently problematic project. In a country whose political class was recruited and reproduced through elite educational institutions, moreover, the basis of access to state power would remain unstable and in constant flux, its claims to represent broader popular forces forever open to question and contestation and to diverse fears, hopes, and fantasies. With such instability and uncertainty already evident even in the heyday of Suharto's New Order in the 1980s, by the early 1990s the process of capitalist development had combined with the regime's policies on religion and education to give rise to an ascendant segment of Indonesia's political class, one making new forms of claims on the representation of Islam. The riots, pogroms, and bombings of subsequent years signaled both the possibilities and the limitations of this trend.

3

Social Transformation, 1965–1998

Konglomerat, Kelas Bawah, Islam

The pattern of class formation that crystallized in the Dutch colonial era left a legacy of instability and dynamism in class relations in postindependence Indonesia. First of all, the very processes and imperatives of accumulation promoted by the country's capitalist class and the forces of the world capitalist economy gave rise to dramatic forms of economic and social change, with major implications not only for the relations of economic production but for class relations and social reproduction more broadly. In addition, an abiding sense of uncertainty—and possibility—stemmed from the "Hidden Force" of the country's working classes, whose noted capacity for mobilization was a source of both fear and hope for the political class that claimed to represent them. Further, the very nature of this political class, its diverse internal composition, and its variegated sources of recruitment also prefigured a strong measure of internal tension and contestation especially between competing *aliran,* currents emerging from different educational institutions, experiences, and networks, whether civilian or military, secular or Christian or Muslim.

The transformation of class relations in Indonesia over the course of the Suharto era involved the crystallization of a new pattern of private capital accumulation and a new basis for the recruitment and reproduction of the national political class in the late 1960s and early 1970s. The tension and dynamism inherent in Indonesia's new phase of capitalist development and its newly consolidated authoritarian regime gave rise also to decisive shifts in class relations in the archipelago—in particular, the emergence of Islam, first as a rubric for mobilization against a regime understood to be dominated by secular nationalists, Christians, and Chinese businessmen, and

44

subsequently as a banner for ascendancy to and attempted dominance of the political class controlling the circuitries of the Indonesian state. The fears, hopes, and fantasies associated with this trend set the stage for violence.

Capitalism with a Chinese Face, Authoritarianism with a Christian Sword

The three decades of authoritarian rule under Suharto (1966–1998) brought dramatic socioeconomic transformation. Economic liberalization in the mid-1960s opened the country to a massive flow of foreign loans and direct investment, followed by the oil boom and the deepening of import-substitution industrialization in the 1970s. World recession and falling commodity prices in the early to middle 1980s forced the government in the direction of deregulation, trade liberalization, and a shift into export-oriented industrialization, with manufacturing increasing its share of exports and of gross national product in the 1990s. Economic growth, averaging more than 7 percent per annum between 1986 and 1996, entailed unprecedented industrialization and urbanization.[1]

This process of capitalist development also had consequences for class relations in Indonesia. Over the course of the first two decades of the New Order, the "Chinese" business class was transformed from a collection of small-scale merchants and moneylenders into an interlocking directorate of commercial, financial, and industrial capital. Huge Chinese conglomerates emerged, such as Liem Sioe Liong's Salim Group and the Soeryadjaya family's Astra Group, with diverse interests ranging from automobile production to banking, food processing, electronics, household appliances, pharmaceuticals, real estate, and shipping. In the cities and major towns of the archipelago the signs of Chinese capital loomed increasingly large on the urban landscape: bank outlets, department stores, factories, residential subdivisions, shopping malls, and supermarkets. The names of major Chinese capitalists and their banks, conglomerates, and commodities—Liem Sioe Liong, Bank Central Asia (BCA), Maspion Group, Indomee—became household words, even as the familiar neighborhood Chinese shopkeeper was transformed into a local retail outlet for this nationwide, if not properly national, business class.[2]

Although the opening of the Indonesian economy to global flows of capital and goods and the active promotion of industrialization by the New Order state helped to promote the rise of the Chinese *konglomerat,* these same trends worked to undermine local and self-consciously indigenous merchant communities, which lacked access to high finance and technology, especially on Java. The cigarette manufacturers of Kudus, the pawnbrokers and moneylenders of Kotagede, and the batik manufacturers of Solo, Yogyakarta, and Pekalongan—small-scale, labor-intensive merchant communities, organized around family production and informal networks of credit and distribution, and lacking in established linkages with the state—found themselves marginalized by the 1980s, as mass production, national market circuitries, and international finance made impressive inroads. The Javanese batik industry, for example, had survived in the 1950s and early 1960s thanks to Soekarno's economic nationalist policies, under which the Gabungan Koperasi Batik Indonesia (GKBI), or Association of Indonesian Batik Cooperatives, enjoyed a monopoly on the import, production, and (subsidized) distribution of raw materials for batik production, and imitation batik products were largely restricted. But with the fall of Soekarno and economic liberalization under Suharto, the late 1960s and early 1970s witnessed a flood of mass-produced, printed, imitation batik products onto the market, and the rise of capital-intensive, high-tech batik production by large "Chinese" firms.[3] Suzanne Brenner has noted, with reference to the batik-producing community of Laweyan, Solo, that "communities like Laweyan . . . had become distinctly marginal to this arena, and many people in these merchant enclaves attributed their marginalization to the very processes of capitalist development that were rapidly advancing in other quarters."[4]

This process of capitalist transformation was overseen by a state in which the political class was regarded as under the control of those educated in secular and Christian schools. In fact, over the course of the first two decades of the New Order, President Suharto devised and installed a set of institutional mechanisms for the recruitment and circulation of this new political class, which in large part was composed of the armed forces officer corps, which had long been dominated by men raised in secular and Christian school systems. As is well known, Major General Suharto came to power in late 1965 in the wake of a coup d'état, and it was his position as commander of Kostrad, the Army Strategic Reserve Command, in Jakarta—and as one of the army's most senior generals—that allowed him to consolidate power, both within the armed forces and in Indonesian society at large. Under Suharto the army assumed a dominant role within the armed forces, the state, and society, and army officers (both active and retired) came to occupy numerous key positions as cabinet ministers, local government officials, heads of state enterprises, members of the regime's pseudoparliamentary bodies, and ranking members of Golkar (*Golongan Karya,* or Functional Groups), the regime's political machine. Institutionally, the armed forces' preeminent position within the state was guaranteed through its appointed representatives in a largely rubber-stamp parliament and the MPR, the body that met every five years to "elect" the president and vice president.[5] The entrenchment in power of the armed forces in general and the army in particular gave rise to a steady stream of officers who had graduated from the Akademi Militer Nasional at Magelang and circulated within key military commands and through most of the core civilian circuitries of the Indonesian state as well.

Yet this pattern of fluid circulation prefigured the internal transformation of the political class. First of all, the long years of Suharto's rule witnessed a steady erosion of the personal loyalty owed by the military leadership to the president himself. With every passing year, even as another annual batch of armed forces officers went into retirement at the age of fifty-five, Suharto too grew older, and his links to the officer corps—through shared personal, generational, and institutional experiences—grew ever more tenuous. In the late 1960s and 1970s he could still fill the uppermost ranks of the military hierarchy with trusted lieutenants from his days in the 1950s and earlier 1960s as commander of the army's Diponegoro (Central Java) Division, the Mandala Command for the Liberation of West Irian, and Kostrad. By the 1980s, however, virtually all his old army cronies had died off, disgraced themselves, or otherwise exhausted their usefulness. The old pattern could be prolonged only through extraordinary reliance on a single longtime protégé from a somewhat later generation: General Benny Murdani, a Catholic, who enjoyed unprecedented authority as Suharto's security and intelligence czar for much of the decade. As one analyst of the Indonesian military concluded in 1985: "It is safe now to say that at no previous time in Indonesia's history has a military man on active service had such complete control of the country's fire power as General Murdani."[6] Yet by the early 1990s, after Benny Murdani's long-postponed but perhaps inevitable demise, Suharto found himself reliant upon a military establishment dominated by officers who had risen up through the ranks having little direct personal contact with—or proven personal loyalty to—their president.

Second, from the early days of his seizure of power in late 1965, Suharto had also relied on civilian networks and bases of support and on constitutional and pseudodemocratic trappings to entrench himself as president and embellish his rule. Student activists, political party networks, and parliamentary figures had been cultivated in the effort to eliminate the PKI from the political scene and to engineer the dethroning of Soekarno; technocrats were enlisted to facilitate the reopening of the Indonesian economy to foreign capital; politicians (and thugs) were hired to manufacture electoral victories for Golkar and to staff the regime's rubber-stamp parliament; businessmen were promoted to oil the political machine and rewire the circuitries of the domestic market. Over time, the role of these civilians grew ever more significant and prominent.

Parallel with the processes of *mutasi* and *regenerasi* of the academy-trained military elite over the years, then, the Suharto era saw patterns of recruitment and circulation of these networks of civilian elites, who were inducted into the New Order regime through Indonesian universities. At first, the regime worked to incorporate remnants of the local aristocracies that had supported the colonial state under the Dutch and had survived and prospered in the postindependence era as the conservative backbone of Soekarno's PNI (Indonesian Nationalist Party) in many parts of the archipelago. In Java and Madura in the late 1960s and through much of the 1970s, the *priyayi* still retained numerous *bupati*ships (a *bupati*, or regent, heads each district, or regency) and, at least in the case of Mohammad Noer in East Java the governor's seat. The role of the Sultan Hamengku Buwono IX of Yogyakarta during this early period—first in the cabinet and later as Suharto's vice president—symbolized the apogee of this trend. In the Outer Islands a similar pattern prevailed, with Golkar typically built upon the bases of local aristocratic privilege and patronage networks previously sheltered beneath the umbrella of Soekarno's PNI. Yet by the late 1970s the centralizing tendencies of the regime, as well as the overabundance of retiring military officers to fill *bupati*ships, provincial governors' seats, and national-level bureaucratic posts, spelled the limits of aristocratic entrenchment, ascendancy, and accumulation in the New Order.[7] Indeed, the bureaucratic-authoritarian Suharto regime imposed a definite ceiling on the accumulation of social and political capital through private family networks—with only the one obvious major exception of Suharto and his relatives. The exigencies of socioeconomic modernization on the one hand and bureaucratic circulation on the other dictated a pattern of recruitment into—and reproduction of—the political class based not on blood but on something dressed up as merit.

In this regard, the *jaringan* (networks) of Indonesian Protestants and Catholics enjoyed a privileged position within the Suharto regime. Indeed, the first decades of the New Order saw the rise to unprecedented social and political prominence of members of Indonesia's small Christian minority. From parish schools scattered throughout the archipelago to seminaries to the Protestant and Catholic students' organizations at the most prestigious universities in the country, some Indonesian Christians enjoyed a clear head start in the multitiered hierarchy of education that fed into the New Order bureaucratic elite, even as their church coffers and business connections were enhanced by growing numbers of wealthy Chinese Protestants and Catholics.[8] University lecturers and student activists affiliated with the Partai Katolik and other Christian groups had joined the rallies against the PKI and Soekarno in the critical first months of the New Order and enjoyed something of a hegemonic position as the regime's leading political operatives for years thereafter. Most notoriously, General Ali Moertopo, close Suharto associate, political fixer, and head of Opsus (Special Operations), cultivated relations with a cluster of Catholic activists who, with Moertopo's blessing, founded the Center for Strategic and International Studies (CSIS) in the early 1970s. This clique of "political technocrats" helped craft the defusion of Konfrontasi, draft the blueprint for the Association of Southeast Asian Nations (ASEAN), build up Golkar and mastermind its first electoral success in 1971, and put an internationally palatable spin on the invasion of East Timor in 1975.[9] Through their positions at Indonesia's top universities, in the ranks of the military academy–trained officer corps, and in the CSIS, Catholics and Protestants thus landed themselves and their protégés in the seats of civilian and military power: in the cabinet, Golkar, its pseudoparliamentary bodies, and key media outlets and other business ventures. Even in the late 1980s, the top economic and security portfolios in the Indonesian cabinet were in Christian hands.

Besides these influential Indonesian Catholics and Protestants, a somewhat broader pool of Westernized and often Dutch-educated intellectuals loosely affiliated with the defunct Partai Sosialis Indonesia (PSI), or Socialist Party, exerted similar forms of influence within the regime and likewise used their patronage and protection to advance the careers and businesses of their former students and other protégés.[10] Best known since the 1950s as the party of highly cosmopolitan, well-educated, Dutch-speaking, secularized administrators and urban professionals, the PSI had never commanded much in the way of a popular electoral base during the period of constitutional democracy and was banned in 1960 for its role in CIA-backed regional rebellions of 1957–59. But its leading members and their ideas and broader sensibility long held positions of privilege and respect in the higher echelons of the bureaucracy and the armed forces, on university campuses, and in the press.[11] Crucially, PSI leaders enjoyed considerable credibility and close contacts among the regime's international backers, especially the U.S. government. With prominent aristocrats and modernist Muslims among its leaders and sympathizers, the more loosely structured PSI network also had a potentially broader purchase than the Catholic *jaringan* centered in the CSIS. These PSI strengths were well recognized by Suharto in the fragile first years of the New Order, as suggested by such early appointments as that of former PSI activist and prominent economist

Professor Soemitro Djojohadikusumo to be minister of trade and industry in 1968 (and a number of his protégés in subsequent years).[12]

In the byzantine politics of Jakarta in the 1970s and 1980s, however, PSI-linked networks were relegated to semioutsider status and viewed as potentially more oppositional than their Catholic rivals based in the CSIS. PSI leaders closely linked with the army's (West Java) Siliwangi Division were soon marginalized in favor of Suharto and his (Central Java) Diponegoro Division cronies.[13] PSI associates and sympathizers were also among those blamed for the so-called Malari riots of January 1974 (see chapter 5), which precipitated the downfall of the avowedly professional security chief General Soemitro, a bitter rival of Ali Moertopo and his CSIS operatives.[14] Subsequent years still saw a handful of "technocratic" and PSI-ish Soemitro protégés occupying cabinet posts, but the ascendancy and long entrenchment of the Catholic general Benny Murdani as security and intelligence czar in the 1980s maintained the upper hand for CSIS.

The two rival networks reached something of a standoff and modus vivendi in Golkar, the People's Representative Assembly (DPR), and the cabinet, on elite university campuses, and in the media, where the Catholic-run *Kompas* evolved into Jakarta's newspaper of record and the PSI-ish magazine *Tempo* became the nation's most respected weekly. Feeding the growing circulation of such publications, the steady flow of students through the nation's top universities over the years reproduced the social bases and sources of recruitment for these two rival networks as they orbited within the upper echelons of civilian power in the regime. Yet these cosmopolitan, Western-educated intellectuals, technocrats, and political operators represented a tiny privileged elite in a country where only a small fraction of the population reached the level of tertiary education.

The Specter and Attraction of Islam

For the first two decades of the New Order, graduates of Indonesia's vast and diverse network of Islamic schools were largely excluded from recruitment into the ranks of the new political class. Based in local institutions of Islamic worship and learning such as the *pesantren* and the *madrasah,* these historically autonomous and socially embedded Muslim networks were marginalized and alienated by the militarizing, centralizing, and Westernizing tendencies of the Suharto regime in the 1970s and 1980s. The *pesantren*-based leaders of Nahdlatul Ulama (NU), for example, had played a crucial role in the student protests and pseudoparliamentary maneuvers that led to Soekarno's downfall in 1966, and NU activists in regions such as East Java had provided the shock troops for the massacres of PKI members and sympathizers. But by the early 1970s, NU was openly at odds with the Suharto regime.[15] The 1971 election saw NU competing intensely with the regime's political machine Golkar for votes in the *pesantren* belt,[16] and subsequent years saw the loss of NU control over the Ministry of Religious Affairs and its forced fusion with other Muslim groups into a single political party, Partai Persatuan Pembangunan (PPP), or United Development Party, which was subjected to heavy-handed government restrictions and interference.[17]

Activists from the modernist Himpunan Mahasiswa Islam (HMI), or Islamic Students' Association, who had also joined in the anti-PKI rallies and anti-Soekarno maneuvers of 1965–66, were likewise deeply disappointed by their lack of opportunities for participation in the regime in the 1970s and 1980s. The modernist Islamic party Masjumi, banned since 1960 for its role in anti-Soekarno regional rebellions, was prevented from regrouping and competing in the 1971 polls, and modernist Muslim leaders were forced to join with their "traditionalist" NU counterparts in the PPP in subsequent electoral contests.[18] Masjumi activists were among those blamed for the Malari riots of January 1974.[19] And intelligence operations masterminded in subsequent years by CSIS patron Ali Moertopo and later by Benny Murdani worked both to discredit certain modernist Muslim groups as fanatics and terrorists and to justify their harsh repression.[20] With *abangan* (nominal or syncretist) Muslims and Christians occupying a hegemonic position in the palace, the armed forces, the cabinet, Golkar, and the DPR in the 1970s and 1980s, many modernist Muslims understandably saw themselves as unfairly excluded from the corridors of power.

Yet even as foreign capital and the predominantly secular nationalist and Christian political class expanded their circuitries throughout the Indonesian archipelago, the New Order era also witnessed the implementation of numerous policies that enhanced the authority and attractive power of Islam. Anti-Communist hysteria in the early Suharto years drove millions of Indonesians to seek refuge in religious identity, institutions, and faith to avoid fatal charges of atheism,[21] and new government regulations requiring all citizens to declare their faith, expanding religious classes in state schools, and impeding interfaith marriages strengthened the public markers and boundaries of religious identities.[22] For example, in the highlands of East Java, where Islamic faith and practices had once been highly attenuated and syncretic, dramatic religious change was evident in the mid-1980s, as observed by the anthropologist Robert Hefner:

Educational programs for *modin* [village-level Muslim religious leaders] and village officials were also expanded, focusing on the importance of celebrating Islamic religious holidays, a correct understanding of the relationship between religion and *adat* custom, and the coordination of mass-based *dakwah* [Islamic missionary] efforts. By 1985 most communities in the region boasted a variety of committees for activities virtually unthinkable years earlier in this region: the public celebration of Muslim holidays, public education concerning the importance of the Ramadan fast, the payment of the *zakat* alms, and the coordination of *takbiran* parades for the proclamation of God's greatness at the end of the fasting month. In the 1980s, highland communities for the first time began to sponsor the *solat ied,* the special once-a-year mass prayer service held the first morning after the end of the fast. Most villages now also boast new or refurbished mosques and prayer houses, complete with powerful loudspeakers. And everywhere throughout the upland region, evening classes for Qur'anic study (*pengajian*) are attracting large numbers of male and female students. . . .

[A] recent study of *dakwah* activities sponsored by the Department of Religion demonstrates that, especially since 1975, there has been a spectacular increase in government-sponsored *dakwah.* Bureau speakers crisscross the province, presenting over five thousand sermons each year. They control regular broadcasts on radio and television and publish a steady stream of pamphlets and books. A consistent theme of their programs is the backwardness of belief in guardian spirits and *dukun* (religious mediums). The department's East Java network of teachers, scholars, and *mubaligh* [Islamic] preachers includes a full sixty-five thousand people, "constituting a well implanted network in rural society and thus a line of transmission as quantitatively important as that available to the Army, the Ministry of the Interior, or National Education."[23]

Thus, over the first two decades of the New Order, millions of Indonesians previously unincorporated within the orbit of Islamic associations and identities were encouraged to understand themselves as Muslims. As they migrated to towns and cities in record numbers in the 1970s and 1980s, moreover, they came to constitute an urban and suburban underclass—*kelas bawah*—available for mobilization not as the Proletariat of the PKI but as the *Ummat* for those who claimed to represent Islam. Whether they came to the cities from the *pesantren* belt on Java or from rural areas in the Outer Islands, where different kinds of religious schools and practices held sway, the vast majority of these new migrants shared a common faith: Islam. As newcomers in the melting pots of Jakarta and

other major Indonesian cities, often without firmly established family networks or community institutions to support them in times of hardship and
uncertainty, they constituted a new and growing (sub)urban constituency
for those who could preach, teach, or invoke an Islam that could incorporate Indonesians from all over the vast, diverse archipelago.[24]

The possibility for mobilization behind the banner of Islam was further
enhanced by the dramatic expansion of Islamic education in Indonesia under the New Order. Government records for the network of traditional,
rural Islamic boarding schools (*pesantren*) list 1,871 schools and 140,000
students in 1942, 4,195 schools and 677,000 students in 1978, and 9,388
schools and 1,770,000 students in 1997.[25] The self-consciously modernist
school network associated with Muhammadiyah, which in the 1960s already comprised 4,600 *madrasah,* several teachers' academies, religious
training schools, and college faculties, claimed well over 100 institutions
of higher education, including 24 universities, by the mid-1990s. At the
same time, the State Islamic Institute (IAIN), or Institut Agama Islam Negara, which was first opened by the Ministry of Religious Affairs in 1960
along the lines of Cairo's Al-Azhar University, had established 14 branches
around the country by the 1990s, even as the branches of Universitas Islam
quadrupled in number during the same period. Likewise, mainstream state
universities throughout Indonesia saw a marked rise in the numbers of students with devout Muslim backgrounds and in the popularity of campus
mosques, prayer and religious discussion groups, and Islamic student organizations.[26] As one observer noted: "Mosques are filled with worshipers,
particularly young adults; *halaqah* and *pengajian* emerge in almost every
university complex and neighborhood; extra religious schooling (*diniyah*)
in the afternoon is crowded with children and teens; the circulation of Islamic books has reached the highest point in Indonesian history; and female students and adults with head-coverings have become a regular
phenomenon on campuses and in public places."[27] In short, by the 1990s
the rising numbers of Indonesians schooled under a distinctly, self-consciously Islamic rubric had become a visible feature of urban society in
many parts of the Indonesian archipelago.

Similarly, the public sphere of modern, urban, middle-class life in Indonesia was increasingly claimed by professionals who defined themselves
as pious Muslims. Indeed, the markers of Islamic piety were now incorporated into the *habitus* of mainstream Indonesian bourgeois propriety and
prestige. Wealthy Indonesian Muslims began to avail themselves of luxury
pilgrimage tour packages to Mecca[28] and to enroll in various institutes,
foundations, clubs, intensive courses, and workshops in Sufi spirituality

and Islamic learning in Jakarta and other major Indonesian cities.[29] In women's fashions, Islamic covering, or *busana Muslimah,* of various kinds assumed unprecedented popularity and prestige.

Alongside the self-consciously Muslim professionals were the swelling ranks of what might be termed "professional Muslims": in other words, men—and, to a considerably lesser extent, women—who made distinctly modern careers through the promotion of Islam. IAIN graduates filled the growing numbers of posts as instructors in religion in state schools, *madrasah,* and *pesantren* and joined the expanding ranks of functionaries in the vast Ministry of Religious Affairs. Books, magazines, and other publications on Islamic affairs proliferated, as did Muslim radio and television talk shows, promoting the rise of "pop Islam" in the form of pious music stars and preachers *(da'i).*[30] In the 1970s and 1980s, for example, the popular music *(dangdut)* and film star Rhoma Irama produced cassettes and films that claimed an audience estimated at more than fifteen million fans. Rhoma Irama introduced his concerts by reading or singing verses from the Qur'an, and described his style as *musik dangdut dakwah*—pop music for spreading Islam. Hiring a personal tutor to teach him Arabic, making the pilgrimage to Mecca, and otherwise stressing the Islamic content of his personal life and his songs and films, he exemplified the possibilities for mixing popular culture with Islam in Indonesia.[31] Equally impressive was the emergence of Islamic preachers as media stars during the same period. In radio and television programs, pamphlets and books, cassettes and calendars, and appearances at major mosques and stadiums in Jakarta and other Indonesian cities, figures such as the popular *da'i* Kyai Haji Zainuddin MZ delivered an Islamic message to millions of Indonesian Muslims.[32]

Overall, then, the New Order promoted the objectification and functionalization of religion. Indonesian Muslims, in a process observed elsewhere as well in the Islamic world, increasingly came to understand their religion, says Gregory Starrett, as "a coherent system of practices and beliefs, rather than merely an unexamined and unexaminable way of life," to think of "knowing Islam" as "a defined set of beliefs *such as those set down in textbook presentations,*" and to put Islam "consciously to work for various types of social and political projects."[33] In towns and cities around the archipelago a plethora of professional Muslims emerged, reminiscent of the "lumpenintelligentsia" described by specialists on the Middle East. With urbanization, mass literacy, and increasing access to modern means of communication (television, radio, cassettes, newspapers, magazines, books), moreover, the corpus of religious knowledge and the locus of religious authority grew ever more decentered, with independent study supplementing lessons in the classroom and sermons in the mosque. According to Olivier Roy:

> The new Islamist intellectual borrows from religion the unifying figure that is lacking in the knowledge proposed by the school. Fragmentary modern knowledge, acquired autodidactically, is integrated within a Quranic intellectual framework, developing, on the one hand, the image of a transcendent totality, the *tawhid* (the oneness of God, which extends to His Creation), in which all knowledge comes together, and, on the other hand, a terminology drawn from the Tradition, supported by the citation of verses, but often positioned as the equivalent of concepts issued from modern ideologies. The two bodies of knowledge (modern through brochures and manuals, Quranic by citation) in fact cover a "do-it-yourself" creation, the juxtaposition of segments of knowledge into a whole whose logic cannot be reduced to the sum of its parts.[34]

Against this backdrop, and in the context and space of the increasingly self-evident and worrying social gap (*kesenjangan sosial*), it is unsurprising that "Islam" had also emerged as a rubric for popular protest in Indonesia by the 1980s. Islam, after all, represented a suitable idiom of protest by outsiders against a regime in which foreign and Chinese capital, Catholics and Protestants, and graduates of secular institutions of higher education were seen to occupy privileged positions. In September 1984, for example, in a much publicized incident, security forces killed dozens of protesters outside a police station in the poor, overpopulated Jakarta harbor district of Tanjung Priok. The protests emerged after the defilement of a prayer house (*musholla*) by soldiers who used gutter water to remove posters described variously as highly inflammatory or merely informative about upcoming religious gatherings and teachings. After an attack on a soldier in retribution and the burning of his motorcycle by local residents, four men were arrested and detained by the police.

In response, Islamic activists in the neighborhood began to organize to demand the local men's release. Prominent in this process was Amir Biki, a student activist in the mid-1960s and a small businessman who had once worked as a subcontractor for the state oil monopoly Pertamina. Now a bearded *haji* who had often spoken publicly against the government, Biki was a local broker of sorts, combining a neighborhood reputation for piety and strong rhetoric with a broad range of contacts in the government, the police, and the military. On the night of September 12, Biki and other speakers spoke out about the poster incident during a religious prayer and teaching session at the local *musholla*. These speeches, which reportedly railed against the government, were broadcast via microphones, amplifiers, and loudspeakers set up around the neighborhood. Later that night a crowd numbering in the hundreds marched to the police station in Tanjung Priok to demand the release of the four men, only to be violently dispersed by army troops who shot dead as many as two hundred of the protesters—including Amir Biki. In the ensuing public outcry, the victims' families and their defenders were pitted against the armed forces commander, General Benny Murdani, a Catholic, with whose encouragement some forty-five residents of Tanjung Priok were imprisoned for their role in "inciting" the attack on the police station. Thus the "Tanjung Priok Incident" (*Peristiwa Tanjung Priok*) came to signify the marginalization and abuse of Indonesia's poor Islamic majority at the hands of an oppressive—and ostensibly Christian-led—regime.[35]

Subsequent years saw further examples of local protests under an Islamic banner against the intrusions of state and capital. The late 1980s and early 1990s witnessed a wave of demonstrations by Islamic organizations against a government-sponsored lottery in East Java and a number of key cities elsewhere in the country. Land disputes in Central Java and Madura likewise brought into the limelight local religious teachers (*kyai*) who positioned themselves as champions of rural communities that were threatened by the cultural, environmental, and social degradation brought on by industrialization and urbanization.[36] And by the mid-1990s the idiom and organizational presence of Islam were prominently implicated also in a series of riots targeting government buildings, Chinese business establishments, and Christian houses of worship. Typically following on the heels of incidents in which the institutions and representatives of Islamic learning and worship were said to have been insulted, these riots were widely seen as instances of popular mobilization against the entrenched interests of Chinese *konglomerat*, Christian professionals, preachers, political elites, and allied elements of the New Order state.[37] In short, the possibilities for popular mobilization under the banner of Islam were clearly expanding during the long Suharto years.

The Rise and Decline of Islamic Populism: PPP, 1973–1998

In the electoral realm the reorganization of political life under the New Order provided not only new constraints on but also new possibilities for the mobilization of Islam. Organizations such as the modernist HMI, or Islamic Students' Association, and Nahdlatul Ulama's youth wing (Ansor) and militia (Banser) played key roles in the violent destruction of the Indonesian Communist Party in late 1965 and 1966; Muslim politicians helped Suharto force out Soekarno and consolidate his own rule during the same period. But by the first New Order elections of 1971, Islamic parties were in open opposition to a government seen as representing secular nationalist and Christian interests at the expense of the majority faith of the country. While Masjumi remained barred from organizational reconstitution and electoral competition, Nahdlatul Ulama mounted a strong—if tightly constrained—campaign against Golkar, the new government political machine, most notably in East Java, the heartland of "traditional" Islam and its *pesantren* belt. NU won more than 18 percent of the vote; the Partai Muslimin Indonesia (Parmusi), claiming much of the modernist vote, captured 7.3 percent, and two smaller parties—PSII and Perti—together gained an additional 3 percent.[38]

Two years later, in 1973, the New Order state reconfigured the political party system, forcing the amalgamation of secular nationalist and Christian parties into the PDI and the fusion of the various Islamic parties into the vaguely named Partai Persatuan Pembangunan (PPP), or United Development Party. Thus the diverse strains of Indonesia's Islamic traditions and associations were submerged within an omnibus party whose room for maneuver was highly constrained within the New Order's political constellation. Not only was Golkar given tremendous advantages (access to state patronage, backing from the bureaucracy and the military establishment, and discretionary treatment within the electoral regulations and their enforcement), but PPP and PDI were restricted (in their freedom to campaign, to raise funds, and to determine their own candidates, leaders, and policies).

Yet it was precisely under these conditions that PPP first began to articulate a distinctively Islamic populist challenge to the status quo in Suharto's Indonesia. In the 1971 elections, as during the Soekarno era, the various Islamic parties appealed to different constituencies, as seen in the strong showing of Nahdlatul Ulama in the *pesantren* belt rural heartland of East Java. But by the 1977 and 1982 elections the combination of the forced fusion of Islamic parties and the process of industrial growth and urbanization under way in the decade preceding 1982 had worked to create a broad constituency for the PPP among the swelling *kampung* (neighborhoods) of the nation's cities and towns. With green flags and banners proudly displaying an image of the Ka'bah (the holy shrine at the core of Mecca) as the party's emblem, PPP election campaigns presented a unique opportunity for popular mobilization on behalf of Islam. Rhoma Irama and his Soneta Group, playfully nicknamed "The Sound of Moslem," performed at PPP rallies; popular *da'i* such as Zainuddin delivered speeches in support of the party. PPP rallies attracted enormous crowds: in 1982, a million people reportedly attended a rally in Bandung; 500,000 supporters were twice massed in key venues in Jakarta; and crowds estimated to number between 200,000 and 300,000 joined in rallies in the East Java towns of Pasuruan and Banyuwangi and in Ujung Pandang (formerly Makassar), the regional capital of South Sulawesi.[39] As John Pemberton observed during the election campaign in Solo:

> Sunday April 11 [1982] officially belonged to PPP. Again, truckloads of PPP followers flanked by motorcyclists roared the streets. . . . [T]here emerged a point of convergence, a destination: Pasar Kliwon, an old market area at the center of Solo's most populous "Arab" quarter and home of one of the city's most powerful mosques. . . . Thousands of mobile PPP supporters, with crowds of spectators following along, poured into a bottleneck that becomes the main street through Pasar Kliwon. All of the energy that high-speed campaigning carries suddenly was transformed into a mass so dense that it barely moved. There were no costumes, police, performers, or reviewing stands; in their place, shouts of "Hidup Ka'bah" and "Allahu Akbar" echoed all around. The boundary between the street and its edges, between followers and spectators, collapsed jubilantly. Whole families leaned out of shuttered windows in the old second-story apartments that line the streets and poured religious bucketfuls of cooling water on those below. That morning there had been keynote speeches by PPP leaders from Jakarta. By afternoon, Pasar Kliwon itself seemed to embody PPP when for the first, and only, time during the long 1982 campaigning in Solo, an entire community was somehow on the move.[40]

Indeed, despite all the obstacles in its path, and all the advantages accorded to Golkar, PPP proved to be a powerful opposition party. In the 1977 elections it received 29.3 percent of the national vote and won a plurality in Jakarta, an outright victory in Aceh, and a strong showing in a number of major regional capitals and other prominent cities. Almost forty regional assemblies (DPRD), or Dewan Perwakilan Rakyat Daerah Tingkat I, were in PPP hands (of a total of 282).[41] In the 1982 elections, the party received 27.8 percent of the national vote, losing its lead in Jakarta to Golkar by a slim margin but retaining its majority in Aceh and a strong presence elsewhere in the country, as seen in the retention of control in twenty-six DPRD.

It was against this backdrop that the Suharto regime moved to rein in PPP and to diminish, domesticate, and in some ways claim for itself the attractive power of Islamic populism in Indonesia. A key accomplice in these moves was the PPP chairman, John Naro, who had worked closely with military intelligence operatives to establish Parmusi in the late 1960s but had no personal affiliation with either Nahdlatul Ulama or Muhammadiyah, the two largest Islamic associations in the country. Even before the 1982 elections, Naro and his allies worked assiduously to purge the PPP parliamentary slate of vocal critics of the Suharto regime, replacing many of them with his own trusted lieutenants. In 1984, moreover, Naro, now firmly entrenched as PPP chairman, even held a party congress in which President Suharto addressed the opening session and during which the multi-faith state ideology called Pancasila was adopted as the party's foundational set of tenets, rather than Islam, and the Ka'bah was abandoned as the party emblem in favor of a star. Although elements of PPP had often proved uncooperative and at times intransigent in parliamentary debates over legislation pertaining to religion in the 1970s, now it was clear that the "Naro-ing" of the party's leadership and views promised a much more cooperative partner for Golkar in the DPR.

Another prominent figure who played a crucial role in the process of weakening PPP was K.H. Abdurrahman Wahid, known as Gus Dur, who assumed the leadership of Nahdlatul Ulama in 1984. Wahid, whose grandfather had been among the founders of NU in 1926, was educated in prestigious *pesantren* in East Java and in Islamic universities in the Middle East, and thus he had impeccable credentials within the interlocking directorate of NU *kyai*. But thanks to his childhood days in Jakarta as the son of a member of the national political elite, Wahid felt comfortable and familiar also with a set of contacts outside NU and with the liberal cosmopolitanism of Jakarta and the West. Deeply disturbed by the role of NU activists in the anti-Communist pogroms of 1965–66 (while he was away in the Middle East), and equally distrustful of the use of Islam as a rubric for popular mobilization or political legitimation, Wahid promoted a very different vision of a multifaith Indonesia governed by tolerance and social quiescence. Already in the early 1980s he had cultivated a new image for the *pesantren* as a focus for community development, and a set of allies and benefactors— Western governments and foundations, Chinese Catholic businessmen, NGO activists—who saw in him and his views for NU's future a reassuring picture of Islam in Indonesia. Indeed, it was with the blessing—and by some accounts, the active encouragement—of President Suharto and military-intelligence czar General Benny Murdani that Wahid assumed the leadership of NU in 1984.

Given NU's increasing marginalization within PPP by the early 1980s, Wahid thus made the momentous decision in 1984 to withdraw NU from its formal affiliation with the party. For one thing, this decision ostensibly allowed Nahdlatul Ulama to concentrate on the social welfare and educational activities that had been its founding purposes in 1926. As with the liberal Muslim intellectual Nurcholish Madjid's slogan "Islam, Yes! Islamic Party, No!" Wahid's move appeared to promote the cultivation of Muslim civil society while abandoning what were clearly futile and self-destructive efforts to transform the state. For another thing, the delinkage of NU from PPP freed up its members to support other parties, most notably Golkar, and thus to avail themselves of the patronage and protection of the New Order state long denied those deemed to be in opposition to the regime. Small wonder that Wahid's move was greeted with approval by many NU *kyai* and by elements in the government which had become worried by the rising tide of Islamic populism articulated by the PPP.[42]

Disappointed by the weakening of PPP's potential as a vehicle for Islamic aspirations and oppositional politics, or drawn away from the party by the repositioning of NU on the New Order landscape, many former PPP supporters abandoned the party in the middle to late 1980s. Already in 1984, many previously committed backers condemned Naro and the PPP for betraying the needs and aspirations of the *Ummat*. Islamic pop star Rhoma Irama, for example, publicly described PPP as a transvestite (*banci*):

> It's not clear where it's going or what it wants. It's also lost its color. Don't even ask if they can represent the aspirations of the Muslim community. Not a chance. That's why I've decided it's better to stop supporting PPP.
>
> In my view, the leaders of PPP have already committed acts that are forbidden by the tenets of Islam [*haram*]. They're too busy fighting over positions and parliamentary seats, while the voice of the Muslim community goes unheard. And if I remain a PPP supporter, that means I support a stance that is at odds with the voice of my heart. And with the religion I believe in: Islam.[43]

Thus, by the next election campaign, it was clear that popular support for PPP had substantially declined. Compared with 1982, its leaders engaged in far less campaigning, and attendance dropped dramatically at party rallies.[44] After the polls, the fall in PPP votes was revealed to be similarly substantial: whereas in 1982 PPP had won 20.8 million votes, almost 28 percent of the electorate, in 1987 the party garnered only 13.7 million votes, less than 16 percent of all votes cast in the election. Both in the NU heartland of rural East Java and in major cities where urban Muslims had previously backed the party in large numbers, PPP suffered a drastic downturn in electoral support. Only in the remote strongholds of Aceh and

Madura did it show resilience in the face of this broad downturn, and nationwide, the party retained control of only four regional assemblies. The 1992 elections confirmed this trend: nationwide, the party won only 17 percent of the national vote, little more than half of its share of the electorate fifteen years earlier. The high tide of Islamic populism had clearly receded.

Islam Domesticated, Displaced, Defiant

Yet the energies represented in electoral form by the PPP did not simply disappear under the weight of government repression and co-optation. Instead, three interrelated new trends were discernible in the late Suharto era of the 1990s after the high-water mark of PPP mobilization in the late 1970s and early 1980s. First of all, the late 1980s and early 1990s saw the Suharto regime move to capture and claim for itself much of the attractive power associated with the institutions and idiom of Islam. As James Siegel has argued, the New Order state constructed a notion of criminality which filled the gap left by the disarticulation of "the people" with the removal of Soekarno and the destruction of the PKI and, over time, attracted to the power associated with this criminality, "took on the form of a criminal in order to obtain this power" for itself.[45] The same process was at work with what Ruth McVey has called the "untamed, dangerous *Islam fanatik.*"[46] By the early 1990s the sign of Islam, once associated with the supposed terrorist group *Komando Jihad* in 1977, the election campaign violence of 1982, and the Tanjung Priok Incident in 1984, was now something that the state tried to appropriate for itself.

The 1980s had seen an unprecedented ascendance of modernist Muslims into the ranks of the urban middle class and into the circuitries of state power. HMI student leaders from elite schools such as Yogyakarta's Universitas Gadjah Mada, Bandung's Institut Teknologi Bandung, and Jakarta's Universitas Indonesia were recruited in record numbers into the bureaucracy, the business world, and Golkar during this period.[47] It was to recognize, reinforce, and rechannel these trends that the Ikatan Cendekiawan Muslim Se-Indonesia (ICMI), or All-Indonesian Association of Islamic Intellectuals, was founded under the leadership of close Suharto associate B. J. Habibie in the early 1990s. As minister of research and technology since the 1970s, Habibie controlled a sprawling empire of state-owned, high-tech enterprises, an enormous state-based patronage empire outside military and technocratic control in the name of high-tech economic nationalism. Through his hold over "strategic industries" and responsibility for infrastructure projects and industrial development schemes, Habibie wielded considerable discretion in government personnel and contracts, and through privileged access to state loans, contracts, and regulatory breaks, he built up an enormous clientele of university-educated, modernist Muslim *pribumi* ("indigenous") businessmen. With Suharto's support, Habibie was elevated to the governing body of Golkar, and various Habibie protégés won key cabinet positions and other plum civilian and military posts. Meanwhile, a steady process of ICMI-*isasi* moved forward in Golkar, in the awarding of state contracts, on many university campuses, and beyond. CIDES (Center for Information and Development Studies), an ICMI-affiliated think tank, soon began to compete with the Catholic CSIS, and its daily newspaper, *Republika,* tried to rival the Catholic-owned *Kompas.* ICMI support and influence soon extended to Islamic publishers, preachers, and pilgrims, into *pesantren, madrasah,* and IAIN, and to figures within both NU and Muhammadiyah. With Habibie at its helm, ICMI incorporated into the national political class an expanding network of Muslim professionals and professional Muslims who claimed to speak on behalf of all Muslims. The Suharto regime could now claim to be promoting—and representing—Islam in Indonesia.[48]

Yet the processes and possibilities of domesticating Islam were constrained both from above and from below. On the one hand, even as the modernist Muslim network moved upward within the political class, the accumulation of wealth and power by the Suharto family imposed a ceiling on any further ICMI-ish ambitions for the foreseeable future. Suharto's children, after all, had also won seats on the governing board of Golkar and begun to lobby for their own minions and allies in the parliament, the armed forces, and the cabinet; and their huge conglomerates continued to capture the juiciest state contracts and monopoly concessions. So long as Suharto was president, his children would remain entrenched at the pinnacle of power, and succession struggles could leave state control in the name of their father, rather than in the hands of those who spoke on behalf of Islam. On the other hand, in Indonesian society the modernist Muslim segment of the political class found its claim to represent Indonesia—or Islam, for that matter—persistently challenged and hotly contested from below. "Islam," after all, was destined to remain an overly ambitious, indeed presumptuous, banner in a nation boasting the single largest Muslim population and the most popular nongovernmental Islamic organizations in the world. The elitist pretensions of middle-class modernist Muslims to represent Islam ran up against the reality of the millions of unschooled and underemployed ordinary Indonesians of the faith. Even in the boom years of the early to middle 1990s, when ICMI was expanding its network, thousands of Muslim youth had left the nation's *pesantren, madrasah,* IAIN, and universities for the job market, only to find opportunities for state or private-sector employment or upward social mobility highly limited.

Compared with the middle-class modernist Muslim professionals and political operators who traced their roots back to the *madrasah,* the social and political advancement of those hailing from the *pesantren* was decidedly more modest.[49] A few steps behind—or below—their *madrasah*-schooled counterparts on the ladder of educational and social hierarchy, such students flocked in record numbers to the expanded network of IAIN and provincial universities, but at elite university campuses the NU-affiliated Pergerakan Mahasiswa Islam Indonesia (PMII), or Indonesian Islamic Students' Movement, was much more modest in its activities and alumni roster than the HMI. With high rates of unemployment for university-educated youth persisting through the boom years of the mid-1990s, it is clear that even those *pesantren* kids who made it as far as college faced an uphill struggle into the new Muslim middle class.[50] Beyond the *pesantren* belt, moreover, where state patronage (via ICMI or PPP or otherwise) had made significant inroads by the 1990s, the broad majority of Indonesian Muslims were poor and unlettered and thus excluded from the kinds of educational experiences and networks that were so crucial for the emergence and ascendancy of the political class that claimed to speak for the *Ummat.*

Into the space previously captured by PPP stepped the other opposition party allowed to compete in New Order elections, the Partai Demokrasi Indonesia. Created as a forced fusion of secular nationalist and Christian parties in 1973, PDI had, like PPP, competed in New Order elections under highly unfavorable conditions, compromised as it was by government restrictions on its electoral campaigns and intervention in its leadership congresses and internal party deliberations. With Protestants and Catholics seated in the party leadership in numbers proportionately far exceeding the Indonesian Christian minority's small percentage of the national electorate, and with secular nationalists represented by conservative remnants of the old Partai Nasionalis Indonesia (PNI), PDI was hardly an obvious vehicle for populist politics. Yet by the late 1980s and early 1990s, just as PPP suffered a wave of desertion by erstwhile prominent supporters and a dramatic decline in its popular following, PDI gained new appeal as a party with reinvigorated Soekarnoist credentials.

As indicated in the scholarly literature on Indonesian history and politics, Soekarno had not only played a prominent role in an unparalleled popular struggle for independence but presided over the period of most populist politics in the immediate aftermath of independence. Thus, James Siegel has noted, the violent removal of Soekarno—and the PKI—in the early years of the New Order had left open a space for "the people"

(*Rakyat*) to reemerge in the political imagination,[51] with the sign of Soekarno—a spectral figure displaced but never fully disavowed—remaining as a touchstone and talisman of sorts for populist mobilization.[52] For millions of working-class Indonesians, the figure of Soekarno signified the long-suppressed possibility of radical, or at least redistributive, politics after years of harsh restrictions on labor organizing and repression of popular protests. "In the kampungs of Surabaya," says the historian Howard Dick of the New Order years, "Sukarno was a local hero, 'one of us.'"[53] For small merchants and artisans marginalized by the rise of the *konglomerat* under the New Order, moreover, the name of Soekarno resonated with nostalgia for what they remembered as the halcyon years of the 1950s and early 1960s.[54]

Against this backdrop, the emergence of Soekarno's children on the political scene in the late 1980s and 1990s attracted popular energies to the PDI, even as the PPP began its decline. In the 1987 elections, Soekarno's son Guruh Soekarnoputra and daughter Megawati Soekarnoputri emerged as popular campaign figures for the PDI, helping the party increase its small share of the national vote by 3 percent while PPP suffered an almost 12 percent downturn at the polls. Megawati, whose role as regional party chairman and chief campaign figure in populous Central Java had attracted considerable crowd and media attention in 1987, resurfaced in 1992 as a leading national-level PDI personality. In 1993, with the blessings of key elements in the military leadership, she was elected to the post of PDI chairperson for 1993–98. The 1997 elections thus loomed large on the horizon as an unprecedented opportunity for a populist PDI challenge, under the sign of Soekarno, to the New Order regime.

In the 1997 elections, however, the forced ouster of Megawati from the PDI leadership sidelined the most popular oppositional figure and left the party in the hands of a crudely government-installed stooge (Soerjadi), thus leaving voters only PPP as a plausible protest vote. If only by default, then, that party regained a considerable measure of its previous popularity at the polls as the choice of protest voters: its share of the electorate rose to 22.5 percent, its best performance since 1982.

The possibility of PPP reemerging from below as a vehicle of popular oppositional energies was clear from the dynamics of the 1997 election campaign. With the slogan "Mega-Bintang" as a recurring reminder that the party (as identified by its logo, the star) could stand in for the sidelined "Mega," PPP *konvoi* (campaign motorcades) attracted huge crowds in such cities as Banjarmasin and Surabaya and held well-attended rallies in the stronghold towns of Pasuruan and Sampang in East Java and Madura. In Central Java, moreover, "Mega-Bintang" reached its apogee, as PPP increased its share of the popular vote by 150 percent in the city of Solo and otherwise registered major gains. In Solo in particular, PPP attracted considerable media attention through the involvement of its local branch in a "whitening" (*putihisasi*) campaign to counteract the "yellowing" (*kuningisasi*) undertaken by zealous Golkar cadres painting the town to match the party color.

The Solo branch of PPP had already gained a certain reputation for populist mobilization under the leadership of the branch chairman, H. Mudrick Setiawan Malkan Sangidoe, who was elected to the post in 1995. Known locally as Mudrick or Gus Drick, he was in many ways typical of local politicians operating within PPP throughout Indonesia. The grandson of K.H. Abu Amar (a prominent local figure in Sarekat Islam in the 1910s and 1920s) on his mother's side, and of K.H. Gozali Khasan Dimejo (a well-known *kyai* and Nahdlatul Ulama activist in the Central Java town of Bagelen, Purworejo) on his father's side, Mudrick had grown up in a pious Muslim family of small-town traders and activists. Educated in Muhammadiyah schools as a child and active in the association as an adult, he had joined the PPP in Solo in the 1970s and worked his way up through the ranks of the local party branch. While helping to manage the family businesses—a small hotel, an antique furniture store—he was a prominent leader of a PPP youth group in Solo and the commander of the party's security unit for the town. As head of the local branch of PPP since 1995, Mudrick had grown more outspoken on local issues than his predecessors, perhaps emboldened by his strong local base as well as his personal connections with local military commanders, both retired and active. In 1995 and 1996 he made a name for himself in Solo and beyond through his vocal criticisms of petty corruption and abuse of authority, especially in connection with local causes such as the bus terminal, street vendors, and a land dispute involving a mosque and school.

With the onset of the election campaign in January 1997, moreover, Mudrick assumed considerable local prominence at the forefront of the local Mega-Bintang phenomenon. At campaign rallies and in public statements quoted in the press, he voiced his backing for the "whitening" campaign on the streets of Solo and otherwise worked to mobilize popular support for PPP, as exemplified by his distribution of more than 600 tons of rice to local residents in the months leading up to the election. Meeting with Megawati in Jakarta, Mudrick also generated considerable local enthusiasm for PPP in Solo, as seen in the estimated 100,000 supporters who attended the party rally in the city.[55] The results of the election were stunning: PPP not only increased its share of the vote by 150 percent but gained fifteen seats in the local assembly to Golkar's twenty. Even though Mudrick soon found himself embroiled in a long court case as the government began to prosecute—and persecute—him for his involvement in encouraging "social disorder" in Solo, it was clear that PPP had reemerged as a party capable of mobilizing popular energies outside and against the New Order state and the national political class. After three decades under Suharto, the Hidden Force of popular mobilization retained its spectral power, with Islam an attractive rubric not fully captured and domesticated by the New Order state via ICMI.

Conclusion

The three decades of the Suharto era witnessed dramatic change in class relations in Indonesia. Fueled by the oil boom, by import-substitution, and then by export-oriented industrialization, economic growth extended the scope and reach of a predominantly Chinese capitalist class in Indonesian society, with urbanization and the deepening commodification of land and labor in suburban industrial zones bringing more and more workers and peasants into the orbit of the *konglomerat*. By the late 1980s and early 1990s, Indonesian newspapers were filled with stories of wildcat strikes, land disputes, and protests by local residents who blamed the construction of dams, bridges, golf courses, industrial estates, and shopping malls for economic marginalization and environmental degradation. Thus government policymakers spoke worriedly of a growing "social gap" (*kesenjangan sosial*) and of a "latent Communist threat" (*bahaya laten komunis*) represented by emerging labor unions, human rights organizations, environmental groups, and student activists.

The figure of Islam stepped into this gap, offering an attractive rubric for the mobilization—or invocation—of this abiding, powerful Hidden Force in Indonesian society. In the first two decades of the Suharto era, after all, Chinese predominance in business and Christian prominence if not preeminence within the New Order state combined with the elimination of the PKI and the government's forced strengthening of religious identities to define the broad mass of the population as an oppressed Muslim majority. As urbanization, economic growth, and the expansion of tertiary education in Indonesia proceeded in the 1970s and 1980s, moreover, self-conscious and devout Muslims in record numbers came to reside in Jakarta and other major cities in the country and to make increasingly strong claims on urban public space: hence the strong showing, against all the odds, of the Islamic PPP in the 1977 and 1982 elections.

It was against the backdrop of these crucial social trends that the New

Order state attempted to defuse and domesticate but draw upon the power of Islam in the late 1980s and early to middle 1990s, most notably through ICMI and Habibie. This latecomer modernist Muslim network ascended to unprecedented prominence and influence within the national political class in the 1990s, asserting its claim to represent the *Ummat* and thus, however implicitly, to assume the leadership of Indonesia, the world's most populous Muslim nation. Yet the ascendance of those who claimed to speak for Islam within the political class in the late Suharto era did not come without attendant ambiguities, anxieties, and ironies—problems that gave rise to and profoundly shaped a wave of religious violence in 1995–97.

4

Buildings on Fire

Church Burnings, Riots, and Election Violence, 1995–1997

The ambiguity and tension inherent in the position of those claiming to represent Islam within the political class in the Indonesia of the middle to late 1990s stemmed from three fundamental problems. First, the ascendancy of a modernist Muslim network, associated with ICMI and Habibie within the political class, ran up against the competing interests and built-in advantages of the Suharto family itself—most notably Suharto's favorite daughter, Siti Rukmana Hardiyanti, better known simply as Mbak Tutut. Over the course of the late 1980s, Suharto's children had begun to emerge as a major force in the business world, their vast, diversified conglomerates enjoying unparalleled access to state loans, contracts, monopoly franchises, and regulatory and tax breaks. By the early to middle 1990s a few of the Suharto children had also won seats on the governing board of Golkar and begun to lobby for their own minions and allies in the parliament, the armed forces, and the cabinet. Meanwhile, their huge conglomerates continued to capture the juiciest state contracts and monopoly concessions, as the announcement in 1996 of Tommy Suharto's "national car" project amply attested. So long as Suharto was president, his children would remain entrenched at the pinnacle of New Order power.

Thus the final years of the Suharto era witnessed the intensification and escalation of tensions between the Suharto family and those ascendant modernist Muslim elements of the political class disappointed if not embittered by the remaining constraints placed on their accumulation of financial, industrial, and political capital. With urban middle-class Muslims grumbling about the onerous tariffs slapped on imported automobiles to protect Tommy Suharto's mostly Korean-produced national car, Amien

68

Rais, chairman of the country's leading modernist Islamic association Muhammadiyah and himself a prominent member of ICMI, launched a public broadside against the Suharto family's business interests, using revelations that surfaced in a series of well-publicized business scandals as the basis for a set of acerbic speeches, articles, and books that led to his forced resignation from the governing board of ICMI.[1] Meanwhile, jockeying for position within the Suharto regime intensified with the approach of the 1997 elections, the 1998 session of the People's Consultative Assembly (MPR) to "elect" the president and vice president, and the approaching moment of *suksesi* (succession) from Suharto to a new president and, perhaps, a new kind of regime.

Second, and at the same time, the claims by modernist Muslim members of the political class to represent Islam and to capture the popular energies long suppressed with the demolition of the PKI and the disappearance of the *Rakyat* from official discourse ran up against challenges from below. "Islam," after all, was an overly ambitious banner in a nation boasting the single largest Muslim population and the most popular nongovernmental Islamic organizations in the world. With their long histories, deep roots in society, and widely divergent theological, institutional, and social underpinnings, NU and Muhammadiyah could hardly be so easily captured—or their leaders co-opted—by an ICMI-based network emanating from the state. In particular, ICMI faced strident and vocal opposition from Abdurrahman Wahid (Gus Dur), the chairman of Nahdlatul Ulama, who had withdrawn NU from PPP in the mid-1980s and worked to forge close ties with Catholic businessmen and secular NGOs in Jakarta, as well as American and European foundations promoting liberal multiculturalism in Indonesia. In general, the considerable autonomy of associational life and the great plurality of views long found in the Indonesian Islamic community made the creation and enforcement of a hegemonic, state-based Islam a very difficult project.

Beyond the realm of Islamic educational institutions and associational activities, moreover, workers, villagers, and poor urban *kampung* dwellers were showing ample evidence of capacity for popular mobilization under decidedly nonreligious banners. With industrialization and urbanization came rising numbers of wildcat strikes, land disputes, and incidents of football hooliganism, plus protests over evictions, environmental problems, and the marginalization of street hawkers, market stall vendors, and small shop owners by the new department stores, supermarkets, and shopping malls appearing on urban landscapes in towns and cities around the country.[2] A fine local example of these broad trends was the series of mass actions witnessed in 1995 in Pasuruan (the East Javanese town allegedly the inspiration for Louis Couperus's depiction of Labuwangi in his novel *The Hidden Force* nearly a century earlier). In 1995 alone, Pasuruan saw the picketing of a cigarette factory accused of landgrabbing, the siege of a village hall after allegations of fraud in the election of the village headman, an attack by knife-wielding peasants on a naval base in a dispute over a mango grove, and the burning of a Korean-owned MSG factory said to be polluting a local river.[3] Even in a town as piously Muslim as Pasuruan, the underclass (*kelas bawah*) was reemerging and mobilizing behind causes other than those located under the rubric of Islam.

The potential for broader forms of popular mobilization behind decidedly non-Islamic banners also loomed large. In April 1994 the East Sumatran city of Medan—after Greater Jakarta and Surabaya perhaps the most important industrial hub in the country—saw a week of major strikes and large demonstrations by workers, many of whom were affiliated with the independent labor union federation Serikat Buruh Sejahtera Indonesia (SBSI), or Indonesian Prosperous Workers' Union. Encouraged by legislation in the United States linking access to the American market with governments' willingness to tolerate independent labor unions, the SBSI had emerged in the early 1990s under the leadership of a Batak Christian labor lawyer in Medan, Muchtar Pakpahan. In a city known for its considerable ethnic and religious diversity, it succeeded in unionizing thousands of workers under a broad-based secular rubric, which the government predictably depicted as reflecting the resurfacing influence of old PKI tactics and remnants in the area. After a month of sporadic wildcat strikes in Medan, when an estimated 25,000 to 30,000 workers, many of whom were affiliated with SBSI, held demonstrations in the city and its environs in mid-April, the protests eventually turned violent, targeting shops, banks, and in one case a factory manager who was killed as he tried to drive into an industrial estate. By May 1, 1994, Muchtar Pakpahan and other SBSI activists were in prison, and further strike actions in Medan were harshly suppressed. But as subsequent strikes elsewhere in the country suggested, the potential for a working-class movement still loomed large with continuing industrialization and economic growth.[4]

Meanwhile, the rise of Megawati Soekarnoputri to the leadership of the Partai Demokrasi Indonesia in the early 1990s attracted considerable popular energies to a political party previously lacking in mass appeal or oppositional orientation. With Megawati's attendance at PDI rallies in the 1992 election campaign drawing huge crowds and helping to boost the party's vote, and with Megawati's childhood friend Gus Dur offering a new support base for her and her party among members of Nahdlatul Ulama, the 1997 elections were expected to produce a popular Soekarnoist challenge to Golkar and the Suharto regime. Although Megawati's forced ouster from the PDI leadership and replacement by a government stooge in mid-1996 had removed the immediate threat of a presidential challenge by secular and Christian elements of the political class in 1997–98, the riots that unfolded in poor urban neighborhoods in central Jakarta after the violent ejection of pro-Megawati forces from the PDI's national headquarters by security forces and their allies in the party made clear that the *Rakyat* could be reclaimed and rechanneled by a national political project other than Islam.[5]

As the third fundamental problem for those claiming to represent Islam politically, the ascendancy of modernist Muslims to the highest echelons of the political class, and of university-educated Muslims within the ranks of the urban middle class in general, threatened to diminish and dissolve the very basis on which Islamic networks and solidarities worked to transcend class differences and to underpin claims to legitimate power and wealth. After all, among the growing numbers of devout Muslims in Golkar and the armed forces officer corps were many who sought patrons and allies beyond ICMI, just as many new members of the rising Muslim middle class were attracted to the same Westernized, liberal cosmopolitanism that had long been the preserve of Indonesians educated in secular and Christian schools. In their use of modern educational institutions and associations as a launching pad for the capture of state power and the construction of a patronage network, modernist Muslims were following in the footsteps of the Christian, secular nationalist, and PSI-ish *jaringan* that had preceded them, from the Dutch colonial era through the first two decades of the New Order. In their accumulation of capital and their assumption of a distinctly bourgeois lifestyle, pattern of consumption, and sense of propriety, many middle-class Muslims came to share the habitus of a class previously dominated by Chinese businessmen, Christian professionals, and the aristocracy. In Aswat Mahasin's analysis:

In their mixing with bureaucrats, Chinese financiers and international partners, they become more cosmopolitan and amorphous (in the sense of eroding the communal sentiments of the past) and argue for more tolerance on the part of the *ummat*. In life-style, they carefully imitate all the middle class symbols, with their conspicuous consumption, urbanism, and of course, patronizing style. But internally, they tend to hold on to and nurture *santri* group solidarity, both to secure their assumed representative status as well as to strengthen their internal control. They have their powerful lobbies which look after student organizations and other *ummat* institutions, which make sure that no sign of radicalization comes to the fore, and which ensure that only acceptable leaders can be elected to their national conventions.[6]

With the rapid and sustained industrialization and urbanization of the New Order years, moreover, came a widening gulf between this class and the workers, peasants, and urban *kampung* dwellers who figured so prominently in daily newspaper reports of wildcat strikes and land disputes. This gulf was increasingly palpable in urban social space and in the experience of everyday life in Indonesian cities. As Howard Dick writes with regard to Surabaya:

> There was also the nagging fear of the mob. Hence, as in Dutch times, kampung people were again coming to be seen as socially alien, unpredictable, uncontrollable. Glossy brochures advertising the new housing estates included reassuring pictures of uniformed security staff, conveying the subliminal message, You will be safe here.
>
> Social stratification was facilitated by the motor vehicle and air-conditioning. The role of the automobile in causing twentieth-century urban sprawl is well recognized. Air-conditioning has been taken for granted but it has allowed Surabaya, like other prosperous cities of Southeast Asia, to turn inside out, to become a city in which people turn their back on the external environment. Instead of improving the harsh external environment by the time-honored means of shade, water, verandahs, and gardens, developers have created artificial indoor environments. The middle class can now live in air-conditioned houses, travel in air-conditioned cars to air-conditioned offices, and enjoy recreation in air-conditioned malls. However, this artificial environment is all private space, what money can buy. The kampung dweller for the most part has to survive without air-conditioning and in public space. As the surface area of concrete, asphalt, and brick increases, so does the ambient temperature in what has always been notorious as a very hot city, especially at the end of the dry season. It is further degraded by the heat and pollution emitted by the other, air-conditioned society. Thus physical comfort is a social divide almost as sharp as [was] skin color in the colonial period.[7]

Thus precisely at the moment when a modernist Muslim network based in ICMI was ascending to the pinnacle of state power, and when devout Muslims were enjoying unprecedented upward mobility in the privileged realms of business, the professions, and the universities, the plausibility of Islam as a rubric for the assertion of claims to represent the broad mass of the population began to come into question.

These increasingly apparent, awkward, and acutely perceived ambiguities and tensions, I argue, prefigured the onset of religious violence in Indonesia in the mid-1990s. Ambiguities and tensions in the position of "Islam" shaped not only the *timing* of the church burnings, riots, and other disturbances that occurred during these years but also their *location,* their *protagonists,* their *targets,* their *mobilizational processes,* and their *outcomes.* Given the difficulty of explaining variance in the pattern of religious violence through rigorous comparative analysis and counterfactual reasoning, I hope to establish the explanatory power of the framework developed above by showing how it illuminates all these aspects of religious violence in the middle to late 1990s in Indonesia, traced over time, across space, and in popular discourse from inception to aftermath.

Church Burnings

The rise of religious violence in Indonesia became apparent in a series of attacks on Protestant and Catholic houses of worship in late 1992. Over the course of that year an increasing number of reports in the media had cited local controversies and disputes concerning Christian religious activities in urban areas predominantly populated by Muslims. When complaints about unofficial church services and accusations of creeping Christianization went unheeded, incidents began to occur.

Residents of a predominantly Muslim neighborhood in East Jakarta, for example, complained to local officials in mid-1992 about a group of Batak Protestants who were reportedly using a house in the area for weekly religious services. After months during which these complaints were ignored, a crowd of residents gathered outside the house on a Sunday morning in early November, eventually attacking a preacher and other members of the group until policemen arrived on the scene. The same month saw assaults on a Protestant church in North Sumatra, a Pentecostal church in the East Javanese town of Pasuruan, and a Catholic church in a village in Wonosobo, Central Java. In these cases, too, Muslim residents had complained about unauthorized church buildings (in one case a church constructed opposite a local mosque), and also behavior by Christian worshipers and preachers deemed insulting to Muslims. In December 1992 a Christmas Eve celebration in a church in Jember, East Java, was disturbed by Muslim youths who attempted to set the church alight with Molotov cocktails.[8]

This trend continued. Between 1992 and 1997, some 145 churches in Indonesia were demolished, burned down, or otherwise forced to close. And not only those churches attacked in the riots discussed here but a number of other Christian houses of worship became objects of crowd violence during these years in various parts of the country. For example, in Indonesia's second city, the East Javanese capital of Surabaya, a set of concerted assaults by crowds numbering in the hundreds on Sunday, June 9, 1996, seriously damaged ten churches and violently disrupted services. These particular attacks allegedly began after a pet dog belonging to a church group urinated on the wall of a mosque, a violation of local Muslim sensibilities that had sparked earlier complaints.[9] But in Surabaya and elsewhere, the visibility, audibility, and perceived opulence of Christian churches, congregations, and schools clearly inspired deeper resentment as well.[10]

Riots on Java, 1995–1997

By 1995 the pattern of religious violence had shifted from small-scale attacks on Christian churches to larger and more sustained incidents of religious rioting. A handful of riots occurred in predominantly Catholic localities in old areas of Portuguese influence in Eastern Indonesia, where the expansion of the centralized Indonesian state had combined with official transmigration schemes, expanding market networks, and spontaneous migration to produce growing Muslim minorities. Alongside the intrusions of Muslim bureaucrats rotated in by Jakarta came the encroachment of immigrant petty traders from Outer Island cities such as Makassar, typically of Bugis ancestry and Muslim faith. Against this local backdrop, and in the context of the national political trends in favor of Islam described above, late 1994 and 1995 witnessed a series of riots in Dili, the capital of the territory of East Timor occupied by Indonesian troops since 1975, with crowds burning Bugis-owned shops and destroying local mosques. These months also saw crowds in towns on the predominantly Catholic island of Flores respond to the desecration—real and rumored—of local churches by attacking shops owned by Muslim migrants.[11]

The year 1995 also marked the onset of a spate of much larger, more sustained, and more widely publicized riots in various towns in Java. In late October, for example, in the midst of legal proceedings against a Catholic public schoolteacher who had beaten a Muslim student, a crowd demolished a courthouse in the East Javanese town of Kediri, home to some of the most prominent of Indonesian *pesantren*. At the end of the same month a crowd attacked a Chinese-owned supermarket and nearby homes, shops, and cars in the West Javanese town of Purwakarta, some one hundred kilometers southeast of Jakarta. The supermarket targeted by the mob had been the site of an incident two weeks earlier, when a Muslim girl on her way home from a local Islamic school stopped with her friends to buy chocolate and found herself accused of shoplifting by the store security guard. In full view of other shoppers, the girl had been slapped in the face, berated by the security guard and the wife of the owner, forced to clean the toilets in the store, and otherwise humiliated before she was handed over to the local police, who promptly released her for lack of evidence.[12]

News of the incident spread around Purwakarta and to nearby towns in West Java such as Subang, Karawang, Cikampek, and Cianjur, circulating from the girl's *pesantren* in Subang to other religious schools in an area of Java well known for its religious piety and dense networks of Islamic schooling.[13] A flyer voicing outrage was reportedly reproduced and passed around. Of special interest was the fact that the girl had been wearing a Muslim head scarf, or *jilbab*, when she was forced to clean the toilets in the "Chinese-owned" supermarket.[14] On October 31 a collection of Purwakarta residents, high school pupils, and other youths gathered outside the store to protest. By the following day the crowd had grown in size—subsequent media reports cited estimates as high as 15,000 participants—and stormed the store, stoning the windows, breaking into the premises, and bringing out goods into the street, where they were burned along with a few cars and motorcycles. A day later the crowd turned on the two houses and a warehouse belonging to the supermarket owner and other Chinese stores in the area as well.[15]

A few weeks later, another riot unfolded in the Central Javanese town of Pekalongan, a few hundred kilometers east-northeast of Purwakarta along the northern coast (*pasisir*) of Java. Pekalongan had been long known as a center of batik production and of Islamic learning, with pious Muslim batik traders—whether Javanese, Sumatran, or immigrant Arab in ancestry—among the leading sponsors and founders of Islamic schools and organizations in the town. The Sarekat Islam had been active in Pekalongan in the 1910s, and the modernist Muslim association Muhammadiyah established a *madrasah* there in the following decade (as did Al Irsyad, another modernist group founded by Hadrami Arab immigrants in the Indies). A number of long-established *pesantren* in Pekalongan associated themselves with Nahdlatul Ulama after that association's founding in 1926, as did new *pesantren* started up by *kyai* in subsequent decades.

In the postwar era, moreover, the steady expansion and elaboration of these schools established urban Pekalongan as a strongly self-consciously Muslim town. By 1980 almost 5,000 *pesantren* students were estimated to be living in urban Pekalongan, with neighborhoods such as Buaran, south of the city center, dominated by *santri*. A thousand more Muslim students filled the town's *madrasah* and, after its founding in the early 1980s, the

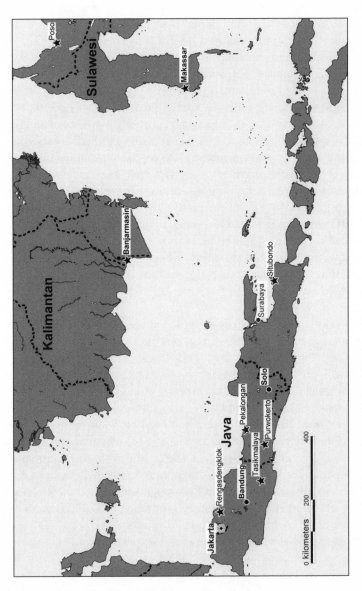

Major sites of religious riots, 1995–1997 (Peter Loud)

campus of Universitas Pekalongan. By the 1980s, moreover, some 17 mosques, 227 *langgar,* and 18 *mushola* were said to be servicing an urban population of nearly 120,000 Muslims in the city of Pekalongan, where nine Protestant churches and a single Catholic church, a Buddhist temple, and a Chinese temple (*klenteng*) catered to the small non-Muslim minority (estimated at 8 percent of the population). As the anthropologist Chantal Vuldy, who worked in Pekalongan, observed in the late 1980s, the Muslim majority enjoyed a special claim to public space in the city:

> On Friday, traditionally a day of worship in Pekalongan (except for local government office workers), at the call of the *imam,* there appears a crowd of men and youths in *sarung palekat* or *batik,* their heads covered with *peci,* a towel or prayer mat in their hands or thrown over their shoulders. The multitude, coming on foot, forms a human river whose ebb and flow ripples slowly across the streets and neighboring alleys at this hot hour of the day. Others, coming from somewhat more distant locations, park their bicycles or motorbikes at the back of the mosque or just in front of it: the sheer number of vehicles attests to the impact of religion on the population and especially on youth.[16]

It was thus in a town strongly marked by Islamic piety, learning, and associational history that a riot took place on the afternoon of Friday, November 24, 1995. Two days earlier, a Chinese storekeeper, recently released from a hospital after four years of treatment for paranoid schizophrenia, had ripped up a copy of the Qur'an on a street in full view of neighbors en route to the neighborhood mosque for early morning prayers. News of this grievous debasement of the Muslim holy book spread rapidly in Pekalongan, its circulation accelerated and amplified by attendance at midday Friday prayers just a few weeks before Ramadan in the devoutly religious town. After the prayers, members of the congregation at the nearby mosque took to the streets, heading for the residence of the man who had insulted their faith. His shop was forced open, its contents spilled out onto the street and set afire. For four hours, the crowd stoned dozens of Chinese stores in the neighborhood. Two Chinese-owned textile factories, resented for their role in marginalizing small-scale batik producers in the town, were also set alight before the rioting petered out in Pekalongan.[17]

Situbondo

On October 10, 1996, nearly a year later, a much larger-scale and more widely publicized riot unfolded in the East Javanese town of Situbondo. A town of some 44,000 residents that served as the capital of a regency with a population well over 500,000, Situbondo was more than 98 percent Muslim and enjoyed a nationwide reputation as a site of Islamic piety and learning. An eminent local religious scholar in Situbondo, K.H. As'ad Syamsul Arifin had served for decades as a prominent member of the national governing bodies of Nahdlatul Ulama, and the town had been the location of the controversial 1984 congress of the organization.[18] Although K.H. As'ad Syamsul Arifin passed away in 1990 at the age of ninety-five, his son K.H. Cholil Lora emerged as a popular religious leader with a large following, especially among local toughs and street children, and a reputation that reached far beyond Situbondo.[19]

More generally, Situbondo's many *pesantren* attracted thousands of students from all over East Java and elsewhere in the archipelago.[20] In particular, the Madurese provenance of many residents, students, and *kyai* helped to connect Situbondo to the major towns of Madura and to centers of Madurese population elsewhere in the country. K.H. As'ad Syamsul Arifin's school, Pondok Pesantren Salafiyah Syafiiyah, alone claimed some 15,000 students. As elsewhere in the *Oosthoek* (East Hook) or *Tapal Kuda* (Horseshoe) of East Java, the combination of a large Madurese population and geographical distance from the court culture of the Central Javanese kingdoms had established a pattern of local religiosity dominated by the kind of Islamic devotion and schooling represented by Nahdlatul Ulama.[21] Indeed, NU had been the strongest party in Situbondo in the 1950s and 1960s, and under the New Order, PPP emerged as a powerful challenger to Golkar in the town, winning 47 percent of the local vote in 1977 and 52 percent in 1982; the party still claimed a sizable minority of votes in 1987 and 1992 even as it suffered a nationwide decline. When K.H. Cholil Lora held forth at *pesantren* in Madura or PPP rallies in Surabaya, he was often met by large crowds of enthusiastic Madurese admirers.

By the 1990s, however, the waning electoral fortunes of PPP, the passing of K.H. As'ad Syamsul Arifin, and the marginalization of Nahdlatul Ulama within the corridors of power in Jakarta combined with economic and social change to suggest downward trends for Islam in Situbondo. The early 1990s saw the arrival of branches of major Jakarta-based Chinese banks, the opening of local Chinese-owned supermarkets and movie theaters, and the onset of a major project for the construction of an oil refinery in Situbondo financed by a consortium that included large Jakarta- and Hong Kong–based firms. In rural areas of Situbondo regency, shrimp farms owned or capitalized by Chinese businessmen had begun to displace rice farms and salt beds along the coast, even as sugar planters in the area suffered a continuing downswing. Meanwhile, the diversity of Protestant denominations in Situbondo had resulted in more than two dozen churches—and very prominent schools—for the tiny Christian population in the town, thus raising suspicions of surreptitious Christianization and questions as to the necessity of so many churches for so few Christians in this stronghold of traditionalist Islam. Some observers pointed to the anomaly that no less than five churches but only three mosques were located along the town's main thoroughfare and claimed that less than half of the churches in the entire regency were properly licensed and registered by the government. In the 1990s, moreover, the construction of a large Protestant church along the main street created considerable controversy, as its size—though justified by projections of the congregation's growth through procreation rather than proselytization—dwarfed other public buildings in the town and inspired rumors that it was the single tallest church in Southeast Asia. K.H. Hasan Basri, chairman of the government's Council of Indonesian Islamic Scholars (MUI), asked, "As a city well known for the Islamic piety of its residents, why is it that when you enter Situbondo, the most prominent building is a church, not a mosque?"[22]

In this context of rising sensitivity as to the position of Islam in Situbondo, in October 1996 a riot unfolded in connection with a court case of alleged blasphemy against Muslims and the Islamic faith. The defendant, as it happens, was neither Christian nor Chinese but rather a twenty-six-year-old Muslim man named Saleh who worked as a custodian at a prominent mosque in Situbondo and as an *ustadz* (junior instructor) for Muslim pupils at a nearby elementary school. According to the original letter of complaint filed against Saleh at a local police station, he had made blasphemous statements in a series of conversations with K.H. Zaini, the head of a *pesantren* in Situbondo and a local leader of the Naqsyabandiyyah, a leading Sufi brotherhood (*tarekat*).[23] Saleh had first approached Zaini in April 1996 for assistance in convincing members of the mosque to turn down the volume of loudspeakers used for sermons and for calling the faithful to prayer, since many members of the mosque were students and devotees of K.H. Zaini. Saleh himself had a different spiritual teacher, a man named Mudarso, who was said to have gained a following of a kind among dozens of local residents.[24]

Questioned by Zaini as to the nature of his spiritual *guru*'s teachings, Saleh reportedly made a number of controversial assertions which, according to Zaini's letter of complaint, he reiterated in subsequent conversations and even wrote down on Zaini's request. Saleh claimed, for example, that his guru had special magical powers, and that among those who respected these powers were none other than the late K.H. As'ad Syamsul Arifin and his son, K.H. Cholil Lora, the two most prominent re-

ligious leaders in recent memory in Situbondo. As for the nature of his beliefs and their relation to Islam, Saleh allegedly made blanket accusations
against *kyai* and castigated them as liars, claiming that through his guru he
had learned how to undertake religious rituals and prayers outside the guidance and guidelines of the established local Islamic authorities. The late
As'ad Syamsul Arifin himself, Saleh claimed, had passed away in a state of
takacer, or imperfection, because he had died in the hospital rather than at
home. As for the pillars of Islamic devotion more broadly, Saleh reportedly
made even more controversial statements, voicing his rejection of claims
that Muhammad was the Messenger of Allah and his assertion that the
Qur'an was of manmade rather than divine origin.[25]

Following this series of conversations, and with Saleh's written statement
in hand, K.H. Zaini filed a complaint with the local police station, accusing Saleh of religious blasphemy and the denigration of Islam. The Situbondo branch of Nahdlatul Ulama, to which Zaini also sent a copy of the
letter, urged him to withdraw and retract the complaint to avoid unnecessary and undesirable controversy and publicity, but Zaini persisted. According to Ahmad Suaedy and others:

> As a prominent local religious teacher and leader of a Muslim brotherhood
> (*tarekat*), Kyai Zaini had relations with many people and had many fol-
> lowers in a number of areas. While awaiting a response from the police,
> Kyai Zaini continued to talk about the problem with Saleh with anyone
> who cared to listen, whether in small gatherings at his house or on occa-
> sions when he was delivering talks at mosques, pesantrens, or amongst the
> members of his *tarekat.* Kyai Zaini also reproduced many copies of the
> "writings" of Saleh, consisting of his assertion that Kyai As'ad's death was
> *takacer,* and he circulated them widely. Over time, Kyai Zaini's efforts had
> created considerable local controversy.[26]

Spurred on by Zaini's legal complaint and the local controversy he had
so assiduously helped to create, the local police eventually arrested Saleh,
and local prosecutors began working on a case against him. At a series of
public hearings held a few months thereafter, with students from Zaini's *pesantren* and members of the local branch of the Naqsyabandiyah *tarekat*
in attendance, as well as many others from Situbondo and beyond, whose
interest in the case had been piqued by Zaini's efforts, the courthouse was
filled to overflowing on each occasion. Students and staff at the *pesantren*
founded by K.H. As'ad Syamsul Arifin also came to observe the proceedings out of interest and obligation to the man whose memory had allegedly
been so grievously insulted by Saleh, as did others representing K.H. Cholil Lora's following as well. Unlike Zaini and his supporters, the followers

and descendants of the late As'ad were reportedly concerned to prevent further controversy or disturbance, and by some accounts the authorities invited one of his daughters to attend and make statements at the trial to reduce the level of tension at the courthouse. But the hearings were marred by anger and violence, with Saleh's testimony causing considerable uproar among those in attendance and the presence of more than one hundred policemen and army troops failing to prevent the crowd from jostling and punching Saleh on one occasion and, on another, attacking and setting alight the car used to transport him.[27]

By the time of the fifth and final hearing of the case on October 10, 1996, as many as 3,000 people were in attendance, the courtroom packed with onlookers, policemen, and army troops, and the street outside the courthouse likewise filled with interested people, many from outside Situbondo. When the guilty verdict and the sentence were announced by the judge—five years minus time already served in detention, the maximum sentence allowed for the offense—the crowd reacted violently, clearly disappointed that the punishment was not more severe. Inside the courthouse, people shouted and jostled with policemen, and Saleh was hurriedly evacuated through the back door amid cries of "Kill Saleh!" Meanwhile, the people outside had begun to throw stones at the courthouse windows, and with fuel obtained from the gasoline station on the street they set the building alight while it was emptying of onlookers, policemen, and others involved in the case.

As the courthouse went up in flames, the rioters turned to the nearby Bukit Zion Bethel Church, whose size and prominence had given rise to such controversy even before its completion in 1995. The church was set on fire, as was another church and a Chinese-owned restaurant on the same street. By the end of the afternoon, crowds now swollen with schoolchildren and *pesantren* students had attacked, demolished, or set on fire twenty-five churches in downtown Situbondo and several outlying areas in the regency, plus two Christian schools and several residences used by preachers and others holding religious services (in one, a Pentecostal minister and his family perished in the fire). Also seriously damaged were two movie theaters, a video arcade, a billiard hall, and a supermarket, all owned by Christian Chinese businessmen.[28]

As the fracas subsided toward evening, security forces began to make arrests. In all, some fifty-four alleged rioters were detained, including many schoolchildren and *santri* from Pesantren Walisongo, the religious school once led by K.H. As'ad Syamsul Arifin and now by his children, including the popular K.H. Cholil Lora. That *pesantren*—many of whose students had experienced difficulties in registering to vote a few months earlier in a case that smacked of discrimination against assumed PPP supporters—was clearly a target of the authorities' attention, as seen in the conspicuous parking of army trucks around its grounds for several nights after the riot. Also targeted in the crackdown in Situbondo were members of the Nahdlatul Ulama security group called Pagar Nusa, whose members were known for their skill in martial arts and for their persistent interference in illegal but "protected" gambling operations in the town. Pagar Nusa members were among those arrested in October 1996, and one local leader of the group was beaten up so badly while in detention that he died in a military hospital that December.[29]

Tasikmalaya

The month of December 1996 also witnessed the unfolding of a riot, similar to the one in Situbondo, on the opposite side of Java, in the southern West Javanese town of Tasikmalaya. Located some 285 kilometers southeast of Jakarta, Tasikmalaya by the 1990s was a regency with a population of more than 1.8 million residents, predominantly rural in character but with a growing urban center where small-scale moneylending, artisanry, and industrial production (e.g., fabrics, handicrafts, bamboo furniture, wooden sandals) were well established. Tasik, as the town was commonly known, also served as an educational hub in southeastern West Java: it boasted five institutions of tertiary education, comprising Universitas Siliwangi, a school of administrative sciences, a law school, and two religious institutes. Indeed, the overwhelmingly (99 percent) Muslim town was home as well to many religious schools, with as many as 900 *pesantren* and more than 60,000 *santri* identified in official estimates, and large numbers of *madrasah* as well.[30]

Tasikmalaya's identification as a devoutly Muslim town was further strengthened by its immersion within larger webs of Islamic associational and political activity. As elsewhere in much of West Java, the strength of Nahdlatul Ulama in the 1950s had been fairly matched if not exceeded by that of Masjumi, giving the two Islamic parties a hegemonic position in local politics during the Soekarno era. In addition, Tasikmalaya had been a major center of recruitment and activity for the armed Darul Islam rebellion that emerged in the early 1950s and petered out in the early 1960s. Under the New Order, the political strength of Islam in Tasikmalaya was still evident in the strong showing of PPP in the 1977 and 1982 elections; its subsequent decline in 1987 and 1992 was attributed to the abandonment of the party by local *kyai* in favor of Golkar. The town boasted a nationally prominent local *kyai*, K.H. Ilyas Ruchyat, who served as the Rois A'am of Nahdlatul Ulama, as well as many lesser-known activists in modernist Muslim circles.[31] Among its many religious schools, Tasik's Pesantren Suryalaya was especially well known as a center of activity for the prominent Sufi order Tarekat Qadiriyyah Naqsyabandiyyah.[32] Like Situbondo, Tasikmalaya hosted a major NU congress (in 1994) and was clearly a town with a strong reputation for Islamic piety, learning, and associational activity.

That said, however, by the mid-1990s the position of Islam in the town had not been perceptibly improved by the emergence of ICMI at the national level and the broader pattern of social and political advancement enjoyed by many middle-class urban Muslims in Indonesia during this period. Not only had PPP lost more and more seats to Golkar in the local assembly in the elections of 1987 and 1992, but Chinese wealth and influence had begun to assume ever greater prominence on Tasikmalaya's urban landscape. Even as the town's small-time moneylenders, artisans, and producers faced increasing competition from larger-scale and more heavily capitalized Chinese-owned banks, factories, and companies, local market vendors and other petty traders found themselves marginalized by newly arrived Jakarta-based supermarket and department store chains such as Matahari and Ramayana, and prominent automobile and motorcycle dealerships as well.[33] The local government adopted a plan to relocate the main marketplace to the site of the bus terminal on the fringe of the town center and to replace it with a modern shopping center owned by a well-known Chinese businessman.[34] The wealth and prominence of Tasikmalaya's tiny Chinese minority were also amply visible in a dozen Christian churches and a handful of Christian schools located in the town.[35]

Yet, as in Situbondo, the riot in Tasikmalaya on the day after Christmas in December 1996 began not with insults to Islam by Chinese or Christian residents but with a dispute involving the local police force, whose members were overwhelmingly Muslim themselves. The dispute can be traced back to December 19 of that year, when a fourteen-year-old *santri* at a small *pesantren* several kilometers from the town center received a beating administered by junior instructors in response to repeated accusations that he had stolen money from his fellow *santri*.[36] The boy's father, as it happened, was a local policeman who learned of the beating and, angered by the punishment, summoned those responsible for administering it to his son. The next day the elderly *kyai* nominally in charge of the *pesantren* and *his* son, who had assumed day-to-day responsibility for the school, visited the police station, but they were sent away by the policeman, who demanded to see those *santri* or *ustadz* who had beaten his son. Finally, in response to a formal police summons, the younger *kyai* and the two *ustadz* responsible for the beating went to the police station on December 23, where the policeman promptly set upon one of the two himself. When the *kyai* tried to intervene, he found himself similarly abused by the policeman and his three underlings, who threw him and the two *ustadz* into an interrogation room where they continued to receive beatings at the hands of the policemen. By the time higher police and civilian authorities were alerted and intervened to stop the abuse, the *kyai* and the two *ustadz* were bleeding heavily and covered with bruises and scars. Later that evening they were released from police custody and returned to the *pesantren*, but the severity of their injuries led the elderly *kyai* to take them straight to the hospital for treatment.[37]

By the next day, December 24, news of the incident had circulated widely in Tasikmalaya and beyond. With dozens of *santri* piling into the ward to visit the beleaguered *kyai* and *ustadz*, the hospital decided to send them back to the *pesantren* to recuperate, thus helping to give rise to false rumors that the *kyai* had died as a result of his injuries. By the end of the day, Christmas Eve, hundreds of *santri* had begun to gather at the main mosque in downtown Tasikmalaya to discuss the case and the possibility of mounting a protest against the policemen, whom the authorities had already removed from the town and detained pending disciplinary hearings. Activists at the local offices of key Islamic student associations such as the NU-affiliated PMII (Indonesian Islamic Students' Movement) and the modernist HMI (Islamic Students' Association) held meetings to discuss the issue, as did student leaders at local universities and PMII and HMI activists in the nearby town of Garut and the West Java provincial capital of Bandung. With rumors spreading throughout Tasikmalaya and beyond on Christmas Day that the *kyai* was dead, news of a joint prayer meeting to be held the next day at the main mosque began to circulate through word of mouth and mimeographed flyers. By the next morning, news of the original incident had reached readers of the chief Muslim Jakarta newspaper, the ICMI-affiliated *Republika*,[38] and dozens of *santri* and Islamic activists from Tasikmalaya, Garut, and beyond had begun to assemble.

It was in this context that a crowd numbering well into the thousands gathered in and around the main mosque in Tasikmalaya on the morning of December 26, 1996, the day after Christmas.[39] The prayer meeting featured a number of speeches by prominent PMII and HMI activists from Tasikmalaya and Garut, reportedly ranging from the conciliatory to the incendiary. Afterward, many members of the crowd and several of the key speakers moved to the nearby regency police headquarters down the street, where a signed statement of concern was to be delivered to the police commander. But at least some members of the huge throng around the station had another message in mind for the police, and soon rocks were flying through the windows of the police station, and a riot was under way. Before long, hundreds of people were storming the town's major department stores and setting them on fire, and other Chinese shops were attacked as well. Crowds also gathered around several churches, demolishing them and setting them alight. By the evening, the rioting had already begun to peter out with the arrival of large numbers of army troops, but the town was still burning and smoking from all the buildings set on fire by the crowd. Among the buildings damaged or destroyed by rioting and fire were 12 churches (of which 4 were burned to the ground), 4 Christian schools, 6 police stations, and more than a dozen other police installations. Damaged or demolished in addition were 7 department stores, 8 automobile and motorcycle dealerships, 6 bank offices, 4 factories and warehouses, 3 hotels, and 89 stores and shops, not to mention the dozens of cars and motorcycles that were set alight by the crowds.[40]

As in Situbondo, a government crackdown was rapidly implemented in the aftermath of the riot. Of the more than 5,000 people estimated to have participated, almost 200 were detained by the security forces. Dozens of young *santri* and schoolboys were quickly released, but more than 120 of the remaining detainees were accused of crimes in connection with the riots, and many of them served short stretches in jail.[41] Chiefly, however, the authorities focused on a handful of prominent local activists from Islamic organizations in Tasikmalaya and Garut who had been involved in earlier protests and were clearly identified as troublemakers. The head of the local branch of PMII in Tasikmalaya, for example, was sentenced to two years in prison for his alleged role in inciting the riot, and the head of the local branch of HMI was awarded a twenty-two-month sentence. Two Tasik-born activists based in Garut, who had long been involved in protests and student organizing activities in Tasikmalaya, were implausibly—but conveniently—named the masterminds of the riot and sentenced to longer terms: eight and ten years, whereas the policemen who had beaten the *kyai* and the two *ustadz* served less than two years for their crimes.[42]

Rengasdengklok

The disturbances in Situbondo and Tasikmalaya in late 1996 were followed by yet another riot in early 1997, in the West Javanese subdistrict (*kecamatan*) town of Rengasdengklok, Karawang regency (*kabupaten*). An overwhelmingly Muslim and predominantly Sundanese town of more than 190,000 residents located 80 kilometers east of Jakarta and just 17 kilometers north of Karawang proper, Rengasdengklok boasted more than 100 mosques and 500 prayer houses by the mid-1990s. The affiliation of local religious scholars, activists, and officials with national-level Islamic groups such as Dewan Dakwah Islamiyah Indonesia (DDII) and Persatuan Islam (called Persis) likewise attested to the central place of Islamic piety in the town. Yet the spillover effects of rapid urbanization and industrialization in the nearby Jabotabek (Jakarta-Bogor-Tangerang-Bekasi) area over the course of the Suharto years had also spurred processes of economic and social change in Rengasdengklok in which non-Muslims assumed highly prominent roles. Most obvious in this regard were the activities of a small circle of local Chinese moguls whose business operations ranged from a rice mill and trading company to an automobile parts factory, a motorcycle dealership, a shopping center (built in 1992), a local bank, and a residential subdivision in the town (developed earlier in the 1990s).[43]

The increasing prominence of these hallmarks of Chinese wealth and economic control in Rengasdengklok—bank branches, department stores, factories, motorcycle dealerships, residential subdivisions, and shopping centers—was accompanied by highly visible markers and deeply felt suspicions of rising Christian influence in the urban landscape. Plans to construct a new Protestant church in Rengasdengklok in the early 1990s, for example, ran aground amid a flurry of rumors, gossip, and anonymous letters (*surat kaleng*) complaining about the proposed scale of the edifice, which, it was said, would dwarf the churches in the regency capital of Karawang. The construction of a stupa-like structure in the middle of a major intersection in Rengasdengklok, sponsored by local Chinese magnates to advertise their companies, likewise attracted controversy: its cone-shaped top was viewed by critics as resembling both the roof of a church and the conical hat often worn by Pope John Paul II. Meanwhile, rumors that Protestant residents were using their homes for unofficial religious services helped to sustain suspicions of surreptitious Christianization in the town.[44]

It was thus amid rising interreligious tensions that a riot unfolded in a back street of Rengasdengklok early on the morning of January 30, 1997, the twenty-first day of the Muslim fasting month of Ramadan. The riot began with an exchange of words between a Chinese resident and a teenager who was banging the drum at two o'clock in the morning to rouse Muslims in the area for the pre-dawn Ramadan meal of *sahur* and prayer. The drum at the prayer house had wakened the Chinese family next door and led to arguments on previous occasions, but on this particular morning the exchange of words escalated to the level of insults, with the teenager called "dog" and "pig" and one of the children in the Chinese family throwing rocks at the prayer house, reportedly breaking a window pane. In short order, a crowd of local residents had gathered and begun to throw stones at the Chinese house, only to be dispersed by policemen summoned by the father of the Chinese family (and allegedly paid "gasoline money" for his troubles).

While many residents drifted away from the scene and went back to sleep after their early morning prayers, others remained, and as word spread through the neighborhood and beyond, a larger crowd began to assemble outside the Chinese family's home beside the prayer house. Located on a busy alley just a few short minutes by foot from the town's market stalls, the site of the early-morning dispute attracted passersby and others whose interest had been piqued by rumors already circulating after daybreak. By six o'clock, several hundred people had gathered, according to subsequent reports. With the crowd hurling rocks at the windows, breaking down the gates, and threatening to burn down the house, a group of policemen arrived to evacuate the besieged Chinese family from their residence—which the crowd promptly demolished, sparing it from fire only because of the entreaties of neighbors worried about the danger to their own homes.[45]

The riot rapidly spread elsewhere in Rengasdengklok. First, a crowd of people moved from the Chinese family's home by the prayer house to the marketplace, where they destroyed the market stall owned by the family. Within hours, a crowd of several hundred people attacked a Protestant church located near a rice bodega said to be owned by the Chinese family. A Chinese *klenteng* and two other churches were likewise attacked, including a Pentecostal church whose congregation reportedly included the Chinese family involved in the original dispute over the sounding of the prayer house drum. A Buddhist temple (*vihara*) was also seriously damaged; the image of a partially dismembered statue of the Buddha hanging from the temple archway was transmitted across the world by the Associated Press, CNN, and *Time* magazine. By the end of the day, dozens of Chinese stores had been demolished, as were such prominent Chinese establishments as the Shelby Plaza shopping center and several banks. A number of cars were vandalized or set afire, and dozens of Chinese homes suffered damage, most notably windowpanes shattered by stone-throwing crowds. Only spray-painted signs claiming "Muslim property" and Muslim prayer mats hung on storefronts and house and car windows saved other property from the rioters' actions.

As the day drew to a close, smoke was still rising from buildings along the main streets of Rengasdengklok, but the riot was winding down. From the very next day (a Friday, as it happened) through the post-Ramadan holiday Idul Fitri in mid-February, army troops remained in Rengasdengklok to reinforce local police efforts to reestablish order in the town and began

Army soldiers look on during the riot in the West Javanese town of Rengasdengklok in January 1997 (AP)

to round up dozens of youths identified as participants in the crowd
violence.[46]

Election Violence: From Java to the Outer Islands, 1997

A few months later yet another wave of rioting unfolded, in Pekalongan,
the same Central Javanese town that had seen an early riot in November
1995. But in contrast with those in Situbondo, Tasikmalaya, and Rengasdengklok, the disturbances in Pekalongan in March and April 1997 occurred in the heat of the 1997 general election campaign and were
intimately, indeed openly, wrapped up with the intensification of competition—not only for votes but also for public space—between the Islamic
PPP and Golkar, the Suharto regime's political machine. The final years of
the Suharto era had witnessed increasing tension and contestation between
the modernist Muslim network (*jaringan*) represented by Habibie and
ICMI, on the one hand, and members of the Suharto family on the other,
most notably Suharto's favorite daughter, Mbak Tutut. With the approach
of the 1997 parliamentary election, and with the 1998 quintennial session
of the People's Consultative Assembly looming on the horizon as the venue

for the "election" of the president and vice president for 1998–2003, competition between these two rival elements in the regime began to escalate, especially with regard to the allocation of parliamentary seats.

Both Habibie and Tutut were represented in the governing body of Golkar and played crucial roles in the selection of candidates for the Golkar slate.[47] Tutut was awarded responsibility for Golkar's campaign in Central and East Java, and with her candidates filling the party's slate for these two provinces, she had a strong interest in maximizing Golkar's margin of victory within this bailiwick. Thus Tutut's close associate (and rumored paramour) General Hartono, the army chief of staff, donned a yellow Golkar jacket and made unprecedented (and highly controversial) statements of army support for Golkar, which carried special weight in the Madurese general's home province of East Java, where he had previously served as regional army commander and where his own network of protégés and clients in the army and otherwise was still strong. In Central Java, moreover, Governor Soewardi was likewise eager to please the president's favorite daughter, who was rumored to be in line to succeed Harmoko, then chairperson of Golkar. Thus Soewardi took special measures to promote Golkar in Central Java to meet his announced target of 70 percent victory, most notoriously through a campaign of "yellowing" (*kuningisasi*), in which the party's official color was painted over city street curbs, the walls of public buildings, and many other prominent public surfaces.

By contrast, Habibie and his supporters had nothing to gain from a strong Golkar performance in areas of the country where the party's slate consisted largely of Tutut proxies, whereas seats won by the Islamic PPP could possibly be used to the advantage of those claiming to represent Islam within the regime. ICMI, after all, included prominent PPP leaders among its members and offered an umbrella under which Muslims had begun to enjoy the fruits of state patronage without the weight (or stigma) of openly, officially supporting the Suharto regime as a whole. With the removal of the popular Megawati Soekarnoputri from the leadership of the PDI, moreover, only PPP remained as a party capable of winning the protest vote (as was suggested by the emergence of the slogan "Mega-Bintang," linking the ousted PDI chairperson to the stars that had replaced the Ka'bah as the PPP symbol). Thus, despite PPP's decisive downturn in popularity and electoral performance in 1987 and 1992, the party reemerged in 1997 as an attractive vehicle of Islamic populism in towns and cities across the country, exemplified by the "whitening" campaign (*putihisasi*) led by Mudrick in the Central Javanese city of Solo.[48]

This resurgent PPP now enjoyed the tacit support, if not active connivance, of elements within the regime linked to Habibie and ICMI, whether through their discretion over the enforcement of campaign regulations or their provision of financial support to the party. For example, the armed forces commander-in-chief, General Feisal Tanjung, an ICMI member and close Habibie associate, had issued a statement distancing himself and the armed forces from Hartono's embarrassingly open assertion that all members of the services owed their support to Golkar. Meanwhile, in Central Java, the "whitening" effort waged by PPP to counter Governor Soewardi's aggressive "yellowing" campaign appeared to have the blessing of the regional army commander, Major General Subagyo Hadisiswoyo, who enjoyed warm relations with Mudrick, PPP's branch chairman in Solo.[49] Beyond the regime, moreover, the conflict between Tutut and Habibie over Golkar trickled down to the major Islamic associations in the country, with Amien Rais, the leader of the modernist Muhammadiyah and a member of ICMI, stepping up his attacks on the Suharto regime, while Gus Dur, chairman of the traditionalist Nahdlatul Ulama, joined Tutut at Golkar campaign rallies in East and Central Java.[50]

Pekalongan

With the 1997 election campaign in Central Java characterized by heightened tension and hostility between Golkar and PPP supporters, in mid-February 1997 scuffles between rival groups of youths affiliated with the two parties broke out in the towns of Temanggung and Banjarnegara, leaving a handful of participants injured and a dozen motorbikes damaged in the fray.[51] In late March of the same year, moreover, the first of a series of riots unfolded in the Central Javanese town of Pekalongan, the same northern coastal town where a riot had occurred in late 1995. It was hardly a surprising site for violent conflict in the election campaign of 1997: the town, after all, was well established as a leading center of Islamic learning, worship, and associational activity in Central Java, and Islam constituted a powerful basis for political party mobilization there as well. In the early postindependence era of constitutional democracy, the modernist Muslim party Masjumi enjoyed considerable support in urban Pekalongan, with Nahdlatul Ulama also faring well in the rural outskirts and surroundings of the town. Under the Suharto regime, PPP consistently performed strongly in Pekalongan, winning a majority of votes, and elected seats in the Regional People's Representative Assembly in every election except that of 1987. In 1992, Pekalongan was the only regency in Central Java where PPP defeated Golkar, thus suggesting itself as the most self-consciously Islamic town in the province.

The push to win 70 percent of the vote for Golkar in the 1997 elections was therefore bound to meet stubborn resistance in Pekalongan, as events in March and April of that year amply illustrated. The first episode of such mobilization occurred on March 24, when a crowd of PPP supporters destroyed a stage that had been set up for a Golkar event in the southern city subdistrict (and PPP stronghold) of Buaran, just outside the well-known Islamic school Pondok Pesantren Alquran. Earlier that same day, clashes had occurred between local residents and members of the police force, who had been taking down PPP flags along the major thoroughfare of the city in preparation for the Golkar shindig (which was expected to feature not only Mbak Tutut and other major party figures but also the well-known Islamic popular music star Rhoma Irama, who had abandoned PPP for Golkar, and the television *da'i* K.H. Zainuddin MZ, who had likewise fallen into the party's embrace). The crowd of youths that gathered in the evening, reportedly armed with rocks and Molotov cocktails, destroyed the stage and burned its remains.

Two nights later, on March 26, rioting occurred again in downtown Pekalongan. Stores along the street leading toward the demolished Golkar stage were attacked, as were telephone booths, the local branch of the Bank Rakyat Indonesia, and a garbage dumpster. According to one newspaper account,

> the crowd took out the goods in the stores and burned them. Four motorcycles were also burned. . . . The next day . . . the street leading up to Pondok Pesantren Alquran . . . was blocked off with burning tires, wood, and garbage. A store selling *batik* dyes on Kertijayan Street became a target of the crowd's rampage, and the dyes were poured out on the street and burned, spewing smoke everywhere. Kertijayan Street and the area around it were blocked off by the security forces. . . . The length of Medono-Kertijayan Street, which at first had been lined with yellow flags, became green (the color of PPP and of Islam more generally).[52]

Local officials estimated that as many as 60 stores had been attacked and set alight and some 23 motorcycles and 2 cars had likewise been destroyed or burned.[53]

In the aftermath of the riot, the government's security forces initiated a crackdown on those elements blamed for the disturbances in Pekalongan. Some thirty-one youths, mostly teenagers, were immediately arrested and detained for their alleged role in the riot, but the focus of the government's attention and accusations lay elsewhere. Following up on charges made by a local lawyer, which received considerable publicity through local and national newspaper and radio reports, the authorities homed in on K.H. Afifudin Musytari HB as a figure responsible for inciting the riot in Pekalongan. The founder and leading light of a *pesantren* on the outskirts of Semarang, the provincial capital of Central Java, Afifudin was a former student in the Pondok Pesantren Alquran in Buaran, where the riot broke out, and he was said to have made an incendiary, inflammatory speech in Pekalongan just a few weeks beforehand.[54]

Afifudin's role in the rioting received further attention following another disturbance that broke out in Pekalongan on the night of April 2, after a series of prayer meetings in various venues in the town led by Afifudin and two other prominent *kyai*. This riot allegedly began as a street scuffle between a gang of youths (possibly affiliated with the pro-government youth group Pemuda Pancasila), who had torn down PPP posters, and a convoy of some fifty young men on motorcycles who were accompanying the *kyai* around town on their local speaking tour. A garbage container was overturned; several stores were broken into, the goods brought out into the street and set alight. Most notable in this regard was a Kawasaki showroom where the windows were smashed in and the motorcycles wheeled out and burned.[55]

Banjarmasin

Although a few minor clashes between PPP supporters and Golkar campaigners occurred again in Pekalongan and elsewhere in Central Java later in April 1997,[56] the biggest election-related disturbance in the country took place in May in the distant Bornean port city and South Kalimantan provincial capital of Banjarmasin. As the center of provincial administration and as a market and transshipment point for the timber, mineral resources, and agricultural commodities from its hinterlands, Banjarmasin had grown steadily over the course of the Suharto era, its population reaching more than 530,000 by the mid-1990s. Three-quarters of the residents were estimated to be of indigenous Banjarese stock, the rest consisting of migrants, whether Batak, Bugis, Javanese, Madurese, or Minangkabau. Most numerous and visible of the immigrants were those from Madura, who were prominent among the city's street vendors and *becak* drivers, and who were known both for their Islamic piety and for their strong support of PPP.[57]

Banjarmasin itself was a city where Islamic devotion had long enjoyed a prominent role. By the 1990s the city boasted more than 100 mosques and almost 900 prayer houses, thus earning it the sobriquet of "the city of one thousand *langgar.*" In the early postindependence era of constitutional democracy, Nahdlatul Ulama and Masjumi had both enjoyed considerable popularity in Banjarmasin. And under the New Order regime PPP performed strongly, capturing 34 percent of the vote in the city even in 1992, its worst election year. In the course of the 1997 election campaign, it also became clear that PPP would pick up votes previously claimed by PDI, as well as many more votes from among the city's recent migrants, especially those from Madura. In fact, the election campaign saw the prominent Madurese *kyai* and PPP leader K.H. Alawy Muhamad traveling to Banjarmasin to bring out the vote. On May 22, the date of PPP's officially allocated final campaign rally, the streets of Banjarmasin were filled with the party's supporters mostly from the port and slum area of Hulu Sungai but also Muslim students from local universities, especially Universitas Islam Kalimantan and IAIN Antasari.

The following day, May 23, was allocated to Golkar, whose supporters had organized a motorcycle *konvoi* and parade around Banjarmasin as well as a set of festivities at a stadium in the city. Because it was a Friday, the Muslim day of worship, the organizers had reportedly decided to delay the campaign rally until the early afternoon, after the end of the midday prayers. In the event, however, Golkar's motorcycle *konvoi* and parade began to circle the city around ten o'clock and was in full swing by the end of the morning. With hundreds of Golkar campaign workers, pro-Golkar youth groups, and government employees filling the ranks of the parade, the rumble of the motorcycles, the honking of horns, the shouting of slogans were inevitably perceived as an annoyance—if not an insult—by those attending midday prayers at various mosques around Banjarmasin. This was especially the case at Masjid Noor, a mosque not far from a major Banjarese market area. Originally a *langgar* founded by a Hadhrami Arab immigrant family, in 1953 it had been renovated and expanded into a mosque by prominent Banjarese merchants and backers of Masjumi. Still known for its political independence in the Suharto era, by the 1990s Masjid Noor was so highly popular with local residents that on Fridays worshipers filled both floors and spilled out onto the nearby street with their prayer mats and towels, sometimes reaching as far as the local marketplace. For this reason, on Fridays the streets were usually blocked off by midmorning and the shops closed up until the afternoon.

But on Friday, May 23, 1997, Masjid Noor's congregation was disturbed by the sound of three motorcycles, driven by Golkar security guards, circling the mosque just as the midday prayer drew to a close. The three cyclists soon found themselves surrounded by members of the congregation, forced off their motorcycles, jostled, and punched around. They reportedly put up a good fight, aided by the arrival of other members of Golkar's security contingent, which consisted largely of street toughs belonging to well-connected gangs that provided "protection" and "security" at nearby markets and shopping malls—most notably the upscale Plaza Mitra just 300 meters east of the mosque. But residents of nearby neighborhoods, many of whom had joined the PPP rally the previous day, also rushed to the scene, even as clashes broke out outside the Masjid Miftahul Ulum between Golkar campaigners who had been crooning away on a karaoke machine during the midday prayer and members of the congregation of the mosque.[58]

Soon, thousands thronged the streets of Banjarmasin to join in the attack on Golkar. Campaigners for the party were forced to shed their yellow Golkar T-shirts; Golkar flags and other emblems were destroyed around the city; and the Golkar regional headquarters, located just 250 meters south of Masjid Raya Sabilal Muhtadin, was sacked, with at least five vehicles belonging to Golkar set afire by the crowd. The home of the local Golkar party treasurer was attacked and burned down, as was a hotel where visiting Golkar dignitaries were rumored to be spending the night. As many government employees and others who had joined the rally in response to pressures from their bosses (or monetary inducements) abandoned their yellow T-shirts for street clothes and joined the crowds, the jubilant throng turned the streets green, the color of PPP and of Islam. According to one report, "the crowds paraded around the city filled with euphoria. Shouts of insults against Golkar predominated. They really controlled the city. The security forces were rendered powerless."[59]

But the crowds on the streets of Banjarmasin did not confine their attacks to Golkar itself. In addition, the stores of Chinese merchants, and Chinese-owned department stores, banks, and shopping malls were stoned, broken into, and set alight, the goods inside looted or brought out into the street and burned. Most prominent in this regard was the destruction of Plaza Mitra: its bookstore, supermarket, cinema, discotheque, car showroom, and Kentucky Fried Chicken outlet were damaged and set on fire by the crowd. Once rumors spread that the Golkar motorcyclists who had disturbed the midday Friday prayer were Christians, churches were also targeted by the crowds. Gereja Katedral, not far from the local Golkar headquarters, was demolished; the Gereja Huria Kristen Batak Protestau (HKBP) was burned down; 9 more churches and a Chinese temple were seriously damaged. By the end of the day, 144 stores, 151 homes, 3 shopping centers, 2 department stores, 5 banks, 4 government offices, 3 restaurants, 2 hotels, 36 cars, and 47 motorcycles were estimated to have been destroyed. Unlike previous election-related violence, moreover, the rioting in Banjarmasin took a terrible toll on human life: more than 120 people were killed on this occasion, the vast majority of them burned alive inside a store in Plaza Mitra.[60]

Postelection Riots: Makassar, September 1997

Although the May 1997 riot in Banjarmasin represented the high point of election-related violence in late Suharto-era Indonesia in terms of loss of life as well as property, it did not signal an end to the kind of disturbances that had plagued the country since 1995. Indeed, early postelection protests by PPP supporters against alleged Golkar fraud turned violent in several towns in East Java in early June 1997, with crowds burning down Golkar offices and other government buildings in Pasuruan, Jember, and the Madurese district town of Sampang, all longtime PPP strongholds.[61] More important, perhaps, September 1997 saw the unfolding of a postelection riot highly reminiscent of earlier episodes in 1995 and 1996, this time in Makassar (then known as Ujungpandang), the regional capital of South Sulawesi.

By the mid-1990s, Makassar was a bustling city of 1.5 million residents and a major administrative, educational, and economic hub for Eastern Indonesia. The port city boasted a precolonial history as a major entrepôt in the archipelago, and its indigenous Makassarese and Bugis merchants, sailors, and fishermen continued to roam far and wide throughout the Dutch colonial and postcolonial eras. In the Suharto era, moreover, well-connected businessmen from Makassar rose to national prominence, most notably Yusuf Kalla, a longtime Suharto associate, Golkar bigwig, and one-time cabinet minister.[62] As regional capital of South Sulawesi, the home province of ICMI chairman and high-tech industrial czar B. J. Habibie, moreover, Makassar was a privileged site for state provision of patronage and opportunities to non-Chinese, Muslim businesses.

In addition, Makassar was distinguished by a long history of Islamic worship, learning, and associational and political activity. The port city had been ruled by a sultanate, and its Bugis traders and seamen were known for their religious devotion. In the early postindependence years, not only was Makassar a stronghold for the Outer Island modernist/mercantile Muslim party Masjumi; it was also a locus of activity for the Darul Islam Indonesia movement, whose supporters waged a protracted guerrilla war in the hinterlands of South Sulawesi against the Soekarno government in the 1950s and early 1960s. Under the New Order, PPP likewise enjoyed considerable strength in the city. Over the course of the Suharto era, moreover, Makassar persisted and evolved as the center of Muslim educational, associational, and business activity in Eastern Indonesia, with its IAIN branch and Universitas Hasanuddin attracting Muslim students from all over Sulawesi, Maluku, and various other islands in the underdeveloped eastern half of the archipelago. By the 1990s, with the expansion of tertiary education, the ascendancy of Habibie and his patronage network, and the rise of local *pribumi* (indigenous) businessmen and political operators such as Yusuf Kalla, the star of Islam burned brightly and was clearly on the rise in Makassar.

At the same time, however, the limits to these upward trends were amply evident to Muslim residents of Makassar in the mid-1990s. Resentful *pribumi* businessmen not only claimed that companies owned by members of Makassar's small Chinese community (of about 40,000) controlled 60 percent of the construction industry, some 70 percent of the retail trade, and 90 percent of banking in the city but complained that Chinese businessmen enjoyed privileged access to credit and unfettered ease in obtaining permits and licenses for their ventures.[63] Urbanization in Makassar during the New Order witnessed the increasing predominance and visibility of Chinese capital in areas of retail trade and city spaces previously held by Muslim merchants. As one report noted in 1997:

> Traditional markets have been replaced by fancy shopping centers, and clearly these new buildings tend to be filled by the Chinese. The Central Market, for example, has now changed its name to Makassar Mall. Many family-owned stores which had sold goods there over many generations have been forced to close since the construction of the new shopping center. They could not afford to pay such high rent. Likewise in two other old markets, Pasar Baru and Pasar Terong. At the beginning of April 1996, these two markets were rebuilt as modern shopping centers. Both of them were constructed by Chinese-owned companies, PT Makasar Prabu Sejati and PT Makasar Putra Perkasa, at the cost of one billion rupiah.[64]

Meanwhile, with population growth came the swelling of urban slum areas filled by Muslim migrants from the city's hinterlands of South Sulawesi and Eastern Indonesia in general, even as Chinese wealth loomed ever larger on the urban landscape. Aside from the new shopping malls, the late 1980s and early-mid 1990s saw the development of exclusive residential subdivisions, the installation of motorcycle and automobile dealerships and showrooms, and the proliferation of bars, discotheques, and karaoke clubs in the city, all identifiably Chinese.[65] In a city that had witnessed attacks on Chinese residents during the tumultuous months of late 1965 and again in 1980—following the rape and murder of a Makassarese housekeeper by a Chinese businessman—a major episode of anti-Chinese rioting during the late Suharto era was hardly surprising.

The riot began on the evening of September 15, 1997, with another murder, this time by an allegedly deranged young man of Chinese ancestry who attacked a street vendor with a knife on a back street in the southern part of the city. The vendor escaped, but two of his customers fell victim to the knife-wielding attacker: a nine-year-old Muslim schoolgirl returning home from evening prayers and her twenty-year-old nanny. Within moments, as the little girl lay unconscious on the street, her nanny bleeding from multiple knife wounds, her attacker was surrounded and assailed by outraged local residents. By the end of the evening, as both he and the girl lay dead in the hospital, a riot began to unfold outside in the city.[66]

Whereas the murderer, an unmarried twenty-three-year-old seller of recycled bottles, was a faceless Chinaman, his innocent victim, as it happened, was the daughter of parents well known in the realm of Islamic education and associational activity in Makassar and elsewhere in South Sulawesi. The girl's father headed an Islamic educational foundation in the nearby regency of Gowa; her mother served as an assistant dean in the Faculty of Islamic Law in the Makassar branch of IAIN and had long been prominent in Islamic associations, most notably HMI; and two of her uncles worked as lecturers at Universitas Hasanuddin.[67]

Thus news of the incident spread rapidly through networks of Islamic students and activists in Makassar. Within hours of the killing on the evening of September 15, a *konvoi* of HMI activists on motorcycles had arrived on the scene and reportedly moved on to initiate the stoning of Chinese shops and the burning of cars elsewhere in the city. The next morning, even as a motorcade of cars and pickup trucks returned to Makassar from the slain schoolgirl's impromptu funeral in Gowa, students burned tires outside the campus of the local IAIN branch, and crowds began to attack Chinese business establishments, including literally hundreds of stores, motorcycle showrooms, bars, discotheques, and banks, burning dozens of cars and motorcyles in the process. The religious inflection of the rioting was clear: a well-established Chinese temple was sacked, while buildings sporting Muslim prayer mats or spray-painted indicators of Muslim ownership were spared.[68] By September 17, as the rioting subsided, nearly 1,500 stores and homes lay in ruins, as did more than 50 bars and nightclubs and 14 banks.[69]

Conclusion: Explaining the Riots

Beginning with Purwakarta and Pekalongan in late 1995, and ending with Makassar almost two years later, in September 1997, the penultimate years of the Suharto era witnessed a series of riots described as religious in nature. But such a label may obscure as much as it illuminates: many observers insisted that the underlying causes were economic rather than religious, and what many described as anti-Chinese riots in 1995–96 were followed by election-related riots in 1997. What remains to be explained is how *all* these riots *were* religious in some sense of the term, and how the specific modalities of this religious violence—its timing, location, protagonists, mobilizational processes, forms, and outcomes—were shaped by the religious constellation in general, and the place of Islam in particular, in the Indonesia of 1995–97.

Timing

A first step in this direction is to consider the *timing* of the riots against the broader backdrop of modern Indonesian history. After all, disturbances like those of 1995–97 have been relatively rarer—and considerably more concentrated—in Indonesia than is conventionally assumed, and their temporal distribution across the twentieth century deserves close consideration. Concerted attacks on Chinese-owned shops, businesses, and homes, Christian (and other non-Muslim) houses of worship, and government buildings in provincial towns and cities in Indonesia occurred in discrete time periods: in the 1910s, in 1963, and in 1980, leaving aside for the moment those incidents of violence which were directly connected with events in Jakarta (see chapter 5).

These earlier discrete time periods have much in common with 1995–97: they all correspond closely with historical moments of especially acute and unsettling urgency, anxiety, and ambiguity as to the position of Islam and of those who claimed to represent Islam in Indonesian society. In the 1910s, for example, the series of riots that targeted Chinese business establishments and residences in various towns along the northern coast of Central and East Java came at a moment when, as historians have noted, "the Chinese" were most clearly seen "to stand in the way of the rise of a native middle class."[70] It was during this decade that Muslim merchants and professionals began to form associations to promote the advancement of modernist Islam in the archipelago, such as the educational and welfare association Muhammadiyah in 1912, and the Sarekat Islam in the same year. Initially conceived as a Chinese-style mutual-help organization or *kongsi* among Muslim batik traders and producers, Sarekat Islam rapidly evolved into the first major mass movement in the Indies, its rallies, strikes, and other activities attracting the participation and attention of hundreds of thousands, if not millions, of indigenous inhabitants, especially on Java.[71] But this same decade also saw a marked surge in the prominence and assertiveness of the immigrant Chinese minority, which occurred in tandem with the rise of the nationalist movement in China at the turn of the century and the Chinese revolution of 1911. In 1900, Chinese merchants had founded the Tiong Hoa Hwee Koan, which began to establish modern Chinese-language schools on Java and elsewhere in the archipelago, and in subsequent years prominent members of the Chinese community began to press the Dutch colonial authorities for new privileges in the Indies, most notably legal status on a par with Europeans and the lifting of restrictions on Chinese travel and residence. The turn of the century had also seen Chinese merchants making inroads in spheres of the economy— batik; *kretek* (clove) cigarettes—previously held exclusively by indigenous Muslim merchants.[72] Thus the riots in various towns in Central and East Java in the 1910s unfolded against the backdrop of a broader push for recognition by forces claiming to represent Islam and, it is worth noting, at a time when these forces were most clearly and self-consciously imitating non-Muslims, notably in their founding of schools and associations modeled on those established by Europeans, Christians, and Chinese.

Some fifty years later, in 1963, a second wave of rioting unfolded in various towns of West Java (and, to a lesser extent, elsewhere on Java) at a moment of seemingly very different yet in crucial ways similar circumstances to those obtaining in the tumultuous 1910s. The late 1950s, for example, witnessed the rise of economic nationalism in Indonesia, as seen in the seizure and expropriation of Dutch businesses in the archipelago in 1957–58 and the declaration of a government ban on "alien-owned" retail stores in rural areas in 1959–60. The 1959 decree clearly targeted Chinese merchants, and although it was unevenly implemented, more than 100,000 Chinese residents left Indonesia in 1960, fearing subsequent restrictions and expropriations to come. The announcement of this decree, it is worth noting, was made by a cabinet minister affiliated with Nahdlatul Ulama at a gathering of "national" businessmen closely linked with NU and other Muslim parties, and the decree was most assiduously implemented—and extended to prohibit Chinese residence in rural areas—in West Java, where Muslim parties enjoyed special strength.[73] Overall, such expressions of "anti-Chinese feeling," Herbert Feith noted, were "most marked among Indonesian business groups determined to expand at the expense of the Chinese" and the right-wing Muslim parties and army officers who represented them, whereas the left-wing president, Soekarno, and the Indonesian Communist Party (PKI) worked to protect Chinese residents from such attacks.[74]

By 1963, Indonesian domestic and international policy was at a major crossroads, with the political constellation in the country marked by rising tension between left- and right-wing forces. On the one hand, the early months of 1963 saw Soekarno engaged in efforts to reach a rapprochement with the United States and in negotiations with the International Monetary Fund (IMF) for a new set of loans and economic stabilization policies. Such developments promised to strengthen the position of the army and of those forces representing Muslim urban middle-class and business interests. On the other hand, the early months of the year also saw increasing moves toward an alliance between the Soekarno regime in Jakarta and the Chinese Communist leadership in Beijing, presaging a leftward tilt in favor of the Indonesian Communist Party (PKI) at the expense of the army and right-wing Muslim parties, whose influence had been diminished since the ban imposed on Masjumi in 1960. Meanwhile, the termination of martial law on May 1, 1963, spelled a diminution of the army's powers, weakening the hand of the strongest remaining anti-Communist force in the country. It was thus, once again, against the backdrop of heightened tensions between social forces identified with Islam, on the one hand, and elements deemed to stand in their path, on the other, that riots targeting Chinese businesses, residences, and houses of worship unfolded in several towns in West Java (and to a lesser extent elsewhere in Central and East Java) in mid-1963.[75]

Some seventeen years later, in 1980, a third wave of similar riots occurred in several towns and cities of Central Java and in Makassar. These riots took place in the context of rising hopes and fears as to the strength of Islam in the country, as marked by the strong showing of PPP in the 1977 general elections and the rising assertiveness of the party in the national parliament (DPR), as well as the considerable interest generated by the Iranian Revolution of 1978–79. Faced with recurring forms of resistance by PPP in the parliament, including several well-publicized walk-outs by party members in protest against various pieces of government-imposed legislation, President Suharto launched a broadside against organized Islam in a speech in Pekanbaru in March 1980. There were certain groups, Suharto charged, which had yet to demonstrate their full commitment to Pancasila, the formal state ideology since independence, which was based on monotheistic but multifaith principles. Here the president was clearly referring to PPP and other Islamic organizations such as HMI, which had refused to accept the five points of Pancasila as their founding principles.[76]

Yet even as the regime's leading security and intelligence officials—most notably (Catholic) General Benny Murdani and (Protestant) Admiral Sudomo—began working to rein in and redirect PPP and other errant Islamic organizations, leading dissident figures in Jakarta launched a protest against this misuse of Pancasila by the president. In May 1980 a group of fifty prominent Indonesians, including many influential retired generals and two former prime ministers, delivered a "Statement of Concern" (*Perny-*

ataan Keprihatinan) to parliament. The members of this "Petition of Fifty" (*Petisi Limapuluh*) were predominantly devout Muslims and included a handful of prominent Muslim leaders affiliated with Masjumi and PPP.[77] This unprecedented public protest against the attack by the Suharto regime on Islam loomed large in the background of the rioting that unfolded in Makassar in May 1980,[78] and in Solo, Semarang, and other towns in Central Java in late November of the same year.[79] Thus the riots of 1995–97 fit within the broader historical pattern of similar disturbances in twentieth-century Indonesia: such riots occurred only during periods of heightened ambiguity, anxiety, and anticipation with regard to the position of Islam and those forces claiming to represent it in Indonesian society.

Location

Second, the geographic pattern of rioting in 1995–97 was also distinctly colored by religious context, as seen in the *location* of riots in provincial towns and cities where the institutions of Islamic learning, association, and political activity enjoyed a special claim on the public sphere. All these sites were known for the Islamic piety of their inhabitants, whether Sundanese as in Purwakarta, Rengasdengklok, and Tasikmalaya; north coastal Javanese as in Pekalongan; Madurese as in Situbondo; Bugis-Makassarese in Makassar; or Banjarese in Banjarmasin. All these towns and cities were well known for their density of *pesantren, madrasah,* IAIN, or other Islamic educational institutions, as well as Nadhlatul Ulama, Muhammadiyah, and other Muslim associational networks, typically including Al Irshad and Persatuan Islam. All had long histories of political organization and activity under the banner of Islam, ranging from the Sarekat Islam's rallies of the 1910s and 1920s to Nahdlatul Ulama and Masjumi in the 1950s and 1960s. And PPP presented a major challenge to Golkar in all these localities from the late 1970s through the 1990s. Most, if not all, these localities it is worth adding, had also been marked by experiences of armed rebellion under the rubric of Darul Islam in the 1950s and early 1960s. That movement for an Islamic state in the early postindependence period was based in areas—West Java, the northern coast of Central Java, South Sulawesi, Aceh, and South Kalimantan—which constituted the hinterlands of the towns and cities where religious riots unfolded in the mid-1990s.[80]

Aside from the historical and sociological depth of their Islamic institutions of worship, learning, and associational and political activity, the towns and cities that experienced major episodes of rioting in 1995–97 were ones in which the tensions between the position of Islam and non-Muslim sources of power, prestige, and wealth had grown especially acute over the course of the New Order era. These sites were, after all, either major Outer Island regional urban centers (Banjarmasin and Makassar) or Javanese provincial towns (Purwakarta, Pekalongan, Rengasdengklok, Situbondo, Tasikmalaya) where small-scale Muslim merchants, moneylenders, and manufacturers faced marginalization in the face of well-capitalized Chinese *konglomerat,* whether Jakarta-based or local in origin. Like the batik and clove traders and producers in Kudus and other towns in Java in the 1910s, smalltime Muslim shopkeepers and entrepreneurs in such towns and cities found themselves dwarfed and dislodged in the 1990s. These sites had witnessed the supplanting of public markets by supermarkets and department stores and shopping malls, the eviction of local residents to make way for business establishments and residential subdivisions, and the marginalization of small local firms by larger companies enjoying greater access to capital and closer cooperation from local officials of the state.

In all these localities, such encroachments and intrusions upon predominantly pious Muslim communities and their livelihoods were seen as involving and benefiting Chinese businessmen, whether Jakarta-based magnates or so-called *konglomerat lokal,* who through the corruption and collusion of government officials were able to ride roughshod over legitimate local concerns.[81] Moreover, the increasing awareness of the glass ceiling imposed by Chinese capital was fairly matched by a growing sensitivity to the anomalous prominence of Christian churches and schools in the midst of predominantly devout Muslim populations: hence the common backdrop of controversies over permits for the construction of new churches, claims of surreptitious Christian services in private residences, and accusations of creeping *Kristenisasi.*

Protagonists and Mobilizational Processes

Third, an examination of the *processes* by which riots unfolded in these towns and cities in 1995–97, reveals the common prominence of institutions of Islamic worship and learning in the protagonists, the nodal points of mobilization, and the discursive points of reference—and rumor—which marked the onset of these disturbances. Time and again, the riots began with perceived insults, violations, and abuses suffered by locally venerated Islamic figures and institutions. In Purwakarta, for example, crowds gathered to protest the humiliation of a young Muslim schoolgirl by a Chinese storeowner who accused her of shoplifting. The news that she had been forced to clean the store toilets while wearing her *jilbab* was deemed particularly offensive just a few short years after government authorities had relented in the face of widespread and well-publicized demands and allowed schoolgirls to wear the Muslim head scarf to classes.[82] Indeed, the *jilbab* had emerged in the 1990s as perhaps the most visible signifier of the extension of claims by Islam on the urban public sphere, with demands for recognition met by the government but pointedly ignored and abnegated in the incident in Purwakarta.[83]

Similar insults to the integrity and public status of Islam were prominent in all the other riots that occurred in 1995–97. The shredding of a copy of the Qur'an in Pekalongan, the beating of the *kyai* (and rumors of his death) at the hands of the police in Tasikmalaya, the blasphemy case in Situbondo, and the dispute over the prayer-house drum in Rengasdengklok all exemplified this shared feature of the riots, as did the killing of the IAIN lecturer's daughter in Makassar. The riots in Pekalongan and Banjarmasin in 1997 likewise arose in the context of heightened tension between supporters of the Islamic PPP and the backers of Golkar in the lead-up to the election of that year and in PPP strongholds where Golkar rallies were perceived as unwelcome and insulting intrusions.

Muslim associations and institutions of learning and worship also played prominent roles in the transmission—and interpretation—of these discursive points of reference, as well as in the process of assembly by which crowds gathered and mobilized. These were localities where "professional Muslims"—religious teachers, members of the local MUI, and branch leaders of the student associations HMI and PMII—were thick on the ground, prominent in local society, and available for service as "fire tenders" and "conversion specialists" who could play crucial roles in stoking the fires of religious tension and providing interpretive frames for the extrapolation of local disputes into larger, interreligious issues.[84] As in the disturbances of 1963 and 1980 (and, no doubt, those of the 1910s), what Stanley Tambiah terms "focalization" and "transvaluation"[85] of the incidents deemed insulting to Islam circulated through networks of *pesantren* and IAIN students—via HMI and PMII branches, *tarekat* groups, and the ranks of the PPP—by means of conversations, telephone calls, and, by the 1990s, photocopied flyers, e-mail messages, and Muslim newspapers and magazines. In virtually every case, the "assembling process"[86] involved mosques, *pesantren*, IAIN, and other sites of Islamic worship and schooling as key locations for mobilization in defense of the faith. In several instances this process was facilitated, accelerated, and amplified by Friday midday prayers at local mosques, or by the backdrop of Ramadan. The role of what Elias Canetti called "riot crystals,"[87] moreover, was typically played by *santri* from the local *pesantren* or HMI students from the IAIN, who rallied their classmates to seek justice or retribution, delivered impassioned speeches at local mosques, and otherwise served as the shock troops of the disturbances.

Targets, Forms, and Consequences

Fourth and finally, the *form and consequences* of the rioting reflected the context of acutely perceived ambiguity, awkwardness, and anticipation with regard to the position of Islam in Indonesian society. The violence of these rioting crowds, after all, was directed not against persons but against buildings and property: stores were damaged and burned down, their goods looted and set alight in the streets, the looting itself overshadowed by this symbolic destruction—rather than consumption—of commodities and economic power. The riots culminated—and, typically without effective intervention from the authorities, subsided—with these fires. As James Siegel has suggested, the burning of Chinese property, Christian churches, and, in many cases, government buildings and Golkar offices can thus be seen as a disavowal, an assertion of the moral status of Islam precisely at the historical moment when those who saw themselves as representing Islam and asserted moral claims to power in Indonesian society on this basis found themselves most unsure of the nature of their identities.[88] After all, like Chinese and Christians before them, Muslim Indonesians were now entering the core circuitries of the market and state power with unprecedented success, and doing so in the name of Islam. Unlike the disturbances of the 1910s, 1963, and 1980, which had typically begun with religious processions, traffic accidents, and other incidents between people who did not know one another, many of the riots of 1995–97 began with disputes between Muslim and Chinese neighbors living cheek by jowl in crowded urban neighborhoods. Thus even as rioters attacked and burned police stations, government buildings, and Golkar offices to voice their demands for public recognition for Islam, writes Siegel, they "destroyed Chinese wealth [and Christian churches] not to shame Chinese [and Christians], but to show that they were unlike them."[89]

As for the aftermath and consequences of these episodes, each riot resulted in a bewildering flood of commentary and analyses variously blaming social inequality, government policy, Chinese/Christian hegemony, or elite conspiracy. But however sociological or conspiratorial the register, all the hand-wringing, breast-beating, and finger-pointing ultimately led to unanswered questions surrounding the representation and recognition of Islam and the Muslim majority of the population. Were the interests and aspirations of Muslims inadequately addressed under the current political and economic system? Who could—and should—speak on their behalf? Was their power to be pathologized or celebrated, suppressed or appropriated?

It is hardly surprising that the onset of economic crisis and political transition in early 1998 heightened fears—and hopes—of the power of the Hidden Force of Islam in Indonesian society. With Habibie, ICMI, and the ascendant network of modernist Muslims waiting in the wings and increasingly impatient for the removal of remaining obstacles to their assumption of power, sensitivities as to the position and status of Islam were at an all-time high in Indonesia. Small wonder that a surge of mobilization in early 1998 by middle-class urban Muslim students and professionals— championed by such figures as the Muhammadiyah chairman (and prominent ICMI member) Amien Rais and crystallizing under the banner of *Reformasi*—was accompanied by a major riot in Jakarta and several other major cities in mid-May of 1998, much as earlier moments of real or potential political transition in Jakarta (1945–46, 1965–66, 1974) had also been marked by violent crowd actions. This was a new and transitional phase of religious violence in Indonesia.

5

Crisis, Conspiracy, Conflagration

Jakarta, 1998

It was in the aftermath of a series of religious riots in various provincial towns and cities that the long-anticipated transition from the authoritarian regime of President Suharto in late 1997 and early 1998 culminated in the May 1998 riots in Jakarta, Solo, and several other cities and the resignation of Suharto later that month. Spates of localized collective violence along similar lines had foreshadowed the onset of previous moments of national-level political transition over the course of the twentieth century. The disturbances that accompanied the rise of the Sarekat Islam in the 1910s, for example, presaged the long-deferred *Revolusi* for independence in 1945–49, which featured many episodes of collective violence alongside the armed guerrilla struggle against the Dutch. The riots in West Java in 1963 were likewise followed by the fall of Soekarno, the assumption of power by Suharto in 1965–66, the anti-Communist pogroms that eliminated the Partai Komunis Indonesia (PKI) during these years. Disturbances developed in Makassar and Central Java in 1980 even as the group of prominent retired military officers and Muslim politicians represented in the "Petition of Fifty" (Petisi Limapuluh) launched the most frontal challenge to Suharto's leadership since his assumption of power in the mid-1960s.

If each of these waves of localized collective violence occurred during periods of heightened ambiguity, anxiety, and anticipation with regard to the position of Islam in Indonesian society, so too did the impetus for national-level transition come in no small measure from those forces and figures who claimed to represent Islam in the country. Studies have shown that the energies, aspirations, and associational and educational networks associated

106

with Islam made an enormous contribution to the struggle for independence during the *Revolusi* of 1945–49. The prominent role of Islamic organizations in the fall of Soekarno and the violent destruction of the PKI
in 1965–66, most notably in the public demonstrations by HMI and parliamentary maneuvers by Nahdlatul Ulama in Jakarta, and the massacres
of alleged PKI members by NU youth (Ansor) and militia (Banser) groups
in East Java, are likewise well known and well documented. In 1980, once
again, the specter of an ascendant, insurgent Islam was evident in PPP's rising popularity, the refusal of PPP and HMI to accept Pancasila's precepts
as their founding principles, and the Petition of Fifty's unprecedented attack on Suharto's misuse and distortion of the state ideology and his attack
on Islam in the name of Pancasila.

Echoes of Malari

More than any other such moment in Indonesian history, the sequence of
provincial disturbances in 1995–97 and mass rioting in Jakarta in May
1998 echoed the series of events that had begun in Bandung in mid-1973
and culminated in what came to be known as the Malari riots in Jakarta in
mid-January 1974. In August 1973, in the West Javanese capital city of
Bandung in the aftermath of a traffic accident and dispute involving a
Muslim teenager in a horse-drawn wagon and three Chinese youths in a
Volkswagen, crowds numbering in the hundreds set Chinese cars and motorcycles on fire and attacked Chinese-owned shops and residences in the
city.[1]

   That rioting and episodes of violent religious conflict elsewhere in the
country unfolded against the backdrop of rising protests by PPP (the then
newly formed Islamic party) and other leading Muslim organizations and
individuals against the government's promotion of a new marriage law.
First introduced by government representatives in parliament in August
1973, the proposed legislation provided for secular administration of marriage laws, which would remove marriage, divorce, and the entire realm of
family law from the religious court system under the Ministry of Religious
Affairs to the secular courts under the Ministry of Justice. Such a shift of
judicial and regulatory powers from religious to secular authorities, and the
elimination of religion as an obstacle to marriage between citizens of different faiths, one former minister of religious affairs warned, threatened to
erase "the limits of religion" in Indonesia.[2] Against statements by the
Catholic leader of Golkar's Parliamentary contingent that excessive religious devotion constrained progress toward national development, PPP

members walked out of parliament, accusing the government of hostility to Islam and espousal of atheist principles similar to those that had been held by the PKI. It was only through the extraparliamentary intervention of the military leadership, represented by General Soemitro, head of the Command for the Restoration of Security and Order (KOPKAMTIB), and General Sutopo Yuwono, head of the National Intelligence Coordination Agency (BAKIN), that the legislation was revised to assuage Muslim concerns, and a compromise bill was crafted with PPP's approval in November 1973.[3]

This series of events reflected—and in considerable measure exacerbated—a set of growing tensions between rival factions, and between conflicting institutional, social, and religious elements, within the New Order regime. On the one hand, President Suharto relied heavily on two retired army generals and longtime close associates from his home province (and longtime army command) of Central Java: Ali Moertopo and Soedjono Hoemardani, both of whom served as Special Assistants to the President (SPRI). Soedjono was best known as a practitioner of Javanese mysticism, a spiritual adviser to Suharto, and a broker of Japanese business interests in Indonesia.[4] Moertopo, the founder and head of the intelligence group OPSUS (Special Operations), had (with Soedjono) helped to establish the Catholic think tank CSIS, the Center for Strategic and International Studies, which served as a hub of policy formation, influence-peddling, and recruitment into the innermost corridors of civilian power in the regime.[5] Both men were thus closely associated with Christian and Chinese political and business interests, and their own preferences for Javanese spiritualism and syncretism, as well as their experiences in the army in the 1950s and early 1960s, inclined them toward strong suspicion of organized Islam.

Still, the key leadership posts in the military establishment were in the hands of officers less intimately connected with—or beholden to—President Suharto and more closely associated with the practices and organizations of devout Islam. General Juwono was a Bugis Muslim from South Sulawesi, thus representing an ethnic group—and an Outer Island area—whose Islamic devotion was not compromised or complicated by the *abangan* spiritualism and syncretism of the Javanese officers who dominated the military establishment. General Soemitro hailed from East Java, the heartland of Nahdlatul Ulama and of traditional Islamic learning and worship, where he had overseen the slaughter of tens of thousands of alleged PKI members in 1965–66 by contingents of Ansor and Banser groups while serving as regional commander for the province. Soemitro thus boasted close contacts and warm relations among many *kyai* and politicians from NU who were now affiliated with PPP.[6]

It was against this backdrop that student protests emerged and began to grow in Jakarta in late 1973. These protests, in which the Muslim university students' association HMI played a leading role, targeted Moertopo and his associates for special criticism, while Soemitro once again assumed the role of a mediator, giving speeches at student demonstrations and otherwise allowing the wave of mobilization to build up in the streets.[7] As the Japanese prime minister, Kakuei Tanaka, arrived in Jakarta for a visit in mid-January, protests against links between the Indonesian government and Japanese businesses in the country grew into full-scale rioting in the city, leaving a trail of burning Chinese and Japanese business establishments in its wake.[8] Implicated in the student protests and, by assocation, the Malari riots, Soemitro was forced to resign his post; the hated SPRI were dismissed and their official functions discontinued. But Moertopo, his close associates, and the Christian and Chinese interests exemplified by CSIS retained considerable influence in the regime for years thereafter.

It is against the background of such earlier moments of national-level political transition and collective violence as Malari, as well as the riots in provincial towns and cities around the archipelago in 1995–97, that the fall of Suharto and the riots of May 1998 must be understood. Many observers have argued—or simply assumed—that it was the economic crisis of 1997–98 which precipitated the student movement, the riots, and the resignation of the longtime president. But Suharto, it should be recalled, had weathered previous economic crises by bending with the winds, bowing to the demands of the IMF and other foreign lenders and investors, and opening up new avenues to ease and accelerate the flow of çapital in Indonesia.[9] Suharto had likewise handled previous waves of student protest through a combination of repression, co-optation, and promises of reform. What was unusual about the final months of 1997 and the first five months of 1998 was the final upward push by ascendant elements of the political class claiming to represent Islam in Indonesia. Yet as in preceding key moments of political transition, mobilization by forces claiming to represent Islam was a crucial motor of national-level political change, and as in earlier transition periods such a push for long-sought recognition and power was accompanied by violence.

In this light, the contrasts and similarities between the riots of May 1998 and the Malari episode of 1974 appear particularly instructive. As in the months and weeks leading up to Malari (*Malapetaka Limabelas Januari*, or January Fifteenth Catastrophe), the spring of 1998 saw a rising tide of student protests in Jakarta and other major Indonesian cities, calling not only for better economic conditions (Turunkan Harga!) but also for an end to corruption—(*Kolusi, Korupsi, dan Nepotisme* (KKN)—and the implementation of major political and economic reforms (*Reformasi*). As in late 1973 and early 1974, moreover, against the backdrop of escalating tensions within the regime, the protests of early 1998 emerged, grew, and flourished between figures closely associated with the personal interests of President Suharto, on the one hand, and those identified with more enduring institutional elements of his regime, on the other. In both instances, student protests targeted the cluster of interests around the palace for special criticism, while enjoying the active encouragement or quiet acquiescence of the supposedly more "professional" officers and the "apolitical" civilian technocrats who held key official posts but much less actual power in the New Order state. Both the Malari incident in Jakarta in mid-January 1974 and the mass rioting in May 1998 developed not only as byproducts of student protests but also, it has been alleged, through the incitement and instigation of agents provocateurs, described as working for Soemitro or his archrival Ali Moertopo in the first instance, and their middle to late 1990s counterparts in the regime in the second.[10]

That said, the key difference between the unfulfilled promise—or threat—of Malari and the fall of Suharto in May 1998 was, in a word, Islam. In 1973–74 the dominant secular nationalist and Christian elements of the Suharto regime found themselves under attack by PPP members in parliament, HMI students in the streets, and other prominent Islamic figures and organizations in the editorial pages of the newspapers and magazines of the day. But neither Soemitro nor Juwono were inclined to associate themselves too closely with the defense of an Islam that was still identified with only a small minority element of the national political class. In 1998, by contrast, it was the Suharto family itself that emerged as the target of student protests, urban middle-class grumbling, and attacks by such prominent Islamic leaders as chairman Amien Rais of Muhammadiyah. By 1998, moreover, the forces identified with Islam were enjoying a much more prominent, if not securely dominant, position within the national political class, as seen in both the student protests and the backroom maneuvering of Vice President (and ICMI chairman) Habibie and his supporters in the parliament, the cabinet, and the armed forces leadership.

Thus the riots in Jakarta and other major Indonesian cities in May 1998 must be understood, if not as religious violence per se, then as part of the process by which the final push for national power was made by forces claiming to represent Islam. Yet in contrast with the provincial disturbances of the preceding three years, in the end neither the rioting in Jakarta nor the broader campaign to force the resignation of Suharto occurred under the sign of Islam. Instead, the identification of these national events with the *massa* (mob) or *Rakyat* in the first instance and the broader forces of

Reformasi in the second foreshadowed the possible absorption, evisceration, or evaporation of Islam at the very moment of its apparent ascendancy to the pinnacle of state power.

January–April 1998: The Struggle for the Vice Presidency

Even as the riot in Makassar was winding down in mid-September 1997, a major economic crisis of national—indeed, regional—proportions was beginning to hit Indonesia. As international investors and lenders suddenly started to abandon long-popular East Asian markets in the latter half of 1997, the Indonesian economy suffered most of all, with the rupiah depreciating 70 percent and the Jakarta stock exchange index falling 50 percent from mid-July 1997 to early January 1998. Indonesia's vulnerability to such rapid fluctuations in world currency markets reflected both extremely high levels of overseas borrowing (especially private, unhedged, short-term debt) and widespread perceptions (and self-fulfilling predictions) that rising cronyism and nepotism were making the economy extremely weak in the face of a crisis.[11] Indeed, the downward spiral of crisis began to accelerate quite precipitously at the end of the year, as uncertainties regarding the stability of the Suharto regime multiplied. In late October 1997 the government announced an austerity program worked out with the International Monetary Fund and began to shut down several ailing local banks, but the rupiah continued to plummet. With the largely appointed People's Consultative Assembly (MPR) due to meet in March 1998 to name the president and vice president for the next five-year term, rumors were rife in Jakarta about Suharto's health, his choice of running mate, and the implications for subsequent succession scenarios.[12]

As early as November 1997, moreover, it became clear that the ongoing trends sketched in chapters 3 and 4 had conditioned the Suharto regime to view and respond to the unfolding crisis in essentially political terms. Early that month the president's son Bambang Trihatmodjo had reacted angrily to the inclusion of his Bank Andromeda among the sixteen private banks targeted for government liquidation, initiating a lawsuit against the cabinet officials responsible and speaking darkly of a conspiracy behind the decision. Significantly, the chief targets of his ire were Bank Indonesia Governor Soedradjad Djiwandono, son-in-law of Partai Sosialis Indonesia (PSI) luminary Soemitro Djojohadikusumo (and a Catholic with close links to CSIS), and widely respected Finance Minister Mar'ie Muhammad, former activist and leader of the Islamic university student group HMI (1966). These officials, Bambang Trihatmodjo's comments suggested, were part of a larger conspiracy to discredit his good name and that of his family. With disparate elements of the political class eager to diminish the growing power of the president's children—and prevent the ascension of Suharto's daughter Tutut to the vice presidency in March 1998—Bambang was absolutely right.[13] Under conditions of incipient economic crisis and heightened international scrutiny, the president's family was certain to find itself on the defensive, even as diverse elements of the established political class—ranging from marginalized Christians to ascendant modernist Muslims—used the opportunity to push "reforms."

Events in December 1997 further intensified these tensions within the political class. In midmonth, Suharto, apparently having suffered a minor stroke, took ten days of rest from his official duties, heightening speculation about his health and the succession question. By the first week of January 1998, rumors had clearly spun out of control and with devastating effects, sending the rupiah from 1,600 to a previously unimaginable level of 10,000 to the U.S. dollar and setting off runaway inflation.[14] A wave of panic buying ensued in markets, stores and supermarkets in various parts of the archipelago.[15]

Against this backdrop, the first two months of 1998 saw the launching of a political offensive by forces supporting the vice presidential candidacy of ICMI Chairman B. J. Habibie in the upcoming March session of the MPR. Part of this offensive focused on Sofyan Wanandi, a businessman of Chinese ancestry and Catholic faith who was known not only for his control over a diversified group of companies, the Gemala Group, but also his close ties to the CSIS (the conservative think tank that represented certain Chinese/Catholic business interests) and to retired military officers such as General Benny Murdani (retired).[16] Wanandi had openly voiced skepticism about the government's willingness to implement the terms of the IMF agreement, publicly refused to join the government-led "Cinta Rupiah" (Love the Rupiah) campaign, and reportedly expressed hopes that the vice president chosen for the 1998–2003 term would be drawn from the armed forces.[17] Rumors later circulating in Jakarta suggested that he had been lobbying for specific vice presidential candidates—including incumbent Try Sutrisno and the army chief of staff, General Wiranto—and that news of his views had angered and alarmed Suharto.[18] In short, Wanandi represented a cluster of Catholic, Chinese, secular nationalist, and military interests opposed to both the Suharto family and the vice presidential candidacy of Habibie.

Sofyan Wanandi and his brother, CSIS board member Jusuf Wanandi, soon found themselves vulnerable to attack. On January 18, 1998, just three days after the signing of the IMF agreement, a bomb exploded in an apartment in Jakarta, leading to an investigation headed by the Greater Jakarta regional military commander, Major General Sjafrie Sjamsoeddin, a close ally of Major General Prabowo Subianto, the president's son-in-law and a backer of Habibie's bid for the vice presidency.[19] The authorities subsequently blamed remnants of the Partai Rakyat Demokrasi (PRD), or People's Democracy Party—a small and shadowy leftist group—for the explosion but also claimed to have "discovered" documents linking PRD activists to the Wanandi brothers and CSIS. Through much of the month of February, front-page articles about the case appeared in newspapers and magazines, demonstrations for the closure of CSIS were held by Islamic activists, and Sofyan Wanandi was brought in for repeated, lengthy interrogations by the authorities.[20]

News of the case faded and then disappeared entirely in early March as the People's Consultative Assembly unanimously "elected" Suharto and Habibie unanimously as president and vice president, respectively. If, as many analysts suspected, the campaign against Sofyan Wanandi and CSIS was at least partly intended to cow Habibie's opponents within business and military circles, then in these terms it could be deemed a success. Yet the attack on Sofyan Wanandi must also be seen against a broader pattern of government actions in January and February 1998, and with an eye to a wider set of consequences.

Indeed, in January and February, ranking Indonesian government officials, including President Suharto, actively began to stoke popular resentments against Chinese businessmen in the country. Spokesmen for the armed forces, for example, issued statements revealing that General Feisal Tanjung then the armed forces commander and a close ally of Habibie, had contacted thirteen of the nation's wealthiest Chinese businessmen to demand that they join the "Cinta Rupiah" campaign and exchange their U.S. dollars for Indonesian rupiah.[21] Subsequent weeks saw mounting official attacks against unnamed currency speculators, described by the military's chief parliamentary representative as "traitors" and by President Suharto himself as part of a "conspiracy" to reduce the value of the rupiah to 20,000 to the U.S. dollar.[22] From the language used, it was abundantly clear to all who cared to read or listen that the president and his minions were referring not only to Sofyan Wanandi in particular but also to Chinese businessmen in general.

In addition, top government officials, both civilian and military, actively encouraged Islamic groups to amplify and act upon these anti-Chinese sentiments. On the evening of January 23, 1998, for example, an estimated 4,000 activists from several key Islamic groups joined 3,000 Kopassus troops for an unprecedented and much-publicized breaking of the Ramadan fast at the Kopassus headquarters in Jakarta. This occasion brought together the then Kopassus commander, Major General Prabowo Subianto, the president's son-in-law, with prominent leaders of Islamic groups such as Dewan Dakwah Islamiyah Indonesia (DDII), or Indonesian Islamic Propagation Council, and the Indonesian Committee for World Muslim Solidarity (KISDI), both well known for their strident attacks on Christian and Chinese predominance in many spheres of Indonesian business and society.[23]

These groups, already mobilized to support Habibie's vice presidential candidacy and to attack CSIS and Sofyan Wanandi, undoubtedly felt further emboldened by Major General Prabowo's generous display of support for their activities.[24] In a variety of publications and public forums—including a mid-February KISDI rally before thousands of supporters at Jakarta's Al-Azhar Mosque—calls were voiced for a struggle against the "traitors" and "liars" Wanandi and his ilk.[25] Activists such as Hussein Umar, secretary general of DDII, set out across the country to spread the message beyond Jakarta. Meanwhile, both national and local government officials made clear that the definition of "treason" to the Indonesian nation would be understood in religiously colored terms.[26] In early February 1998, for example, following a meeting with Suharto, the government-created Majelis Ulama Indonesia (MUI), or Council of Indonesian Islamic Scholars, called for a *jihad nasional* against "speculators and hoarders," terms defined broadly enough to cover the thousands of—mostly Chinese—shopkeepers, merchants, and businessmen scattered across the archipelago.[27]

In short order, local officials began to push for more concrete steps in this direction. In Solo, for example, the head of the Islamic PPP contingent in the municipal assembly called publicly for Matahari, a prominent Chinese-owned department store chain, to lower the prices of its merchandise, especially primary commodities, to avoid the wrath of residents.[28] In cities and towns in Java and various other parts of the country, newspapers were soon awash with reports of local police and military officials investigating and punishing suspected hoarders.[29] However this new crime was defined, it was clear that shopkeepers and merchants were now burdened with new "protection" costs on top of previous exactions and the rapidly rising wholesale cost of goods. In addition, as the falling rupiah and resultant inflation sent prices of essential commodities rocketing upward, local authorities, from *bupati* (regents) to regional military commanders, began to requisition amounts of "nine basic goods" for sale at specially organized distribution centers called *pasar murah*.[30] Many local Islamic groups soon launched parallel efforts, encouraging hopes about the possible role of *pe-*

santren and *madrasah* as distribution centers to replace the much disparaged Chinese-owned shops and marketing networks.[31]

In short, a wide variety of government statements and more concrete actions throughout January and early February 1998 worked to create an atmosphere of public, officially sanctioned suspicion and resentment toward not only national *konglomerat* such as Sofyan Wanandi but also the thousands of Chinese shopkeepers, merchants, and businessmen scattered throughout the Indonesian archipelago. These steps were taken in a country whose government and majority population had long stigmatized its Chinese minority as foreign and predatory and had shown considerable sympathy for heavy restraints on the unfettered operation of the so-called free market. And since the most dramatic and broadly felt effects of the current crisis—rapidly rising prices—were first being experienced directly via Chinese-owned shops and stores throughout the country, it was small wonder that many Indonesians saw local Chinese shopkeepers as profiting rather than suffering from the crisis, as perpetrators rather than victims of the conspiracies and crimes referred to by Suharto and his minions. With newspaper articles reporting almost daily about police and military riot-simulation exercises in various parts of the country, the stage was set for further disturbances. And in fact, in the months of January and February 1998 a series of small-scale riots took place in a number of towns and cities around Indonesia, most notably in areas known for their Islamic piety, such as the northern coast of Java and parts of Sumatra, Sulawesi, and Lombok.[32]

In virtually all cases, these riots took the form of attacks on Chinese-owned shops, supermarkets, or department stores, with looting and destruction of goods.[33] Despite the privations that accompanied the deepening economic crisis, the broad pattern was characterized by the destruction—rather than the confiscation—of goods, even those most heavily in demand. In the West Java regency of Majalengka, for example, when hundreds of residents gathered demanding lower prices on primary commodities and gasoline, they seized petroleum drums and other goods from the stores and burned them in the street.[34]

Catholic and Protestant churches were also targeted by the rioting crowds, leaving dozens of Christian houses of worship damaged, burned, or entirely destroyed by mid-February, according to one estimate at the time.[35] Reports that some riots were started by outsiders who arrived in trucks or motorcycle convoys led various local and foreign journalists to conclude that many of these incidents had in fact been staged by elements within the regime.[36] Although the riots did not lead to any mass killings or spread much beyond ephemeral, local episodes, they understandably helped to create—or at least exacerbate—a climate of anticipation with regard to larger-scale violence. Small-town Chinese shopkeepers closed their premises and maintained an especially low profile (even during the traditionally cacaphonous Chinese New Year); many of their wealthier counterparts in the big cities reportedly purchased open airplane tickets for Singapore or Hong Kong.

Meanwhile, the dramatic and in some instances exaggerated coverage that the riots received in foreign media led to growing international worries regarding "social unrest" in Indonesia.[37] Foreign governments issued statements of concern, dispatched special envoys to see Suharto, and ordered their embassies to prepare emergency evacuation measures for their citizens on Indonesian soil. The IMF, facing a wave of criticism for its alleged mishandling of the crisis and mounting prospects of a deteriorating situation in Indonesia, began to signal its own recognition of the need to reevaluate and perhaps renegotiate the agreement signed in mid-January 1998.

As the March 1998 session of the People's Consultative Assembly opened in Jakarta, however, the appearance of order was rapidly restored. The riots halted abruptly, and Suharto and Habibie were unanimously chosen president and vice president by the tightly controlled, mostly appointed MPR, without a single interruption in the proceedings such as had occurred in 1988 and 1993. A wave of military reassignments saw the president's son-in-law Prabowo Subianto promoted to the command of KOSTRAD, the Army Strategic Reserve Command, and awarded the rank of lieutenant general. Other key military rotations left such crucial operational positions as army chief of staff, special forces (KOPASSUS) commander, and Greater Jakarta regional military commander in the hands of close Prabowo associates and allies. Yet the new armed forces commander and defense minister, General Wiranto, and his allies in senior staff positions and other regional command posts, appeared to constrain Prabowo's well-known ambitions, even as the retirement of the outgoing armed forces commander, General Feisal Tanjung, and other key ICMI-affiliated generals deprived Habibie of allies at the very top of the military hierarchy.

The new civilian leadership slate likewise left Habibie—and the broader Islamic forces he represented—in a highly awkward and ambiguous position within the regime. On the one hand, Suharto had installed Habibie as vice president, selecting him—by design or default—instead of his own much-despised daughter Tutut or the incumbent Try Sutrisno, a retired general widely viewed as the choice of Christian, secular nationalist, and military elements in the political class. Tutut was too controversial, especially in the context of the economic crisis, and Try was too untrustworthy, especially given his ties to the retired General Benny Murdani and the precedent of his having been nominated—without Suharto's blessings—for the position by a military MPR delegate in 1993. On the other hand, Suharto's choices for the new cabinet tended to pass over ICMI's well-publicized wish list in favor of close Suharto family friends and allies: presidential golfing and business partner Mohammad "Bob" Hasan (Suharto's first and only Chinese cabinet member) as minister for trade and industry; daughter Tutut as minister for social affairs; and her long-rumored paramour retired General Hartono as minister of internal affairs.[38] The choice of Hasan as minister of trade and industry—and of a close Tutut ally as the new minister of finance—seemed to guarantee that Suharto family interests would not be unduly compromised by the new agreement forged in April with the IMF, one viewed by some analysts as considerably more "flexible" than the one signed almost three months earlier.[39]

With Tutut expected to assume the leadership of Golkar in the party's October 1998 congress, and her close associate Hartono exercising enormous influence as head of the Ministry of Internal Affairs, ICMI's star now appeared to be fading, Habibie's elevation to the vice presidency notwithstanding. Indeed, officials close to Suharto were careful to remind journalists of the ambiguities in the constitution surrounding succession in the event of the president's sudden death or incapacitation, and some emphasized the temporary caretaker role of a "troika" composed of the ministers of defense, foreign affairs, and internal affairs—none of whom were allied with Habibie. Against the opposition of PPP, moreover, Suharto pushed new legislation through parliament in March granting the president special powers in the event of a national emergency. Suddenly, for those forces in the political class claiming to represent Islam, the window of political opportunity appeared to be rapidly closing.

March–May 1998: The Final Push

It was against this backdrop that the spring of 1998 witnessed the emergence and growth of a student movement in Jakarta, much along the lines of late 1973 university campus demonstrations that had preceded the Malari riots of January 1974. The attacks on Sofyan Wanandi and CSIS, and on "hoarders and speculators" more broadly, could not but contribute to the circumstances that kept local and foreign businessmen alike from making new investments and other long-overdue decisions. The dynamics set in motion by these measures, including the riots, likewise further weakened the stability and value of the rupiah in January and February, increasing the already enormous and unsustainable levels of foreign debt owed by local companies and the Indonesian government itself. Consequently, the new agreement signed with the IMF in mid-April 1998, though in some ways more flexible than the mid-January deal, was based on much more pessimistic forecasts: higher debt levels, higher inflation, and negative economic growth (−4 percent) for the year rather than stagnation. The impact of these dramatically downward trends was now all too evident in rapidly rising unemployment, costs of living, scarcities, and hardships for millions of Indonesians. IMF disbursement of funds, moreover, was now conditional on monthly assessments of Indonesian progress on economic reform.[40]

Meanwhile, the adventurist anti-Chinese scapegoating in January–February and the increasingly nepotistic personnel and policy decisions in March–April had begun to exacerbate internal tensions within the regime and rising dissension within the political class more broadly. The rapid ascendancy and multifarious activities of Lieutenant General Prabowo and his allies had embittered avowedly more "professional" officers in the military establishment and rallied them around the new armed forces commander and defense minister, General Wiranto, who had maintained a stoic, melancholy public silence in the preceding months, punctuated by his attack on the anti-Chinese campaign as "garbage."[41] The dismissal of regime "technocrats" such as Soedrajad Djiwandono and Mar'ie Muhammad and their replacement with more pliable Suharto family flunkies had likewise dismayed many established elements of the political class, ranging from associates of the Catholic think tank CSIS to alumni of the modernist Muslim student association HMI to members of the long defunct technocratic Socialist Party (PSI) and its influential network within the elite. ICMI activists were also bitterly disappointed that their own (well-publicized) wish list of cabinet ministers had mostly been scotched by the appointment of Mbak Tutut's favorites in March.

With Sofyan Wanandi and the CSIS network on the defensive, it was now the turn of the old PSI network of Westernized liberals and technocrats to mobilize urban middle-class sentiment against the regime. In March, women from Universitas Indonesia and other elite circles, led by the famed astronomer Professor Karlina Leksono, formed a group called Suara Ibu Peduli (Voice of Concerned Mothers) and protested outside government offices against the rising price of milk and other failings of the regime.[42] More impressive, perhaps, was the self-proclaimed vice presidential candidacy of the former environment minister Emil Salim, the only open challenge to Habibie. Salim's candidacy failed to stimulate an *interupsi* in the MPR in March, but it did win vocal support from such old PSI luminaries and fellow former cabinet ministers as Soemitro Djojohadikusumo, Mohammad Sadli, and Selo Soemardjan, as well as respected Islamic scholar Nurcholish Madjid, a former chairman of the Islamic university students' association HMI.[43] Knowledgeable observers suggested that Salim's vice presidential bid also elicited quiet sympathy in the upper ranks of the military establishment (where the PSI network had long enjoyed influence) and broad support in middle-class circles.

Indeed, March and April 1998 saw the emergence and spread of antigovernment student protests at college campuses in many parts of the archipelago, including the elite universities that had long served as nodal points in recruitment for and reproduction of the New Order.[44] By the end of April, moreover, growing evidence suggested that the students' demands for *Reformasi* now enjoyed solid legitimacy and support, both within the regime and among key constituencies in Indonesian society at large.[45] PSI-ish university lecturers, deans, and rectors soon began to appear and speak out at campus rallies, and luminaries such as Emil Salim and Selo Soemardjan voiced their support on such occasions and in newspaper columns.[46] Retired generals soon joined their ranks.

Further, beyond these circles, elements of the long ascendant but increasingly frustrated modernist Muslim network within the political class also began to mobilize against the regime. Muhammadiyah chairman (and Universitas Gadjah Mada lecturer) Amien Rais had emerged as a vocal critic of Suharto in mid-1997, distanced himself from ICMI, in the face of the anti-Chinese campaign of January-February 1998, adopted a strong stance against the government and its narrow sectarianism. By late April he had emerged at the forefront of the *Reformasi* campaign and enjoyed the support of a broad range of student groups at university campuses around the country.[47]

In the face of student mobilization, evidence of internal strain and discord within the regime soon began to surface. A few top government officials spoke darkly of vague conspiracies behind the student protests, but more and more figures in the cabinet and the parliament embraced the vague notion of *Reformasi* and the process of public dialogue with student leaders. In the military establishment, for example, although Army Chief of Staff Soebagyo, a pliant Prabowo ally, issued stern warnings, dismissive comments, and thinly veiled threats to the students as protests endured and grew week after week, by contrast, Wiranto-linked regional commanders— such as East Java's Major General Djadja Suparman—had proved much more accommodating since early March, and by early May, General Wiranto himself had assumed a leading role in the dialogue with some student leaders.[48] A similar split could be discerned in the diverging responses to news that student activists had been abducted and allegations that armed forces personnel were responsible. Even as rumors linking the abductions to Prabowo and his allies began to circulate in Jakarta, Armed Forces Commander Wiranto categorically denied official military involvement, condemned whatever "rogue elements" (*oknum*) had committed such misdeeds, and ordered an immediate investigation.[49]

It was in the context of these broadening popular protests and deepening regime divisions that the government announced its drastic reduction of fuel subsidies on the evening of Monday, May 4.[50] Doubtlessly designed, and perfectly timed, to force IMF approval and disbursement of funds despite misgivings about the pace and extent of reform implementation since the signing of the April 10 accord, this move hiked gasoline prices by 70 percent, diesel by 60 percent, and kerosene by 25 percent literally overnight.[51] That evening, long lines for fuel created huge traffic jams in the streets of Jakarta and Surabaya. For the first time, student protests spilled out into the streets in several major cities; demonstrators stopped traffic for hours outside the regional assembly in Surabaya; and Medan experienced mass rallies and rioting.[52]

With President Suharto out of the country to attend an international conference in Cairo, protests, riots, and rumors filled the streets of Jakarta and other major cities from Surabaya to Medan, Samarinda, and Makassar.[53] Prominent figures in ICMI began calling for a cabinet reshuffle and a special MPR session on Suharto's return.[54] Student protests continued to grow, and confrontations with police and military authorities became more frequent and more heated. In the late afternoon of May 12, after hours of protests in and around elite Trisakti University in northwest Jakarta, security forces opened fire and shot four students dead, wounding several others.[55] The killings, suspected to be the premeditated handiwork of elements in the security forces, generated widespread public outrage.[56]

On May 13, thousands joined a burial ceremony for the slain students, bringing crowds to the streets outside the University. Scattered rioting and looting broke out in the main boulevard abutting Trisakti and in a few other locations in north, west, and central Jakarta, with crowds attacking shopping complexes, banks, department stores, and Chinese shops. The next morning the rioting spread throughout the greater Jakarta area: crowds converged on nodal points of Chinese commercial power, and the Chinatown area of Glodok was especially hard hit. Rioting also spread to other cities, most notably Solo,[57] with smaller disturbances in Medan, Palembang, and Surabaya. With Jakarta still smoldering and tens of thousands of armed policemen and military troops taking to the streets, the riots finally petered out the next day.[58]

Jakarta residents returning from Friday midday prayers on May 15, 1998, survey the damage on the streets of the nation's capital from the riots earlier that week (AP)

May 1998: Riots and Resignations

The riots of May 1998 were unprecedented in their scope, violence, and impact. Subsequent reports estimated that more than 1,000 people had lost their lives; many others had suffered beatings, rapes, and other indignities; and countless shops, homes, and other private property had been lost to burning, looting, and wreckage.[59] Although many of those who died were protesters or looters killed by security forces or trapped inside burning buildings, Chinese residents of Jakarta were targeted for violent abuse and were victimized in countless incidents—most notably the rapes of more than a hundred women in various parts of the city—acts of violence and brutality unseen in previous riots.[60] Fearful for their lives, some 150,000 residents (chiefly Chinese Indonesians and Western expatriates) fled the country, mostly by airplane to nearby Singapore or Hong Kong.[61]

Like the shootings at Trisakti University on May 12, the riots in Jakarta on May 13–15 bore traces of instigation and orchestration by elements in the armed forces, with suspicions focusing on the KOSTRAD commander, Lieutenant General Prabowo Subianto. Media and NGO accounts sketched a pattern of instigation and coordination by groups of men who initiated the rioting and carried out the rapes; they were described in terms that suggested military-backed *preman* (thugs or gangsters) as well as military troops in mufti.[62] Evidence also implicated well-connected notorious gangsters such as Anton Medan and the anti-Chinese activist Ki Gendeng Pamungkas.[63]

Suspicions about the Trisakti shootings and security forces' behavior during the riots pointed vaguely in the direction of Prabowo and his military academy classmate and longtime close friend Major General Sjafrie Sjamsoeddin, Jakarta's regional commander. But subsequent revelations published by the Jakarta weekly magazine *Tajuk* were later to prove far more specific and sensational: according to an interview with an anonymous member of KOPASSUS, troops from KOPASSUS, KOSTRAD, and Kodam Jaya (the Greater Jakarta Regional Command) had been assembled as early as March 1998 and readied for undercover operations by Prabowo and Sjafrie Sjamsoeddin. Together with Jakarta-based *preman* and several hundred civilians brought in from as far afield as East Timor and Irian Jaya, these forces were then mobilized on May 12 and assigned targets for "riot" activities, including rapes of "Chinese" women. The military operation, under the rubric of a Gerakan 12 Mei Orde Baru (May 12 New Order Movement), was apparently intended to justify a harsh military crackdown in Jakarta and to precipitate both the immediate dismissal of Wiranto and the elevation of Prabowo and his allies to the top command posts in the armed forces.[64] Observers variously described Prabowo as acting at Suharto's behest to disrupt and discredit the student movement, or as working to help Habibie and his supporters force upon Suharto a cabinet reshuffle and special Session of the MPR.

Although similar forms of sensationalism, speculation, and conspiracy theorizing had also emerged in the wake of the riots that unfolded around the country in 1995–1997, the evidence of military instigation and orchestration in May 1998 was much more compelling. A joint fact-finding team of investigators assembled by the government and staffed by prominent human rights lawyers and other researchers issued a six-volume report that presented eyewitness accounts and other evidence in support of such a pattern.[65] The team concluded: "Agents provocateurs, generally not local residents, athletic in appearance, some wearing elements of school uniforms, did not participate in the looting, and immediately left locations [of rioting] after buildings or goods were set alight. These agents provocateurs also were responsible for bringing or preparing various implements for destroying and burning buildings, such as metal crowbars, flammable solvents, cars, molotov cocktails, and so forth."[66] A special team of researchers likewise uncovered considerable evidence of direct military involvement in the rapes of Chinese women in Jakarta and, despite serious threats and intimidation (including the rape and murder of one of its staff members), circulated its findings in the Jakarta press and before an international audience.[67]

Investigations of the events of mid-May 1998 in Solo, the most affected city after Jakarta, also implicated the security forces in the process by which student protests at a local university had developed into large-scale rioting. In a pattern reminiscent of Jakarta, eyewitnesses noted that crowd actions had been led by small groups of well-built men, sometimes arriving on motorcycles or scooters, variously clad in school uniforms or masking their faces in bandanas. These *provokator* reportedly set fire to tires, cars, or other goods in the streets, pried open doors with crowbars, stoned shop windows, and otherwise initiated or incited attacks on Chinese-owned commercial establishments in Solo.[68]

Further evidence of military involvement was apparent in the looting and destruction visited upon the Ramayana department stores in the Jakarta area, as revealed in an insurance case in which I served as an expert witness. The Ramayana department stores suffered more losses and damages than any other retail chain, and the 26 damaged or burned-down stores (of 29 total) scattered around the Jakarta area suggest two striking features of the overall pattern and process of the rioting in May 1998. First of all, virtually all these stores were located in close proximity to major toll roads or thoroughfares in the greater Jakarta area, mostly at busy intersections and junctures where there were clearly other major business establishments such as banks and large shopping complexes, of which the Ramayana stores were merely a small part. Even the stores located in Bekasi and Tangerang, suburbs to the east and west of Jakarta, were found along the main toll roads. The virtually simultaneous occurrence of rioting at these scattered sites around the greater Jakarta area fit well within a pattern of instigation, orchestration, and coordination by military elements using the main arteries of the city to transport troops in mufti and other subcontracted groups to incite rioting, rape, and the burning of goods and buildings.[69] The handful of stores in the central Jakarta were likewise very much accessible via major boulevards.

Second, and perhaps more revealing, many of the stores were located in close proximity to key military installations, ranging from army headquarters to complex housing units of the main military commands linked to the instigation of the riots: namely, Kodam Jaya, KOPASSUS, and

KOSTRAD. One store was located little more than 1,000 meters from the Kodam Jaya complex, and another was situated a mere 500 meters from army headquarters.

Eyewitnesses interviewed in connection with an insurance case involving the Ramayana stores, moreover, volunteered information that tended to confirm the pattern of military involvement noted in many other reports. Witnesses at some stores claimed to have observed the arrival of athletic-looking men with crew cuts—usually dropped off by trucks or vans, or arriving in motorcycle convoys—who came equipped with rocks, gasoline, or other materials useful for carrying out attacks on stores and other buildings. Witnesses in other locations emphasized the role of men whom they identified as *preman,* gangsters or thugs, in organizing and mobilizing crowds, men who in some instances were said to have "cased the joint" at least a few days before the riots. There was even one witness who claimed to have seen army troops lock looters in the mall in Karawaci on the southern outskirts of the city.[70]

Yet however much the rioting can be attributed to such deliberate scheming, its consequences clearly exceeded the realm of conspiracy. On May 15, President Suharto returned home early from Cairo; security forces began to reassert law and order on the streets of Jakarta; and the government restored the fuel subsidies.[71] With a cabinet reshuffle reportedly imminent, a final round of rotations at the highest echelons of New Order power was in the offing, albeit not the one foreseen by Prabowo or President Suharto.[72] Indeed, the lingering horrors of the rioting in the streets a few days earlier combined with fearful anticipations of imminent and irrevocable reshuffles in the civilian and military hierarchies to undermine internal regime solidity in the face of continuing protests and mounting calls for Suharto to step down. In the wake of the riots, prominent figues representing the full spectrum of the political class—including Adi Sasono, the secretary general of ICMI—had joined opposition leader Amien Rais in a fifty-member Majelis Amanat Rakyat (MAR), or Assembly of the People's Mandate, and called for Suharto's resignation.[73]

Against this backdrop, rising fears of displacement in the imminent reshuffle and contingency plans for a possible special session (*sidang istimewa*) of the MPR soon precipitated the withdrawal of support for Suharto from within even the innermost circles of the regime. If, as many feared, Mbak Tutut was about to assume the stewardship of Golkar and Lieutenant General Prabowo the command of the armed forces, the moment for a preemptive strike had arrived.

First to defect were civilian elements loosely affiliated with Habibie, ICMI, and, through this network, the HMI students and Muhammadiyah leaders on the streets. On May 18 the fraction heads of the DPR—including current Golkar chief and DPR speaker Harmoko and armed forces fraction leader Lieutenant General Syarwan Hamid, both Habibie allies—publicly called on the president to resign, thus claiming the hitherto rubber-stamp parliament as a new locus of authority and the vice president as legal successor.[74] Two days later, with thousands of student protesters still occupying the parliament grounds, Economic Coordinating Minister Ginandjar Kartasasmita and thirteen other cabinet members submitted their resignations. Like their counterparts in the DPR, many of these ministers enjoyed a close association or tactical alliance with Vice President Habibie and shared a common distaste for the now ascendant Mbak Tutut and her minions in Golkar, the cabinet and the parliament.

In the military establishment, meanwhile, a set of countermoves and a process of internal consolidation appear to have proceeded in response to the emerging disarray and defections in civilian circles. Rumors in early May had suggested growing support in top military circles for a cabinet reshuffle or, if necessary, a special session of the MPR, and Armed Forces Chief of Staff for Social and Political Affairs Lieutenant General Susilo Bambang Yudhoyono, a Wiranto ally, had initiated consultations with (mostly PSI-ish) civilians about a package of political reforms. After the Jakarta riots and the DPR chiefs' defections, moreover, a series of meetings among the top military brass reportedly led to an emerging consensus in support of the immediate convening of a Dewan Reformasi (Reform Council) and the holding of new elections within a matter of months. It was perhaps with this plan in mind that General Wiranto publicly rejected parliamentary leaders' May 18 date for Suharto's resignation and Habibie's assumption of presidential powers.[75]

Yet Suharto's inability to recruit credible figures to join a new Cabinet or a Dewan Reformasi, the continuing growth of student and middle-class protests, and the unraveling of the regime through internal defections undermined this attempt to defuse, if not resolve, the crisis. On the evening of May 20, Wiranto reportedly informed Suharto that he could no longer guarantee the security of his regime. The next morning, Suharto announced his resignation, and Habibie assumed the presidency.[76] With the chairman of ICMI now occupying the pinnacle of state power, the ascent of Islam in Indonesia appeared to be reaching its apogee.

Conclusion

The series of events culminating in Suharto's resignation and Habibie's assumption of the presidency in late May 1998 were driven in no small measure by the forces associated with the promotion of Islam in Indonesian society and state. The campaign for *Reformasi*, after all, had been championed by Amien Rais, the chairman of Indonesia's preeminent modernist Islamic association, Muhammadiyah, and Muslim student associations were among the most prominent groups behind the student protests at university campuses in Jakarta and other major cities around the country.[77] In addition, the internal defections that brought about the unraveling of the Suharto administration were led by a Trojan horse, as it were, of civilian and military elements linked to Habibie, ICMI, and a broader set of networks associated with Islam.

Beyond the maneuvers and machinations within the Indonesian political class, the resurfacing threat of the Hidden Force in the streets of Jakarta had also been carefully, consciously nurtured in circles associated with the promotion of Islam inside and outside the Suharto regime. In January and February 1998, for example, high-ranking military officers, civilian officials, and political operators had launched a highly public attack on Jusuf and Sofyan Wanandi, the Catholic think tank CSIS, and Chinese business (and Christian influence) more broadly. Crying out against Catholic political conspiracies and calling for jihad against—self-evidently Chinese—financial speculators and commodity hoarders, these elements insisted that the economic crisis signaled not the opportunity for reform in the sense of a rollback of state intervention in the economy but instead the imperative of expanding the regulation of the market in the name of a higher—that is, Islamic—moral economy of sorts. It was in this climate that the scattered—and seemingly far from spontaneous—food riots of January and February 1998 unfolded in towns along the northern coast of Java and in other localities known for their Islamic piety.

It was later, with the apparent instigation and orchestration of Lieutenant General Prabowo Subianto and his allies, moreover, that the rioting and the rapes unfolded in Jakarta, Solo, and a few other cities in mid-May of the same year. Together with his military academy classmate and close associate Major General Sjafrie Sjamsoeddin, the Greater Jakarta regional commander at the time, Prabowo had been publicly cultivating ties with Islamic groups known for their strident opposition to Chinese and Christian interests in Indonesia, and he had taken the initiative in the campaign against the Wanandi brothers and CSIS in a show of strong support for Habibie's bid for the vice presidency.

In the hope of defending his presidency and the interests of his family, it appears, Suharto had encouraged the anti-Chinese campaign of January–February 1998, endorsed Habibie as his vice president in the March MPR session, exacerbated the hardship of urban residents by slashing fuel subsidies in early May, and perhaps knowingly absented himself from Indonesia to attend a meeting in Cairo just as rioting began to unfold first in Medan and then in Jakarta and elsewhere. If, as many commentators have suggested, Suharto had come to distrust Habibie, Prabowo, and the broader forces associated with Islam inside and outside the regime, perhaps he acquiesced in their advancement and their activities in early 1998 with an eye toward a well-timed dismissal and disavowal of "adventurist" and "sectarian" elements in his regime (including extended family members and friends) as an effective strategy for silencing domestic and foreign criticisms and calls for reform: hence his continuing reliance on the seemingly more secular and "professional" General Wiranto, and his public courting of liberal, antisectarian Muslim intellectuals such as Nurcholish Madjid and Abdurrahman Wahid in the final days of his rule.

The public debate and political fallout that arose from the ashes of the Jakarta riots were strongly colored by questions concerning the role of Islam in the violence and the position of Islam in an emerging post-Suharto Indonesia. The public outcry against the mass rapes of Chinese women led to predictable stalling, obfuscation, and denials on the part of civilian and military officials, as well as a pattern of harassment, intimidation, and violence against nongovernmental organizations that had initiated an investigation of the events of May 13–15, 1998 in Jakarta (as noted, one investigator was raped and murdered). A number of Islamic publications, moreover, focused attention on a Jesuit priest, Romo (Father) Sandyawan Sumardi, SJ, who had led the efforts of a group called Team of Volunteers for Humanity (Tim Relawan untuk Kemanusiaan) to document both the mass rapes and the broader pattern of instigation and orchestration of the rioting. Sandyawan's group began publicizing its findings as early as July 1998, and Sandyawan also served as a member of an official joint fact-finding team constituted by key government agencies and nongovernmental organizations, which concluded its inquiries into the riots and published an executive summary of its findings in October of the same year.

Sandyawan had already attracted considerable invective from both government officials and certain Islamic publications for his alleged role as patron of the leftist Partai Rakyat Demokrasi (PRD), or People's Democracy Party. The PRD had been blamed for the rioting that had followed the storming of PDI headquarters on July 27, 1996, by government forces in connection with the forcible removal of Megawati Soekarnoputri from the leadership of the party. PRD activists had been rounded up and imprisoned, and Sandyawan, who was publicly identified as a mentor to the party's leaders, was picked up for questioning. His name resurfaced in early 1998 in the controversy surrounding Sofyan Wanandi and his alleged support for the PRD, which was accused of planning bomb attacks and other terrorist activities in Jakarta.

Sandyawan, in other words, had long been identified as a key link in the chain between Christian generals, Chinese businessmen, and liberal-to-leftist activist groups attempting (whether through unions, political parties, or NGOs) to build a mass base by means of (secular) class-based appeals to workers, peasants, and the urban poor. His pioneering role in investigating the riots and documenting the rapes, then, soon came to serve as a lightning rod for criticism and skeptical commentary by certain voices claiming to speak on behalf of Islam.[78] Official and nonofficial efforts to investigate the riots, to document mass rapes, and to pursue suspicions of military influence and involvement, those voices insisted, were driven by partisan forces eager to discredit the new government, to put President Habibie and his allies on the defensive, and to drum up international—especially U.S.—media and government scrutiny of the situation in Indonesia in order to strengthen the hand of Christian and Chinese interests. Likewise, they cast the removal of Prabowo and his allies from key military commands in Jakarta in late May 1998, Prabowo's dismissal from the armed forces in August of the same year for his role in the kidnapping, torture, and disappearance of student activists, and accusations that he had masterminded the May riots in Jakarta as efforts to marginalize a valiant defender of Islam in the military establishment.[79] Behind calls for truth, justice, and respect for human rights in the wake of the riots, they declared, lurked an anti-Islamic agenda pushed by self-interested Christians, Chinese, and their domestic and foreign allies.

Indeed, both in Habibie's assumption of the presidency and in the rioting in Jakarta and elsewhere, the ambiguities and obstacles constraining the full ascendancy of Islam were in ample evidence by mid-1998. Within the anti-Suharto protest movement of early 1998, after all, leading modernist Islamic associations and modernist Muslim figures had occupied a prominent, if not preeminent, role by identifying themselves with the broader campaign for *Reformasi*, joining hands with secular liberal, traditionalist Muslim and Christian groups who shared the goal of ousting the longtime president and his family. Within Golkar, the DPR, and the cabinet, Habibie and his supporters had likewise succeeded in undermining Suharto's position only through tactical alliances with cliques and factions against Mbak Tutut and other members of the president's family.

Within the military establishment, the evident adventurism of Lieutenant General Prabowo Subianto and his associates had led to distrust, disavowal, and eventual dismissal, first by the embittered outgoing Suharto and then by the nervous newcomer Habibie. On May 21, the day of

Suharto's resignation and Habibie's assumption of the presidency, Minister of Defense and Armed Forces Commander Wiranto issued orders for Prabowo's transfer from the command of KOSTRAD to head the Army Staff College (*Seskoad*), even as Prabowo's close ally Major General Muchdi Purwopranyono was removed from his post as commander of KOPASSUS. Prabowo's previous support for Habibie (and vehement demands for his recognition) notwithstanding, the new president acquiesced in these moves and in subsequent rotations (*mutasi*) to marginalize Prabowo and his allies within the armed forces. Even though objections from various quarters prevented the two Christian generals originally designated to replace Prabowo and Muchdi from assuming the KOSTRAD and KOPASSUS command posts,[80] Wiranto's continuing tenure as minister of defense and armed forces commander signaled a reversal for Islamic elements within the military establishment.[81] Thus neither in the final ascent to power nor in the formal assumption of authority was Islam the sole— or the supreme—motive force.

These obstacles to the consolidation of a more assertively, unproblematically Islamic regime under Habibie reflected more than just the particular constellation of factional politics in Jakarta in the months leading up to Suharto's resignation. Christians, Westernized liberals, and secular nationalists, after all, continued to exert considerable influence within both the civilian and the military circuitries of the regime, the university campuses, and the middle classes more broadly; and the exigencies of the economic crisis in Indonesia underlined the important role of established interlocutors capable of restoring the country's credibility (and thus its credit flows) with the IMF, the World Bank, and the financial markets. Within the ranks of ICMI and the "new Muslim middle class" it claimed to represent, moreover, ambitious Muslim professionals—businessmen, politicians, intellectuals, military officers—in many ways had much more in common with their Christian and secular nationalist counterparts than with the "professional Muslims"—*ulama* and other Islamic educators, preachers, and publicists, officials of the vast Ministry of Religious Affairs—whose faith they supposedly shared. By 1998, ICMI's think tank CIDES had begun to look much like CSIS: its Jakarta daily *Republika* mirrored the well-established Catholic newspaper *Kompas,* even as HMI alumni from elite universities around the country competed with other entrenched cliques within the political class for state business contracts, positions in Golkar, seats in parliament, and territorial commands in the armed forces.

As graduates of state primary and secondary schools, Indonesian (and sometimes Western) universities (or the Armed Forces Academy), these Muslim professionals were profoundly socialized and deeply absorbed within the secular circuitries of the modern Indonesian state. Habibie held a Ph.D. in aerospace engineering from a German university rather than any qualifications pertaining to Islamic jurisprudence or Qur'anic exegesis. Prabowo, schooled overseas before entering the Armed Forces Academy, was the son of a secular, Western-educated father (the PSI luminary and respected economist Sumitro Djojohadikusumo) and a Catholic mother; even his most ardent defenders did not pretend that he was a "good Muslim." Not only was "*Reformasi*" a more palatable public rubric than "Islam" for the campaign to oust Suharto and the effort to promote the new Habibie regime in the eyes of domestic and foreign audiences, but even among many of those affiliated with ICMI or closely associated with Habibie, the "Islam" in whose name they had organized and mobilized was largely a matter of affiliation within the political class, rather than a marker of devout religious faith. Hence their deep ambivalence and concern in the face of Prabowo's entanglement with such groups as KISDI and Dewan Dakwah, and his adventurist activities culminating in the May 1998 riots.

The ambiguous and awkward position of Islam was evident even in the riots themselves: in the process of mobilization, the actors and targets involved, and the understandings that accompanied and ensued from the violence. Unlike the disturbances in various provincial towns and cities in 1995–97, for example, the rioting in Jakarta in mid-May 1998 was not a response to a perceived attack on prominent Islamic figures and institutions. In fact, the fatal shootings of four students on May 12 took place at Trisakti University, which was known as an elitist institution catering in no small measure to Chinese and Christians youths. In contrast with the role of *pesantren*, mosques, and local branches of various Islamic organizations in facilitating, encouraging, and initiating crowd mobilization against Chinese shops and Christian churches in Pekalongan, Situbondo, Tasikmalaya, Makassar, and elsewhere in 1995–97, moreover, there was no evidence that Islamic groups such as KISDI or DDII played a role in orchestrating the May riots in Jakarta, and there were very few cases of churches and temples attacked or damaged during the mayhem.

Finally, instead of the references to Islam found in the slogans, graffitti, and other forms of expression that came with the provincial disturbances of the preceding three years, the rioting in Jakarta in mid-May 1998 was described by participants and observers in secular terms, as the mobilization of "the mob" (*massa*) or "the People" (*Rakyat*). Spray-painted messages on storefronts such as "*Milik Muslim*" (Muslim-owned) appeared interchangeably with "*Milik Pribumi*" (Native-Owned) as defensive markers of non-Chinese identity rather than as rallying cries of religious mobilization. The targeting of Chinese business establishments was variously understood to reflect the privations and grievances of ordinary Indonesians (i.e., the *Rakyat*) or the insatiability and barbarity of the unruly *massa*.[82] As one eager participant told an observer at the time, "The People are shopping, 100 percent discount!" (Rakyat belanja, diskonto seratus persen).[83] The forms assumed by the Hidden Force—and the hopes and fears thus inspired—now appeared to be those of nation and class, rather than those of Islam. Small wonder that expressions of shock, revulsion, and fear in response to the riots and the rapes circulated throughout the political class, irrespective of religion. Even those Islamic groups enthralled by the possibilities of popular mobilization against Chinese and Christian elements in Indonesian society, and angry that first Prabowo and then the new Habibie regime would be smeared and saddled with responsibility for the violence, refrained from openly claiming the May riots on behalf of the *Ummat*.

Thus the Jakarta riots of May 1998 revealed the constraints on the possibilities of escalating popular mobilization behind the banner of Islam from the provincial town riots of the preceding years to the national level. In the early months of 1998, prominent national figures claiming to represent Islam had engaged in unprecedented inflammatory rhetoric and instigatory activity against the Chinese, yet the popular response—limited and orchestrated as it was—came in a distinctly un-Islamic idiom. Even as the avowed representatives of Islam appeared to be assuming the reins of national state power in Jakarta, the hold of Islam on the broad mass of Indonesian society remained very much in doubt. This doubt, and other doubts and anxieties that came into view with the transition from Suharto's authoritarian rule, helped give rise to new forms of religious violence in the country.

6

From Lynchings to Communal Violence

Pogroms, 1998–2001

With the ascension of B. J. Habibie to the presidency in late May 1998 came the much anticipated elevation of Islam to the seat of national state power in Indonesia. Habibie, after all, had long served as the chairman of ICMI, the All-Indonesia Association of Islamic Intellectuals, and more generally as the patron and promoter of a broad variety of modernist Muslim activists and organizations seeking patronage and protection from the state. Although many individual Muslims had reservations about Habibie's own piety, honesty, and effectiveness as a leader, his ascension to the presidency represented a major triumph for a wide range of groups organizing under the banner of Islam.[1] His cabinet included prominent members of ICMI, and other politicians affiliated with a number of modernist Islamic organizations assumed formal and informal positions of power and influence in his administration. Never before had forces favoring the so-called Islamization of Indonesian state and society enjoyed such proximity to power. Small wonder that Amien Rais, chairman of Muhammadiyah and champion of the university campus–based campaign for *Reformasi* and Suharto's resignation, helped to wind down student protests in late May and early June 1998 with pronouncements that the new Habibie administration deserved a six-month trial period.

At the same time, however, the position of Habibie—and of Islam more broadly—remained fragile within the Indonesian state; the powers of the new president and his allies were circumscribed and challenged from both within and without. The retention of General Wiranto, former Suharto adjutant, as minister of defense and armed forces commander in chief, for example, signaled the limits of Habibie's influence within the powerful military establishment, even as the realities of the Asian economic crisis dictated further subordination of Habibie's famously "nationalist" pet projects to the austerity and discipline of an IMF restabilization program. Also in Golkar, the long-dominant party in parliament (and in the People's Consultative Assembly tasked with selecting the president and vice-president), Habibie's position soon appeared precarious. Within weeks of his elevation to the presidency, a bitter fight for the Golkar party leadership surfaced, in which Akbar Tanjung, a Habibie ally and former head of the modernist Islamic student association HMI, only narrowly defeated General Edy Sudrajat, a former defense minister and longtime subordinate of the powerful Catholic military and intelligence czar of the 1980s, General Benny Murdani. The position of Islam within the Indonesian state, it was clear, was far from hegemonic, and the possibilities for promoting substantive Islamization remained highly circumscribed.

The Habibie Interlude

It was in this context of evident insecurity and uncertainty that President Habibie initiated a process of liberalization. The summer of 1998 witnessed the loosening of restrictions on press freedoms and the release of scores of political prisoners, even as greater freedom of association encouraged the formation of literally dozens of new political parties. Before the end of the year, moreover, plans for a general election in mid-1999 had already been announced, with many of the restrictions of the long Suharto era lifted to allow for much freer competition. This move in the direction of democratization was soon accompanied by shifts toward decentralization: the passage of two important pieces of legislation on regional autonomy in 1999 devolved considerable administrative and fiscal powers to regencies (*kabupaten*), cities (*kotamadya*), and, to a lesser extent, provinces (*propinsi*), while allowing local assemblies (DPRD) to elect regents (*bupati*), mayors (*walikota*), and governors (*gubernur*), hitherto essentially appointed by the Ministry of Home Affairs in Jakarta.

Given the overwhelming majority of statistical Muslims in Indonesia as well as the Islamizing trends in the country noted by countless observers since the 1980s, many figures within the Habibie administration understandably hoped that the political space opened up by these moves would be occupied in large measure by forces rallying behind the banner of Islam. After nearly a decade of claiming to represent not just Islam but millions of Indonesian Muslims, this segment of the national political class projected considerable self-confidence in this regard. What constraints continued to circumscribe and threaten the new regime could be ascribed to powerful enemies within the Indonesian state (e.g., residual secular and Christian influence in the military) and the international arena (i.e., Christian and Jewish conspiracies to contain Islam and oppress Muslims throughout the world). Against these essentially external, hostile, and parasitic forces stood the Habibie administration as the organic representative of Indonesian society, a society of Muslims. Dissent from within this society—continuing student demonstrations and other protests against the regime—was demonized as the work of Communist agitators and their dupes, said to be secretly backed by Christian generals, businessmen, and politicians, if not the CIA and Mossad.[2]

Yet with the movement toward political liberalization, democratization, and decentralization initiated by Habibie, the claims to represent Islam in Indonesia fell under increasing strain and strife, for the fixity and boundaries of all sorts of identities in the country were undermined and in some cases overwhelmed by a multiplicity of competing interpellations. Within ICMI and its satellite organizations, after all, a broad diversity of modernist Muslims had long coexisted, ranging from nondevout seekers of patronage to pious but highly Westernized Muslim liberals to committed Islamists of decidedly puritan hue. More important, perhaps, the authority of ICMI and the various Islamic activists and organizations that sought protection and patronage under Habibie's wings had always rested on its embeddedness within the central state apparatus of a closed authoritarian regime, and on its access to the perquisites, privileges, and prestige of state power. This narrowly modernist Muslim stream within the political class lay like a small oil slick upon the vast ocean of Indonesian Islam, with its rich diversity of Muslim institutions of education, association, and worship historically independent from state control and its huge population across the sprawling archipelago of avowed believers much poorer, more rural, and much more modestly educated than those who, from the pulpits of state power in Jakarta, claimed to speak on their behalf.

Hopes that Habibie and his allies could win the elections of mid-1999 were destined to be dashed. The administration party Golkar suffered a precipitious decline to 22 percent of the vote; a welter of modernist Muslim-led parties (PPP, PAN, PBB, and PK) totaled only another 21 percent. By contrast, the decidedly ecumenical Partai Demokrasi Indonesia—Perjuangan (PDIP), or Indonesian Democratic Party of Struggle, led by Megawati Soekarnoputri—the daughter of Indonesia's national hero and first president—placed first with nearly 34 percent of the vote. The Partai Kebangkitan Bangsa (PKB), or National Awakening Party, led by Abdurrahman Wahid—longtime head of the "traditionalist" Muslim association Nahdlatul Ulama—came in third after Golkar with 12.7 percent.

With this election result, the possibility of cobbling together a winning coalition of Golkar and allied Islamic parties to (re)elect Habibie in the People's Consultative Assembly (MPR) was foreclosed, and the threat of a Megawati presidency loomed large. Thus in the October 1999 MPR session, the main Islamic parties—PPP, PBB, PAN, and PK—formed a "Central Axis" (*Poros Tengah*) in support of the liberal traditionalist Wahid as president, forcing the "secular nationalist" Megawati to settle for the vice presidency instead. With this outcome, and as Wahid refused to reward his erstwhile Central Axis supporters with cabinet seats or other concessions, by the end of 1999 Islam had experienced a rapid decline and reversal of fortunes from its apogee in the preceding year. After a transitional administration dominated by modernist Muslims and protective of Islamist groups, Indonesia was now ruled by a president identified with traditionalist Islam, liberalism, and accommodation with Christians, and a vice president whose party included large numbers of non-Muslims (more than one-third of its parliamentary slate) and few prominent members with any history of Islamic schooling or association. By mid-1999 the notion of Islam as a universalist faith and force in Indonesia, so seemingly ascendant in the years leading up to 1998, had fallen prey to the divisive and particularistic dynamics of competitive elections.

The Eclipse of the Religious Riot

The pattern of dramatic change—and abiding uncertainty regarding the position of Islam in the Indonesian public sphere prefigured three decisive shifts in the pattern of religious violence from mid-1998 through 1999. First, after several years of disturbances targeting Chinese business establishments and non-Muslim houses of worship in provincial towns and cities around the archipelago, and in the wake of the May 1998 riot in Jakarta (and several other cities), the familiar repertoire of anti-Chinese riots and church burnings disappeared from the stage of Indonesian public life. Although in the first weeks and early months after the rioting in Jakarta there were numerous reports of harassment and intimidation suffered by Indonesians of Chinese ancestry around the archipelago,[3] the phenomenon of religious rioting described in chapter 4 soon petered out and vanished from view.

To be sure, the first year following Suharto's resignation did witness a handful of riots in some ways reminiscent of the disturbances of 1995–97. In late June 1998, for example, several hundred students from *pesantren* in the Central Javanese town of Purworejo congregated in the town center after Friday midday prayers to demand the closing of local gambling outlets. The crowd then proceeded to attack and burn several gambling venues plus a handful of nightclubs, karaoke bars, discotheques, and a movie theater. The crowd also set upon four churches—three Protestant, one Catholic—and the house of a Protestant minister, leaving a trail of broken windows and pews in its wake before dispersing for evening prayers at the local mosque and a police escort back to various *pesantren*.[4] Christian groups listed more than a dozen cases of attacks on churches in various other parts of Indonesia in the first six months following Suharto's resignation and Habibie's ascension to the presidency.[5] September 1998 witnessed assaults on Chinese shops in the Central Javanese town of Kebumen and the East Sumatran city of Medan,[6] and in early January 1999 an attack by a crowd of rickshaw drivers on a police station in the West Javanese town of Karawang spilled over into the looting of some Chinese shops and minor vandalism in a handful of non-Muslim houses of worship.[7] Similar but smaller-scale disturbances were also reported in various parts of the archipelago in the second half of 1998 and into 1999.

But none of these incidents unfolded in response to perceived insults or slights to Islam, its local representatives, or local institutions of Islamic worship and education, and little of the violence appears to have been directed at the specifically religious targets—churches and temples—so prominent in the riots of previous years. Instead, the attacks on Chinese businesses—supermarkets, rice mills, shrimp farms, stores—in 1998–99 fit well within a broader pattern of strikingly secular mobilization in localities around the archipelago. Popular claims to property—land occupations, lootings—grew ever bolder with the worsening economic crisis, the widening of freedom to organize, and the uncertainty regarding previously fixed guarantees of state protection.[8]

Insofar as religious violence was concerned, the fading of attacks on Chinese property, non-Muslim houses of worship, and government buildings by crowds mobilized under the banner of Islam during this period represents an important change worthy of examination. For contrary to suppositions of deep-rooted "ethnic hatred" or "economic resentment," the rising tide of unemployment, inflation, and hardship for ordinary Indonesians across the country and the easing of authoritarian restrictions on popular mobilization did not combine in 1998–99 to spell a return to anti-Chinese riots, much less an escalation in the frequency or violence of such disturbances. Instead, with the assumption of power in Jakarta by forces closely identified with the promotion of Islam, it was the shift in the constellation of religious authority in Indonesian state and society that prefigured the disappearance of religious rioting of a certain kind. If in 1995–97, after all, the *upward* push for the recognition of Islam in Indonesian society had pitted the defenders of the faith against the stubborn residues of Christian and Chinese power in the hierarchies of state and market, with Habibie's ascension to the presidency in mid-1998 the push for recognition was no longer *upward* but rather *downward* and *outward*. For with the effective capture of state power in Jakarta, the greatest expectations and anxieties as to the position of Islam in Indonesia no longer centered on a fixed hierarchy located within a centralized state but were redirected and diffused within the broader, murkier realm of Indonesian society.

The Emergence of Islamic Vigilante Groups

A second shift in religious violence in the latter half of 1998 was the emergence, especially in Jakarta, of state-sanctioned—and subcontracted—vigilante groups mobilized under the banner of Islam. The final years of the Suharto era had already witnessed the occasional mobilization of rowdy, small-scale protests against perceived nodes of Christian influence and antiregime activity (e.g., the Catholic-run think tank CSIS, the Catholic-owned newspaper *Kompas,* the Christian/secular nationalist PDI) in Jakarta, as well as attacks on student demonstrations, which were caricatured as the work of Communist remnants and Christian conspirators in Indonesia. These incidents had seen the mobilization of dozens, if not hundreds, of militant activists affiliated with such Islamic groups as Dewan Dakwah Islamiyah Indonesia DDII or (Indonesian Islamic Propagation Council) and KISDI (Indonesian Committee for Solidarity with the Muslim World) and recruited through a network of allied mosques and Islamic schools. The lumpen quality of many such recruits was perhaps best exemplified by the participation of many residents from Tanjung Priok, the tough port area of Jakarta where survivors and families of victims of the security forces' atrocities in 1984 (see chapter 3) were said to harbor bitter resentment against the foes of Islam. Such incidents had been understood to enjoy the blessings of powerful elements in the regime, such as Lieutenant General Prabowo Subianto, who were working hand in glove with the leaders of DDII and KISDI.

With the ascension of Habibie to the presidency in May 1998, this embryonic and sporadic pattern of Islamic vigilante activity began to crystallize into a more hardened and consistent form. Just hours after Suharto's

resignation on May 21, such groups—reportedly in coordination with senior military officers such as Prabowo—began preparing an assault on the
grounds of the national parliament to disperse student protesters and defend the fledgling Habibie administration. Months later, in preparation for
a special session of MPR (the supraparliamentary body then tasked with
choosing the president and vice-president and ratifying constitutional
amendments), a more sustained and serious campaign along these lines was
mounted against student protests and elite maneuverings to force out Habibie in favor of a presidium of opposition leaders and civic figures. With the
apparent support of Defense Minister and Armed Forces Commander in
Chief Wiranto and his lieutenants, a number of Islamic groups were tapped
to provide recruits to the Pasukan Keamanan (Pam) Swakarsa, or Volun-
tary Security Units, which joined police and military troops in providing
"security" for the MPR in its November 1998 special session. As the Habibie administration worked to insulate MPR members from rising pressures
to take steps against Suharto and his family, to pass legislation reducing the
military's role in politics, and to expedite and expand the process of holding general elections, more than 100,000 Pam Swakarsa members were
recruited and armed with bamboo sticks, sharpened spears, and other
makeshift weapons. Recruited in large part through KISDI, DDII, and
newly minted groups such as Forum Umat Islam untuk Keadilan dan Kon-
stitusi (Furkon), or Forum of Muslim Believers for Justice and the Constitution, and Front Pembela Islam (FPI), or Front for the Defenders of Islam,
Pam Swakarsa members were drawn from poor neighborhoods scattered
around the greater Jakarta area, and from towns and villages elsewhere on
Java and Madura, and were allowed to use the Istiqlal and Al Banna
mosques in Central Jakarta as their temporary quarters.[9] Wearing green
and white caps and headbands bearing the basic Muslim confession of
faith—"There is no God but God"—in Arabic script, these Pam Swakarsa
members represented themselves as defending not only the MPR and the
Habibie administration but Islam as well. The provision of official blessings by the government's Council of Islamic Scholars (MUI), training and
weapons by the security forces, and funds to pay "volunteers" by top-rank-
ing military officers, Islamic activist leaders, and, allegedly, the Suharto
family, bolstered the efforts of the Pam Swakarsa forces to guarantee the
success of the MPR's special session.[10]

In the event, this success was achieved only at the expense of widespread
incidents of violence. With the massing of both unarmed student protesters and stick- and spear-wielding Pam Swakarsa members on the streets of
Jakarta in November 1998, the city witnessed scattered skirmishes and attacks in the streets and back alleys during the weeks leading up to and

through the MPR's special session.[11] Dozens of student protesters suffered beatings at the hands of the Pam Swakarsa, and a handful were shot dead by the security forces, while a number of Pam Swakarsa members fell wounded—in a few cases, fatally—at the hands of angry crowds of Jakarta residents. Even as senior government officials, both civilian and military, adopted a stance of distance and disavowal in the wake of these events, Islamic activists remained publicly proud of their violent defense of the regime. Just as some Pam Swakarsa members had told reporters before the special session that they were "ready to wage jihad" against Communist students supported by non-Muslim forces such as CSIS, Benny Murdani, and (the "Chinese" Catholic businessman) Sofyan Wanandi, so did Furkon activists later describe the fatalities of November 1998 as "risks of struggle" worth shouldering in light of the "success" of the MPR special session.[12]

But even as Pam Swakarsa units were disbanded in late November 1998, more enduring forms of state-backed vigilante violence under the banner of Islam endured. In August 1998, activists had founded the FPI with the evident blessing—and rumored active support—of Major General Djadja Suparman, new commander of the Greater Jakarta Regional Army Command and a close ally of Defense Minister and Armed Forces Commander-in-Chief Wiranto. The FPI not only participated in securing the MPR session in November of that year but also developed a more sustained presence and repertoire of activities in the Jakarta area and a few other cities. Led by Indonesians of Hadhrami Arab extraction, clad in body-length white tunics and headdresses in a distinctly and self-consciously Middle Eastern style, hundreds of FPI members would reappear on subsequent occasions in 1999 and 2000, wielding sabers and machetes and claiming to speak in the name of Islam. On a number of occasions, armed FPI members numbering in the hundreds surfaced to attack student demonstrations against the Indonesian armed forces (Tentara Nasional Indonesia, or TNI). During Ramadan in those years, moreover, the FPI led a number of well-publicized raids on bars, nightclubs, discotheques, brothels, and gambling outlets, violently attacking the premises of these establishments and quickly dispersing their clients with saber- and machete-wielding antics.[13] For several years after 1998, such FPI "sweepings" were said to allow the group—and its backers in the security forces—to extort protection payments from the owners of numerous recreational, gambling, and entertainment establishments in Jakarta and a few other cities.[14]

After years in which violence under the banner of Islam—attacks on government buildings, Chinese property, and non-Muslim houses of worship—reaffirmed a push to make claims on the public sphere and the state by a mobilized *Ummat,* by late 1998 this new form of violence—crudely armed Islamic militia attacks on student protesters and on seamy business establishments—in the name of the faith had emerged as a subcontracted, supplementary form of state power. From Islam as a banner of sometimes violent, often disruptive, popular mobilization *from below,* "Islam" now reappeared as a rubric for regime consolidation and legitimation *from above,* with violence and disruption in the name of the faith represented as an *excess* variously deployed and disavowed by those in civilian and military seats of state power according to the ebb and flow of the political tides.

"Horizontal" Violence: Gang Warfare, Mob Lynchings, and Communal Conflict

Meanwhile, a third and broader shift in the nature and direction of religious violence became evident in the months following Habibie's ascension to the presidency: the emergence of seemingly "horizontal" conflict of a popular and highly murderous nature. As could be expected, the effects of the first change of president in three decades in Jakarta were soon to trickle down to the cities, towns, and villages of the archipelago in terms of access to state power and patronage. With the removal of the certainty and the centralization of state power in the Suharto era, and their replacement by a transitional form of government moving toward competitive elections and the deconcentration and decentralization of state power, the fixity of the very hierarchy connecting localities to the center was undermined, as were the boundaries of the jurisdictions governed by those asserting authority within this hierarchy.

Under Suharto's New Order, the circuitries of power connecting villages to towns to provincial cities to Jakarta had been centrally wired in the national capital and coursed through the military, the civil service, Golkar, pseudoparliaments, and schools and universities. Competition for power and patronage within the political class was thus confined and channeled— vertically, as it were—within the state's coercive and ideological apparatuses, as rival networks defined by educational and religious affiliations and identities fought for coveted appointed positions (e.g., military commands, governorships, seats in the various pseudoparliamentary bodies) and associated privileges (e.g., construction contracts and criminal franchises). Against this backdrop, the demise of the New Order and the promise of competitive elections carried significant implications. Instead of individuated competition channeled vertically and confined laterally within the state, various streams or *aliran* within the political class now found themselves competing—collectively and horizontally, as it were—not (only) in and for the state, but (also) in and for society. Thus the boundaries of identities and interests in Indonesian society, long determined by a fixed, hierarchical source of recognition firmly anchored in the state and centered in Jakarta, were left in flux.[15]

The implications of this loosening and shifting of boundaries were evident in a variety of violent new conflicts. In some cases, these were boundaries over property and territory, as seen in countless seizures of land and fights over control of mines, forests, and shorelines. In numerous other cases the boundaries concerned were those of local criminal rackets, with rival gangs in Jakarta and other cities initiating *antar-kampung* (interneighborhood) skirmishes to determine the extent of their turf claims under conditions of indeterminate or fluctuating franchise. More broadly, with the deconcentration of power in Jakarta and the move toward decentralization in the provinces, the very boundaries of administrative units came into question, with local politicians vying for the subdivision (*pemekaran*) of countless villages, regencies, and provinces in the months and years after Suharto's fall from the presidency.

In many cases, contestation involved boundaries of collective identities—whether those of community, clan, ethnicity, or religious faith—whose fixity was no longer assured. Thus the months after Suharto's fall saw the proliferation of cases of *main hakim sendiri,* mob lynchings of suspected thieves by members of village and neighborhood communities, especially on Java.[16] Meanwhile, in November 1998 a violent skirmish took place on the island of Sumba between hundreds of members of two rival clans—one affiliated with the local *bupati,* the other with the head of the local assembly—armed with spears and knives, which left a reported 100 casualties in its wake.[17] Coordinated attacks on Madurese immigrant communities, already witnessed in early 1997 in parts of West Kalimantan, subsequently recurred in the province and spread to areas of Central Kalimantan, with armed gangs—claiming to represent the proudly "indigenous" Dayak and later Malay ethnic groups—effecting the "cleansing" of tens of thousands of "outsiders" from these localities.[18]

It is hardly surprising, then, that much of the horizontal violence that began to unfold in 1998–99 assumed the form of specifically *religious* pogroms. For reasons already amply suggested, religious faith had long served in Indonesia as the primary marker of public identities insisted upon—and enforced by—the state, and as a key determinant of point of entry into the political class. Not only was the ascension to the presidency of a politician closely identified with Islam thus experienced beyond Jakarta in terms of religiously coded local repercussions for the distribution of state offices and patronage, but the turn toward open politics and competitive elections laid open the question of the very basis of claims to religious authority and state power. If, under a centralized, closed authoritarian regime, claims of representation had been imposed and enforced from above, now under conditions of political openness and competition the boundaries of religious authority had to be affirmed from without and from below. Thus the first few years after Suharto's fall saw, for example, groups identified with rival Protestant sects clashing in violent skirmishes in the tiny island of Nias off the northwestern coast of Sumatra,[19] and the burning and destruction of dozens of homes identified with members of a "Medi" cult by their Muslim neighbors in a village in the West Javanese town of Tasikmalaya.[20] Beyond such highly localized conflicts, moreover, came larger-scale episodes of violence under the sign of Islam and religious faith, as seen first in the case of the antiwitchcraft campaign on Java, and then in the Muslim-Christian pogroms in Maluku and Central Sulawesi.

Java: Antiwitchcraft Campaigns

The first new form of large-scale collective violence to emerge in the months following the resignation of Suharto and the ascension to the presidency of Habibie assumed the form of an antiwitchcraft campaign centered in and around the East Javanese regency of Banyuwangi. Unlike the 1995–97 provincial riots in which crowds targeted Chinese business establishments, churches and temples, and government buildings in regency towns and cities in Java and beyond, this campaign saw groups of residents of rural villages and hamlets lynching accused practitioners of malign magic (*dukun santet*) in mob killings often involving defenestration, decapitation, and other mutilations of their victims' corpses. The killings grew in frequency over the course of July and August in Banyuwangi and neighboring regencies such as Jember and then peaked in September and October 1998 before subsiding, only to recur in similar spates in nearby southern Malang and West Javanese towns such as Ciamis and Sukabumi in 1999 and 2000. By some estimates, more than 160 accused sorcerers had been killed in Banyuwangi and other towns of East Java by October 1998,[21] and dozens more lost their lives in the subsequent episodes of antiwitchcraft campaigns in southern Malang and the Ciamis area in 1999–2000.[22]

These killings unfolded against the backdrop of a long history of alleged sorcery and in the context of a broad spectrum of religious beliefs and practices in rural Java. As the anthropologist Clifford Geertz famously de-

scribed in his 1960 classic *The Religion of Java,* the networks of traditionalist and modernist Islamic schools scattered across Java coexisted with
mystical sects, shrine-based cults, and local *dukun* (healers and practitioners of magic). Geertz reported no reported instances of collective violence
against the *dukun santet* in the 1950s, when he conducted his fieldwork:
"Any attempt to organize public opinion against an accused sorcerer," he
claimed, "would be almost certain to fail."[23] Yet by the early mid-1980s,
given the rising tensions and changes in the position of Islam in national
politics in general, and in the position of the traditionalist Islamic association Nahdlatul Ulama in rural Java in particular, a wave of violent, often
deadly, attacks on *dukun santet* in hamlets and villages in various parts of
Java was reported in the press.[24] In late 1997 and early 1998, moreover, as
economic crisis and internal regime tensions deepened in Indonesia, mob
lynchings of accused sorcerers in the East Javanese towns of Banyuwangi,
Bondowoso, Jember, and Situbondo once again attracted media attention,[25] leading to public discussion of possible antiwitchcraft legislation to
be drafted by the national parliament.[26]

The early killings occurred during a period of heightened tension and uncertainty as to the position in Indonesian society of Nahdlatul Ulama in
particular and of Islam more broadly. The emergence of ICMI as a nexus
of Islamic influence and patronage in the early to middle 1990s had caused
growing concern among the leaders of NU, who viewed ICMI as a vehicle
for the promotion—and imposition—of modernist Islam at the expense of
the more traditionalist and syncretic form of religious worship and schooling embodied in NU's network of mostly rural Islamic boarding schools
(*pesantren*) and in the Sufi brotherhoods (*tarekat*), which overlapped with
and extended the influence of NU's traditional Islamic scholars, the *ulama*
or *kyai.* With the elections of 1997 and the approach of the March 1998
session of the People's Consultative Assembly, which saw the election of
ICMI chairman B. J. Habibie as Suharto's vice president, moreover, the
trend of modernist ascendancy within the Indonesian state and inroads in
Indonesian society appeared only to accelerate, much to the dismay and
distress of NU leaders.

This palpable sense of threat was already evident in the aftermath of the
riots in Situbondo and Tasikmalaya in late 1996, as I discovered in many
discussions with NU activists over the course of an eight-month stint in East
Java in 1997–98. At the time, conspiracy theories circulating in NU circles
attributed the disturbances to efforts by ICMI leaders and their allies in the
armed forces to discredit Nahdlatul Ulama and its chairman, K. H. Abdurrahman Wahid (Gus Dur), as weak and ineffectual in the face of ordinary Muslims' rising intolerance and impatience with slow progress in the

promotion of Islam. In the first weeks of 1998, as Habibie manuevered to win the vice presidency, and as a series of reportedly instigated food riots unfolded in towns around Java, violent clashes between groups of NU youths and the police over the protection of gambling and prostitution during the fasting month of Ramadan were reported in rural areas along the borders of the East Javanese towns of Bondowoso and Jember.[27]

With Habibie's assumption of the presidency in May 1998, uncertainty and anxiety surrounding Nahdlatul Ulama's position in Indonesian society only deepened, especially in the NU heartland—the so-called *pesantren* belt—of rural East Java. In no small measure, this anxiety stemmed from threats "without" and "above," as modernist Muslims' entrenchment in the seats of state power in Jakarta spelled increasing encroachment within the Ministry of Religious Affairs, patronage and influence in mosques and schools around the country, and the possibility of legislation promoting the standardization of Islamic practices and teachings and the imposition of other regulations in the name of a distinctly modernist Islam.[28]

Yet in equal measure, this anxiety arose from "within" and "below," as the immediate moves toward greater openness and liberalization in politics and the impending shift to a system of competitive elections raised questions as to NU's claims to represent—in both senses of the term—the broad mass of Muslims in rural Java. Even in areas of Java well known as NU strongholds, the organization's strength was hardly uniform across the rural landscape, instead radiating out of the most established *pesantren* and gradually fading away in their hinterlands. Intermarriage among the children of prominent *kyai*, the founding of new *pesantren* by inspired former *santri*, and the networks of various Sufi *tarekat* served as spokes of these interlinked local wheels of the NU machine, producing and reproducing webs of traditionalist Islamic worship and schooling across the Javanese countryside and supporting an overlay of official NU organizations— youth, women's, students', martial arts—and small pockets of NU influence within the local agencies of the state. Yet inside and beyond these webs of NU authority—even at their most densely interwoven—were to be found alternative, competing forms of religious practice and association, including mystical sects, shrine-based cults, and practitioners of healing and magic, as well as apathy and indifference with regard to matters of spirituality and faith.[29] Thus the anxiety accompanying the dramatic political shifts of mid-1998 concerned the broader constellation of religious authority among Muslims—devout, and "statistical," "modernist," and "traditionalist"—in Indonesian society, and the position of Nahdlatul Ulama therein.

This kind of anxiety was perhaps most pronounced in localities along the fringes of the *pesantren* belt, where NU's authority coexisted uneasily—and competed quietly—with other sites and sources of spiritual authority. Banyuwangi, where the killings of alleged sorcerers were concentrated, stood out as a particularly rich arena of religious diversity and contestation. Banyuwangi, after all, was notable not only for its geographical location at the easternmost point of Java, its proximity to the neighboring Hindu island of Bali, and its own distinctive regional dialect (Bahasa Osing) but also for its distinctive religious history and complexion. The Banyuwangi regency of the late 1990s lay at the center of what had once been the principality of Blambangan, known first as a refuge for residual elements of the pre-Islamic kingdom of Majapahit when the conquering Muslim coastal empire of Mataram consolidated its hold over much of the Javanese countryside in the sixteenth and seventeenth centuries, and later as the last Hindu-Buddhist realm on Java to fall to the Dutch East India Company and its client sultans in the late eighteenth century.

Eager to promote the integration of Banyuwangi (the new name for the regency and the town constructed north of the ruins of Blambangan) and concerned about the influence of nearby independent Bali, the Dutch actively encouraged—indeed, essentially imposed—a process of Islamization on the area. The formal acceptance and adoption of Islam in the local society was clearly matched by subterfuge and resistance, especially in the more remote, upland areas, and by the continuing strength of other forms of religious devotion.[30] In the twentieth century, moreover, as plantation agriculture in Banyuwangi began to attract large numbers of Madurese (as well as Javanese and Balinese) to this remote economic, cultural, and religious frontier,[31] the regency's immigrants came to constitute nearly 50 percent of the local population by 1930, the highest percentage anywhere on Java.[32] Even in the 1990s, census figures suggested continuing diversity in Banyuwangi, with only 67 percent of the population self-identifying as Javanese at the turn of the century.[33]

The combination of imposed Islamization and immigration from without produced an especially diverse religious landscape in Banyuwangi, in which traditionalist Muslims affiliated with NU lived cheek by jowl with neighbors oriented toward very different sources of spiritual power. Accompanying this diversity was a high level of religious tension. As described by Andrew Beatty, an anthropologist who conducted fieldwork in the early 1990s in a village in the regency,

> in rural Banyuwangi . . . typically we find pantheistic mysticism, spirit cults, and normative piety coexisting in great intimacy within a single social framework. . . . In rural Banyuwangi, difference is constructed within

the same space, and thus with greater intensity. The pious Muslim, when he rolls out his prayer mat in public view, is all too aware of his next-door neighbour who sits on the front doorstep pointedly ignoring the call-to-prayer. The group of mystics who gather in the evenings to expatiate in loud voices on the meaning of this or that do so in allusions which seem designed to trouble, but not quite offend, more orthodox auditors on the other side of the bamboo wall. And the visitor to the local shrine during the fasting month takes a devious route with her basket of offerings, equally anxious about the blessing she seeks and the criticism she must avoid.[34]

These tensions had a very real basis in recent historical experience. Indeed, the linkage between the boundaries of religious identity, on the one hand, and the wielding of power and violence, on the other, was well established in the Banyuwangi of the late 1990s. The anti-Communist pogroms of 1965–66 hit rural East Javanese regencies such as Banyuwangi especially hard and involved many local members of NU-affiliated youth and martial arts groups in the atrocities.[35] In their wake came mass "conversions" to the official religions formally acknowledged by the Indonesian state—mostly to Islam, of course, but also in smaller numbers to Hinduism and Christianity—by residents anxious to avoid the charge of atheism associated with the outlawed PKI.

Yet these conversions failed to produce uniformity of Islamic practice or belief in rural Banyuwangi, or to eliminate sources of religious tension and conflict. As Beatty related in the early 1990s:

> in Banyuwangi, there is a popular association (rarely, of course, attested in fact) between magical powers, even sorcery, and expertise in Arabic. Two modins [muezzin] of the past generation in Bayu were reputed to be sorcerers and were blamed for causing numerous deaths. Modin S was eventually killed by a mob; modin P fled and turned into a weretiger who haunts Alas Purwo, the eastern forest. Several descendants of these "sorcerers" were forbidden to learn Koranic recitations by their parents as it would later open them to accusations of sorcery.[36]

A history of religious diversity and tension was also found in many other key localities on Java, where large numbers of *dukun santet* killings took place in 1998–99. Southern Malang, for example, was located along the borders between the Oosthoek zone of NU-led traditionalist Islamic worship and heavy Madurese settlement, on the one hand, and the supposedly more syncretic Hindu-Buddhist or Javanist practices associated with the dynastic realms of Central Java, on the other.[37] Ciamis was likewise a pe-

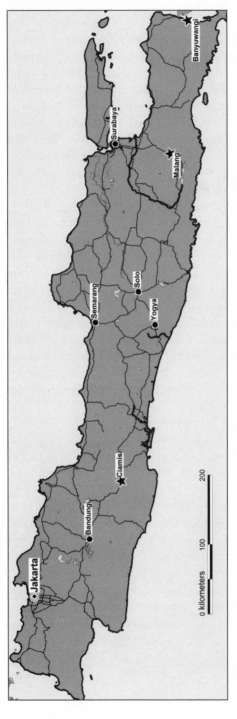

Antiwitchcraft campaigns on fringes of upland Java: Banyuwangi, Ciamis, Malang (Peter Loud)

ripheral locality in the predominantly Sundanese region of West Java
known as the Priangan, which had remained largely free of Central Javanese influence in the eras of Majapahit and Mataram and within which
small nodes of NU influence coexisted uneasily with a diversity of religious
practices ranging from more modernist Islamic orthodoxy to local healers,
cults, and sects.[38] As Ben White noted: "The hilly southern region of West
Java, stretching from Pandeglang and Lebak to the West to Tasikmalaya in
the East is the least irrigated, the least densely populated and the relatively
least accessible part of West Java. . . . [I]t has had until the 1990s much of
the character of a pioneer settlement region."[39]

Overall, the topography of *dukun santet* killings in 1998–99 was characterized by the concentration of violence on the fringes of the upland regions of Java, where, as elsewhere in Southeast Asia, the universalistic
scripturalist religions largely failed to climb. As the anthropologist Robert
Hefner wrote with regard to upland Pasuruan, for example, "The highlands remained predominantly Javanese, and their religious traditions
strongly Javanist (*kejawen*), with few orthodox Muslim influences. Mountain religion emphasized festivals at guardian-spirit shrines rather than
mosque services or daily *solat* prayer."[40] In the mountainous areas of
Banyuwangi, southern Malang, and Ciamis, the traditionalist Islamic religious practices and webs of political affiliation associated with Nahdlatul
Ulama ran up against more localized spiritual practices on the one hand,
and more secular nationalist political affiliations (PNI and PKI in the
1960s; PDIP and Golkar in 1998–99), on the other. Overall, the attacks on
alleged sorcerers in Java in 1998–99, though seemingly scattered widely
across the landscape of East and West Java, were in fact concentrated in
upland frontier zones along the fringes of NU's political and religious
authority.

It was thus amid of the broad tensions and uncertainties surrounding
the position of Islam in Indonesia in 1998–99, and in local settings characterized by considerable diversity and contestation in religious practice
and association, that the process of collective violence against supposed
witchcraft unfolded. At first, these killings remained highly local and particularistic. In one village in Jember, for example, the alleged sorcerer was
a certain Pak Sufi, a farmer who had recently moved to the village and attempted to assume the position of prayer leader at the local Islamic prayer
house (*langgar* or *musholla*), an elected post also contested by a certain Imron, who enjoyed considerable local respect among the faithful. According
to the account provided by local residents to members of an NU fact-finding team,

two days after Pak Imron's election as prayer leader, responsible for daily instruction in studying the Qur'an, he suddenly began to suffer from a stomach ache. He was examined by a doctor at the local clinic, but the ailment could not be treated. Finally, he was brought to a *kyai* who was said to be able to cure mysterious diseases. This *kyai* said that it was Pak Sufi who had caused the ailment. The *kyai* also advised Pak Imron not to seek revenge. Pak Imron also approached Pak Sufi, and asked him not to use the "black magic" in his possession. On this occasion, Pak Sufi admitted his guilt and begged Pak Imron's forgiveness.[41]

Pak Imron apparently recovered, in due course, but Pak Sufi developed a local reputation as a practitioner of black magic who could cause illness in those who came into conflict with him. One night in late October 1998, Pak Sufi went missing. His body was discovered in a nearby river two days later, the skull crushed by a heavy blunt object of some kind. Members of his family were said not to have shed a single tear for his passing; they reportedly told the police that Pak Sufi had in fact been a *dukun santet* and thus that an autopsy and investigation of his murder would be unnecessary—or, rather, unwanted.[42]

In Rogojampi, a subdistrict of Banyuwangi where nearly two dozen killings took place, the fate of a certain Pak Ruslan was similar. "Every person who had a problem with him always ended up dead by unnatural causes," a neighbor subsequently told investigators. "There were some who went blind before they died; there were also some whose bellies swelled up before they died. . . . If he hadn't had magical powers, he wouldn't have dared to mess around with other men's wives so openly. He also wouldn't have managed to divert other farmers' irrigation to his rice fields with such success."[43] Given these allegations, news of attacks on sorcerers elsewhere in Banyuwangi in the autumn of 1998 provided the occasion for local residents to go after Pak Ruslan. Late one night a group of local youths approached Ruslan's residence, which he had left abandoned, perhaps forewarned of their impending arrival. The youths cut the electric supply, stoned the windows, and looted and demolished the empty house. Early the next morning the same group found Pak Ruslan in a neighboring village, brought him back to his home, and hacked him to death. His body was left for hours in the open air before a neighbor rallied local residents to organize a hasty burial. Pak Ruslan's family did not even insist on the customary Islamic ceremony of *tahlilan* before his burial, apparently fearing the reaction of other residents.[44]

Many other killings, as reported in the media and as described by villagers interviewed by researchers, followed along these highly localized lines: local figures with local reputations for local witchcraft were killed by groups of local residents, often after long periods of suspicion and a series of warnings. The killings were clearly premeditated, perpetrated as they were by attackers who gathered by night and left grotesquely disfigured corpses in their wake. Rather than being disavowed, these killings were explained—and excused—by local residents in terms of revenge for individual acts of black magic carried out by the victims.[45]

Yet over the course of October 1998 the accumulation of dozens of cases of individual killings began to create a broader climate in which supralocal understandings of the violence came into view. Already in February 1998, in the wake of a series of attacks on local sorcerers, the *bupati* of Banyuwangi had ordered the subdistrict heads (*camat*) to compile lists of suspected *dukun santet,* which prompted subsequent meetings with village headmen (*kepala desa*) around the regency. This process, and follow-up instructions issued by the regent in September of that year, evidently heightened awareness of a climate in which suspected *dukun santet* were under threat, and generated diverse conspiracy theories as to the involvement of local officials in the killings.[46]

By July 1998, moreover, newspaper reports had begun to include accounts of killings carried out by outside intruders dressed as ninjas in black costumes and masks, as seen in foreign action films. According to one study of the news coverage,

> the term *ninja* first appeared in the mass media on July 20th, 1998. At that time, a certain Paiman, 40 years old, and his wife Jamirah, 45 years old, were killed. They were both residents of Kutorejo hamlet, Kendalrejo village, Tegaldlimo subdistrict. These two victims were attacked by a crowd of roughly one hundred people. They were tied up and dragged out of their house, then dragged and beaten along the road for about a kilometer until they were dead.
>
> The term *ninja* then reappeared on August 3rd, 1998, when in Babakan hamlet, Kedayunan village, Kabat subdistrict, an old farmer, Zainuddin, 60 years old, was killed in front of his wife and children. The police arrested eight suspects charged in connection with these two murders, while 175 other local residents who were deemed only to have played supporting roles were not detained. The evidence seized consisted of a 3 meter-long bamboo stick, four stones, and four meters of elastic cord.
>
> It remained unclear how these two events were linked with the mention of *ninjas*. There was no specific image—for example, that the killers wore masks, or wore black costumes, or various other plausible trademarks of *ninja* as seen in films. Some believe that the term *ninja* first emerged in the

mass media. In other words, it was the mass media that sparked the use of the term *ninja*—without any indication as to what the journalists were referring to.[47]

These reports of ninjas leading attacks on villagers in various towns in Java recalled the supposed use of ninja costumes by Special Forces units of the Indonesian Armed Forces in the occupied territory of East Timor.[48] Such associations reinforced fears and rumors in NU circles of conspiracies launched by modernist Muslim elements of the Habibie regime and the military establishment,[49] or by recalcitrant elements of the ousted New Order regime, whether the former president Suharto himself or his son-in-law Prabowo, the former *KOPASSUS* commander and close ally of hard-line modernist Muslim groups such as KISDI and DDII.[50] Prabowo had been dismissed from the armed forces in the summer of 1998 in connection with revelations of his role in the abductions of student leaders and other opposition figures in the final months of Suharto's rule, but fear of Prabowo— and of his remaining network of supporters in the military—remained strong. Whether pro-Habibie elements trying to intimidate their enemies or Prabowo seeking revenge and reasserting his power as a "spoiler," sinister forces in Jakarta were suspected of using their assets in the security forces to harass and intimidate NU in its strongholds.[51] The rumors generated by the accounts of ninjas were accompanied by stories of death threats issued in unsigned letters and anonymous phone calls, with low-level members of the security forces and local criminal elements undoubtedly exploiting the opportunity to extort money from residents fearing accusations of black magic and attacks in the night.[52] Sporadic rumors and media reports of mentally deranged men allegedly armed, paid, and "dropped" in villages in East Java with instructions to commit murder likewise contributed to the widespread climate of fear in many villages in rural Java.[53]

Over the months of late 1998, as the individual killings of suspected village sorcerers began to assume the features of a broader antiwitchcraft campaign, the local anxieties and tensions in remote areas of upland rural Java were thus increasingly accompanied by supralocal apprehensions of impending attacks on *kyai* and on Nahdlatul Ulama as a whole. Even in the bustling city of Surabaya, the capital of East Java, fear of such attacks in late 1998 was reportedly widespread in NU circles:

The *santri* (*pesantren* pupils) became acutely sensitive. When rumors circulated that K.H. Soleh bin Zeid Al Yamani, the caretaker of the Majelis Taklim As Salafi in Kampung Nyamplungan, Surabaya, had been slaughtered by *ninja,* for example, more than a thousand *santri* laid waste to a local police station where the killer *ninja* were reportedly being held. In fact, the *kyai* was alive and well, and remains so to this day.[54]

Such rumors allowed the networks of *kyai* and other organizations associated with Nahdlatul Ulama to appropriate for themselves the local fears and tensions so evidently pronounced in the killings of *dukun santet* in rural Java in 1998. Recast in this light, the focus and target of the violence was NU itself, and those responsible for the violence were not local villagers mobilized from below and within zones of NU influence but rather outside elements infiltrating from above and without.

This tendency to explain—and to appropriate—the *dukun santet* killings as an external attack on NU was accompanied by efforts to reassert the authority of the *kyai* and of the organization of Nahdlatul Ulama as a whole in rural Java, most notably in those fringe areas where the episodes of violence were concentrated. These efforts assumed two forms. First of all, local *kyai* began to administer *sumpah pocong*, special oaths (often including key phrases in Arabic), to be publicly sworn by accused *dukun santet* before local residents in order to determine their innocence or guilt. One well-known *kyai* in rural Jember reportedly administered dozens of such oaths. For example:

> Pak Di and Syahlan were asked to bathe and then wrapped up in white sheets like corpses and laid down in the mosque. Some villagers came to witness the ceremony. Beforehand, Kyai Luthfi gave a brief introduction about the *sumpah pocong* oath and about the sanctions of Allah on those who betrayed the oath. Then Kyai Lutfhi initiated the oath-taking. Both Pak Di and Syahlan followed Kyai Luthfi in swearing "before Allah, I am not a *dukun santet*. May the wrath of Allah rain down on me and my family if I am not telling the truth."[55]

Another suspect who was granted mercy through *sumpah pocong* administered by Kyai Luthfi was Nur, aged sixty, a resident of the same area of Jember:

> For nearly a decade, he had been shunned by other villagers because he was believed to be a *dukun santet*. If Nur offered someone something to eat, they wouldn't touch it. Likewise when Nur went out into the village, people always treated him very cautiously, so that he wouldn't spread his black magic. So when news of the killings of *dukun santet* began to spread, Nur also became very cautious, fearing that he would be lynched by a mob. After some time, he approached Kyai Luthfi and asked him for protection

and help in convincing people [that he was not a sorcerer]. Kyai Luthfi offered to administer a *sumpah pocong*, and Nur agreed to take the oath. Local residents were invited to attend the oath-taking ceremony. Nur was made up like a corpse—and asked to sign a document drawn up by Kyai Luthfi. Just as with Syahlan and Djunaidi, people who had previously treated Nur with suspicion now lined up to ask for his forgiveness. Eventually, many people even came to visit him in his home.[56]

Second, accompanying the reassertion of the authority of the *kyai* through the *sumpah pocong* was the reinforcement of Nahdlatul Ulama's organizational powers in terms of its claims to represent and to police its constituent members. In parts of Java such as the Banyuwangi-Jember area, the NU youth group Ansor and militia Banser began to project their authority in the final months of 1998 through the organization of local security measures: strengthening neighborhood watches (*ronda*) and otherwise heightening surveillance against "outsiders" of various kinds.[57] The subsequent wave of killings in southern Malang and the Ciamis area in 1999 provoked a similar reaction.[58] In response to the perceived threat of further *dukun santet* killings and ninja incursions, these NU groups—which had played a crucial role in the anti-Communist pogroms of 1965–66 in East Java—thus mobilized violence under the banner of Nahdlatul Ulama to restore peace and order to to the troubled border zones of NU's authority in rural Java.

Regency-Wide Interreligious Pogroms: Poso, Central Sulawesi

Just as 1995–97 saw the pattern of religious rioting begin in Java and then spread to the Outer Island cities of Banjarmasin and Makassar, so too did 1999–2001 witness a replay of Java's 1998–99 murderous attacks on sorcerers. These interreligious pogroms in the Central Sulawesi regency of Poso and the Eastern Indonesian island province known as Maluku—like the *dukun santet* killings in Banyuwangi, Malang, Ciamis, and elsewhere in Java—targeted religious "others" and "outsiders" (including immigrants) and worked to (re)establish religious authority structures and boundaries during a period of great uncertainty and anxiety.

Unlike the attacks on individual sorcerers in the villages and hamlets of rural Java, however, the violence in Poso and Maluku from late 1998 through 2001 was notably collective as to both its perpetrators and its victims: armed groups attacked entire neighborhoods and villages with murderous intent and effect.

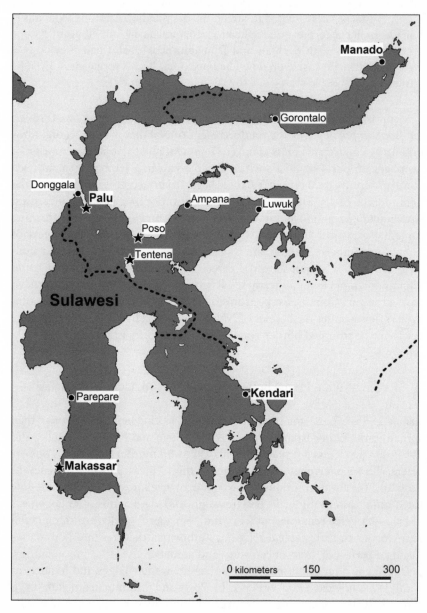

Sulawesi (Peter Loud)

This new pattern *pogroms* was made possible by at least three features of the settings in which it unfolded. First of all, in contrast with the anti-witchcraft campaigns along the fringes of Nadhlatul Ulama's strongholds on Java, with their overwhelming Muslim majorities, these interreligious pogroms occurred along the boundaries between the officially recognized faiths of Islam and Christianity, with Protestant churches claiming sizable congregations in these localities and constituting important alternative structures of authority and access to state power to those provided by their Islamic counterparts. Second, compared with the more economically developed and diversified setting of Java, with its clearer division between (predominantly Chinese) business and government, poorer and more peripheral Central Sulawesi and Maluku were local economies in which access to the agencies of the Indonesian state loomed even larger for the accumulation of capital, status, and wealth, and in which local business and politics were more fully overlapping. Third, these local constellations of religious authority and political economy combined with the approaching elections of 1999, decentralization, and the redrawing of administrative boundaries (*pemekaran*) to create tremendous uncertainty and anxiety along the local borders—and within the local hierarchies—of religious faith, not only among Islamic and Christian ecclesiastical establishments but also among rival Muslim and Protestant networks of local politicians, businessmen, gangsters, civil servants, and (active and retired) military and police officers.

These commonalities set the stage for similar patterns of interreligious violence in Poso and Maluku in 1998–2001. Both localities witnessed collective violence across the religious divide: armed groups identifying themselves as Christians and Muslims engaged in violent pogromlike attacks on entire neighborhoods and villages populated by residents identified as believers in the opposing religious faith. Both localities, moreover, saw hundreds, indeed a few thousands, of people killed in the process, the violence leaving a trail of destruction (burnt-out homes, houses of worship, schools, and shops) and displacement (tens or even hundreds of thousands of refugees) in its wake. Further, the two localities experienced similar shifts and transformative effects in the modalities of violence, as local patterns of segregation, policing, and militarization along religious lines crystallized and hardened during the course of 1999, 2000, and 2001. Yet for all these similarities between Poso and Maluku, their differences are also worthy of consideration, in particular with regard to the scope and scale of violence. I examine first the regency-wide pogroms in Poso before turning to the province-wide pogroms in Maluku.

In Poso, the violence began with small-scale fighting between rival youth gangs in the eponymous capital town of the regency in late December 1998; it recurred and escalated into a sustained wave of murderous attacks on entire neighborhoods and villages by crudely armed groups in April–June 2000 and June–July 2001, then shifted to a spate of coordinated paramilitary attacks on individual neighborhoods and villages in October–December 2001 before subsiding into more sporadic shootings, bombings, and nighttime raids from 2002 onward.

These shifts in the *forms* of violence in Poso reflected the kinds of *locations, protagonists,* and mobilizational *processes* in and through which they unfolded. As a location for interreligious violence in 1998–2001, the regency of Poso was notable for its role as a major Outer Island hub of Protestant population, proselytization, and political power, and a center of Christian ecclesiastical activity and authority. The consolidation of Dutch control over this part of Central Sulawesi in the first two decades of the twentieth century had been accompanied, assisted, and in no small measure achieved by the activities of Protestant missionaries from the Dutch Reformed Church (and by organizations such as the Salvation Army elsewhere in the province). Although Islam was well established among the residents of the coastal areas of Central Sulawesi, it had largely failed to climb inland and upland, leaving the animist highlands of the province available for conversion to Christianity. Protestant missionary schools operating under the Ethical Policy of the colonial regime drew highlanders into their orbit with increasing success in the final decades of colonial rule, forging the crucial linkages between literacy, Protestant education, and entry into the state bureaucracy. These schools combined with the codification of customary law (*adat*) and the promotion of indigenous ethnic To Pamona identity to produce among highlanders kinds of supralocal connections and conceptions of collective identity very different from those emerging among the lowland, coastal Muslim population through *pesantren* networks, Sufi *tarekat,* the Hajj, and, increasingly, modern forms of Islamic education and association, most notably under the rubric of the Al-Khaira'at organization based in nearby Palu.[59]

This division persisted and deepened with Indonesian independence, under the rubric of the Gereja Kristen Sulawesi Tengah (GKST), or Central Sulawesi Protestant Church, established in 1947 and headquartered in the town of Tentena in the southern highlands of Poso regency. Still funded by the Dutch Reformed Church and assisted by foreign missionaries, the GKST evolved over the first half-century of independence into a complex organization boasting more than three hundred congregations and an array of schools, hospitals, clinics, development projects, and so on by the turn of the twenty-first century. As in the late Dutch colonial era, writes the anthropologist Lorraine Aragon, the Suharto regime appreciated Protestant assistance in "creating nuclear family households, defining individual economic responsibilities, increasing ties to the national and global economies, introducing biomedicine, and expanding school attendance," and in promoting "the acceptance of national regulations, the use of money, government rhetoric concerning the benefits of progress, and regional record keeping."[60] The GKST therefore served as a major channel for access to the state, through its network (*jaringan*) of school graduates entering the police, the military, the civil service, and Golkar. Indeed, as detailed by anthropologists who studied the church's history, the GKST itself evolved into a somewhat statelike set of local authority structures. Its congregations were divided into evangelization groups, composed of closely related families, which met weekly for ceremonial feasts and sermons by the church elders, who were chosen by the governing body of the congregation. The elders thus came to serve as lay preachers, as authority figures within extended family circles, and—given their privileged access to the diverse resources, services, and networks of the GKST—as major local power brokers among a predominantly poor rural population.[61]

Against this backdrop, the holding of genuinely competitive elections, the process of devolution of fiscal and administrative powers to the regency (*kabupaten*) level, and the shift from the central government's appointment of regents (*bupati*) to selection by local assemblies (DPRD) all combined to create considerable expectation and anxiety with regard to the structure of religious authority and power in Poso in 1998–2001. The final years of the Suharto era—and the brief Habibie interlude—had witnessed increasing success on the part of Muslim political-cum-business networks in the regency in extending their presence and influence into realms previously dominated by Protestants. This success in Poso reflected both the national political conjuncture and the local culmination of several decades of increasing Muslim integration into the market (e.g., in copra-producing coastal areas), into state educational institutions (including new local universities), and into the ranks of the local bureaucracy. By the 1990s this trend was apparent both within the local corridors of the state, as ICMI- and HMI-affiliated civil servants and politicians claimed positions and patronage powers once held by Protestants, and along the local circuitries of the market, as Muslim migrants (most notably Bugis from South Sulawesi)[62] established new moneylending and marketing networks and bought up land in the hills of the regency in the midst of a worldwide cocoa boom.[63] Researchers noted a pattern of land sales by families seeking cash to fund their children's university education and to pay the bribes necessary to obtain positions in the local bureaucracy.[64] Overall, these trends reproduced within the Muslim population of Poso similar patterns of exploitation and inequality, and parallel structures of power and authority, to those found among Christians in the regency. As for the impact of these trends on Protestant highlanders in Poso, Aragon concludes:

> Family-based farming of cash crops also generated new wealth, but again mostly for ambitious Muslim migrants and urban merchants, including Chinese ones. Although Pamona and other highland Protestants did grow some cash crops such as cloves, coffee, and cacao, highlanders remained primarily subsistence rice farmers. Few became involved in market activities beyond the sale of small crop surpluses in exchange for basic supplies or cash needs. While Muslim Bugis or Makasar migrants became middleman traders or worked for private businesses through their patron-client networks, Protestant highlanders traditionally had no capitalist business experience and much more localized exchange networks. Many ran up high-interest debts to immigrant salespeople, whose kiosks offered credit, and so found their next season's produce already owed before harvest.
>
> Highlanders traditionally left their ancestral villages only for higher education, church employment, or civil service jobs, if they could obtain them. As non-Pamona bought up or were allotted lands through transmigration programs, many Pamona youths found themselves landless as well as jobless by the end of the Suharto regime. Opportunities for social mobility depended upon personal connections to members of the regional bureaucracy. Indigenous groups' access to positions remained available mainly to descendants of the precolonial nobility, and Protestants' ties to recognized aristocracies were fewer than those of Muslims. Although a small percentage of Protestant Pamona leaders did increase their economic standing dramatically during the New Order, the mass of Pamona and other highland Protestant farmers did not.[65]

Meanwhile, Protestant church leaders, politicians, businessmen, and gangsters in Poso in the 1990s had found an increasingly attractive alternative to Golkar in the PDI, the Indonesian Democratic Party. The PDI had deep roots in Poso, having incorporated the Soekarno-era Protestant party Parkindo (which polled 26 percent and won second place in Poso in the 1955 elections),[66] and held its annual national congress in the regency in 1997.[67] Thus the processes of democratization and decentralization in Poso came with the opportunity—for some, the imperative—of mobilizing Protestant voters to halt (and reverse) the apparent religious trends of the preceding several years, if not through Golkar then via the PDIP, the Indonesian Democratic Party of Struggle, headed by the popular Megawati Soekarnoputri. Likewise, for members of local Muslim political-cum-business networks in Poso, the possibility of a fragmented Muslim vote, divided among Golkar, PPP, the new Islamic parties, and even PDIP, threatened a loss in control over the local assembly (DPRD) and, with decentralization, key local executive posts as well.[68] Legislation creating a new regency of Morowali out of eastern Poso in September 1999 further narrowed the margin between the numbers of Christians and Muslims registered as residents and as voters, thus heightening the uncertainty—and the urgency— of political mobilization along religious lines.[69]

The opportunity or imperative of mobilizing voters in Poso along religious lines in 1998–2001, however, came at a time when the established structures of local religious authority and identity appeared to be in danger of losing their certainty, their coherence, their distinctiveness, and their power. By the 1990s, migration patterns had made the town of Poso increasingly diverse, in ethnicity, language, and religion,[70] as Lorraine Aragon noted:

> Protestants besides Pamona included Minahasans, Balinese, and Chinese as well as Mori, Napu, and Bada' people from within the regency. Muslims included Arabs, Javanese, Bugis, Makasar, Mandar, Buton, and Kaili people as well as Tojo, Togian (Togean), and Bungku people from the regency. The small Catholic minority was comprised of Minahasans and Chinese, as well as migrants from former Portuguese colonies such as Flores. Balinese were the only Hindus.[71]

Thus the GKST, though still dominant among the To Pamona people of the Poso highlands, could no longer claim to speak on behalf of all Christians in the regency. Likewise, the established mosque and school network associated with the Al-Khaira'at organization, with its headquarters and university in nearby Palu, now competed with local branches of such national organizations as Nahdlatul Ulama, Muhammadiyah, Persatuan Islam, Sufi *tarekat* such as the South Sulawesi–based Khalwatiyya,[72] and other streams of Islamic devotion and affiliation for worshipers and pupils among Muslims of Javanese, Bugis, Makassarese, and other origins in Poso.[73]

Alongside the diversifying and destabilizing effects of immigration on religious affiliations and authority structures in Poso came more subtle—and in some ways more subversive or homogenizing local trends accompanying capitalist development, the expansion of modern education and communications, and the imposition of national state religious policies. For much as the local cliques of Muslim businessmen, bureaucrats, politicians, and gangsters within and beyond Poso in the 1990s resembled those of their

Protestant rivals, so too did the local marketing and moneylending networks of (Muslim) Bugis entrepreneurs begin to mirror those of their (Christian) Chinese counterparts and competitors.[74] In the organization of religious life, moreover, further parallels emerged, as Christian and Muslim associations and schools alike worked to mediate between the needs of their respective flocks (*jemaah*), on the one hand, and the opportunities and pressures of state and market, on the other. Thus, for example, the Al-Khaira'at school system had modernized over the years, culminating in the formally recognized Universitas AlKhairaat in Palu, which offered secular degrees in agriculture, aquaculture, and medicine alongside its selection of religious studies. More broadly, Aragon observed a "process of supra-ethnic convergence of local Christianity and Islam" during the course of fieldwork in Central Sulawesi (mostly in neighboring Palu) in the 1980s:

> The longer I lived in Central Sulawesi, the more convinced I became that Christian and Muslim practices in Palu were conforming to each other. Christmas became, like the Muslim holiday in Lebaran, a weeklong visiting holiday where Christian and Muslim employees alike were invited to visit and eat at their superiors' homes. Christians who were invited to their Muslim coworkers' homes on Lebaran returned the invitations at Christmas, and vice versa. Common gifts such as jars of cookies, Western-style frosted layer cakes, or cases of imported soft drinks were exchanged both within and across religions at the major holidays.
>
> As any visitor to Muslim regions of Indonesia knows, mosques of the past decades have used the miracle of electronic amplification to broadcast their five-times-daily calls to prayer throughout the surrounding community. In urban areas, these amplified chants in classical Arabic reverberate loudly in a manner that only the most hearing impaired could ignore. In the late 1980s, Christian churches similarly began to adopt the use of loudspeakers for their services. They then broadcast the ministers' words not only to their in-church congregations, but, like the mosques, also beyond the church walls to all those thinking they might sleep through the words of God.
>
> Muslim services in Palu also began to include sermons comparable in format and length to those given in the Christian churches. One Protestant missionary wife claimed that local Muslim leaders were imitating her husband's sermon topics and delivery style. Even within Muslims' and Christians' minor discourses of rivalry, there was religious convergence. Christians disparaged goats as unclean Muslim animals, just as Muslims decried pigs as unclean Christian livestock. . . . Christian and Muslim institutions similarly contended to pull villagers away from their ancestral and family orientations towards compliance with a more remote state and

God wielding more awesome powers. These common goals of modernization, at least in Central Sulawesi, made Christianity and Islam companions and peers as well as erstwhile adversaries.[75]

Thus the location and timing of religious violence in Poso were associated with a local conjuncture that threatened to undermine the foundations of religious authority in the regency. This local conjuncture was one in which the dominant structures of religious authority faced unprecedented uncertainty as to their strength, their solidity, and their claims on the local population, in the face not only of unsettling sociological trends but also of sudden political change. Under the Suharto regime, Protestant and Muslim hierarchies of authority had been subordinated to, and partially submerged within, a highly centralized authoritarian state, beneath which they found shelter, stability, and patronage. With competitive elections now determining the composition of the local assembly, and thus the selection of the new regent and the distribution of patronage and power in Poso, the period 1998–2001 broadened the field, the forms, and the fruits of contestation between these hierarchies, underlining the imperative of voter mobilization for gaining access to state power on the one hand, and for making claims to religious constituencies on the other.

The significance of this local conjuncture for determining the location and timing of violence in Poso was confirmed by the spatial and temporal pattern of the pogroms that unfolded in the regency beginning in late December 1998 and recurring in major episodes in 2000 and 2001. The violence first occurred near the turn of the year 1999, against the backdrop of the approaching national elections amid mounting uncertainty, excitement, and anxiety about the impending selection of new local officials, most notably the new *bupati*, for Poso. Violence began on the occasion of a major religious holiday with fighting between thuggish groups of young men at a major node of economic and criminal activity—and contestation—in the center of town and along the borders between a Protestant and a Muslim neighborhood. This first episode fell on December 24, 1998, as Protestants celebrated Christmas Eve and Muslims observed the fasting month of Ramadan, with youths from the adjoining neighborhoods of (Protestant) Lombogia and (Muslim) Kayamanya engaged in fisticuffs and knife fights around Poso's central bus terminal. On the following day, Christmas, the fighting resumed and spread, with Muslim youths stoning a store blamed for sheltering Christian gang members and selling alcohol during Ramadan, and then attacking other Christian shops, restaurants, and beer halls as well to enforce a ban on the sale of liquor during the holidays—a ban agreed upon by the authorities as well as some local religious leaders.

As Protestant youths fought back, the violence continued and spread, fueled by rumors of church and mosque burnings and the like. From Lombogia, the home of influential Protestant civil servants and retired military officers, the news reached other Christian neighborhoods in Poso town and Protestant villages south of the town and the GKST headquarters in Tentena. From neighboring Kayamanya, the home of many Muslims affiliated with Al-Khaira'at, word likewise traveled to other urban and rural areas by means of local Muslims' familial, associational, and market circuitries. Consequently, the days following Christmas Eve witnessed the arrival of truckloads of machete-wielding men, both Protestant and Muslim, from various areas of Poso and the spread of crudely armed attacks by these rival mobs on homes, shops, and other buildings within urban Poso and in villages along the major roads into town. By the end of December, as the security forces restored order, hundreds of people had been wounded, mostly Protestants and Catholics, and hundreds of (again, mostly Christian) homes destroyed.[76]

Beyond the personal injuries suffered and property destroyed, the rioting also worked to heighten suspicions across the religious divide, to strengthen the boundaries and lines of authority within each religious community, and to sharpen the organization and instruments of violence on both sides. The displacement of hundreds of families whose homes were destroyed and the flight of hundreds more in the face of continuing intimidation and fear of further attacks created hundreds of Internally Displaced Persons (IDPs), mostly within Poso regency, and hardened both the pattern of segregation and the resolve for retribution among the local population.

In the aftermath of the events of late December 1998, moreover, the role of networks of local Protestant and Muslim politicians, businessmen, and gangsters in inciting and organizing the violence had come into view. For example, a prominent Protestant member of the Poso regional assembly (DPRD) who was a vocal supporter of the candidacy of the incumbent regional secretary (*sekwilda*), a fellow Protestant, for the *bupati*ship, was identified as a major organizer of the convoy bringing truckloads of crudely armed men into Poso town during the rioting. He was subsequently arrested, tried, convicted, and sentenced to fourteen years in prison for his role in the violence but died of apparently natural causes in mid-2000. The younger brother of the incumbent *bupati*, a Muslim, was likewise charged with inciting anti-Christian violence through a campaign of flyers, banners, and graffitti in December 1998; he was eventually convicted and sentenced to two years in jail.[77]

These same local networks were evident in egging on and orchestrating the second major episode of violence in April 2000. This second episode came in the wake of the election in October 1999 of a (Muslim) Golkar figure as the new Poso *bupati,* beating rival Protestant and Muslim candidates backed by local PDIP and PPP branches, respectively. It also unfolded in the midst of a losing campaign to elevate the defeated PPP candidate to the position of Poso *sekwilda,* the second most powerful position in the regency. Indeed, the violence began just one day after a local paper published a story based on an interview with a PPP assemblyman in Poso who issued the warning, as the mid-April headline proclaimed, "Poso Likely to Face Riots Again."[78]

Like the first episode, the second began with a fight between rival Protestant and Muslim youth gangs at Poso's central bus terminal. This fighting spilled into the Protestant neighborhood of Lombogia and beyond, with the burning and looting of houses and churches and the flight of hundreds of Protestants (and Catholics) over the next few days. When riot police called in to disperse the crowds shot and killed three Muslims, a group of local Muslim businessmen and politicians met with the *bupati* and the provincial governor to demand the transfer of the police chief (a Javanese officer at odds with the group), the dropping of charges against the former *bupati*'s brother for incitement of the December 1998 violence, and the awarding of the *sekwilda* post to the losing PPP candidate for the *bupati*-ship. But when none of these demands were met, the attacks on Protestant neighborhoods resumed, with Muslim residents of Poso town reportedly reinforced by groups of crudely armed coreligionists from nearby coastal villages. A new level of coordination and organization was apparent in the use of cell phones and walkie-talkies, the wearing of white headbands by armed Muslim groups (likewise red headbands by armed Christian groups), and the conduct of "sweeping" operations in Muslim neighborhoods which led to the hacking to death of several Protestants. By the end of April the violence had wound down, but at least seven Protestants and three Muslims were reported killed; dozens more were seriously wounded; and with hundreds of homes, shops, churches, and other buildings destroyed, the extent of the damage and displacement far exceeded the more limited violence of December 1998.[79]

In addition, the preponderance of casualties, damage, and suffering inflicted on Poso's Christian population in this second episode helped to prefigure a third wave of violence and vengeance just a few weeks later, from late May 2000 through July of that year. Like the previous two episodes, this one began in a key area of Poso town but on this occasion with a nighttime attack on the Muslim neighborhood of Kayamanya by a small but well-armed gang of Christian thugs. This group had reportedly participated in the paramilitary training of hundreds of men in a village outside the town with the sponsorship of local Protestant politicians, businessmen, civil servants, and retired police and army officers; it was led by a notorious *preman* (gangster), a Catholic from Flores who had migrated to Poso in the 1970s.[80] On arrival in Kayamanya, members of this group began attacking local residents, killing several before fleeing the area and hiding in a nearby Catholic church, which was subsequently burned down by a Muslim crowd after the group made its escape. The fighting spread, with "red" and "white" squads of armed men clashing and launching attacks on neighborhoods and villages in and around urban Poso, and hundreds—indeed, thousands—of Muslim residents fleeing as large numbers of armed Christian groups began to stream into the town. On May 28, led by the aforementioned Catholic gangster from Flores, the gang attacked a village of Javanese transmigrants outside Poso town, killing dozens (at least seventy) men in a local *pesantren* and holding dozens more women and children hostage (and sexually assaulting the women) for several days.[81] Other Muslim areas in and around urban Poso, and as far south as the predominantly Protestant town of Tentena, were also set upon by armed "red" squads, and hundreds of Muslim homes and shops were laid waste.

Such attacks, and Muslim counterattacks, persisted sporadically into June and July 2000, as security forces gradually reduced the violence. Eventually they made dozens of arrests, including that of the by now notorious Catholic gangster from Flores; he was subsequently tried, convicted, and in due course sentenced to death along with two of his compatriots. But not until August 2000, with hundreds of riot police and army troops now posted in Poso, and representatives of both Protestant and Muslim communities in the regency participating in a "peace accord" attended by then President Wahid as well as provincial governors from around Sulawesi, did the violence largely subside—for almost a year.[82]

Punctuated by occasional small-scale skirmishes and other incidents, this uneasy peace was interrupted by the recurrence of large-scale violence in mid-2001, against the backdrop of rising tensions between local (Muslim) Golkar, PPP, and (Protestant) PDIP politicians over the selection of a Muslim as the new *sekwilda* for the regency.[83] By late June 2001, reports suggested a pattern of escalating attacks by armed groups on villages in Poso and in the new neighboring regency of Morowali, leaving in their wake a growing trail of casualties, burned-down homes and houses of worship, and refugees. In one particularly brutal and well-publicized incident, more than a dozen Muslim villagers—mostly women and children—were killed by an armed Christian group in early July 2001.[84] Although the infusion of new police and army forces into Poso helped to bring a temporary halt to the violence in mid-July, the final months of 2001 saw a new wave of

Local fighters armed with makeshift rifles move on after torching homes during the final phase of interreligious violence in Poso, Central Sulawesi, before the signing of the Malino accords in December 2001 (AP)

armed attacks, now characterized by the use of automatic weapons and full-scale military operations across the religious divide. The mobilization of armed groups numbering in the hundreds resulted in the razing of dozens of villages, leaving scores of casualties and displacing hundreds or thousands of residents: a human rights group based in Palu reportedly estimated that more than 140 people had been killed and nearly 2,500 homes destroyed by the end of 2001.

This intense militarization of the conflict came after the arrival in Poso of paramilitary forces affiliated with Laskar Jihad (see Chapter 7) and other Islamic groups working to assist Muslim forces in the regency. Non-Muslim areas—including, for the first time, Hindu Balinese transmigrant settlements—appear to have borne the brunt of the violence, as seen in the reported preponderance of their residents among the casualties and fleeing refugees.[85]

Yet the arrival of the first Laskar Jihad forces in Poso in July 2001 coincided with the elevation of PDIP leader Megawati Soekarnoputri to the presidency, a development which in due course spelled stronger support and protection for non-Muslims in Central Sulawesi. In fact, October–December 2001 saw army units squaring off against Laskar Jihad and other

Muslim forces in Poso and reportedly engaging in atrocities such as summary executions, abductions, and torture on a number of occasions. By the end of the year, more than 3,000 police and army troops had been stationed in Poso, with senior armed forces officers in Jakarta promising major training exercises and, if need be, the rapid deployment of additional troops to Central Sulawesi in the months ahead. Late December 2001, however, saw the signing of the so-called Malino accords by a broad range of local figures from Poso after talks organized by Coordinating Minister for People's Welfare Yusuf Kalla, a prominent Golkar official and Bugis businessman from South Sulawesi. Thus, the violence of 1998–2001, which had led to the killings of hundreds of men, women, and children, the destruction of dozens of houses of worship and more than 16,000 homes, and the displacement of tens of thousands of people, was followed in 2002 by a precipitous decline in collective violence in Poso.[86]

Overall, in contrast with 1998–2001, the period beginning in January 2002 saw a marked shift from waves of sustained warfare between armed groups numbering well into the hundreds to more sporadic, individuated, and clandestine forms of violence across the local religious divide. As the prominent human rights activist Arianto Sangaji, based in Central Sulawesi, has noted, since the end of 2001, conflicts in Poso and neighboring Morowali have assumed three forms: (1) shootings, (2) bombings and bomb threats, and (3) clandestine attacks on villages or neighborhoods, typically undertaken under the cover of night, with the perpetrators often taking special care to disguise their identities.[87] The first year following the Malino peace accords, a significant number of such incidents began with the bombing of four churches on New Year's Eve, 2001–2002, and peaked in a string of bombings and shootings in July and August 2002.[88] The next year, by contrast, was by and large more peaceful; local observers recorded only 19 bombings, 19 shootings, and 3 fatalities in all of 2003, with most of the incidents occurring in the regency capital town of Poso Kota, neighboring coastal Poso Pesisir, and the adjacent new regency of Morowali.[89]

With a second redistricting of Poso regency in December 2003[90] and the approach of the 2004 elections, however, incidents of violence in Poso and Morowali began to increase in frequency and intensity, starting with a series of violent attacks on villages in the two regencies in October 2003.[91] The parliamentary elections of April 2004, which saw an apparent victory in (now Christian-majority) Poso for a coalition of PDIP and the new Protestant evangelicals' Partai Damai Sejahtera (PDS), or Prosperous Peace Party, were likewise followed by a string of killings, as the election of a new *bupati* in 2005 loomed on the horizon.[92] Yet even this recrudescence of violence consisted of isolated attacks and assassinations, rather than a relapse into the large-scale, collective mobilization and warfare of 1999, 2000, and 2001, suggesting that a measure of reequilibration had been reached in Poso over the subsequent years.

Such reequilibration, of course, had been achieved at considerable cost and through the violent redrawing of religious boundaries and reconstitution of hierarchies of authority on both sides of the religious divide. More than a thousand people are estimated to have been killed in Poso during the peak years of violence in 1999–2001, with many more sustaining injuries and enduring untold suffering, and with thousands of homes and dozens of churches, mosques, and other buildings damaged or destroyed in the process. In addition, the violence forced tens of thousands of IDPs to flee their homes, neighborhoods, and villages and seek refuge among their coreligionists elsewhere within Poso, in neighboring regencies in Central Sulawesi, or beyond the province itself.[93]

That the pogroms proved effective in sharpening—and simplifying—the boundaries of religious identity and authority in Poso, could be seen in the obstacles impeding the repatriation of IDPs and in the gerrymandering of a mostly Protestant rump regency—with less than one-half of the original Poso population—by hiving off the two new, mostly Muslim, regencies of, first, Morowali and then Tojo Una-Una. The pogroms also proved instrumental for the reconstitution of local religious authority structures in Poso and its two new neighboring regencies. Both Protestant and Muslim networks of politicians, businessmen, civil servants, policemen, military officers, and gangsters came to enjoy greater coercive powers within their respective religious communities, thanks to the evolution of policing and surveillance structures and the elaboration of arms smuggling and other illegal activities—all ostensibly defensive in nature and responsive to self-evident threats from without.[94]

Yet even as the violence in Poso generated waves of IDPs well beyond the regency's borders and attracted flows of financial support, fighters, and weapons from Christian and Muslim networks elsewhere in Sulawesi and beyond, its contagious effects did not create serious, sustained interreligious conflict of a province- or regionwide scale.[95] Beyond the original regency of Poso, after all, the rest of Central Sulawesi was more solidly Muslim: 78 percent of the population province-wide and ranging from 68 percent in the Banggai Islands to 93 percent in Buol.[96] With regard to interparty conflict, moreover, the stabilizing effects of this strong Muslim majority at the provincial level were evident in Golkar's 54.5 percent showing in Central Sulawesi in the 1999 elections and virtually identical performance in all its regencies, with the PDIP claiming only 14 percent of the vote, PPP less than 11 percent, and no single other party more than 2.5 percent overall. Given such demographic clarity and electoral stability, neither the threat nor the promise of electoral mobilization along religious lines—within Golkar and beyond—were sufficiently demographically compelling to encourage violent mobilization beyond Poso, where redistricting had left local Muslim and non-Muslim populations (and their respective political networks) approaching virtual parity and facing considerable uncertainty and anxiety in the face of the political changes of 1998–2001.

Province-Wide Interreligious Pogroms: Maluku and Maluku Utara

In these same years a set of parallel pogroms unfolded across the religious divide in Ambon, the provincial capital of Maluku, and spread to other localities in this vast archipelagic province. As in Poso, the violence in Maluku began with a knife fight in a bus terminal in the capital, grew into attacks by crudely armed groups on urban neighborhoods, and radiated out into the hinterlands with similar assaults in various towns and villages on various islands scattered around the province. As in Poso, with the ensuing militarization and segregation along religious lines, such large-scale collective mobilization had largely subsided in Maluku by 2001, giving way to more individuated forms of violence such as bombings, drive-by shootings, and nighttime attacks. This pattern reflected features of Maluku similar to Poso's as a *location* for religious violence and a similar *conjuncture* as a backdrop for its initiation, as well as a similar set of local *protagonists* and *mobilizational processes* which were crucial for its unfolding. Compared with Poso, however, the interreligious pogroms of Maluku were distinguished by the greater scale and scope of the violence, which spanned from the provincial capital of Ambon to towns and villages throughout the vast Moluccan archipelago, leaving thousands of casualties, and hundreds of thousands of people driven from their homes and communities on islands scattered around Maluku.

As in Poso, the linkages between localities and larger centers of power in Maluku and beyond had long been mediated by religious identity. Islam in the Moluccas was first propagated under the auspices of the Ternate (an island and town in North Maluku) sultanate, whose influence extended through much of eastern Indonesia and as far afield as the Philippine archipelago in the years prior to European contact.[97] Roman Catholicism was imported in the sixteenth century by the Portuguese, who established a network of forts and small settlements in the Moluccas during the heyday of the spice trade.[98] The Dutch East India Company, which replaced the Portuguese as the sole purchaser of Moluccan spices in the seventeenth century, brought Protestant missionaries first to the island of Ambon and the fort town of the same name and later to other islands of the Moluccan archipelago. Dutch missionary schools provided not only religious instruction but also practical education to Protestants for the purposes of preparing low-level civil servants for the colonial regime. As the Dutch colonial state extended its hold over the Netherlands East Indies in the late nineteenth century and in the "Forward Movement" of the early twentieth century, and as the colonial bureaucracy expanded its functions and personnel under the Ethical Policy declared in 1902, so did the numbers of Protestant civil servants, teachers, missionaries, and soldiers leaving the Moluccas for other islands of the archipelago correspondingly increase.[99]

Protestants from the island of Ambon were thus disproportionately well represented among the ranks of civil servants, professionals, and missionaries throughout the Dutch East Indies, and particularly in the Dutch colonial army, the Koninklijk Nederlandsch-Indisch Leger (KNIL), or Royal Netherlands-Indies Army. The number of Ambonese Protestant recruits into the KNIL grew enormously in the late nineteenth and early twentieth centuries, and the pattern of recruitment, organization, and quartering of soldiers "served to create a degree of competitiveness and a strong identification with the ethnic group and the status accorded to it by the authorities," according to Richard Chauvel.[100] By the 1930s an estimated 16 percent of the Protestant population of Ambon was living outside the Moluccas, and as clerks, professionals, and soldiers under the Dutch, they and their families enjoyed a higher level of material welfare and a closer degree of identification with the colonial regime than did the Muslim residents of the island.[101]

It was thus a group of Ambonese Protestants who had served in the KNIL who led successive local efforts to establish the Negara Indonesia Timur (State of East Indonesia), the Republik Indonesia Timur (Republic of East Indonesia), and finally the Republik Maluku Selatan (RMS), or Republic of South Maluku, during the transition to Indonesian independence in the late 1940s and early 1950s. Yet despite their initial ambivalence about inclusion in the Republic of Indonesia, the head start enjoyed by such educated Ambonese Protestants was evident well into the Suharto era in their predominance locally (and, in relative terms, nationally) within the security forces, the civil service, the university belt, and the professional classes. This head start was, inter alia, a linguistic one. Since the early nineteenth century a creolized Ambonese Malay had replaced local languages among the Protestant population in the South Moluccas, reinforced by "schools, sermons, [and] company directives," thus facilitating the adoption of the Malay-based national language, Bahasa Indonesia, in the twentieth century.[102]

Meanwhile, however, the termination of the Dutch clove monopoly, the collapse of the spice trade, and the relegation of the Moluccas to the status of an economic backwater combined to help establish a different and more limited pattern of extralocal linkages for Muslims in Maluku. The phasing out of the clove monopoly in the 1860s and improved interisland transportation in the late nineteenth century facilitated closer contact with Muslims elsewhere in the Netherlands East Indies, and small but growing numbers of Muslims began to leave the Moluccas as sailors, traders, and pilgrims. This pattern of slowly increasing circulation and interaction with Muslims from elsewhere in the archipelago began to draw the distinction between Muslim and Protestant elites in Maluku more sharply in the early twentieth century, as the former increasingly identified themselves in Islamic, and Indonesian, terms, whereas the latter tended to view their identities and interests as closely linked to the continuation of Dutch colonial rule.[103] Yet the limits of such patterns of supralocal circulation and sense of connectedness among the Muslims of the Moluccas were evident in the persistence of local dialects in Muslim villages, in sharp contrast with the rise of the Ambonese Malay lingua franca in Protestant areas of the islands.[104]

With independence, however, the defeat of the Ambonese Protestant–led Republik Maluku Selatan in the early 1950s, and the termination of Ambonese Protestants' colonial-era advantages within the bureaucracy and the armed forces in particular, Muslims in Maluku began to experience gradual upward social mobility along the pathways paved by their Protestant counterparts, through increasing access to education and employment opportunities within the Indonesian state.[105] The ascendancy of educated Muslims in Maluku into the political class accelerated in the Suharto era, as economic development, state expansion, and urbanization eroded the Protestants' hegemonic position, most notably in the provincial capital city of Ambon. By the 1990s, Protestants there and elsewhere in Maluku faced rising competition from Muslims in schools and in the armed forces, the bureaucracy, Golkar, and the DPRD, and in business (both legal and illegal). Suharto's shift toward state promotion of Islamicization at the national level coincided with local demographic trends: rising numbers of Butonese (and, to a lesser extent, Bugis and Makassarese) immigrants from Sulawesi and high birth rates among local Muslims began to tip the population balance in favor of Muslims (59 percent province-wide in 1997) and, even in the Protestant stronghold of Ambon city, 42 percent.[106]

Thus, as in Poso, local political-cum-business networks in the Maluku of the late Suharto era were incorporated into the national political class through a pattern of linkages defined—and divided—by religion. Indeed, just as Maluku's Protestant civil servants, army officers, and members of Golkar engaged in intermarriage and nepotistic practices with their coreligionists in the universities, the professions, business, and the criminal underworld, so too did the province's Muslim political networks operate as channels for patronage and protection linking Muslim towns and villages around the province with Ambon City and Jakarta. As the political scientist Jacques Bertrand, who conducted extensive fieldwork in Ambon, noted:

> The state sector became divided into sections controlled by each group. A particularly interesting example was the University of Pattimura (UNPATTI). The powerful Education Faculty (FKIP), one of the largest faculties in the university, was almost exclusively staffed with Christians well into the 1990s, while other departments included more Muslims. Within the regional and municipal bureaucracies, such tendencies were common. Christians resented the growing presence of Muslims in areas they previously controlled, while Muslims saw their advancement as a just redress since they have been previously marginalized in the region.[107]

Against this backdrop, the resignation of Suharto and inauguration of B. J. Habibie in May 1998 carried particular significance for Maluku. Habibie, after all, had served throughout the 1990s as the head of ICMI, the Association of Indonesian Islamic Intellectuals, and under this national umbrella, well-connected Muslims in Maluku could be expected to enjoy considerably enhanced local advantages in getting appointments to civil service posts, army commands, seats in parliamentary bodies, university lectureships, and preferential treatment within various business and criminal ventures.[108] Indeed, as in Poso, the last five years of the Suharto era had already witnessed marked trends along these lines, as a Muslim governor in Maluku began to fill the top positions in the local bureaucracy with fellow Muslim allies, cronies, and clients.[109]

Yet beyond the immediate implications for local Muslim and Protestant patronage networks of Habibie's rise to the presidency in mid-1998, the approach of competitive elections in mid-1999 and the devolution of considerable powers to elected local assemblies legislated later that year represented a major challenge to existing religious identities, boundaries, and structures of authority in Ambon and elsewhere in Maluku. In obvious ways, local shifts in the distribution of state patronage and in the discretionary use of state regulatory power raised tensions along and across the borders between Muslims and Protestants, as did the impending shift to a system in which freely elected local officials would wield much more power over their constituencies. After all, the boundaries between Muslims and Protestants in Maluku appeared to be sharply defined and securely fixed in spatial terms, in a pattern of segmentation into local units of official religious homogeneity.[110] Religious boundaries thus tended to conform to village boundaries, and even in those rare localities where religious diversity was found, segregated settlement patterns divided not only Muslims and Christians but even Protestants and Catholics.[111]

This pattern, observable both in villages scattered throughout Maluku and in urban neighborhoods (*kampung*) in Ambon city,[112] was reinforced by government policies prohibiting interfaith marriages, expanding religious instruction in schools, and promoting a pattern of recruitment into the bureaucracy through networks based on religious affiliation. In this context, competition for state offices, public works contracts, and legal and illegal business franchises was understood according to the zero-sum logic of a highly divided society. Given the considerable ambiguities about land titles and village boundaries in rural Maluku, gang turf in urban Ambon and administrative units throughout the province, the uncertainties attending the regime change, the approaching elections, *pemekaran* (redistricting), and decentralization all made for heightened tensions along religious lines in the months following the fall of Suharto. The impending division of the province into predominantly Muslim (85 percent) Maluku Utara and a rump Maluku with virtual parity between Muslims and non-Muslims (49–50 percent) in September 1999 only exacerbated the problem.

Yet in perhaps somewhat less obvious ways, the shift to an open, competitive, and decentralized system of organizing power in Indonesia was also accompanied by heightened uncertainty and anxiety as to religious identities and structures of authority *within* the Muslim and Christian communities. Anthropological writings on the villages of Ambon, after all, stressed the persistence well into the Suharto era of religious beliefs and practices that transcended the Muslim-Protestant divide, patterns of enduring alliance (*pela*) and mutual assistance between villages of different official faiths, and understandings of local property and authority relations based on suprareligious customary law (*adat*) and aristocratic lineage.[113] Ethnographic work on other parts of Maluku likewise revealed a broad spectrum of diversity and change in the religious beliefs and practices of those registered as Muslims and Christians in the province, with "conversion" a recent and ongoing process for many official believers, even well into the 1990s.[114] Patterns of migration to and within Maluku—especially

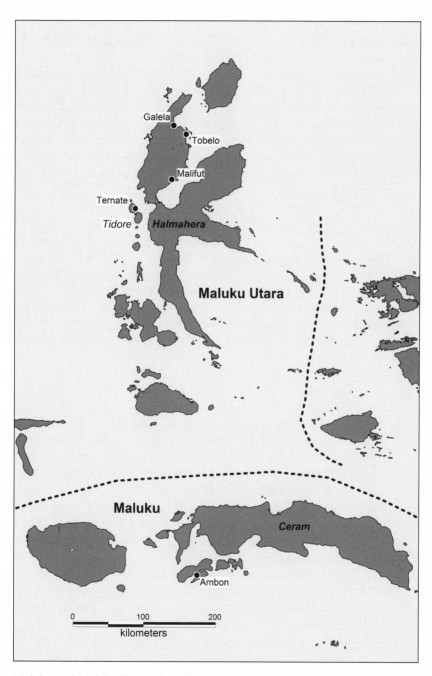

Maluku and Maluku Utara (Peter Loud)

by (Muslim) Butonese from Sulawesi—were cited by observers in the same period as increasing the diversity of religious practices and heightening the "ethnicizing" tensions between both Christian and Muslim "natives," on the one hand, and immigrant "outsiders," on the other, over economic resources, property relations, village elections, and other issues.[115]

Against this backdrop, the dominant structures of power associated with Protestantism and Islam in Maluku, much like their counterparts in Poso, were haunted by rising doubts and fears as to their authority, identity, and coherence. On the Protestant side, the Gereja Protestan Maluku (GPM), or Maluku Protestant Church, greatly resembled the GKST in Central Sulawesi in its internal authority structure and discipline, and its well-established links to state power. As Gerry van Klinken has noted, the GPM

> is by far the largest non-government organization in the province. Its structure exactly parallels that of local government. Its youth wing, Angkatan Muda Gereja Protestan Maluku (AM-GPM) has thousands of affiliated branches. All Protestant young people are socialized in the elements of an extremely formal religion through a constant round of activities that takes the dedicated believer away from home most nights of the week. Most prominent Protestant Ambonese are therefore also prominent church leaders.[116]

The establishment of the GPM in 1935, its ensuing institutional detachment from the Dutch Reformed Church, and the end of Dutch rule in the 1940s had favored localizing trends and accommodation with non-Christian practices.[117] Yet expanding access to modern education and contact with the outside world combined with the increasing encroachment of other Christian denominations and the promotion of Islamic reformism in Maluku in subsequent decades to promote rising concern with the everyday religious beliefs and practices of those claimed as belonging to the church. As one anthropologist, Dieter Bartels, noted: "After World War II some young Christian ministers were given the opportunity to study at prestigious theological schools in Europe and the United States. As these ministers gained leadership positions within the church, they were striving to achieve universally accepted standards of Protestantism and thus determined to 'purify' Moluccan Christianity by ridding it of ancestor veneration and any customs contrary to Christian beliefs."[118]

Meanwhile, the Seventh Day Adventist church had already established a small congregation in Ambon in the 1920s, and in the postwar, postindependence period the GPM "saw a number of other Protestant denominations, mostly of evangelical and Pentecostal character, growing much faster.

In psychological and institutional aspects the GPM was not yet fully on its way to abandoning the character of a dominant religion."[119] Over the years the sizable Catholic population in Southeastern Maluku had expanded as well, as had the numbers of Catholic migrants to Ambon city. Missionary activities in Maluku provided by Protestant churches from elsewhere in Indonesia and beyond likewise increasingly encroached on the GPM's established turf.[120]

At the same time, the poverty and isolation of sparsely populated, archipelagic Maluku was combining with the associational diversity and limited state institutionalization of Islam in the Netherlands Indies, and early postindependence Indonesia more generally, to limit the possibilities for promoting universalistic understandings of the faith among the scattered and still mostly poorly schooled Muslims of the Moluccan Islands. Bartels claimed: "The degree of indigenization of Islam varied widely from village to village, but in one region it was carried so far that people ultimately came to believe that Islam was brought to the Moluccas by the Prophet himself. On the island of Haruku, the pilgrimage [to] Mecca came to be viewed as unnecessary, but was performed at a special sacred site in the mountains behind the villages."[121]

Over the three decades of the Suharto era the expanding circuitries of the market, the state bureaucracy, and the school system began to draw more and more Muslims in Maluku into the orbit of more modern understandings of Islam, as promoted by both the state's official policies on religion (*agama*) and the diverse outreach (*dakwah*) activities of various Islamic associations such as Muhammadiyah and Al Khaira'at. Thus, as Richard Chauvel had already observed in the early 1980s: "A situation has therefore developed, in which, within both religious communities there has been pressure for reform. Under attack have been those elements of common *adat* heritage which Christians and Moslems share."[122] These pressures, as Bartels further noted, went well beyond the strictly "religious" realm:

> The people battling in the political arena are often identical or allied with religious purists and fanatics within the religious structures of Islam and Christianity. These people are outward directed. That is, they tie in with other organizations on the national level and beyond. They perceive Islam or Christianity as universal truths and thus as mutually incompatible. Extremists among them demand the "purification" of religion from beliefs which are not in line with pan-Islamic or pan-Protestant beliefs. Thus they have launched attacks on beliefs that God is one and the same for Christians and Moslems, and they have demanded the discontinuance of ancestor veneration and most of *adat*—all of which would lead to a further weakening of interfaith ties.[123]

Against this shared and enduring concern about *adat,* the persistence of local aristocratic influence, religious syncretism, and rising ethnic diversification in Maluku, the hierarchies of Protestant and Muslim power in the province were nevertheless notable for their increasing *similarities,* rather than differences. After all, in contrast with the final decades of Dutch rule in the archipelago, the half-century since Indonesian independence had witnessed the evolution of Muslim networks of power in Maluku strikingly similar to those established by their Protestant counterparts: through the modern school system into the civil service and local legislative and executive offices, the police and military, the universities, the media, the professions, and the world of business and criminality. The same decades had likewise seen commensurate linguistic shifts in the direction of homogenization: Ambonese Malay now served—as it had for almost two centuries for Protestants—as a lingua franca among Muslim speakers of whatever Moluccan language or dialect, and Bahasa Indonesia was increasingly used by Muslims and Protestants alike.[124] By the late 1990s, direct personal memories of the violent events of the transition to independence, when the mostly Christian forces backing the Republik Maluku Selatan had fought bitterly against the mostly Muslim supporters of integration into Indonesia, were increasingly distant and dying with the aging men and women who had participated in these events.[125]

By the end of the twentieth century, moreover, more and more privileged Muslims in Maluku than ever before were attending the same state schools and universities, viewing the same television programs and movies, speaking the same linguae francae, and jockeying for advantage within the same state and market circuitries as Protestants. By the mid-1990s, in the provincial capital city of Ambon, the newly built Ambon Plaza shopping complex combined Chinese, Bugis, and Butonese storefronts and drew Christian and Muslim consumers and flaneurs alike.[126] Thus the attractive powers of the national state and the global market threatened if not to dissolve, then to diminish the differences between the most privileged local representatives of the two religious faiths.

It was thus against the locally increasing ambiguity, uncertainty, and anxiety with regard to the structures and boundaries of religious identity and authority in Maluku that interreligious pogroms in this province unfolded in 1999–2001. These began, moreover, in a national context of dramatic political movement and change, with the ascendancy of Habibie to the presidency in mid-1998 and the holding of competitive elections in mid-1999. As the fledgling Habibie administration forged a working alliance with a number of militant Islamic groups in Jakarta, civilian and military elements in the regime worked with some of these groups (e.g., Front Pembela Islam) as well as local gangsters (*preman*) to recruit and mobilize pro-government auxiliary forces in the streets to counter student demonstrations in Jakarta in November 1998 during the special session of the MPR. By November the impact of this new pattern of mobilization and linkages between elements in the military, pro-Habibie Islamic groups and Jakarta gangs and protection rackets had begun to erode the long-standing advantages of Christian groups in the criminal underworld of the national capital. This trend percolated down into rivalries between well-connected Christian and Muslim Ambonese gangs operating in the protection rackets of the Jakarta underworld.[127]

On the night of November 22, 1998, a major street fight outside a gambling casino in the area of Ketapang in Central Jakarta—involving Christian and Muslim Ambonese gangs, local residents, and members of militant Islamic groups—resulted in several deaths and the burning of seven churches.[128] Rumors that the riot had been deliberately instigated as part of a larger conspiracy spread rapidly in Jakarta, in Ambon, and elsewhere in Maluku, especially after the violent attack on a Muslim neighborhood in Kupang, West Timor, a week later, during a march organized by a Christian youth congress to protest the church burnings.[129]

The fallout from events in Jakarta soon trickled down to Ambon city and Maluku more generally. The process was no doubt accelerated by the return (by some accounts, the expulsion) of dozens of Ambonese *preman* to their home province in time for Christmas and Ramadan, and rising anticipation of the recently announced and rapidly approaching June 1999 elections. Thus violent competition over the fluctuating boundaries of power shifted downward, as it were, to local protection rackets in Ambon precisely as electoral mobilization was getting under way in a province where tight demographic margins between Muslims and Christians combined with the sociological and religious trends sketched above to produce considerable uncertainty and anxiety. If rival Christian and Muslim gangs in Jakarta and Ambon city had previously been part of competing networks of active and retired military officers, bureaucrats, businessmen, and politicians associated with Golkar, the possibility of a strong showing by the secular nationalist PDIP in the upcoming elections foreshadowed not only mass defections by Christians (and potentially by Muslims) but also a broadening of the arena and the weapons of contestation.[130]

Thus, as in Poso, interreligious pogroms in Maluku began to unfold around the turn of the new year at a key local node of economic and criminal activity in Ambon city: a bus terminal.[131] On January 19, 1999, on the Muslim holiday of Idul Fitri, a dispute apparently broke out there between a (Protestant) minibus driver and two (Muslim) Bugis youths demanding

A resident of Ambon walks past gutted shops and homes on a street demolished during the first phase of interreligious violence in the city in January 1999 (AP)

(in the Protestant version of events) protection money or (in the Muslim version) rent payment to the owner of the minibus, then escalated into fighting between residents of two adjacent *kampung* in the city of Ambon, one Protestant, the other Muslim. News of the violence began to circulate, and groups of hundreds of crudely armed Christian and Muslim young men, carrying knives, lead pipes, and various incendiary devices, attacked neighborhoods across the religious divide in Ambon city and villages elsewhere on Ambon island, hacking to death dozens of victims and burning to the ground hundreds of houses and other buildings.[132] This kind of violence continued sporadically into February, spreading to the nearby Central Maluku islands of Haruku, Seram, and Saparua and leaving dozens dead, hundreds wounded, and thousands of homes, shops, churches, mosques, and other buildings burned or otherwise destroyed.[133] By early March, as this first phase of violence began to subside, more than 100 casualties were reported, and as many as 70,000 refugees were said to have fled Ambon.[134]

The trouble in Ambon created a self-reinforcing climate of mounting mutual suspicion, fear, resentment, and vengefulness. In many neighborhoods and villages in Maluku, Protestant and Muslim *posko* (communications or command posts) sprang up, as did elaborate local security arrangements for issuing advanced warning, arming residents, and launching preemptive strikes against outsiders. Churches and mosques soon emerged as major nodes in these formations of violence, serving as major sites of paramilitary mobilization, planning, communication, coordination, and rearmament. This trend not only hardened the divisions between Christian and Muslim communities but further spurred the reconstitution of neighborhood and village gangs as crudely armed local militias, sporting variously red (Christian) or white (Muslim) bandanas and other clothing to distinguish themselves as defenders of their respective religious communities and faiths.[135] In Ambon, local observers noted at this juncture, "everyday social life is segregated: red market, white market, red and white speedboat quays, red and white pedicabs (*becak*), red and white minibuses, red and white banks, and so forth."[136]

This pattern of hardening segregation and militarization along the religious divide crystallized around the structures of the intertwined political, business, and ecclesiastical networks established by Protestants and Muslims within and beyond Ambon province. By February 1999, security forces had begun to intervene directly in the conflict, occasionally firing on crowds during disturbances and in several instances leaving casualties in their wake. Local Christian and Muslim leaders were soon trading accusations that various police and military units, whether based in Ambon or drawn from elsewhere in the archipelago, were guilty of bias and collusion in their handling of the conflict.[137] Given the prominence of retired military and police officers in the rival Protestant and Muslim networks of politicians, clerics, businessmen, and gangsters in Ambon and elsewhere in Maluku, partisan involvement in the fighting by "organic" members of the security forces in the province was something of a foregone conclusion.[138] Meanwhile, back in Jakarta, Islamic organizations and political parties tried to rally Muslims to protect their coreligionists in Ambon and spread accounts blaming the violence on the Ambonese Christian community, on the virtually extinct movement for an independent Republik Maluku Selatan, and on a broader anti-Islamic conspiracy of national and international dimensions.[139] Drawing on their considerable connections in Jakarta (especially in the military establishment, the business community, and the PDIP), as well as church networks in North America and Europe, Christians in Maluku likewise organized support networks in the name of self-defense.

In this context, as in Poso, the shift to competitive elections was played out in Maluku through violent mass mobilization along severely divided religious lines. In the June 1999 elections, Protestants scored a victory with a slim majority in Ambon and a clear plurality in the province for the Partai Demokrasi Indonesia-Perjuangan, whose local representatives in the DPRD were overwhelmingly Protestants and whose national chairman, Megawati Soekarnoputri, won the vice presidency and considerable influence in Jakarta. Although Muslim voters in Maluku were split among Golkar, PPP, and other Islamic parties, their avowed patrons and protectors in Jakarta succeeded in scotching Megawati's presidential bid and in maintaining a toehold in the newly installed Wahid administration.[140] More important, these Jakarta-based champions of Indonesian Islam had begun to develop an interest in supporting jihad in Maluku, not only to help their beleaguered coreligionists but also to protect and promote a stronger sense of religious boundaries in the national arena, where political parties and figures commanding multifaith constituencies, such as the PDIP's Megawati, were winning millions of votes—and dozens of parliamentary seats—at their expense.

Even more than in Poso, this pattern of hardening sectarian division and mobilization—of arms, money, and (mis)information—combined with continuing uncertainties and anxieties over local boundaries to guarantee the continuation and spread of violent interreligious conflict in the vast archipelagic province. As elsewhere in Indonesia, Maluku had seen the proliferation of fictive villages during the New Order as a local strategy for the acquisition of government subsidies, and the extent of village-owned communal lands and the widening of competition in elections for village headmen (*pilkades*) guaranteed that this patchwork of claims on local resources would be hotly contested between neighboring communities divided by religious affiliation.[141] Meanwhile, the passage of new legislation promising "regional autonomy" had begun to devolve considerable powers to the level of the regency (*kabupaten*), where local demographic and electoral constellations often amplified the sectarian implications of the June 1999 provincial and national election results. At the same time, moves to create—or gerrymander—new administrative districts and regencies, and the formation of the new province of Maluku Utara in September 1999,[142] spurred mobilization and maneuvering over the windfall of new state offices, resources, and regulatory powers. With such rising concern over shifting boundaries and sites of authority, it is unsurprising that a society already locally segregated and translocally segmented along lines of religious identity and association would see a vicious cycle of rumors, conspiracy theories, and self-fulfilling prophecies of interreligious violence in subsequent months and years.[143] The flow of tens

of thousands of refugees from Ambon and other sites of earlier violence—
"carrying with them," noted Philip Winn, an anthropologist working in
the Banda Islands in 1999, "stories, fears and rumors"[144]—only strengthened these dynamics.[145]

Indeed, the months immediately following upon the June 1999 elections
witnessed the resumption and spread of the pogroms in the Moluccan archipelago.[146] In August 1999, for example, fighting broke out in North
Maluku, just a month before its official reconstitution as a new province
and on the occasion of the formal inauguration of the new district of Malifut in the regency of North Halmahera.[147] This new district was to con-
sist of some sixteen villages populated by transmigrants resettled from the
nearby island of Makian in 1975, and eleven additional villages identified
with the more established local Kao and Jailolo ethnolinguistic groups. For
years, the transmigrants' settlement and cultivation of land in the area had
run up against the resentment and resistance of the "indigenous" Kao and
Jailolo, whose representatives' claims to *adat* land rights grew only more
vociferous with an Australian mining company's discovery in the 1990s of
gold in Malifut. This dispute acquired a strongly religious complexion,
since the Makianese transmigrants were Muslim, the Kao and Jailolo predominantly Protestant. Malifut, moreover, had come to serve as a Muslim
bottleneck choking off the southward spread of Christianity from predominantly Protestant North Halmahera by the *Gereja Masehi Injili Halmahera* (GMIH), or Evangelical Church of Halmahera, and the largely
American-staffed New Tribes Mission based in the northeastern district of
Tobelo.[148] The Kao and Jailolo thus won backing for their claims from
Protestant politicians and the Sultan of Ternate (who counted on Christian
backing for his ambition to assume the governorship of the new province),
while the Makianese enjoyed the support of Muslim politicians in Maluku
and Jakarta.[149]

Against this backdrop, a pattern of "cascading" and escalating violence
unfolded in North Maluku in the second half of 1999.[150] First, the sched-
uled inauguration of the new district of Malifut in August 1999 was
marked by the outbreak of fighting between crudely armed groups from
Kao/Jailolo and Makianese villages. The fighting persisted for several days,
leaving a handful of casualties but dozens of homeless or displaced families in its wake. Violence recurred and escalated in October 1999 with a
wholesale Kao and Jailolo attack that razed all sixteen Makianese villages,
left dozens of Makianese casualties, and forced some 16,000 Makianese
residents to flee to Ternate and Tidore. Then, the presence of these Makianese IDPs and the circulation of a forged letter from the head of the
GPM in Ambon to the head of the GMIH in Tobelo, calling for the Chris-

tianization of North Maluku and the "cleansing" of Muslims from the province, combined to provoke attacks on Protestants in Tidore and then Ternate in November 1999.[151]

The violence in Tidore and Ternate, in turn, prompted mobilization by armed followers of the Sultan of Ternate and by forces loyal to his rivals for the governorship (including the Sultan of Tidore and a PPP politician who assumed the *bupati*ship of Central Halmahera), and also resulted in the flight of Protestants from the two towns to safe havens in North Halmahera and North Sulawesi. In yet another twist, late December 1999 saw groups of armed men from among these IDPs from Ternate and Tidore, and from local Protestant villages, launch attacks on Muslim villages in the predominantly Protestant North Halmahera district of Tobelo, where the headquarters of the evangelical GMIH was located. These assaults, which began on the day after Christmas and lasted into the first week of the new year, left hundreds of Muslim villagers in Tobelo and neighboring Galela dead (including more than 200 slaughtered in a local mosque) and forced the flight of thousands more.[152] By the end of January 2000, official sources estimated that more than 1,600 people had been killed in Maluku Utara since August 1999 and tens of thousands displaced by the violence.[153]

The massacre in Tobelo combined with a wave of attacks by Protestants on Muslims in other parts of Maluku to spur new forms of violent mobilization in avowed defense of Islam elsewhere in Indonesia. Fighting in Ambon city had broken out on Christmas Day 1999 and led to the burning of one of the GPM's most prominent churches in the capital by an armed Muslim crowd, followed by the burning of two mosques later the same day by a similar Protestant mob.[154] Widely circulated media reports of these events, which fell on a major Christian holiday and in the midst of the Muslim fasting month of Ramadan, had helped to precipitate the massacre in Tobelo, where tensions were reportedly already running high with the arrival of Protestant refugees from Ternate and Tidore the previous month. A similar dynamic was evident in the Central Maluku town of Masohi, where attacks by armed Protestant groups on Muslim villages in late December and early January left dozens of casualties and hundreds more homeless, violated, wounded, and otherwise traumatized. The alleged participation of Protestant police and military personnel (and the reported acquiescence of the Protestant *bupati*) in the violence in Masohi combined with the killing of 27 Muslims in Ambon on Christmas Day, the massacre of hundreds of Muslim villagers in Tobelo, and the flight of tens of thousands of Muslim IDPs from Maluku and Maluku Utara to draw increasingly vociferous condemnations of Christian atrocities and expressions of concern for Muslim welfare in Maluku from Islamic organizations and political parties in Jakarta.[155] For example, Amien Rais—chairman of the MPR, leader of the National Mandate Party (PAN), and longtime head of Muhammadiyah—joined other leading politicians at a rally in early January in Jakarta, attended by an estimated 100,000 militants, in calling for jihad to save Muslims in Maluku.

The wave of Protestant violence against Muslims in Maluku also spurred both old and new forms of religious violence elsewhere in Indonesia. On January 17, 2000, for example, prominent Islamic leaders, including a dean from the local university, the heads of local Islamic associations and schools, the leaders of a local Islamic militia, and the Jakarta-based Islamic labor leader and ICMI member Eggi Sudjana,[156] held a *tabligh akbar* (major public gathering) in a field in the city of Mataram, the largest urban center on the predominantly Muslim island of Lombok ("island of a thousand mosques") and the capital of the province of West Nusa Tenggara. The *tabligh akbar* was announced as a venue for raising funds for Muslim victims of the violence in Maluku and for expressing solidarity and concern among the faithful. But the event was preceded by the dissemination of a letter by some of the organizers demanding that Christians in Lombok come forward to issue public condemnations of the atrocities committed by Protestants in Maluku in the preceding weeks and threatening dire consequences in the event of continuing Christian silence on the issue. An estimated 2,000 Islamic activists attended the gathering, many of them sporting white bandanas with the inscription *Allahu Akbar* (God is Great) written in Arabic on their foreheads. Afterward, some of these activists began to attack buildings identified as belonging to the small Christian minority in Mataram; they burned Protestant and Catholic churches, schools, shops, and homes over the next two days and drove some 3,000 Christians to seek refuge in local police and military installations or in non-Muslim sanctuaries beyond Lombok, such as Bali, Manado, and Papua.[157]

Meanwhile, as in Poso in June–July 2001, the wave of violence in late December 1999 and early January 2000 which gave rise to calls for jihad in Maluku resonated among many Muslims elsewhere in Indonesia and spurred the mobilization and deployment of Laskar Jihad units to the Moluccan archipelago in the spring of 2000. Indeed, it was this wave of anti-Muslim violence in Maluku that occasioned the very creation of Laskar Jihad (see chapter 7), whose paramilitary and other operations in Ambon, North Maluku, and elsewhere in the Moluccas preceded and foreshadowed their arrival and activities in Poso more than one year later. Already in late January 2000, then, in the aftermath of the huge rally in Jakarta, dozens of Muslim volunteers were arriving in Ambon and other parts of Maluku to provide medical, logistical, and paramilitary support to their beleaguered coreligionists. In April 2000, moreover, a well-organized paramilitary group also called Laskar Jihad was formed on Java.

By May 2000, an estimated 3,000 Laskar Jihad recruits—and hundreds of similar Muslim paramilitary troops—had reportedly arrived in Maluku, setting in motion a new phase of interreligious violence, one characterized by a high level of militarization. As in Poso, Laskar Jihad forces brought with them military training, heavy automatic weapons, sophisticated forms of radio communications, and close links with elements in the armed forces. Thus June and July 2000 witnessed a fresh wave of aggressive paramilitary attacks on vulnerable Protestant areas, including an assault on a Protestant village in Galela district abutting the GMIH stronghold in the Tobelo district of North Maluku, and the razing of Waai, a Christian village sandwiched between two Muslim villages on the east coast of Ambon island. These assaults claimed dozens of Protestant casualties and proved highly effective in "cleansing" thousands more Protestant residents from these border zones.[158] Even with the declaration of a civil emergency in Maluku by President Abdurrahman Wahid in late June 2000, Laskar Jihad–led attacks on Protestant areas persisted, allegedly aided and abetted by elements of the armed forces.[159] By early 2001, eight Protestant villages and towns in Ambon had been occupied by Muslim forces, and hundreds or even a few thousand Protestants on small islands elsewhere in Central Maluku were reportedly forced to convert to Islam to ensure their survival.[160]

Yet as in Poso in late 2001, these paramilitary operations of Laskar Jihad from mid-2000 through mid-2001 heralded a pattern of effectively stalemated and thus subsiding interreligious violence in Maluku and Maluku Utara. By 2001 the violence in the Moluccan archipelago had effected a pattern of enduring religious segregation and simplification, with the Laskar Jihad–led assaults serving to eliminate some of the remaining anomalies of Protestant pockets inside—and impeding the connection of— Muslim zones.[161] By 2001, moreover, Protestant and Muslim villages and towns throughout the two provinces had come to feature "red" and "white" armed groups ready for mobilization and plugged into their respective interlocking directorates of local politicians, bureaucrats, businessmen, criminal networks, and retired and active police and military personnel. Local election results—PDIP's outright victory in Ambon city and strong plurality in (predominantly Christian) Southeastern Maluku, and its weaker showing against Golkar and PPP in (predominantly Muslim) Central Maluku—also worked to clarify the new distribution of civilian-controlled state patronage along religious lines.

Meanwhile, the security forces' efforts to control the violence in Maluku had been led since mid-2000 by a "Yon Gab" (Combined Battalion), drawn from various crack units of the armed forces and comprising people of mixed faiths from locations outside Maluku—commanded by a (Hindu) Balinese general. This Yon Gab, increasingly pitted against Laskar Jihad and other Muslim forces and involved in defending local Christian communities against Muslim offensives, was widely perceived and resented among Muslims as biased in favor of Christians. In mid-2001 it undertook a serious offensive culminating in an attack on a Laskar Jihad contingent in the provincial capital of Ambon in June 2001 which led to the deaths of more than a dozen armed Islamic militants.[162]

With the rise to the presidency of Megawati Soekarnoputri in Jakarta in mid-2001, moreover, came the violent removal of Laskar Jihad elements from Maluku and Maluku Utara and the strengthening of protection for Christians in the two provinces, many of whom were affiliated with the now ruling PDIP. The latter half of 2001 saw a diminution of Laskar Jihad strength and activism in the two provinces and, more generally, a pattern in which incidents of violence across the religious divide were kept to a minimum. Complaints against the Yon Gab by Muslim leaders in Maluku and their counterparts in Jakarta led to the withdrawal of that battalion and its replacement by a large contingent of KOPASSUS troops in November 2001, but the basic pattern continued. It was in this context that in mid-February 2002 the leaders of the Christian and Muslim communities in Maluku signed an agreement to resolve the conflict in the province. The terms of the agreement included promises to facilitate the removal and prosecution of "outside" parties, to surrender the huge numbers of loose firearms accumulated by armed groups on both sides, and to form an independent commission to investigate the roots of the conflict and the various crimes committed since its inception.[163]

Signs of improving conditions in Maluku were reported by a variety of sources in subsequent months of 2002. In Ambon city, for example, observers noted the removal of barricades between some neighborhoods of different faiths and the opening of marketplaces and other shopping areas in which Christians and Muslims freely mixed.[164] Reports of conditions elsewhere in Maluku were likewise cautiously optimistic, noting evidence of reduced interreligious tensions and small trickles of returning refugees. In the predominantly Muslim new province of North Maluku (Maluku Utara), security conditions were said to have reached a point where civil emergency status was no longer warranted.[165]

Clearly, the sheer size and strong stance of the security forces contributed to the downturn in the violence. The leader of Laskar Jihad was arrested in May 2002 and put on trial for inciting violence in Maluku, and the group came to face continuing, if not increasing, restrictions on its presence and operations in Maluku in the months leading up to its formal disbandment in October of the same year.[166] More generally, hundreds, if not thousands, of weapons were surrendered around Maluku in the weeks before the armed forces' imposed deadline of June 30, 2002, and the regional army commander initiated sweeps for remaining loose firearms in subsequent weeks.[167]

That said, incidents of violence nevertheless continued to mar the uneasy calm setttling in around the provinces of Maluku and Maluku Utara. Most tragic was an attack on a Christian village in Ambon in late April 2001 which claimed twelve lives and was blamed on Laskar Jihad and allied local Muslim forces.[168] Also quite revealing was a subsequent armed encounter between KOPASSUS troops and elements of the local Riot Police Brigade (Brimob), which drew renewed attention to the involvement in the conflict of active and retired members of the security forces in the conflict and to the predatory aspects of "peace-keeping."[169]

Yet overall, as in Poso, by 2001 interreligious violence had peaked in Maluku and Maluku Utara and had begun to subside. In subsequent years, incidents of armed combat across the religious divide in Maluku were very infrequent and limited in their scope, leading to the lifting of civil emergency status in the province in late 2003. Ambon and other localities were occasionally troubled by drive-by shootings and other assassinations, as well as bombings and the discovery of explosive materials clearly intended for imminent use.[170] The upsurge of religious tensions and mobilization accompanying the April 2004 parliamentary elections, however, and the annual anniversary of the founding of the RMS later that month, led to a much more dramatic recrudescence of violence in Maluku than in Poso. A Protestant procession in Ambon city celebrating the occasion on April 25 was assaulted by crudely armed groups of Muslim youths, who went on to lead attacks on Protestant neighborhoods in the city over the following week, claiming the lives of more than a dozen residents and leaving homes, churches, and a Christian university building burned to the ground. More than twenty Muslim residents of Ambon were also killed in the clashes, mostly shot dead by the security forces. Yet even this episode, which knowledgeable observers suggested owed much to the machinations of rival police and army units in Ambon, did not lead to a resumption of violence elsewhere in Maluku or Maluku Utara.[171] Overall, as in Poso, even with tens of thousands of IDPs still encamped in and around Ambon and scattered elsewhere around the islands of the Moluccan archipelago, and with the thorny questions of repatriation, compensation, and reconciliation left essentially unresolved, large-scale collective violence of a pogromlike nature appears to have largely disappeared from the two provinces since the end of 2001.

Conclusion: Pogroms, 1998–2001

The antiwitchcraft campaigns on Java in 1998–99 and the interreligious pogroms in Poso and Maluku in 1999–2001 all represented a decisive shift in the pattern of religious violence in Indonesia from the preceding phase of riots in 1995–97. This shift was evident in the very *forms* that violence assumed, with murderous attacks on individuals (in Java) and entire neighborhoods and villages (in Poso and Maluku) replacing, as it were, the earlier exclusive focus on the burning of buildings and property. The shift was also quite evident in the new *locations, protagonists,* and *mobilizational processes* in and through which the violence unfolded in parts of rural Java in 1998–99 and in Poso and Maluku in 1999–2001. The very ways in which this violence was *religious* were also markedly different from those of the riots of the previous years.

As suggested by the virtual disappearance of the kind of religious riots seen in 1995–97, the emergence, spread, transformation, and fading of religious pogroms in 1998–2001 reflected a national *conjuncture* that shaped the nature and direction of violence at that time. Most obviously, this conjuncture was one in which the forces associated with the promotion of Islam in Indonesian public life were first launched into the seats of state power in Jakarta, soon embattled from without and within, and eventually eclipsed and ousted from power. The effects on the national political stage of this precipitous rise and fall of Islam in 1998–2001 rapidly trickled down through the distribution of power and patronage in provinces, regencies, towns, and villages around the Indonesian archipelago. The local effects were especially destabilizing in localities where the *jaringan* connecting local networks of politicians, civil servants, (retired and active) military and police officers, businessmen, and gangsters to Jakarta were defined and divided along religious lines, and where local boundaries of authority—and balances of power—were redrawn through *pemekaran,* the formation of new districts, regencies, and provinces (most obviously in Maluku Utara).

Such palpable tremors of political realignments rippling across the archipelago at this conjuncture, moreover, were accompanied by deeper, perhaps somewhat less discernible, tectonic shifts in the very structures of religious identity, authority, and power in Indonesia. The anthropologist

James Siegel has argued that the loosening of the centralized authoritarian state's surveillance and control during the political liberalization initiated by Habibie in the latter half of 1998 called into question not only the established hierarchies of power and patronage in Indonesia but also the very source and structure of recognition and identity for Indonesians around the archipelago.[172] This state of uncertainty was profoundly destabilizing for religious institutions—whether Nahdlatul Ulama, Al-Khaira'at, Gereja Kristen Sulawesi Tengah, or Gereja Protestan Maluku—which in one way or another had secured niches beneath and within the New Order state and thus kept at bay persistent questions about the boundaries of their authority and identity.

That this state of uncertainty was also profoundly destabilizing for many people is perhaps best exemplified by a villager in Banyuwangi, described by Siegel, who found himself wondering—and asking others—whether he might, in fact, be a *dukun santet*. "This man could not tell from his own interrogation of himself whether he was a sorcerer. He asks how he is seen by others, and he thinks that they may know something about him that he does not know himself." The villager's self-doubts provide something of an extreme limit case of the implications of the breakdown of recognition and sociality for the onset of violence. "The feeling of being possessed—if not the posing of the question 'Am I a witch?'"—Siegel argues, was a precondition for the outbreak of the antiwitchcraft campaign on Java in 1998–99:

> It indicates that, at a certain moment, there was not merely uncertainty about identity, which means that one doubts who one is, as though one had a range of known possible identities. To be a witch, at least in Java, is to be invested with a power heterogeneous to all social identity. Thus there is also the possibility that one could be someone completely different from anything or anyone one knows. The impossibility of relying on social opinion opens up infinite possibilities within the person. But these possibilities are not the ones imagination presents.
>
> Accused of witchcraft, I can find no reflection of myself. I therefore ask, "Am I a witch?," but I do so futilely. To ask this question is to say that I cannot put myself in the place that others once placed me. I can no longer see myself as they saw me at an earlier time in my everyday identity. Earlier I would be able to say, "I am not a witch," because I would not be able to find in myself the confirmation that the accusations of my neighbors were true. But under conditions that prevailed during the witch hunt, self-image disappeared as multiple possibilities of identity thrust themselves forward. "Witch," under that condition, is a name for the incapacity to figure oneself.

The difference between witch and murderer of witch collapses when both are thought to be inhabited by death and feel it urgent to kill to save themselves. They are governed by the feeling that death is already present in them and in those near to them. The capacity to die replaces social identity. To rid themselves of it they must kill. They have the attributes of the witch. They hope that murder will restore normality.[173]

As Siegel suggests, this radical uncertainty—and the ensuing violence—recalled another conjuncture in modern Indonesian history, the period of anti-Communist pogroms in 1965–66, not just in rural East Java but elsewhere in the archipelago as well. Those years, after all, had witnessed sudden, rapid regime change; the breakdown of established structures of power and patronage, recognition and identity; and a climate of widespread fear (and not just among those Indonesians affiliated with the Partai Komunis Indonesia): fear of being killed by the Communists, as well as fear of being accused of—and killed for—being a Communist oneself.[174] As the state-led anti-Communist pogroms proceeded, with hundreds of thousands killed and an equal or greater number imprisoned for their affiliation with the PKI, many Indonesians sought refuge in religion—if not spiritually, then for protective identity. For in the face of the fatal association of atheism—or lack of official religion (*agama*)—with Communism and the pressing imperative of identification (in all senses of the word), millions of Indonesians sought to obtain national identity cards—*Kartu Tanda Pengenalan* (KTP)—which required a declaration for one of the five supposedly monotheistic faiths officially acknowledged by the state: Islam, Protestantism, Catholicism, Hinduism, and Buddhism. Thus in the years stretching from the massacres and mass jailings of 1965–66 to the Suharto regime's first experiment with elections in 1971, millions of Indonesians converted to an official *agama* so as to avoid the stigma of "not yet having a religion" (*belum beragama*) and thus suspicion of Communist identity.[175] This process of linking citizenship to religion continued for years, as seen in the wave of conversion sweeping the remote Southeastern Maluku island of Aru in the mid-1970s in advance of the 1977 elections, as recounted by the anthropologist Patricia Spyer.[176] More than the regional rebellions of the 1950s in Maluku and Sulawesi, the fall of Suharto in mid-1998 thus recalled the violence of 1965–66 and the subsequent consolidation of new—official, "statistical"—religious identities and religious authority structures that it had issued.

Such recollections were thus doubly troubling, both as omens of the uncertainty and violence accompanying regime change, and as reminders of underlying doubts about religious identities, boundaries, and hierarchies, doubts that owed so much to the violence of this earlier era. As Spyer has argued, these religious identities, boundaries, and hierarchies had long rested on the logic of seriality, on "numbers, statistics, and the range of enumerative practices with which they [were] associated."[177] In this context, the competitive elections and decentralization already looming on the horizon in 1998 and replacing centralized authoritarian rule in 1999 heightened worries about the numbers of the faithful—numbers of converts, numbers of voters—who could be claimed for each flock (*jemaah*).

It is thus against the temporal backdrop of this distinctive national conjuncture of 1998–2001 that the geographical distribution and spread of the pogroms in specific *locations* around the Indonesian archipelago during this period must be situated. Indeed, following the logic of seriality stressed by Spyer, it is striking that all the major episodes of communal violence during this period unfolded in provinces where the statistical distribution of religious faith was least concentrated, all of which were found in the cluster of eight provinces with between 30 percent and 85 percent Muslim populations—and electorates. According to the 2000 census, Maluku was only 49 percent Muslim after the creation of Maluku Utara (85 percent Muslim); Poso was only 56 percent Muslim, in 78 percent Muslim Central Sulawesi.[178] Thus the PDI had long established roots in all these localities, and the possibility of a destabilizing shift—of votes, DPR and DPRD seats, and eventually *bupati*ships and governorships—from Golkar to PDIP loomed large on the horizon. Meanwhile, the statistically solid Muslim regency of Banyuwangi stood out as the site of the tightest electoral margin— 45.5 percent to 43.9 percent—in East Java between the most popular Islamic parties, PKB (41.9 percent) and PPP (3.5 percent), on the one hand, and the major ecumenical parties, PDIP (32.7 percent) and Golkar (11.1 percent), on the other.[179] All the sites of large-scale religious violence in 1998–2001, in other words, were localities in which high levels of electoral uncertainty prevailed.

In such settings, increasing apprehensions about the numerical and electoral strength of statistical religious others thus combined with abiding anxieties about the weakness and fragmentation internal to religious communities themselves. The tensions observed by anthropologists along the upland fringes of Nahdlatul Ulama's strongholds in East Java in the late 1990s, for example, owed as much to the challenges from below represented by rival local sources of spiritual authority—healers, Javanist groups, shrine-based cults—as they did to conspiracies from above among modernist Muslims entrenched in the state in Jakarta. Likewise, the established positions of GKST and Al-Khaira'at in Poso were increasingly threatened over the years, not only by competition across the official religious divide but by rising ethnic, associational, and denominational diversity and fragmentation within their respective realms of pastoral care. Similarly, the ecclesiastical authority of their counterparts in Maluku ran up against the enduring influence of *adat* and aristocratic lineage, the proselytizing efforts of outside missionaries (evangelical Protestant, Catholic, and Muslim), and the destabilizing effects of immigration.

Meanwhile, by the turn of the twenty-first century, the attractive powers of modern secular education, the national state, and the market had drawn increasing numbers of Christians and Muslims into their orbit, encouraging discernible trends toward cultural, linguistic, organizational, and social homogenization across the religious divide. These trends were perhaps most visible in everyday life in Maluku's provincial capital city of Ambon, where Protestant and Muslim neighborhoods and houses of worship were often found in close proximity (as reports of the violence of early 1999 make clear), and where more and more Ambonese and migrants of different faiths mingled in the streets, the schools, the shops, and the offices of government with every passing year. If in the 1955 elections the vast majority of voters in Poso and Maluku had backed sectarian political parties clearly identified with one or another religious faith—Masjumi for Muslims, Parkindo for Protestants—by the time of the elections of 1999 the avowedly ecumenical orientation of the two most popular parties (PDIP and Golkar) signaled the possibility of overriding, if not erasing, religious differences in the political realm.

In such settings, moreover, the local ecclesiastical establishments had come to assume quasi-statal and para-statal forms, their religious identities intimately bound up with associational, educational, economic, and political hierarchies. This pattern was perhaps less clearly or completely articulated in the East and West Javanese rural strongholds of Nahdlatul Ulama, which was well known for its rather decentralized, familial, and personalistic organizational structures, its relative distance from the modern state school system and other secular state institutions, and its disavowal of pretensions to represent all Muslims under the banner of Islam. In the more peripheral, less developed Outer Island localities such as Poso and Maluku, by contrast, this pattern was much more fully articulated—in part thanks to the relatively more modernized, rationalized, and capitalized structures of local Protestant churches; in part because of the greater importance of the offices and resources of the state. As the anthropologist P. M. Laksono wrote of the remote island town of Tual in Southeast Maluku district:

Civil servants are the backbone of urban society. By the end of the 1980s nearly all the rupiah flowing into the district came from civil service salaries. Almost no rupiah came in outside the government budget. Agriculture is just subsistence. There is practically no export—just a little copra and marine products. The big fishing trawlers that frequent Tual harbor are Taiwanese and pay their money to Jakarta. The whole of society depends on the state—even if only as a labourer at a school building site.[180]

In such localities, moreover, religious institutions and identities had from their inception been political in the sense of close identification with religiously segmented networks connected to the state. Lorraine Aragon observed of the Protestant-Muslim conflict in Poso, "This fight is not about religious doctrines or practices, but about the political economy of being Protestant (or Catholic) and Muslim."[181] Likewise, in Ambon and in other parts of Maluku, the political scientist Gerry van Klinken concluded,

> joining the Protestant or the Muslim community means being part of a network that not only worships God in a certain way but does practical things for its members—provides access to friends in powerful places, for example, or protection when things get tough. These networks extend up the social ladder to influential circles in Jakarta. And they extend downward to street level, where gangs of young men provide the protective muscle that an inefficient police force cannot provide.[182]

These distinctive features of the *timing* and *location* of the antiwitchcraft campaigns and interreligious pogroms of 1998–2001 help to explain both the *protagonists,* the *targets,* and the very *processes of mobilization* through which the violence unfolded. In contrast with the unarmed urban crowds that emerged and dispersed virtually overnight in response to incidents involving institutions of religious learning and worship in the provincial town riots of 1995–97, these later pogroms were marked by distinctly different forms of agency and, it is worth noting, religiosity. Thus in the killings of accused *dukun santet* in the villages of rural East and West Java in 1998–99, for example, crudely armed groups of local youths launched coordinated attacks, but, as James Siegel has pointed out, even after several months of such killings, the victims remained *local* individuals, and the perpetrators continued to act not in the name of Islam, or of Nahdlatul Ulama, or even of "the village" but instead as purely *local* murderous mobs (*massa*):

In a village, some took action against a witch. Each group that did so acted separately and one by one. . . . The witch hunts were the actions of clusters of unselfconscious young men who not only did not, but in my opinion could not, act "in the name of." They lacked the ability to see themselves in assumed identities such as "Christian" or "Muslim" at the moment of the attacks.[183]

By contrast, in Poso, Ambon, and various parts of Maluku and Maluku Utara, the perpetrators of violence had the discursive means of identifying themselves and their victims—collectively—along clear official religious lines. Yet what is so striking in the characters and events at the outset of the pogroms in those localities is the prominence of seemingly "secular" disputes between "secular" groups in "secular" settings—turf wars between urban youth gangs around bus terminals, competition between politicians over state offices, the inauguration of a new district or province—and the apparent absence of churches, mosques, and religious schools from the original violence. Rather than students from religious schools, neighborhood and village youth gangs—defined and divided along religious lines and connected to the religiously segmented local networks of politicians, civil servants, retired and active military and police officers, and businessmen—quickly emerged as the foot soldiers in the interreligious policing and warfare that these networks increasingly organized and equipped along paramilitary lines in the towns and villages of Poso, Maluku, and Maluku Utara.

Early on in these pogroms, churches and mosques came to function as command and communications posts, and as the source of networks for the accumulation and dissemination of (dis)information, weapons, and explosives, as is suggested by the range of accusations against clerics affiliated with Al-Khaira'at, GKST, GMIH, and GPM during this period. This devaluation of the specifically spiritual content of religion was also evident in the early reversion to red and white headbands and other items of clothing to distinguish the opposing sides, and the tendency to use "color war" terms of reference—and other equally profane lingo—instead of a more religiously coded idiom. The very need for such markers in Poso and Maluku further highlighted the anxieties about religious identity, as did the reported prominence of recent converts, refugees, and other outsiders in the violence—perhaps best exemplified by the leading role of the Flores-born Catholic gangster in the massacre of Muslim villagers in Poso in late May 2000.[184]

In all these settings, the unfolding of religious violence produced similar local effects and followed similar patterns of internal transformation. In

Banyuwangi, southern Malang, and other areas of rural Java, for example, the local killings of suspected local *dukun santet* in 1998–99 were in due course appropriated by the leaders of Nahdlatul Ulama as a campaign against the organization and gradually brought to a halt with the reassertion of NU's authority. Suspected *dukun santet* were administered *sumpah pocong* by local *kyai,* and neighborhood watch groups (*ronda*) were strengthened with the deployment of NU youth and martial arts militia (Ansor and Banser) to various towns and villages. In Poso, Ambon, and other parts of Maluku and Maluku Utara, moreover, the pogroms of 1999–2001 effected the spatial segregation and simplification of Christian-Muslim communities seen in other sites of interreligious violence elsewhere around the world, producing what Allen Feldman described as an "interlocking binary spatial grid and inside/outside polarities," with the "proliferation of interfaces, the barricading, and the influx of refugee populations" reorganizing towns and villages into a highly militarized and religiously coded topography.[185]

Such processes were accompanied—and expedited—by the reconstitution of the two opposing religious communities into militarized hierarchies organized and equipped for interfaith warfare. In a pattern reminiscent of shifts observed in sites of sectarian violence elsewhere in the world, the years 1999–2001 in Poso, Maluku, and Maluku Utara thus saw a shift from more spontaneous rampages by crudely armed crowds to more carefully coordinated, large-scale attacks by heavily armed paramilitary groups, and then a reversion to sporadic bombings, drive-by shootings, and quick raids and arson attacks across the well-established and tightly guarded religious divide.[186]

Thus by the end of 2001, the large-scale collective violence between Protestants and Muslims of the preceding few years had run its course and subsided into small-scale disturbances to the formal and informal settlements that had crystallized in these religiously divided localities. In large measure, the fading of pogroms followed from the internal transformation of the violence itself: the successes of "cleansing" worked to (re)establish religious boundaries and hierarchies and thus greatly reduce the uncertainties and anxieties so evident in 1998–99. In no small measure, moreover, the disappearance of pogroms from Poso, Maluku, and Maluku Utara by late 2001 reflected the imposition of local constraints on interreligious violence from without and above, as seen in the the deployment of thousands of police and army troops to these localities, the signing of formal peace accords, and the religiously coded gerrymandering of new districts and provinces. By late 2001, after all, the weak and vulnerable administration of President Abdurrahman Wahid had been ousted and replaced by one headed by Megawati Soekarnoputri, whose leadership of the decidedly ecumenical PDIP and strong position in the national parliament and in the military establishment guaranteed stronger protection for non-Muslims throughout Indonesia.

This national constellation combined with shifts in the international arena in the aftermath of the September 11, 2001, attacks on New York and Washington, D.C., to spell the forced eviction of Laskar Jihad from Poso, Maluku, and Maluku Utara and its effective elimination in due course. But as the formation of that paramilitary group had already fore-shadowed in early 2000, the gradual disappearance of Christian-Muslim pogroms in the provinces and the effective dislodging of Islam from state power in Jakarta also prefigured the emergence of new forms of religious violence in Indonesia, under the distinctive sign of jihad.

7

Jihad and Religious Violence in Indonesia, 1995–2005

In contrast with the riots and pogroms observed in Indonesia in the preceding decade, the turn of the twenty-first century witnessed a discernible shift to a new form of religious violence in the country, one identified with the sign of jihad. This jihad, in the narrow sense of the term, assumed the form of armed paramilitary assaults on Christian neighborhoods and villages in Maluku and Poso in 2000–2001, and terrorist bombings elsewhere in the country from 2000 through 2004. These new forms of religious violence in Indonesia differed markedly from preceding patterns in at least three ways. First of all, they lacked the seemingly more spontaneous, sporadic, and popular character of the riots of 1995–97 and the pogroms of 1998–2000 with their attacks by crudely armed crowds on buildings, neighborhoods, and villages; these were replaced by completely premeditated, carefully planned and coordinated activities by small groups of heavily armed, trained, full-time *jihadi* fighters and conspirators. Not only the identity of the perpetrators but also the very nature of the agency associated with the violence had clearly changed.

Second, the pattern shifted from local forces and focuses of violence to ones of national and international scale. In the riots of 1995–97 and the pogroms of 1998–2000, the violence was directed by townspeople against other townspeople, villagers against other villagers, sometimes even neighbors against neighbors. In the paramilitary activities of armed groups operating in Maluku and Poso, by contrast, recruits from Java and other parts of the Indonesian archipelago were mobilized for a broader, arguably more national, struggle across the religious divide. In the explosions that punctuated the years from 2000 through 2004, moreover, the targets shifted

196

from the local Christian churches bombed on Christmas Eve 2000 to sites of foreign and distinctly Western influence and intrusiveness, such as night-clubs and hotels. These bombings were also carried out by full-time *jihadi* activists who counted Malaysians and other foreign nationals among their numbers, and whose international orbit included Muslim rebel–controlled zones of the southern Philippines, safe havens in Malaysia and Thailand, and training camps in Afghanistan and Pakistan.

Third, the pattern shifted to one in which the purveyors of religious vi-olence appeared to be exclusively Muslim in faith and Islamist in intention, and in which Protestants, Catholics, and other non-Muslims seemed to fig-ure solely as targets and victims. The religious riots of 1995–97, by con-trast, had included a series of attacks by Catholic crowds on Muslim mosques and shops in Eastern Indonesian areas such as Flores and the In-donesian-occupied territory of East Timor. In the religious pogroms of 1998–2000, moreover, some of the most egregious instances of large-scale collective violence were perpetrated by Christians against Muslims and claimed large numbers of victims of both faiths. But the activities of heav-ily armed and trained extralocal paramilitary groups in Maluku and Poso in 2000–2001, and the detonation of bombs in various locations in 2000–2004, were undertaken solely by Muslims acting under an Islamist banner.

To be sure, considerable financial and logistical assistance was provided to armed Christian groups in Maluku and Poso by Christian businessmen, military officers (retired and active), and politicians in Jakarta and else-where in Indonesia, and Protestant and Catholic churches in Western Eu-rope and North America also offered various forms of support. But these Christian forces, like the avowedly neutral agencies of the Indonesian state, were careful to distance themselves from acts of violence against Muslims and to define their involvement in terms of helping to defend vulnerable mi-nority communities under threat. Against the rallying cry for jihad among Muslims in Indonesia and beyond, no corresponding call for a new set of Crusades was openly voiced by Christian leaders in the archipelago or else-where, no supralocal paramilitary groups were recruited and dispatched to Maluku or Poso, and no bombing campaign against mosques around the country or Muslim embassies in Jakarta came to pass.

In short, the turn of the twenty-first century witnessed a notable nar-rowing of religious violence in Indonesia. This narrowing was evident in the decline—rather than escalation—of interfaith violence in religiously di-vided localities around the archipelago, and in the diminishing scale and frequency of violent crowd actions in such settings. Religious violence, it became clear, was increasingly the preserve of small numbers of full-time specialists in isolated pockets, rather than of entire communities of faith across the country. Neither the various local contests for *bupati, walikota,* and *gubernur,* nor the creation of new regencies, cities, and provinces after 1999, nor the parliamentary and presidential elections of 2004 gave rise to new waves of large-scale collective violence across the religious divide.[1] Aside from sporadic bombings, drive-by shootings, and nighttime attacks that peaked as the 2004 national elections approached, even Maluku and Poso remained free of the wholesale pogroms of the turn of the century.[2]

Instead, the religious violence that unfolded in the first five years of the new millennium in Indonesia assumed two forms associated with the pursuit of jihad, in the narrowest and most murderous sense of the term. First of all, the period beginning in early 2000 witnessed the formation and deployment of armed paramilitary groups in areas of Maluku and, by mid-2001, in the troubled Central Sulawesi regency of Poso. In Maluku Utara, for example, small groups of nonlocal Muslim fighters began to arrive in late January 2000, a few weeks after the massacre of Muslim villagers in Tobelo and the other atrocities by armed Christian groups in Maluku in December 1999 and early January 2000 (see chapter 6). As of April 2000, moreover, as many as 2,000 armed Muslim fighters affiliated with Laskar Jihad had appeared in Ambon, following weeks of paramilitary training in Bogor, West Java.[3] They rapidly asserted leadership over local armed Muslim forces and initiated a new wave of attacks on Christian areas. By June and July of that year, groups of such fighters, armed with automatic weapons and sophisticated radio communications equipment, had launched coordinated assaults on isolated or otherwise vulnerable Protestant villages in Maluku Utara, on Ambon island, and, by late 2000, on the neighboring island of Seram.[4] These attacks, which left hundreds of casualties, appeared to enjoy the active support of certain elements in the armed forces. Yet by the end of 2000, efforts to restrain and repel Laskar Jihad by less sympathetic elements in the armed forces were well under way, led first by a Yon Gab (Joint Battalion) under the command of a Balinese Hindu general, and later by KOPASSUS (Special Forces) troops. These efforts, which included well-publicized incidents of torture and summary executions of Laskar Jihad members, contributed to a marked decline in Muslim violence against Protestant neighborhoods and villages in Maluku.[5]

Meanwhile, a somewhat similar pattern was observed in Central Sulawesi, where small numbers of armed Muslim fighters—known as Laskar Jundullah—were sent first by Islamic groups in the South Sulawesi capital of Makassar, and in Jakarta in the months following the June 2000 massacre of more than 100 Muslim villagers in Poso. By July 2001, moreover, hundreds of armed Muslim fighters affiliated with Laskar Jihad had begun to arrive in the wake of renewed large-scale attacks by armed Christian

Hundreds of members of Laskar Jihad wave swords and shout slogans during public rally in Jakarta in April 2000 (AP)

forces on Muslim villagers in Poso. At first, these self-styled *mujahidin* set
up guard posts in critical areas along the borders between Muslim and
Christian neighborhods and villages, while moving to train and reorganize
local armed Muslim groups. By late November 2001, Laskar Jihad forces
had initiated large-scale assaults on Christian neighborhoods and villages
in Poso, leading to widespread anticipation of an attack on the Protestant
town of Tentena and a rising national and international outcry. By early
December, however, a major infusion of army troops had brought this campaign to a halt and facilitated the imposition of a peace accord.[6]

By the end of 2001, then, Laskar Jihad had been largely defanged, driven
out of the two main sites of interreligious violence in the country, and
threatened with irrelevance or extinction. Laskar Jihad next launched a
campaign in late 2001 against gambling and prostitution during Ramadan
in the East Javanese town of Ngawi, responding to public protests with various forms of intimidation. Following the alleged abduction of a local PDIP
politician by Laskar Jihad members, a crowd of PDIP supporters stormed
the offices of a local Islamic organization that was hosting Laskar Jihad in
Ngawi. Local police forces, which had stood by during the PDIP goons' attack, arrested dozens of Laskar Jihad members and sent them off to

Surabaya for weeks of detention in jail.[7] By May 2002, the head of the organization, Ja'far Umar Thalib, was arrested in connection with the murder of one of his own members, who had been stoned to death for committing adultery.[8] In October of the same year, the group was formally disbanded.[9]

This pattern of paramilitary mobilization and forced demobilization in 2000–2002 was accompanied, and extended, by a second form of violence: a bombing campaign that claimed hundreds of lives in Jakarta and elsewhere in the archipelago from 2000 through 2004.[10] Already in late April 1999, just a few short weeks before the parliamentary elections of that year, a bomb exploded late one night in an office inside the complex of the Istiqlal Mosque in Jakarta, a site identified with the accommodation between Islam and secular nationalist forces in Indonesia (*istiqlal* is Arabic for Independence), and known to have been designed by a Protestant architect. The mosque, said to be the largest in Southeast Asia, was viewed by some knowledgeable Islamists as a sacrilegious symbol of Islam's subordination to secular state power and, at the same time, seen by a broader audience of Muslims as one of the premier national sites of Indonesian Islam. The Istiqlal Mosque was thus both a legitimate object of *jihadi* violence and a target whose partial destruction and desecration could be blamed on non-Muslims and thereby used to heighten interreligious tensions and Islamic solidarities on the eve of Indonesia's first free and competitive elections since 1955.[11]

By the end of 2000, moreover, this early bombing experiment had been resumed with a Christmas Eve series of deadly explosions at nearly forty different churches around the Indonesian archipelago. The bombs, which left 19 dead and more than 100 wounded, exploded in churches in cities from Sumatra to Jakarta, Bandung, and other towns on Java, to Mataram on Lombok.[12] During 2001, a series of subsequent bombs and bomb threats targeted a handful of individual churches around the country.

But in 2002 the targets of such explosions shifted from Indonesian Christian churches to sites of foreign—and largely Western—influence and intrusions of a seemingly more secular nature. In October 2002, car bombs exploded at two nightclubs catering to foreign tourists in a resort area on Bali, an island known for the Hindu faith and strong PDIP allegiances of its inhabitants. Accompanied by several other small explosions, the bombs killed nearly 200 people, the majority of whom were young Australian tourists.[13] These explosions were followed by the—apparently suicide—car bombing of the American-owned Marriott Hotel in Jakarta, reportedly a favorite U.S. Embassy staff haunt, which left 10 dead and 150-plus wounded in August 2003.[14] A year later, in September 2004, a second apparent suicide car bomb attack on the Australian Embassy in Jakarta left at least nine casualties and manifold injuries and damages in its wake.[15] This pattern of single annual detonations persisted into 2005: October of that year witnessed a second attack in Bali, with bombs in three restaurants killing more than thirty people.[16] These explosions, along with less well-publicized bomb attacks on Philippine targets (the ambassador's residence in Jakarta in August 2000, the consulate in Manado in October 2002), represented a discernible change in the form, frequency, and focus of religious violence in Indonesia, from the more localized and mobilizational pattern of preceding years.

Protagonists: Jihadist Networks, Persis, and Al-Irshad

The turn of the twenty-first century also witnessed a corresponding transformation in the protagonists—that is, the perpetrators—of religious violence in Indonesia. In the riots of 1995–97, after all, the key catalytic role had been played by local boys enrolled in Islamic schools and affiliated with Islamic students' associations in the very towns and cities where the disturbances occurred. Likewise, in the pogroms of 1998–2000 the murderous attacks on neighborhoods and villages in Maluku and Poso had been undertaken by local youths armed and mobilized by local networks of politicians, civil servants, active and retired military and police officers, businessmen, gangsters, and clerics. In the paramilitary activities in Maluku and Poso of 2000–2001 and the bombing campaign of 2000–2005, by contrast, broader supralocal networks with national and transnational affiliations were mobilized for religious violence.

This shift had already become apparent in the paramilitary mobilization associated with Laskar Jihad that began in early 2000. The formation of Laskar Jihad was announced in a massive rally in the Central Javanese city of Solo in April of that year, with a certain Ja'far Umar Thalib as its supreme leader. In early 1998, Thalib had established an organization known as Forum Komunikasi Ahlusunnah wal-Jama'ah (FKAWJ), or Communications Forum of the Sunna and the Community of the Prophet, which was based outside Yogyakarta, Solo's rival as a center of aristocratic lineage and culture in Central Java. The FKAWJ included a recently founded *pesantren* and surrounding "intentional community" and incorporated into its orbit Muslim students from the cluster of universities in Yogyakarta, Solo, and other towns and cities of the province. By the time of the formation, paramilitary training, and deployment of Laskar Jihad troops in early 2000, FKAWJ's broader flock would exceed 40,000 with affiliated internet sites and publications reaching many more potential sympathizers.[17]

Meanwhile, the various bombings of 2000–2004 were attributed to another Central Java–based Islamic school network, the Pesantren Al-Mukmin in Ngruki, Sukoharjo, on the outskirts of the city of Solo. Among those arrested, detained, and in due course convicted for the bombings were a number of alumni of the Ngruki *pesantren* and of other *pesantren* and *halaqah* (discussion groups) founded by Ngruki graduates around the country, as well as former students of a *pesantren* operated in Malaysia by the Ngruki school's founders while they were in forced exile from the mid-1980s through the late 1990s.[18] Indeed, in August 2000, K.H. Abu Bakar Ba'asyir, the surviving founder of the Ngruki *pesantren*, was elected to head the Majelis Mujahidin Indonesia (MMI), or Council of Indonesian Mujahidin, at the founding congress of that organization in Yogyakarta.[19] In subsequent years, Ba'asyir was accused of serving as the spiritual—if not operational—leader of what American, Australian, Indonesian, Malaysian, Philippine, and Singaporean intelligence agencies identified as Jemaah Islamiyah,[20] a clandestine network of Ngruki graduates and other Islamist activists held responsible for undertaking the various bombings of 2000–2004.[21]

In contrast with the religious identities, affiliations, and institutional trappings associated with the protagonists of the riots of 1995–97 and the pogroms of 1998–2000, the evident centrality of FKAWJ and Pesantren Ngruki to the activities of Laskar Jihad and Jemaah Islamiyah, respectively, marked the purveyors of jihad in two ways. First of all, at their core, the two hubs of jihadist recruitment and indoctrination were located in the heartland of Central Java, a region long described by anthropologists and other observers as home to Islamic practices and solidarities inflected by Javanism, mysticism, syncretism, and pre-Islamic Hindu-Buddhist influences.[22] The province had been a stronghold of the PKI in the 1950s and early 1960s, and it had served as a major source of votes for the ecumenical, secular nationalist PDIP in the 1999 elections. Based on the outskirts of Yogyakarta and Solo, respectively, the FKAWJ and Pesantren Ngruki had also emerged in the shadow of the rival centers of Javanese aristocratic court culture—and of the prominent secular universities—which loomed so large in both cities.[23] Like those who established Muhammadiyah in Yogyakarta and Sarekat Islam in Solo in the 1910s, the founders and followers of FKAWJ and the *Pesantren* Ngruki in more recent years launched their proselytizing efforts in the least puritanical, least pious Muslim area of Indonesia, and in the face of widespread indifference, skepticism, and hostility from their supposed coreligionists.[24] Indeed, the vast majority of Laskar Jihad recruits interviewed for one study came from remote Central Javanese villages and families whose understandings and practices of Islam were fully at odds with those espoused by the group. [25]

Second and more specifically, both the FKAWJ and Pesantren Ngruki traced their origins and affiliations to the educational and associational umbrellas of Al-Irsyad and Persatuan Islam (called Persis), organizations closely identified with Indonesia's Hadhrami Arab immigrant minority and with the strictest interpretations and applications of Islam in the archipelago. Ja'far Umar Thalib, for example, the head of FKAWJ and Laskar Jihad, was himself the son of a Hadhrami immigrant and Al-Irsyad activist, had attended the Persatuan Islam school in Bangil, East Java, and then the Saudi Arabian–sponsored Institute for Islamic and Arabic Studies in Jakarta, where he was a leader of the student organization affiliated with Al-Irsyad. Similarly, Ba'asyir, along with his cofounder of the Pesantren Ngruki, Abdullah Sungkar, was the son of a Hadhrami immigrant and had graduated from Universitas Al-Irsyad. The curriculum of the Ngruki *pesantren* was likewise said to draw heavily on the system of learning established in Persatuan Islam's leading schools.[26] Despite evident differences in tactics (paramilitary activities versus clandestine bombings) and in ideological goals (Islamization of Indonesian society versus the establishment of Islamic law, state, and caliphate), the two networks clearly shared a common ancestry in Al-Irsyad and Persatuan Islam.[27]

Those two organizations had been founded in the early twentieth century by Muslims of Hadhrami Arab descent and by others influenced by the teachings of modernist Islamic scholars in the Middle East. From their inception, Al-Irsyad and Persis schools placed great emphasis on the study of Arabic and, far more than the more Westernized *madrasah* of Muhammadiyah, prepared their students for higher education in centers of Islamic learning far from the Indonesian archipelago. In their religious teachings and practices, Al-Irsyad and Persis were also more openly and stridently antagonistic toward the influence of Christianity in the archipelago and toward the accretions of local customs, the worship of saints and shrines, and the mysticism of Sufis and Javanists alike.[28] As Howard Federspiel noted with regard to Persatuan Islam, its reputation "lay less with its organizational accomplishments in education, buildings or organization, than it did with the creation of an esprit de corps, a distinctive character, an outlook and an ideology that saw Islam as the very center of life with all matters directly dependent on that conviction."[29]

Although the founders and first students of Al-Irsyad and, to a lesser extent, Persis were predominantly drawn from among the immigrant

Hadhrami Arab community in the Indies, by the 1930s the vast majority of students were, by assimilation or ancestry, Indonesians. Yet the fact that these schools fed into an overseas education network promoted a "sense of separateness" and an "outward orientation, back to the Middle East," encouraging students to understand "that their center was not 'here' in the Indies, but rather 'there' in the heartland of the Arab world."[30] Thus Al-Irsyad and Persis activists were understandably ambivalent toward Indonesian nationalism, supporting the struggle against Dutch colonial rule on, the one hand, but opposing the construction of a secular nation-state in its stead, on the other. Although they contributed their energies to the *Revolusi* that led to Indonesian independence in 1945–49, many members of these groups were understandably dissatisfied with the place granted to Islam in the new nation-state and its constitutional democracy; they showed sympathy for the Darul Islam rebellion in areas such as West Java, South Sulawesi, South Kalimantan, and Aceh in the 1950s and early 1960s. A leading figure in Persis, Mohammad Natsir, headed the modernist Islamic party Masjumi and briefly served as prime minister in the early 1950s. But Masjumi's involvement in the CIA-backed regional rebellions of 1957–59 led to the forced dissolution of the party in 1960 and the punishment or political neutralization of many of its members.

Although Al-Irsyad and Persis thus entered the 1960s on the very fringes of Indonesian politics, their enduring transnational linkages, combined with the sociological and political trends of the time, allowed their networks of schools—and their aspirations for Islam in Indonesia—to survive, grow, and prosper in subsequent decades. Masjumi, banned for its role in supporting regional rebellions, by the 1960s could no longer provide an umbrella of state patronage and protection as it had in the early years after independence. So despite their contributions to the anti-Communist campaigns of the 1965–66, activists from these circles found themselves utterly marginalized and at times actively persecuted by the seemingly Christian-dominated New Order state. In this context, Al-Irsyad and Persis activists devoted themselves to the crucial tasks of religious schooling and proselytization. Their efforts were nurtured by DDII, the umbrella group founded by Mohammad Natsir and other former Masjumi leaders in 1967, which drew on donations from Saudi Arabian and other foreign sponsors as well as those from sympathetic Indonesian professionals, businessmen, and government officials. As industrialization and urbanization in the 1970s and 1980s brought millions of Muslim migrants to Jakarta and other major Indonesian cities, DDII established hundreds of *pesantren* and *madrasah* and constructed thousands of mosques in an attempt to capture the hearts and minds of this growing new constituency. It was in this context that Abu Bakar Ba'asyir, a former activist in the Masjumi-linked Gerakan Pemuda Islam Indonesia (Indonesian Islamic Youth Movement) in the early-mid 1960s, and the host of a talk show on a DDII-sponsored Solo radio station eventually banned by the government, helped to found the Pesantren Al-Mukmin in Ngruki, Sukoharjo, in the early 1970s.

DDII was especially successful in its *dakwah* activities in the campus mosques of state universities in major Indonesian cities, including Institut Teknologi Bandung, Institut Pertanian Bogor, Universitas Gadjah Mada in Yogyakarta, Universitas Airlangga in Surabaya, and Universitas Indonesia in Jakarta.[31] Thanks to its access to scholarships offered by Saudi-sponsored and other international Islamic organizations, Dewan Dakwah was also able to facilitate study in the Middle East, with Laskar Jihad founder Ja'far Umar Thalib just one among the many winners of DDII scholarships for Islamic schooling in Saudi Arabia and Pakistan.

By the 1990s, moreover, with the demise of Benny Murdani and the rise of Habibie and ICMI, well-connected Dewan Dakwah activists enjoyed new freedom to preach and to publish, as well as unprecedented access to state patronage and support. Through their inclusion in Habibie's vast patronage empire, such activists extended their influence among government-funded students pursuing postgraduate technological and scientific degrees in Europe and North America, and among the ranks of university lecturers, journalists, publishers, and other "professional Muslims" in Indonesia. By the turn of the twenty-first century, Dewan Dakwah had established a nationwide network of affiliated schools, mosques, organizations, and activists. For many years, the urban middle-class constituency of Persis and Al-Irsyad, the high levels of educational achievement with which their schools were identified, and the relative wealth of the small Hadhrami immigrant merchant elite had given these associations influence far beyond their small numbers, as amply evident in Natsir's leadership of Masjumi in the 1950s. These advantages were all the more evident in the heyday of ICMI and Habibie in the 1990s, as seen in the prominence of Al-Irsyad luminary Fuad Bawazier and of various DDII-affiliated figures during this period.[32] But after years of sponsoring new mosques and schools around the archipelago, this network had also extended its influence somewhat further down the social scale, especially among more modest recent migrants to the growing cities and towns of the country.[33]

It was a network clearly crucial for the promotion of jihad in the first years of the new century. DDII's monthly magazine, *Media Dakwah*, and similar publications such as *Sabili* and *Suara Hidayatullah*, drew attention to atrocities against Muslims in Maluku and Poso, attacked the government in Jakarta for its complacency and complicity, and advertised—if not openly advocated—violent mobilization against Christians in these sites of interreligious violence.[34] Moreover, DDII activists and affiliates in various Muslim parties worked to raise money to support Muslim communities—and Muslim fighters—in Maluku and Poso, and in some cases helped to organize the smuggling of weapons and the insertion of trained jihadists into these areas.[35]

Meanwhile, the longer history of DDII support for the likes of the Ngruki network became evident with the identification of the jihadists accused of the bombings of 2000–2004. For among the Ngruki alumni and other activists named as the bombers were some who had spent time—as had Ja'far Umar Thalib of Laskar Jihad—in the 1980s and early 1990s in Afghanistan and in training camps for *mujahidin* in Pakistan along the Afghan border. The Saudi-sponsored Muslim World League (Rabitat al-'Alam al-Islami), which DDII founder Mohammad Natsir long formally served as a prominent member, funded the recruitment of *mujahidin* from throughout the Muslim world to join in the struggle against the Soviet occupation of Afghanistan, and a small number of Indonesians, Malaysians, and Muslim Filipinos joined their ranks over the course of the 1980s. These Southeast Asian *mujahidin* joined Arab volunteers largely recruited by the Muslim Brotherhood (in Egypt) and other, more radical Islamist groups in camps run by the Afghan leader Abdul Rasul Sayyaf, who enjoyed enormous financial and logistical support from the Saudi religious establishment and the Saudi and Pakistani intelligence services but had virtually no social or political base of his own in his country.[36] In the early 1990s, as various Afghan commanders competed for control, the U.S. government began to apply pressure on Saudi Arabia and Pakistan to withdraw support from Sayyaf and his largely non-Afghan *mujahidin,* whose broader *jihadi* orientation and close collaboration with the likes of Osama bin Laden were well established.[37] But small numbers of Indonesians continued to come to Afghanistan for training well into the 1990s. Thus the narrow stream of Indonesian recruits who came to train at the camps associated with Sayyaf and bin Laden flowed from the broader currents of Al-Irsyad, Persatuan Islam, and DDII.[38]

The Indonesian lineages of the *jihadi* groups engaged in paramilitary activities in Maluku and Poso in 2000–2001 and the bombing campaign of 2000–2004 were clearly more important than their alleged international affiliations with the global terrorist network of Al-Qaeda. Ja'far Umar Thalib, the head of FKAWJ and Laskar Jihad, after all, distinguished himself within Indonesian Islamist circles as a harsh public critic of Osama bin Laden and Al-Qaeda.[39] More important, perhaps, the early identification of the bombing campaign of 2000–2004 with the coherent terrorist organization named Jemaah Islamiyah, led by K.H. Abu Bakar Ba'asyir and staffed by Indonesian *mujahidin* returning from Afghanistan, was gradually undermined by journalistic reportage and investigative research. The very use of the term "Jemaah Islamiyah," it was revealed, appeared to have originated with Indonesian government officials concerned to justify—legally and politically—prosecution of members of an identifiable organization, and as with "Al-Qaeda" it is not entirely clear at what point and to what extent those ostensibly participating in this putative body came to use the term among themselves.[40] The assiduous but unsuccessful efforts by Indonesian government officials to prove that Ba'asyir was directly engaged in the planning and perpetration of the bombings likewise gave way to increasing doubts as to his effective operational involvement, much less leadership role, in clandestine terrorist activities. In the place of the clear caricature of a tightly organized and disciplined Al-Qaeda franchise outlet, a much hazier, messier picture of a loosely organized network of like-minded activists, acting together on an ad hoc basis, came into view.

Indeed, in-depth research published in the wake of the bombings has suggested that from its inception Jemaah Islamiyah was part and parcel of a broader Islamist network in Indonesia, one that included the veterans of the Darul Islam rebellion of the 1950s and early 1960s as well as some of their children.[41] Revealingly, the founding congress of the MMI that elected Ba'asyir as its *amir* was held August 5–7, 2000, to commemorate the anniversary of the proclamation of an Islamic State of Indonesia (Negara Islam Indonesia) by Darul Islam leader Sekarmadji Maridjan Kartosoewirjo on August 7, 1949. More important, perhaps, many of the proverbial foot soldiers of the bombing campaign of 2000–2004—"the people who drive the cars, survey targets, deliver the bombs, and most often risk arrest, physical injury, or death"—were evidently recruited from *pesantren* founded or led by teachers tied to the Darul Islam movement.[42] Even the more senior figures in this terrorist network and the supposedly tight-knit group of cadres who trained and fought together in *jihadi* camps in Afghanistan in the 1980s and early 1990s—or in the southern Philippines in subsequent years—were drawn from families and schools closely associated with Darul Islam or, like the founders of the Ngruki *pesantren,* incorporated into the broader family of Darul Islam veterans over the course of the Suharto era.[43] Yet the remnants of the Darul Islam movement that survived the defeat of its various armed regional insurgencies in the 1950s and early 1960s were characterized by notable factionalism, a pattern that persisted through the long Suharto years and well into the twenty-first century. Indeed, the very years of the bombing campaign (2000–2004) witnessed the irruption of a series of controversies involving Darul Islam activists publicly trading charges of sectarianism, co-optation, and betrayal of the cause.[44]

Such controversies also served as reminders of the well-established pattern of Indonesian government infiltration of the Darul Islam movement, and of the accumulated evidence, both documentary and circumstantial, suggesting government foreknowledge or involvement in the *jihadi* activities of 2000–2004. The complicity of elements of the Indonesian Armed Forces in the training, deployment, and mobilization of Laskar Jihad in Maluku and Poso in 2000–2001 was noted by many contemporary observers. But the historical record of links between the Indonesian intelligence apparatus and clandestine *jihadi* networks is well established and dates back to the early Suharto era. Already in the middle to late 1960s, cooperation between the Suharto regime and previously marginalized Islamist groups was evident in the early phases of the overthrow of Soekarno and the extermination of the PKI. In the lead-up to the first New Order elections of 1971, moreover, Suharto's close associate Ali Moertopo, then head of the notorious Opsus (Special Operations) outfit, worked to reassemble and mobilize the disparate remnants of the Darul Islam movement, providing patronage—and anti-Communist pep talks—in exchange for active participation in the campaign of Golkar, the pro-Suharto political machine, at the polls. Thus the resurrection of the Darul Islam movement in the 1970s and the subsequent emergence of the supposed terrorist group Komando Jihad later in the same decade have often been attributed to Moertopo.[45]

Less well known but of equal significance is the long history of intelligence surveillance and infiltration of the Ngruki network of K.H. Abu Bakar Ba'asyir. It was in the context of close monitoring of Pesantren Al-Mukmin in Ngruki, Sukoharjo, after all, that Ba'asyir and the school's co-founder, Abdullah Sungkar, had been arrested and imprisoned in the late 1970s, and in the wake of their flight into exile in Malaysia in 1985 (to avoid additional prison sentences), the caretakers of the *pesantren* agreed to allow the security service and its agents an active role in the management of the school.[46] In 1989, moreover, the members of an Islamic intentional community founded by Ngruki graduates in a remote village in the Sumatran province of Lampung were massacred by army troops led by a certain Colonel A. M. Hendropriyono.[47] In subsequent years, as he rose to positions of considerable prominence and power in Jakarta, Hendropriyono made assiduous efforts to achieve some kind of reconciliation with the survivors and family members of victims of this massacre, providing them with financial assistance, employment in his various businesses or placement in government posts, and even land for resettlement during his stint as minister for transmigration in the late 1990s.[48] Thus when Lieutenant General Hendropriyono (retired) assumed in 2001 the leadership of the Badan Intelijen Negara (BIN), or National Intelligence Agency, he had already cultivated a coterie of clients and informants from within the Ngruki network. It was against this backdrop that police investigators, journalists, and other researchers discovered numerous links (e.g., cell phone conversations) between Indonesian intelligence and army officers and some of the activists arrested and charged with the bombings of 2000–2004.[49]

In short, the very forms of identity and intentionality identified with the promotion of jihad in 2000–2004 differed markedly from those associated with the preceding periods of religious riots (1995–97) and pogroms (1998–2000). The paramilitary mobilization in Maluku and Poso, on the one hand, and the bombing campaign around the country, on the other, represented carefully planned and coordinated initiatives by small groups of full-time fighters and conspirators engaged in round-the-clock jihad. Thus at first glance, the identification of the perpetrators—the "whodunit" of investigative and prosecutorial work—would appear to suffice as an explanation for the violence of 2000–2004. Indeed, in contrast with the local affiliations of the rioters and pogromists of earlier years, the troops of Laskar Jihad and the bombers of Jemaah Islamiyah were distinguished by their association with Islamic organizations—Al-Irsyad, Persatuan Islam, and DDII—known for their strict puritanism, their strident anti-Christian, antisecular, and anti-Semitic rhetoric, and their strong transnational connections to Salafi and Wahhabi currents in Saudi Arabia and Pakistan, as well as to the global jihad of Osama bin Laden and Al-Qaeda in Afghanistan and beyond.

Yet aside from the lingering doubts suggested above, the fingering of these jihadists leaves essentially unanswered basic questions as to the timing and trajectory of their jihad. For the Persatuan Islam journal *Pembela Islam* (Defender of Islam) was already bewailing the weaknesses of Muslims in the face of a dynamic Christianity in the 1930s, and Dewan Dakwah activists were railing against *Kristenisasi* and the closet secularism of liberal, Western-educated or -influenced Muslim intellectuals throughout the 1990s. Yet at no point during these years did any of the thousands of students and graduates of Al-Irsyad and Persis schools in Indonesia take up arms or explosive materials, and indeed only a very small fraction within the broader family of such Islamic activists did so in the peak years of jihad in 2000–2004.[50] Even the attribution—and reduction—of this jihad to Al-Qaeda and its operatives, or, alternatively, to Indonesian intelligence and its agents provocateurs, leaves the crucial questions unanswered: Why no paramilitary mobilization or bombing campaign *before* 2000? Why these particular forms of so-called jihad? Why the rapid rise and fall of Laskar Jihad? Why the shift from Indonesian targets to foreign, Western ones? Finally, why instead of more religious violence in Indonesia, its apparent reduction by 2005 to a single annual explosion?

Timing: The Discursive, Sociological, and Political Context of Jihad

The answers to those questions lie in no small measure in the discursive, political, and sociological context of 2000–2004, and in the shifting position of Islam within this context. As already spelled out with reference to the riots of 1995–97 and the pogroms of 1998–2000, this book has argued that the modalities of religious violence in Indonesia—its timing, location, forms, targets, protagonists, and processes of mobilization—have been decisively shaped by the broad constellation of religious authority in the country and by the possibility of articulating claims to represent (in both senses of the term) Islam in the world's most populous majority-Muslim nation-state. This argument extends to the forms of so-called jihad observed in Indonesia in 2000–2004.

Indeed, the conjuncture that served as the backdrop to paramilitary mobilization in Maluku and Poso and bombings around the archipelago was one distinguished by a new configuration of religious authority and power in the country. In contrast with the preceding decade of steady ascendancy and rising assertiveness by forces associated with the promotion of Islam in the Indonesian state and the public sphere, the turn of the century saw the eclipse and evisceration of the Islamist project in the country, in a rather sudden and dramatic reversal of fortunes. This trend was already visible on the horizon with the inauguration of the Habibie administration in mid-1998, as it battled against forces within and beyond the state to contest its efforts to represent Islam and to reposition the faith in public life in Indonesia.

In the elections of June 1999, moreover, the fiction of a united Muslim population universally represented by Habibie and allied forces dissipated in fragmentation and factionalism among a welter of Islamic parties, and dissolved in the face of strong electoral showings by non-Islamist parties among Muslim and non-Muslim voters alike. Indeed, a clear plurality of the vote (34 percent) was won by Megawati Soekarnoputri's Indonesian Democratic Party of Struggle known for its Soekarnoist lineages, its secular-nationalist, ecumenical, and syncretist orientation, and its sizeable non-Muslim constituencies and membership. More than one-third of the members of parliament elected on the PDIP ticket were non-Muslims (mostly Protestants), and virtually none of its Muslim MPs claimed a background of Islamic education or associational activity.[51] By contrast, parties with Islamist agendas and affiliations—Partai Persatuan Pembangunan (United Development Party), Partai Bulan Bintang (Crescent Star Party), Partai Keadilan (Justice Party)—achieved less than 20 percent of the vote, with the Partai Amanat Nasional (National Mandate Party) of Muhammadiyah's Chairman Amien Rais winning 8 percent under an avowedly ecumenical banner and with token non-Muslims in its ranks. The universalistic claims made under the sign of Islam were fully revealed as partisan, particularistic, and rather poorly received even among the broad mass of the Muslim population.

Frank admission of defeat in the aftermath of the June 1999 elections was avoided only thanks to the peculiarities of Indonesia's inherited, early postauthoritarian system for indirect election of the president by the People's Consultative Assembly (MPR) in October of the same year. The group of Muslim parties known as the Central Axis (Poros Tengah) cobbled together a coalition in the MPR to defeat the candidacy of the PDIP chairwoman Megawati Soekarnoputri and to elect longtime Nahdlatul Ulama (NU) chairman and National Awakening Party (PKB) leader Abdurrahman Wahid as president instead. But Wahid was quick to turn on his erstwhile supporters, removing from his cabinet or otherwise marginalizing ministers associated with the various Muslim parties and centralizing power in the hands of close associates drawn from traditionalist NU circles (including family members) and from the ranks of the secularized, liberal Muslim and Christian groups with which he had long allied himself and NU. As a figure long associated with the promotion of religious tolerance, moreover, Wahid was especially concerned about the protection of Indonesia's minority faiths and extremely opposed to other Muslim leaders' efforts to rally public support for jihad in Maluku and Poso. Thus the same Central Axis parties' leaders who had publicly rejoiced at the election of a prominent Muslim figure to the presidency soon spoke in terms of Wahid's betrayal of their trust and support and began conspiring to effect the early demise of his presidency. In mid-2000 and again in mid-2001, these Muslim parties and other anti-Wahid forces used the occasion of the annual session of the MPR first to censure the president and then to compel his early removal from office.[52]

Thus the context for the onset of jihad in 2000 was one of disappointment if not despair with regard to the precipitous decline and ongoing reversal of Islam's gains in the 1990s. The country's new president and most prominent Muslim leader, after all, was no longer a champion of Islamicization but instead a representative of Indonesian Islam known to be comfortable and cooperative with Western liberal, Christian, Javanist, secular, and even Jewish elements in Indonesian society and beyond.[53] Outside the narrow realm of formal politics, moreover, the processes of democratization and decentralization unfolding since 1999 gave rise to manifold alternative interpellations—by spokesmen for *adat*, for aristocratic claims to traditional authority, for various ethnic identities and loyalties, for indigenous peoples, and for a variety of local and national causes—which crosscut and competed with the articulation of claims in the name of Islam.[54] Against this backdrop, the atrocities committed by armed Christian groups against Muslim communities in various parts of Maluku and North Maluku in the last week of December 1999 and the first week of 2000 signaled the apparent obliviousness and apathy of the Wahid administration, the mainstream media, and the broad mass of the Muslim population in the face of threats and indignities to Islam. It was thus not only to assist vulnerable coreligionists in areas of interfaith conflict but also to reassert and reawaken seemingly lapsed religious sensibilities and solidarities that the call for *jihad* was issued in the early months of 2000.[55] This call was met first with paramilitary mobilization in Maluku and then—on the first anniversary of the Christian attacks on Muslims in Ambon, Tobelo, and elsewhere of late 1999—with the Christmas Eve 2000 bombings of churches around the archipelago.

Even though this initial phase of jihad expanded to Poso in July 2001, conditions in Indonesia and beyond spelled its termination and transformation in subsequent months. Mid-2001 witnessed not only a massacre of Laskar Jihad troops in Ambon by the security forces but further defeats for Islam in Jakarta. The Central Axis parties had failed to prevent the election of the PDIP's Megawati Soekarnoputri to the vice presidency in 1999, and this position combined with the strength of her party's contingent in parliament and her close connections to elements in the military establishment to make her the eventual replacement for President Wahid in July 2001. Although the Central Axis had worked assiduously against a Megawati presidency in 1999, raising doubts as to her Muslim faith and about the suitability of a woman president in the light of Islamic doctrine, by mid-2001 the leaders of these parties were climbing on board the bandwagon that would bring her to the palace. Hamzah Haz, the Chairman of PPP, agreed to serve as Megawati's vice president; PBB leader Yusril Izha Mahendra stayed on as minister of justice in her administration; and representatives of PAN and PK accepted token seats in the new cabinet.[56]

This acquiescence in the elevation of Megawati to the presidency came at a considerable price. First of all, it served as a public acknowledgment of the real limits to Islamist advancement through parliamentary party politics. By 2001, after all, the various Islamic parties had essentially given up on their avowed efforts to insert key phrases about Islamic law into the constitution. Within each Islamic party, this pattern of co-optation and co-operation with the Megawati administration gave rise to considerable grumbling—and threats of rebellion—from less well-connected and ac-commodating elements: the popular *da'i* K.H. Zainuddin M.Z., for exam-ple, who created a new party among dissatisfied elements in PPP, and the self-proclaimed fundamentalist Ahmad Sumargono, a prominent activist in DDII and its close affiliate KISDI, who tried to challenge Mahendra's lead-ership of PBB.[57]

In addition, the co-optation of the various Muslim parties by 2001 al-lowed Megawati to pursue the kind of ecumenical, secular nationalist agenda with which the PDIP had long been identified, while offering scant protection to the Islamic activists who had mobilized with these parties' en-couragement—and with accompanying military protection—in the pre-ceding years of the Habibie and Wahid administrations. Thus the months following Megawati's ascension to the presidency witnessed the continua-tion and escalation of the crackdown on Laskar Jihad by the security forces, leading to its forced demobilization and virtual disappearance from Maluku and Poso by early 2002 in the wake of the peace accords imposed on these two areas, the arrest of Ja'far Umar Thalib in early May, and the disbanding of the group in October of the same year.

But the networks of Muslim politicians, bureaucrats, businessmen, cler-ics, and retired and active police and military officers who had mobilized to support their coreligionists in Maluku and Poso faced a broader cam-paign of government harassment and intimidation as well. Most prominent in this regard was the well-publicized arrest and imprisonment in Manila in March 2002 of three Indonesian Muslim activists on clearly trumped-up charges of smuggling explosives, a move allegedly made by the Philippine authorities at the urging of the new head of the National Intelligence Agency, (retired) Hendropriyono. Among the three activists was Tamsil Linrung, who served as national treasurer of both Amien Rais's party (PAN) and DDII as well as a leading figure in the DDII-sponsored group KOMPAK, which was active in its support of jihad in Maluku and Poso. Also arrested was Agus Dwikarna, deputy head of the South Sulawesi branch of PAN, fellow KOMPAK activist, member of Majelis Mujahidin Indonesia, leader of a South Sulawesi group calling for the implementation of Islamic law, and alleged founder of Laskar Jundullah, the group of armed Muslim fighters active in Poso.[58] Following arrests made in Malaysia, the Philippines, and Singapore in early 2002, moreover, accusations of in-volvement in terrorist activities led to the onset of police investigations and legal proceedings later the same year against the Ngruki *pesantren* co-founder and MMI leader K.H. Abu Bakar Ba'asyir.[59]

It was in this climate of decisive domestic and international developments that a bombing campaign against foreign, Western targets began to unfold in 2002. The inauguration and entrenchment of the Megawati administration in mid-2001 had spelled the decline and defeat, if not effective disappearance, of the Islamist project in national parliamentary politics, even as accompanying social trends worked to undermine efforts to strengthen religious solidarities among Muslims. Although the new government in Jakarta appeared to prioritize the promotion of Chinese business and the protection of Protestant communities—and PDIP politicians—in Maluku and Poso through peace accords, a crackdown on Laskar Jihad and other Muslim paramilitary forces, and religiously coded gerrymandering in these areas, the complicity of Muslim politicians and the complacency of the Muslim population at large were amply apparent.

Meanwhile, the onset of the "Global War on Terror" in the aftermath of the September 11, 2001, attacks on New York and Washington, D.C., soon encouraged the pursuit of Muslim fighters involved in the jihad in Maluku and Poso and the persecution and prosecution of a broader range of Islamic activists supporting their struggle. As early as November 2001, for example, U.S. Deputy Defense Secretary Paul Wolfowitz, a leading hawk in the George W. Bush administration and a former ambassador to Jakarta, warned that "going after Al Qaeda in Indonesia is not something that should wait until after Al Qaeda has been uprooted from Afghanistan."[60] Accusations of Al-Qaeda training camps in Poso, connections to *mujahidin* in Ambon, and linkages with Abu Bakar Ba'asyir and Jemaah Islamiyah were soon issued by high-ranking foreign government officials, reported in the Indonesian media, and acted upon by the military, police, intelligence, and judiciary arms of the Megawati administration. In tandem with widely publicized arrests and accusations by authorities in neighboring Malaysia, the Philippines, and Singapore eager to demonstrate their commitment to the War on Terror, American pressures helped to expedite and escalate a crackdown on the networks of *jihadi* fighters and conspirators which had emerged and expanded in Indonesia in the preceding years.

In short, the shift of the form and focus of jihad from paramilitary mobilization in areas of interreligious conflict to bombing of foreign, Western targets in 2002 reflected the new constellation of power relations and religious authority in Indonesia that had begun to crystallize at the time. This new constellation was one in which the space for the promotion of Islam in the national parliamentary arena had dramatically shrunk, and in which the channels of quiet collaboration between *jihadi* activists and sympathetic elements in the state and the political class were rapidly being closed down. It was also a constellation, moreover, in which the banner of Islam no longer seemed to carry the potential to mobilize and unify significant numbers of Indonesian Muslims, either as crowds or as voters or as supporters of jihad.

Against this political, sociological, and discursive backdrop, the internationalization of the bombing campaign represented the extrusion of the internal contradictions and limitations of the Islamist project in Indonesia, with externalization forestalling if not foreclosing a belated acknowledgment and acceptance of defeat. This attempt to restore the visibility and viability of Islam at the moment of its virtual evisceration or absorption coincided with an international conjuncture—the rise to global prominence of Al-Qaeda and Osama bin Laden and the retaliatory War on Terrorism—which accorded foreign, especially Western, targets special priority and prestige. Yet the specific timing, locations, protagonists, and forms of jihad reflected the peculiarities of Indonesian conditions in particular.

The significance of the Indonesian political, sociological, and discursive context is especially apparent against the backdrop of preceding episodes of jihad in recent Indonesian history, first in the paramilitary mobilization associated with the Darul Islam movement of the 1950s and early 1960s, and then in the bombing campaigns of the mid-1980s. The proclamation of the Negara Islam Indonesia (Islamic State of Indonesia) in mid-1949, after all, represented a break with the conciliatory stance of Republican leaders during the *Revolusi* by a group of Muslim independence fighters led by S. M. Kartosoewirjo, a protégé of the founder of Sarekat Islam and a one-time associate of Soekarno. With independence, moreover, the favoritism shown toward graduates of secular schools in the staffing of the Indonesian state (including the army), the forced demobilization of the "irregular" guerrilla groups that had contributed so much to the energies of the *Revolusi*, the rejection of special provisions for Islam and Islamic law in the constitution in favor of the multifaith (but monotheistic) Pancasila, and the growing divisions among Muslims that accompanied constitutional democracy all contributed to a rising sense of disappointment and disenchantment among those who had mobilized against the Dutch under the banner of Islam. Thus the early 1950s saw the emergence of the Darul Islam movement, with armed guerrilla groups from the *Revolusi* mobilized against the embryonic Indonesian state as late as the early 1960s in West Java, South Sulawesi, South Kalimantan, Aceh, and some northern coastal towns of Central Java.[61]

This early episode of jihad in reaction to the decline and defeat of a previously ascendant Islam in Indonesia recurred in the form of a bombing campaign in the 1980s, during the peak years of Christian—and, in particular, Catholic—influence in the Suharto era. As noted in Chapter Three above, the early to middle 1980s witnessed a set of humiliating defeats for forces identified with the promotion of Islam in Indonesia. After the strong performance of the Islamic PPP in the 1977 and 1982 parliamentary elections, the Suharto regime embarked on a campaign to defang the threat of a populist Islam. This campaign included the imposition of more subservient pro-government figures within the PPP leadership, the promotion of the liberal accommodationist Abdurrahman Wahid as the new chairman of Nahdlatul Ulama, the encouragement of Wahid's withdrawal of NU support for PPP, and the passage of legislation insisting that all organizations accept the precepts of Pancasila—rather than, say, Islam—as their founding and guiding principles. As this campaign proceeded into the mid-1980s it provoked—in one or the other sense of the word—a violent reaction in the name of Islam. This reaction was first evident in the Tanjung Priok incident in September 1984, but that massacre of Muslim residents by the security forces was followed by a subsequent wave of government repression and apparent Islamist reprisals. Even as Muslim preachers and other activists accused of inciting violence in Tanjung Priok and elsewhere in the country were arrested, imprisoned, and put on trial in late 1984 and early 1985, a series of bombings around the Indonesian archipelago targeted diverse sites of non-Muslim power and influence: a Chinese-owned bank and a Chinese-owned shopping mall in Jakarta in October 1984; a Catholic church and a Protestant seminary elsewhere on Java on Christmas Eve of the same year; the world-famous ruins of the pre-Islamic kingdom of Majapahit in Borobodur, Central Java, in January 1985; and a tourist bus bound for Bali in March of that year.[62]

Against the backdrop of the Darul Islam rebellion(s) of the 1950s and early 1960s and the bombings of the 1980s, the jihad observed in Indonesia in the early years of the twenty-first century thus appears less as the product of—essentially exogenous—Wahhabi or Salafi influence, Afghanistan experience, or Al-Qaeda outreach than as the most recent variation on a well-established, recurring theme in Indonesian history. The activists recruited for jihad in Maluku and Poso in 2000–2001 and for bombings around the country in 2000–2004, after all, seem to have been drawn from the very same networks as those involved in the Darul Islam movement of the 1950s and the bombing campaign of the mid-1980s. These networks, it should be stressed, do not appear to have been involved in any form of religious violence in Indonesia in the intervening decades, which were free of armed insurgencies and terrorist bombing campaigns. Their engagement in full-time, full-blown jihad of one kind or another came only under certain specific circumstances: in the wake of rising popular mobilization and increasingly assertive claims on the public sphere and the state articulated in the idiom of Islam, and during a period of decline, defeat, disappointment, and disentanglement from state power for those forces most closely associated with the promotion of the faith. Thus the jihad of recent years in Indonesia should be understood not as evidence of an ascendant, insurgent Islam but as a symptom of the weakness of those who have tried to mobilize in its name, with both sore losers and ungracious winners involved in its perpetration.

Conclusion: Jihad and Religious Violence beyond Indonesia

My argument with regard to context for jihad in Indonesia since 2000 is supported by evidence concerning the backdrop for the bombings and other terrorist attacks of recent years in other parts of Southeast Asia and elsewhere in the Muslim world. In the Philippines, for example, the rash of bombings around the country identified with the shadowy Abu Sayyaf group in 2002–5 came in the aftermath of the breakdown of live-and-let-live arrangements between the government and the Moro Islamic Liberation Front (MILF) in Muslim areas of Mindanao and the Sulu Archipelago, the unprecedented attacks on MILF camps in such areas by government troops, the forced exile and subsequent arrest and imprisonment of former Moro National Liberation Front (MNLF) chairman and governor of the Autonomous Region of Muslim Mindanao, Nur Misuari, and the deployment of U.S. and Philippine troops to Abu Sayyaf's strongholds in Basilan and Sulu.[63] Similarly in Thailand, the killings and bombings of the same years ascribed to Muslim insurgents in the southern part of the country accompanied the inauguration and entrenchment of a new prime minister in Bangkok, one unencumbered by indebtedness to Muslim-elected MPs and unwilling to countenance or continue well-established special arrangements for Muslim minority areas in the South.[64] Even in neighboring Malaysia, the alleged organizing efforts and armed raids attributed to hitherto unknown groups such as Al-Maunah and Kumpulan Mujahidin Malaysia during this period emerged as part of the decline and defanging of the Islamic party PAS after its strong showing in the 1999 elections.[65] Throughout Southeast Asia, in other words, terrorist jihad was waged in the face of deteriorating political conditions for the avowed representatives of Islam, broader trends that signaled the diminishing potential for achieving unity among Muslims, and simultaneous pressures from beyond the region for crackdowns on Islamic activists.

As argued by other scholars, such a pattern was already observable in the 1990s in other parts of the Muslim world. After the euphoria generated by the Iranian Revolution in the late 1970s, the successful struggle against the Soviets in Afghanistan, and the gains made by the Muslim Brotherhood and various Islamist parties in legal, parliamentary politics in Algeria, Egypt, Jordan, Kuwait, Tunisia, and Turkey in the 1980s, the 1990s witnessed a notable decline for forces promoting Islam in these countries, through a combination of exhaustion, accommodation, and repression.[66]

This trend was first apparent in 1992, with the military's overturning of the Front Islamique du Salut or the Islamic Salvation Front's (FIS) election victory in Algeria, the imposition of new restrictions on the Muslim Brotherhood's role in public life in Egypt, and the subsequent wave of retaliatory terrorist violence by militant Islamist groups in these two countries.[67] By 1997, moreover, a broader set of Islamist defeats had occurred in the political arena: the election of the "reformist" president Mohammed Khatami in Iran, the forced removal of the Islamist prime minister Necmettin Erbakan in Turkey, and coups reducing Islamist influence in Pakistan and Sudan. The revolutionary élan associated with the Islamist project of the 1980s had evaporated, as Islamist movements and parties were increasingly inclined to accommodate secular state authorities and to accept legal, parliamentary niches of influence, and as avowedly Islamic states in Afghanistan, Iran, Malaysia, Pakistan, and Saudi Arabia were discrediting the notion of faith as the basis for moral regeneration, social transformation, and legitimate rule. Islamism, it became clear, was destined to go the way of Euro-Communism, as Olivier Roy explained:

> It has "social-democratized" itself. It no longer offers a model for a different society or a brighter future. Today, any Islamist political victory in a Muslim country would produce only superficial changes in customs and law. Islamism has been transformed into a type of neofundamentalism concerned solely with reestablishing Muslim law, the *sharia*, without inventing new political forms, which means that it is condemned to serving as a mere cover for a political logic that eludes it—a logic in which we ultimately find the traditional ethnic, tribal, or communal divisions, ever ready to change their discourse of legitimization, hidden beneath the new social categories and regimes.[68]

The decline of the Islamist project, moreover, reflected not only the inherent antinomies of its intellectual foundations[69] and the contradictions (or shallowness) of its sociological basis in the new urban middle and working classes[70] but broader and deeper shifts within Islam itself. In the 1970s and 1980s, urbanization, the expansion of educational institutions and opportunities, and the emergence and spread of new circuitries of communication and representation (e.g., radio, television, the Internet) in Muslim countries were said to have created new Muslim publics and to have facilitated the objectification and functionalization of the faith by new Islamic intellectuals (a "lumpenintelligentsia") outside the religious establishment.[71] Yet by the 1990s the destabilizing, debilitating effects of these trends on Islam were also apparent: a widespread crisis of the social authority of the faith in the face of its "deterritorialization," not only through urbanization and internal migration within Muslim countries but also through globalization and the movement of Muslims in growing numbers to Western Europe. Combined with the creeping parliamentarization of the Muslim world, these trends rendered the projection of claims to represent Islam as a coherent body of beliefs or as a unified body believers, increasingly difficult.[72]

Viewed against this backdrop, the global jihad attributed to Osama bin Laden and al-Qaeda can be understood along the lines of the preceding analysis of Laskar Jihad and Jemaah Islamiyah in Indonesia. As in Indonesia, the shift to terrorist violence occurred after many years of expansion in the visibility and power of Islam in the public sphere and within the circuitries of state power, as part of a process of forced demobilization by erstwhile state sponsors of previously sanctioned violence against nonMuslims, and in the face of rising evidence of decline, disappointment, and defeat for the Islamist project. As in Indonesia, this global jihad took as its form and focus first paramilitary mobilization on the frontiers or borders of the Muslim world—Afghanistan, Bosnia, Chechnya—rather than the heartlands of the faith, and then terrorist bombings of Western, but strikingly secular targets in bastions of non-Muslim power. As in Indonesia, this pattern reflected the extrusion of declining, if not fully defeated, Islamist projects at the national level into the grander, global arena and the externalization of the internal limitations and contradictions of this project onto the Western, and especially American, "Other."[73]

Beyond these arguments with regard to jihad in Indonesia and beyond, the broader analysis presented in successive chapters of this book is also of broader relevance to the study of religious violence in a variety of forms and contexts in world history. After all, neither the alarmist and accusatory thrust of the "terrorist expert" literature nor the "whodunit" logic of the International Crisis Group's more impressive reports has addressed—much less answered—crucial questions with regard to the timing, location, targets, forms, and protagonists associated with religious violence in Indonesia. Fingering and following the footsteps of the "bad guys," it has been shown, hardly suffices as an explanation for when, where, whom, and how they strike. An alternative analytical approach is required.

In recent years, the body of scholarship associated with "social movements theory" has begun to encroach upon the study of religious violence in the Islamic world and to incorporate the likes of Al-Qaeda and Jemaah Islamiyah within its analytical grid.[74] Religious violence, the theory posits, is a form of collective action, which, like protests and peasant rebellions and political campaigns, can be understood in terms of available opportunities, resources, and ideologies for mobilization.[75] Through this lens, the timing of religious violence can be seen to reflect shifts in "political opportunity structure" for believers and representatives of a given religion; the perpetrators of violence can be identified through the "mobilizing structures" and "social networks" of religious worship and education; and the forms and targets (the "repertoires") of violence can be linked to the "collective action frames" associated with the faith. In the case of Indonesia, it is easy to see how these terms could be applied to describe the contexts and contours of successive phases and forms of religious violence since 1995, and to imagine how this book in its entirety could be restylized along these lines.

But the putative advantages of descriptive clarity—or conformity—afforded by such use of social movements language[76] are not accompanied by commensurate assistance in the task of explanation. Social movements theory, after all, remains an essentially actor-centered approach in which the agents of mobilization provide the starting point for analysis. Yet the perpetrators—crowds, criminal gangs, conspirators—have been the least accessible and identifiable elements of religious violence in Indonesia, and not only the agents but the very forms of agency associated with this violence have shifted from the "spontaneous" riots of 1995–97 to the more coordinated pogroms of 1998–2001 to the full-time jihad of subsequent years. There is neither a stable set of actors nor a discernible "movement" nor a consistent form of mobilization around which to organize a narrative account, much less an explanatory analysis, of the pattern of religious violence in Indonesia during this period; indeed, the fundamental question of identity—of who is a Muslim and who speaks on behalf of Islam—has remained open and essentially unanswered.

This broader question as to the inherently problematic nature of religious identity in Indonesia has served as the point of departure of this book. Successive phases and forms of religious violence in Indonesia since 1995, I have argued, have reflected shifts not just in the structures of political opportunity for Muslims in the country but also shifts in the discursive, political, and sociological structures of religious identity—and in *the structures of anxiety about religious identity itself.* Both the possibilities for representing Islam as a coherent body of beliefs and a unified body of believers *and* the potential for the dissolution of the boundaries of the faith shaped the timing, location, targets, forms, protagonists, and kinds of agency associated with, first, riots, then pogroms, and then jihad. Thus the riots of 1995–97, unfolding when and where established hubs of Islamic piety and learning ran up against the circuitries of Chinese capital, Christianity, and the secular state, assumed the form of a public disavowal—through the burning of goods and buildings—of desire for incorporation into this profane realm. These riots broke out in the context of rising claims on an authoritarian state and a limited public sphere for Islam, but also amid increasing ambiguity as to the nature of these claims and in the context of increasing popular mobilization behind alternative, non-Islamic banners.

Likewise, the pogroms of 1998–2001, taking place when and where local hierarchies and boundaries of religious authority—whether Muslim or Protestant—appeared to be under greatest strain and threat of dissolution, and assumed the form of murderous collective attacks on religious "others" and the violent reassertion of the local borders and power structures of religious faith. These pogroms were carried out against the backdrop of the rise and fall of an administration in Jakarta identified with the promotion of Islam, in the midst of a shift from centralized authoritarian rule to competitive elections and regional autonomy, and in the shadow of electoral realignments and sociopolitical trends that crosscut established religious divides. Finally, in 2000 the call for jihad, emerging when and where the protection and promotion of Islam appeared to have been most grossly neglected and violated, assumed the form of spectacular displays of terror against non-Muslims in sites of Christian population and Western power. This jihad emerged in the wake of the dramatic defeat of Islam in the elections of 1999, against the backdrop of presidential administrations increasingly susceptible to secular, syncretist, and Christian influence, and amid the broader dissolution of Islam as a unifying force in the parliamentary arena and in the public sphere in general.

Throughout these successive phases of religious violence in Indonesia since 1995, the targets and forms of violence observed reflected the extrusion or externalization of tensions and contradictions internal to the structures of religious identity and authority associated with Islam. In the riots of 1995–97, the attacks on Chinese-owned businesses and property, Christian churches, and government buildings occurred at the peak of pious Indonesian Muslims' success in joining the ranks of the university-educated urban middle class and entering the core circuitries of the capitalist market and the secular state, while the much-discussed "social gap" (*kesenjangan sosial) among Muslims* was at its very widest. Similarly, in the pogroms of 1998–2001, the attacks on "sorcerers" in Java and across the Muslim-Christian divide in Maluku and Poso unfolded as the fixity and force of Islamic and Protestant boundaries and hierarchies faced unprecedented threats of diversification, dissent, and defection *from within* these religious communities. Finally, in the jihad of 2000–2004, the paramilitary assaults on Christian villages and the bombings first of Christian churches and then of foreign, secular targets were undertaken just as the promotion of Islamic law appeared to have faded from the parliamentary arena and the public sphere and to have become the exclusive preserve of a narrow, secretive, sectlike group. Nothing illustrates this point more clearly than reports that members of Jemaah Islamiyah swore an oath of loyalty (*bai'at*) to K.H. Abu Bakar Ba'asyir, a personalistic practice identified with the mystical Sufi brotherhoods (*tarekat*) so abhorred by those advocates of a more puritanical, and more universalistic, view of Islam.

Yet to understand these tensions and contradictions as essentially internal to religion—and to Islam in particular—in a disembodied, theological sense is to ignore and obscure their embeddedness within a broader constellation of this-worldly power relations. As stressed throughout this book and traced from the Dutch colonial era up through the end of the twentieth century, the institutions of religious education and association have occupied a special niche within the matrix of class relations in the Indonesian archipelago. But this privileged position for religious institutions has always been accompanied by ambiguities, uncertainties, anxieties, and expectations, given the contradictions and changes within and between the diverse educational and associational currents (*aliran*) in Indonesian public life. These ambiguities, uncertainties, anxieties, and expectations have prefigured the violence accompanying a period of dramatic social and political change in Indonesia. Religious violence in Indonesia has thus been revealed to be "about" religion in some sense—not in the conventional sense of religious belief or interreligious intolerance but in the broader sense of religious authority, identity, and boundaries.[77]

If this book has from its very title appeared to focus on religious violence perpetrated under the banner of Islam in the world's most populous majority-Muslim country, it has also implicated the forces of Christianity and secularism, which have so often been relegated to un-self-interested-victim or innocent-bystander status in recent accounts of jihad. Instead of depicting Christians in Indonesia as a vulnerable minority, this book has stressed the role of armed Christian groups in initiating violence in Maluku and Poso and in perpetrating some of the worst interreligious atrocities, leaving an overall body count for religious violence from 1995 to 2005 in which

Muslims are all too well represented. More important, perhaps, the book has shown how the pattern of linking religious education and association to state power in Indonesia was one established first by the Dutch colonial regime and the various Protestant missionary efforts that thrived under its aegis, with Islamic segments of the political class largely following in Christian footsteps.

Finally, the book has revealed how supposedly secular, ecumenical, or religiously neutral and disinterested forces—the capitalist market, the coercive and educational apparatuses of the modern state, competitive electoral democracy and decentralization—have been imposed and experienced in a religiously coded fashion in Indonesia. As of this writing, the success of these forces in defanging, demobilizing, and domesticating the threat of Islam in Indonesia is apparent in the broad pattern of interreligious peace, in the predominance of politicians and parties with decidedly non-Islamist agendas in a largely consolidated multiparty democracy, and even in the strikingly secular appeal of the supposedly "fundamentalist" Justice and Prosperity Party (PKS) as a foe of corruption and a promoter of reform. Yet even what can be billed as a triumph for multifaith tolerance or secularism in Indonesia has been accompanied by forms of scapegoating and sacrifice reminiscent of the very religious fanaticism so easily, and so smugly, demonized today.

Notes

Chapter 1. Indonesia

1. Donald L. Horowitz, *The Deadly Ethnic Riot* (Oxford: Oxford University Press, 2002).

2. See, for example, Arjun Appadurai, "Dead Certainty: Ethnic Violence in the Era of Globalization," *Development and Change* 29, no. 4 (October 1998), 905–925.

3. See, for example, Jack Snyder, *From Voting to Violence: Democratization and Nationalist Conflict* (New York: W. W. Norton, 2000); and Michael Mann, "The Dark Side of Democracy: The Modern Tradition of Ethnic and Political Cleansing," *New Left Review* 235 (May/June 1999), 18–45.

4. See also Benjamin Barber, *Jihad vs. McWorld: How Globalism and Tribalism Are Reshaping the World* (New York: Ballantine Books, 1996); and Amy Chua, *World on Fire: How Exporting Free Market Democracy Breeds Ethnic Hatred and Global Instability* (New York: Doubleday, 2003).

5. See, for example, Rohan Gunaratna, *Inside Al Qaeda: Global Network of Terror* (London: C. Hurst, 2002), especially 174–203.

6. See, for example, Zachary Abuza, *Militant Islam in Southeast Asia: Crucible of Terror* (Boulder: Lynne Rienner, 2003), as well as the several reports published by the Jakarta office of the International Crisis Group and written by the respected Indonesia specialist Sidney Jones, referred to below.

7. See chapters 4 and 5 below.

8. See chapter 7 below.

9. See, for example, James T. Siegel, "Suharto, Witches," *Indonesia* 71 (April 2001), 27–78; Gerry van Klinken, "The Maluku Wars: Bringing Society Back In," *Indonesia* 71 (April 2001), 1–26; Lorraine Aragon, "Communal Violence in Poso, Central Sulawesi: Where People Eat Fish and Fish Eat People," *Indonesia* 72 (October 2001), 45–79; and Gerry van Klinken, "Indonesia's New Ethnic Elites," in Henk Schulte Nordholt and Irwan Abdullah, eds., *Indonesia: In Search of Transition* (Yogyakarta: Pustaka Pelajar, 2002), 67–105.

10. Jacques Bertrand's recent book, by far the most coherent, comprehensive, and compelling account of political violence in late twentieth-century Indonesia, situates ethnic conflict against the backdrop of "critical junctures" that saw major institutional reforms or reworkings of the country's "national model." But this framework is not developed as a tool

for disaggregating the violence and explaining variation in its timing, location, targets, forms, and consequences. See Jacques Bertrand, *Nationalism and Ethnic Conflict in Indonesia* (Cambridge: Cambridge University Press, 2004).

11. For critical treatments of secularism in India and Turkey, see T. N. Madan, "Secularism in Its Place," *Journal of Asian Studies* 46, no. 4 (November 1987), 747–760; Ashish Nandy, "The Politics of Secularism and the Recovery of Religious Tolerance," in Veena Das, ed., *Mirrors of Violence: Communities, Riots, and Survivors in South Asia Today* (Delhi: Oxford University Press, 1990), 69–93; and Yael Navaro-Yashin, *Faces of the State: Secularism and Public Life in Turkey* (Princeton: Princeton University Press, 2002).

12. "To determine a war of religion as such, one would have to be certain that one can delimit the religious. One would have to be certain that one can distinguish all the predicates of the religious. One would have to dissociate the essential traits of the religious as such from the political or the economic. And yet, nothing is more problematic than such a dissociation. The fundamental concepts that often permit us to isolate or to pretend to isolate the political—restricting ourselves to this particular circumscription—remain religious or in any case theological-political." Jacques Derrida, "Faith and Knowledge: The Two Sources of 'Religion' at the Limits of Reason Alone," in Jacques Derrida, *Acts of Religion* (London: Routledge, 2002), 63. As Carl Schmitt famously wrote in 1934: "All significant concepts of the modern theory of the state are secularized theological concepts, not only because of their historical development—in which they were transformed from theology to the theory of the state, whereby, for example, the omnipotent God became the omnipotent lawgiver—but also because of their systematic structure, the recognition of which is necessary for a sociological consideration of these concepts." Carl Schmitt, *Political Theology* (Cambridge: MIT Press, 1985), 36.

13. Talal Asad, "The Construction of Religion as an Anthropological Category," in Talal Asad, *Genealogies of Religion: Discipline and Reasons of Power in Christianity and Islam* (Baltimore: Johns Hopkins University Press, 1993), 29.

14. See, for example, Paul R. Brass, *Theft of an Idol: Text and Context in the Representation of Collective Violence* (Princeton: Princeton University Press, 1997).

15. For wide-ranging treatment of the diverse forms of violence observed in early post-Suharto Indonesia, see Freek Colombijn and J. Thomas Lindblad, eds., *Roots of Violence in Indonesia: Contemporary Violence in Historical Perspective* (Leiden: KITLV Press, 2002).

16. Jack Goody, "Bitter Icons," *New Left Review* 7 (January/February 2001), 5–15.

17. Michael Sells, *The Bridge Betrayed: Religion and Genocide in Bosnia* (Berkeley: University of California, 1996), 13.

18. See Barrington Moore Jr., *Moral Purity and Persecution in History* (Princeton: Princeton University Press, 2000); Regina M. Schwartz, *The Curse of Cain: The Violent Legacy of Monotheism* (Chicago: University of Chicago Press, 1997); Rodney Stark, *One True God: Historical Consequences of Monotheism* (Princeton: Princeton University Press, 2001); and Rodney Stark, *For the Glory of God: How Monotheism Led to Reformations, Science, Witch-Hunts, and the End of Slavery* (Princeton: Princeton University Press, 2003).

19. Goody, "Bitter Icons," 13.

20. Talal Asad, *The Idea of an Anthropology of Islam*, Occasional Paper Series (Washington, D.C.: Georgetown University Center for Contemporary Arab Sudies, 1986), 15.

21. Gregory Starrett, *Putting Islam to Work: Education, Politics, and Religious Transformation in Egypt* (Berkeley: University of California Press, 1998), 13.

22. Samuel P. Huntington, *The Clash of Civilizations and the Remaking of World Order* (New York: Simon & Schuster, 1996).

23. Immanuel Wallerstein, "Islam, the West, and the World," *Journal of Islamic Studies* 10, no. 2 (1999), 109–125.

24. Giovanni Arrighi, Terence Hopkins, and Immanuel Wallerstein, *Anti-Systemic Movements* (London: Verso, 1989).

25. See Manuel Castells, *The Information Age: Economy, Society, and Culture*, vol. 2, *The Power of Identity* (Oxford: Blackwell, 2004), 20, 108–144.

26. Jacques Derrida, "'Above All Else, No Journalists!'" in Hent de Vries and Samuel Weber, eds., *Religion and Media* (Stanford: Stanford University Press, 2001), 62.

27. Hent de Vries, "In Medias Res: Global Religion, Public Spheres, and the Task of Contemporary Comparative Religious Studies," in de Vries and Weber, *Religion and Media*, 23.

28. Arend Lijphart, *The Politics of Accommodation: Pluralism and Democracy in the Netherlands* (Berkeley: University of California Press, 1968).

29. For early treatments of the parallels—and points of transmission—between the Dutch and Indonesian patterns, see W. F. Wertheim, "From Aliran towards Class Struggle in the Countryside of Java," *Pacific Viewpoint* 10, no. 2 (September 1969), 1–17; and Ruth McVey, "Nationalism, Islam, and Marxism: The Management of Ideological Conflict in Indonesia," in Ruth McVey, ed., *Nationalism, Islam, and Marxism* (Ithaca: Cornell Modern Indonesia Project, 1971), especially 18–26. For a thoughtful recent discussion that pays closer attention to Christianity in Indonesia, see Albert Schrauwers, *Colonial "Reformation" in the Highlands of Central Sulawesi, Indonesia, 1892–1995* (Toronto: University of Toronto Press, 2000), especially 35–40, 237–242.

30. See, in particular, Dale F. Eickelman and Jon W. Anderson, eds., *New Media in the Muslim World: The Emerging Public Sphere* (Bloomington: Indiana University Press, 1999).

31. Starrett, *Putting Islam to Work*, 9–10.

32. See, for example, Gilles Kepel, *The Prophet and Pharaoh: Muslim Extremism in Egypt* (London: Al Saqi Books, 1985).

33. See, for example, Robert A. Pape, "The Strategic Logic of Suicide Terrorism," *American Political Science Review* 97, no. 3 (August 2003), 343–361.

34. See, for example, Roxanne L. Euben, *Enemy in the Mirror: Islamic Fundamentalism and the Limits of Modern Rationalism* (Princeton: Princeton University Press, 1999).

35. See, for example, Roger D. Petersen, *Understanding Ethnic Violence: Fear, Hatred, and Resentment in Twentieth-Century Eastern Europe* (Cambridge: Cambridge University Press, 2002).

36. See, for example, Horowitz, *Deadly Ethnic Riot*, 102–109.

37. As is made clear in subsequent chapters, this book borrows heavily from Siegel's work and can in no small measure be understood as merely a fleshing-out of the historical, political, and sociological context that remains largely implicit—if well understood—in his writings.

38. For a lucid and amusing exposition of these arguments using the language of Hegel and Lacan, see, for example, Slavoj Zizek, "Enjoy Your Nation as Yourself!" in Slavoj Zizek, *Tarrying with the Negative: Kant, Hegel, and the Critique of Enjoyment* (Durham, N.C.: Duke University Press, 1993), 200–237.

39. Sigmund Freud, *Moses and Monotheism* (New York: Vintage Books, 1939).

40. See Sigmund Freud, "The Taboo of Virginity," "Group Psychology and the Analysis of the Ego," and "Civilization and Its Discontents," in James Strachey, ed., *The Standard Edition of the Complete Psychological Works of Sigmund Freud* (London: Vintage Books, 2001), 11:199, 18:101, and 21:114 respectively. See also the thoughtful discussion in Anton Blok, *Honour and Violence* (Cambridge: Polity Press, 2001), 115–135.

41. René Girard, *Violence and the Sacred* (Baltimore: Johns Hopkins University Press, 1977), 51.

42. Charles Tilly, *The Politics of Collective Violence* (Cambridge: Cambridge University Press, 2003), 77.

43. Appadurai, "Dead Certainty," 908–909.

44. For an illuminating analysis of the emergence of "civil society" along these lines, see Eva-Lotta E. Hedman, *In the Name of Civil Society: From Free Elections to People Power in*

the Philippines (Honolulu: University of Hawaiʻi Press, 2006), especially chap. 7, "Watching the Watchers: The Spectacle of Civil Society," 142–166. In this respect as in many others, I am deeply indebted to Hedman's work.

45. See Mark Juergensmeyer, *Terror in the Mind of God: The Global Rise of Religious Violence* (Berkeley: University of California Press, 2003); and Natalie Zemon Davis, "The Rites of Violence: Religious Riot in Sixteenth-Century France," *Past and Present* 59 (1971), 51–91.

46. "Struggles over ethnic or regional identity . . . are a particular case of the different struggles over classifications, struggles over the monoply of the power to make people see and believe, to get them to know and recognize, to impose the legitimate definition of the divisions of the social world, and, thereby, to make and unmake groups. What is at stake here is the power of imposing a vision of the social world through principles of division which, when they are imposed on a whole group, establish meaning and a consensus about meaning, and in particular about the identity and unity of the group, which creates the reality and the entity of the group." Pierre Bourdieu, *Language and Symbolic Power* (Cambridge: Polity Press, 1991), 221.

47. Werner Schiffauer, "Production of Fundamentalism: On the Dynamics of Producing the Radically Different," in de Vries and Weber, *Religion and Media*, 440.

48. For somewhat similar arguments along these lines with regard to India, see Brass, *Theft of an Idol*; and Paul R. Brass, *The Production of Hindu-Muslim Violence in Contemporary India* (Seattle: University of Washington Press, 2003). Note, however, Brass's repeated insistence that the role and responsibility of individuals for acts of violence should not be diminished and dismissed by reference to "discourse."

49. Brass, *Theft of an Idol*, 280.

50. Brass, *Production of Hindu-Muslim Violence*, 33–34.

51. Michel Wieviorka, *The Making of Terrorism* (Chicago: University of Chicago Press, 2004), 291. Emphasis in the original.

52. Ibid., 297.

53. See: Olivier Roy, *Globalised Islam: The Search for a New Ummah* (London: Hurst, 2004); Olivier Roy, *The Failure of Political Islam* (Cambridge: Harvard University Press, 1995); and Gilles Kepel, *Jihad: The Trail of Political Islam* (Cambridge: Harvard University Press, 2000).

54. Roy, *Globalised Islam*, 289.

55. As Slavoj Zizek has noted: "Fantasy does not simply realize a desire in a hallucinatory way. . . . [A] fantasy constitutes our desire, provides its co-ordinates; that is, it literally 'teaches us how to desire.' . . . [F]antasy mediates between the formal symbolic structure and the positivity of the objects we encounter in reality—that is to say, it provides a 'schema' according to which certain positive objects in reality can function as objects of desire, filling in the empty places opened up by the formal symbolic structure." Slavoj Zizek, *The Plaque of Fantasies* (London: Verso, 1997), 7.

56. Sigmund Freud, "Extracts from the Fliess Papers," in Strachey *Standard Edition*, 1:247.

57. Zizek, *Plaque of Fantasies*, 32.

Chapter 2. Situating "Islam" in Indonesia

1. E. P. Thompson, *The Making of the English Working Class* (New York: Pantheon Books, 1963), 9.

2. For a survey of Chinese migration to Southeast Asia over the centuries, see Anthony Reid, "Flows and Seepages in the Long-term Chinese Interaction with Southeast Asia," in Anthony Reid, ed., *Sojourners and Settlers: Histories of Southeast Asia and the Chinese* (Sydney: Allen & Unwin, 1996), 15–49.

3. Of course, the same period also witnessed a massive flow of Chinese migration to the Americas as well as a similar exodus from parts of the Indian subcontinent (which greatly affected British Burma and Malaya and, to a lesser extent, French Indochina). For a fine overview of these demographic trends, see Walton Look Lai, *Indentured Labor, Caribbean Sugar: Chinese and Indian Migrants to the British West Indies, 1838–1918* (Baltimore: Johns Hopkins University Press, 1993), 19–49.

4. Maurice Freedman, "The Handling of Money: A Note on the Background to the Economic Sophistication of Overseas Chinese," *Man* 59 (1959), 64.

5. See Armando Cortesao, ed., *The Suma Oriental of Tomé Pires.* 2 vols. (London: Hakluyt Society, 1944), 1:182; H. J. de Graaf and Th. G. Th. Pigeaud, *Chinese Muslims in Java in the 15 and 16 Centuries: The Malay Annals of Semarang and Cerbon,* trans. and ed. M. C. Ricklefs (Clayton, Victoria: Monash Papers on Southeast Asia), 1984; and Denys Lombard and Claudine Salmon, "Islam et Sinité," *Archipel* 30 (1985), 73–94.

6. On this point, see Mason Hoadley, "Javanese, Peranakan, and Chinese Elites in Cirebon: Changing Ethnic Boundaries," *Journal of Asian Studies* 47, no. 3 (August 1988), 503–518.

7. G. William Skinner, "Creolized Chinese Societies in Southeast Asia," in Reid, *Sojourners and Settlers,* 66–67.

8. See Peter Carey, "Changing Javanese Perceptions of the Chinese Communities in Central Java, 1755–1825," *Indonesia* 37 (April 1984), 1–47.

9. Ibid., 16.

10. James R. Rush, *Opium to Java: Revenue Farming and Chinese Enterprise in Colonial Indonesia,1860–1910* (Ithaca: Cornell University Press, 1990), 87.

11. James Rush, "Placing the Chinese in Java on the Eve of the Twentieth Century," *Indonesia* 1991 (special issue: The Role of the Indonesian Chinese in Shaping Modern Indonesian Life), 17–18.

12. On these trends, see Takashi Shiraishi, *An Age in Motion: Popular Radicalism in Java, 1912–1916* (Ithaca: Cornell University Press, 1990), 35–37.

13. Jamie Mackie, "Towkays and Tycoons: The Chinese in Indonesian Economic Life in the 1920s and 1980s," *Indonesia* 1991 (special issue: Role of the Indonesian Chinese), 83–96.

14. Edna Bonacich, "A Theory of Middleman Minorities," *American Sociological Review* 38 (October 1973), 583–594.

15. John S. Furnivall, *Colonial Policy and Practice: A Comparative Study of Burma and Netherlands India* (New York: New York University Press, 1944), 304–305.

16. Mary F. A. Somers, "Peranakan Chinese Politics in Indonesia" (Ph.D. diss., Cornell University, 1965), 231. See also Donald E. Willmott, *The National Status of the Chinese in Indonesia* (Ithaca: Cornell Modern Indonesia Project, 1961), 29–34.

17. G. William Skinner, "The Chinese Minority," in Ruth T. McVey, ed., *Indonesia* (New Haven, Conn: Human Relations Area Files, 1963), 112–113.

18. Ibid., 113; Willmott, *National Status,* 70–89.

19. Somers, "Peranakan Chinese Politics," 194–214.

20. Pramoedya Ananta Toer, *Hoakiau di Indonesia* (Jakarta: Bintang Press, 1960). This book was banned and its author imprisoned in the early 1960s by the Soekarno regime for its arguments along these lines. In 1998 a new edition was issued by the Jakarta publishing house Garba Budaya.

21. Charles A. Coppel, *Indonesian Chinese in Crisis* (Kuala Lumpur: Oxford University Press, 1983), 52–68, 99–176; Mely G. Tan, "The Social and Cultural Dimensions of the Role of Ethnic Chinese in Indonesian Society," *Indonesia* 1991 (special issue: Role of the Indonesian Chinese), 113–125.

22. See Mackie, "Towkays and Tycoons," 83–96.

23. See Harold Crouch, *The Army and Politics in Indonesia* (Ithaca: Cornell University Press, 1980), 273–303.

24. On "market corruption," see James C. Scott, *Comparative Political Corruption* (Englewood Cliffs, N.J.: Prentice-Hall, 1972), 57–75.

25. See Benny Subianto, "Potret Konglomerat Lokal," in Andreas Harsono, ed., *Huru-Hara Rengasdengklok* (Jakarta: Institut Studi Arus Informasi, 1997), 89–108.

26. See James T. Siegel, *Solo in the New Order: Language and Hierarchy in an Indonesian City* (Princeton: Princeton University Press, 1986), 232–254.

27. Dede Oetomo, *The Chinese of Pasuruan: Their Language and Identity* (Canberra: Australian National University, Research School of Pacific Studies, Department of Linguistics, 1987), 58.

28. Yoon Hwan Shin, "The Role of Elites in Creating Capitalist Hegemony in Post-Oil Boom Indonesia," *Indonesia* 1991 (special issue: Role of the Indonesian Chinese), 128.

29. On this point, compare Oetomo, *Chinese of Pasuruan*, 103–116; and Siegel, *Solo in the New Order,* 240–245.

30. Benny Subianto, "The Politics of Chinese Indonesians after the Fall of Soeharto's New Order," paper presented at the 52nd Annual Meeting of the Association for Asian Studies, San Diego, March 9–13, 2000.

31. John Pemberton, *On the Subject of "Java"* (Ithaca: Cornell University Press, 1994); Suzanne Brenner, *Domesticating Desire: Women, Wealth, and Modernity in Java* (Princeton: Princeton University Press, 1998).

32. On both points, see Jennifer Alexander and Paul Alexander, "Protecting Peasants from Capitalism: The Subordination of Javanese Traders by the Colonial State," *Comparative Studies in Society and History* 33, no. 2 (April 1991), 370–94.

33. Alexander Gerschenkron, *Economic Backwardness in Historical Perspective* (Cambridge: Harvard University Press, 1962).

34. See, for example, Jan Breman, *The Village on Java and the Early-Colonial State* (Rotterdam: Comparative Asian Studies Programe, Erasmus University, 1980), especially, 10, 15, and 42.

35. On Java, see Robert E. Elson, *Village Java under the Cultivation System, 1830–1870* (Sydney: Allen & Unwin, 1994), 158. On West Sumatra, see Joel S. Kahn, *Constituting the Mingkabau: Peasants, Culture, and Modernity in Colonial Indonesia* (Oxford: Berg, 1993), especially 70–74, 187–191. On Maluku, see Dieter Bartels, "Guarding the Invisible Mountain: Intervillage Alliances, Religious Syncretism, and Ethnic Identity among Ambonese Christians and Moslems in the Moluccas" (Ph.D. dissertation, Cornell University, 1977), 26.

36. Carol Warren, *Adat and Dinas: Balinese Communities in the Indonesian State* (Kuala Lumpur: Oxford University Press, 1993), 3.

37. Elson, *Village Java,* 29.

38. See, for example, Robert E. Elson, "Aspects of Peasant Life in Early 19th Century Java," in David P. Chandler and M. C. Ricklefs (eds.), *Nineteenth and Twentieth Century Indonesia: Essays in Honour of Professor J.D. Legge* (Clayton: Monash University Centre of Southeast Asian Studies, 1986), 71.

39. Elson, *Village Java,* 49–67.

40. Peter Burns, "The Myth of Adat," *Journal of Legal Pluralism* 28 (1989), 1–127, especially 17–37.

41. Shiraishi, *An Age in Motion,* 20–21.

42. Victor V. Magagna, *Communities of Grain: Rural Rebellion in Comparative Perspective* (Ithaca: Cornell University Press, 1991), 19.

43. See, for example, Eric R. Wolf, "Closed Corporate Peasant Communities in Mesoamerica and Central Java," *Southwestern Journal of Anthropology* 13, no. 1 (Spring 1957), 1–18.

44. Robert Cribb, *Historical Atlas of Indonesia* (Richmond, Surrey: Curzon Press, 2000), 137.

45. Clifford Geertz, *Agricultural Involution: The Processes of Ecological Change in Indonesia* (Berkeley: University of California Press, 1963), 89. For a critical treatment of the many problems with Geertz's account of "agricultural involution" in Java, see Benjamin White, "Agricultural Involution and Its Critics: Twenty Years After," *Bulletin of Concerned Asian Scholars* 15 (1983), 18–41.

46. Geertz, *Agricultural Involution*, 90.

47. Joshua Barker, "Surveillance and Territoriality in Bandung," in Vicente L. Rafael, ed., *Figures of Criminality in Indonesia, the Philippines, and Colonial Vietnam* (Ithaca: Cornell University Southeast Asia Program, 1999), 95–127.

48. See ibid., 97, citing N. Niessen, "Indonesian Municipalities under Japanese Rules," in Peter J. M. Nas, ed., *Issues in Urban Development* (Leiden: Research School, CNWS, 1995), 125–127.

49. Barker, "Surveillance and Territoriality in Bandung," 122–126.

50. Hans Antlov and Sven Cederroth, eds., *Leadership on Java: Gentle Hints, Authoritarian Rule* (Richmond, Surrey: Curzon Press, 1994).

51. See, for example, Koentjaraningrat, "The Village in Indonesia Today," in Koentjaraningrat, ed., *Villages in Indonesia* (Ithaca: Cornell University Press, 1967), 386–405, especially 391–398.

52. Clifford Geertz, *The Religion of Java* (Chicago: University of Chicago Press, 1960), 11–85; Robert R. Jay, *Javanese Villagers: Social Relations in Rural Modjokuto* (Cambridge: MIT Press, 1969), 206–216.

53. Wolf, "Closed Corporate Peasant Communities."

54. Robert R. Jay, *Religion and Politics in Rural Central Java* (New Haven: Yale University Southeast Asia Studies, 1963), 42 (emphasis added).

55. Frank L. Cooley, "Allang: A Village on Ambon Island," in Koentjaraningrat, *Villages in Indonesia*, 153. See also Frank L. Cooley, *Ambonese Adat: A General Description* (New Haven: Yale University Southeast Asia Studies, 1962).

56. Clifford Geertz, "Form and Variation in Balinese Village Structure," *American Anthropologist* 61 (1959), 991.

57. John R. Bowen, "On the Political Construction of Tradition: Gotong Royong in Indonesia," *Journal of Asian Studies* 45, no. 3 (May 1986), 545–561.

58. Tsuyoshi Kato, "Different Fields, Similar Locusts: Adat Communities and the Village Law of 1979 in Indonesia," *Indonesia* 47 (April 1989), 89–114.

59. Pemberton, *On the Subject of "Java,"* 238–239.

60. Ibid., 242.

61. Bartels, "Guarding the Invisible Mountain," Paschalis Maria Laksono, "Wuut Ainmehe Nifun, Manut Ainmehe Tilor (Eggs from One Fish and One Bird): A Study of the Maintenance of Social Boundaries in the Kei Islands" (Ph.D. diss., Cornell University, 1990), 123–124.

62. Warren, *Adat and Dinas*, 7–8.

63. Magagna, *Communities of Grain*, 21.

64. See, for example, P. de Kat Angelino, "De Leak op de Bali," *Tidjdshcrift voor Indische Taal-, Land- en Volkekunde* 60 (1921), 1–44; Jay, *Javanese Villagers*, 299–302; Siegel, *Solo in the New Order*, 41–52; and Ronny Nitibaskara, "Observations on the Practice of Sorcery in Java," in C. W. Watson and Roy Ellen, eds., *Understanding Witchcraft and Sorcery in Southeast Asia* (Honolulu: University of Hawai'i Press, 1993), 123–133.

65. See Bartels, "Guarding the Invisible Mountain."

66. Louis Couperus, *The Hidden Force* (Amherst: University of Massachusetts Press,

1985). The original Dutch novel, *De Stille Kracht,* was published in 1900; its title is perhaps more literally translated as "The Silent Force."

67. Benedict Anderson, "Languages of Indonesian Politics," in *Language and Power: Exploring Political Cultures in Indonesia* (Ithaca: Cornell University Press, 1990), 133.

68. See Ann Laura Stoler, "Working the Revolution: Plantation Laborers and the People's Militia in North Sumatra," *Journal of Asian Studies* 17, no. 2 (May 1988), 227–247; and Rex Mortimer, *The Indonesian Communist Party and Land Reform, 1959–1965* (Melbourne: Monash University, 1972).

69. Pemberton, *On the Subject of "Java,"* 237.

70. Shiraishi, *An Age in Motion.*

71. Benedict R. O'G. Anderson, *Java in a Time of Revolution: Occupation and Resistance, 1944–1946* (Ithaca: Cornell University Press, 1972).

72. See Audrey R. Kahin, ed., *Regional Dynamics of the Indonesian Revolution: Unity from Diversity* (Honolulu: University of Hawaii Press, 1985).

73. See: James T. Siegel, *A New Criminal Type in Jakarta: Counter-Revolution Today* (Durham, N.C.: Duke University Press, 1998).

74. Ibid., 51.

75. See, for example, John Pemberton, "Notes on the 1982 General Election in Solo," *Indonesia* 41 (April 1986), 1–22.

76. Heather A. Sutherland, *The Making of a Bureaucratic Elite: The Colonial Transformation of the Javanese Priyayi* (Kuala Lumpur: Oxford University Press, 1979).

77. See, for example, Lorraine V. Aragon, *Fields of the Lord: Animism, Christian Minorities, and State Development in Indonesia* (Honolulu: University of Hawai'i Press, 2000); R. William Liddle, *Ethnicity, Party, and National Integration: An Indonesian Case Study* (New Haven: Yale University Press, 1970); and Edward Peake, "Tradition, Christianity, and the State in Understandings of Sickness and Healing in South Nias, Indonesia" (Ph.D. thesis, University of London, 2000).

78. Gavin W. Jones, "Religion and Education in Indonesia," *Indonesia* 22 (October 1976), 19–56.

79. For early treatments of the parallels—and points of transmission—between the Dutch and Indonesian patterns, see W. F. Wertheim, "From Aliran towards Class Struggle in the Countryside of Java," *Pacific Viewpoint* 10, no. 2 (September 1969), 1–17; and Ruth McVey, "Nationalism, Islam, and Marxism: The Management of Ideological Conflict in Indonesia," in Ruth McVey, ed., *Nationalism, Islam, and Marxism* (Ithaca: Cornell Modern Indonesia Project, 1971), especially 18–26.

80. See Arend Lijphart, *The Politics of Accommodation: Pluralism and Democracy in the Netherlands* (Berkeley: University of California Press, 1968).

81. Albert Schrauwers, *Colonial "Reformation" in the Highlands of Central Sulawesi, Indonesia, 1892–1995* (Toronto: University of Toronto Press, 2000), 14.

82. Deliar Noer, *The Modernist Muslim Movement in Indonesia 1900–1942* (Kuala Lumpur: Oxford University Press, 1973).

83. On somewhat similar patterns of traditional schooling in Morocco, see Dale F. Eickelman, "The Art of Memory: Islamic Education and Its Social Reproduction," *Comparative Studies in Society and History* 20 (1978): 485–516.

84. Martin van Bruinessen, "Pesantren and Kitab Kuning: Continuity and Change in a Tradition of Religious Learning," in Wolfgang Marschall, ed., *Texts from the Islands: Oral and Written Traditions of Indonesia and the Malay World* (Bern: Institut fur Ethnologie, 1989), 124. See also Martin van Bruinessen, "Kitab Kuning: Books in Arabic Script Used in the Pesantren Milieu," *Bijdragen tot de Taal-, Land-, and Volkenkunde* 146, nos. 2–3 (1989), 226–269.

85. See, for example, Zamakhsyari Dhofier, "Kinship and Marriage among the Javanese Kyai," *Indonesia* 29 (April 1980), 47–58.

86. See, for example, Zamakhsyari Dhofier, *The Pesantren Tradition: The Role of the Kyai in the Maintenance of Traditional Islam in Java* (Tempe: Arizona State University Program for Southeast Asian Studies, 1999); and Sidney Jones, "The Javanese Pesantren: Between Elite and Peasantry," in Charles F. Keyes, ed., *Reshaping Local Worlds: Formal Education and Cultural Change in Rural Southeast Asia,* Monograph Series (New Haven: Yale University Southeast Asia Studies, 1996), 19–41.

87. Benedict R. O'G. Anderson, "Language, Fantasy, Revolution: Java 1900–1950," in Daniel S. Lev and Ruth McVey, eds., *Making Indonesia: Essays on Modern Indonesia in Honor of George McT. Kahin* (Ithaca: Cornell University Southeast Asia Program, 1996), 26–40; John D. Legge, *Intellectuals and Nationalism in Indonesia: A Study of the Following Recruited by Sutan Sjahrir in Occupation Jakarta* (Ithaca: Cornell Modern Indonesia Project, 1988); Rudolf Mrazek, *Sjahrir: Politics and Exile in Indonesia* (Ithaca: Cornell University Southeast Asia Program, 1994); and Mavis Rose, *Indonesia Free: A Political Biography of Mohammad Hatta* (Ithaca: Cornell Modern Indonesia Project, 1987).

88. See Richard Chauvel, *Nationalists, Soldiers, and Separatists: The Ambonese Islands from Colonialism to Revolt, 1880–1950* (Leiden: KITLV Press, 1990), 25–38; and David E. F. Henley, *Nationalism and Regionalism in a Colonial Context: Minahasa in the Dutch East Indies* (Leiden: KITLV Press, 1996), 80–115.

89. See, for example, Taufik Abdullah, *Schools and Politics: The Kaum Muda Movement in West Sumatra (1927–1933)* (Ithaca: Cornell Modern Indonesia Project, 1971).

90. James T. Siegel, *The Rope of God* (Ann Arbor: University of Michigan Press, 2000), 11, 57–58.

91. See, for example, Anderson, *Java in a Time of Revolution,* especially 1–109; and Audrey Kahin, "Struggle for Independence: West Sumatra in the Indonesian National Revolution" (Ph.D. diss., Cornell University, 1979).

92. Clifford Geertz, *The Social History of an Indonesian Town* (Cambridge: MIT Press, 1965), 127–128.

93. Ruth McVey, "Nationalism, Revolution, and Organization in Indonesian Communism," in Lev and McVey, *Making Indonesia,* 96–117.

94. Joel Eliseo Rocamora, *Nationalism in Search of Ideology: The Indonesian Nationalist Party, 1946–1965* (Quezon City: Philippine Center for Advanced Studies, University of the Philippines, 1975), 49.

Chapter 3. Social Transformation, 1965–1998

1. See Hal Hill, *The Indonesian Economy since 1966: Southeast Asia's Emerging Giant* (Cambridge: Cambridge University Press, 1996).

2. Richard Robison, *Indonesia: The Rise of Capital* (Sydney: Allen & Unwin, 1986).

3. On these trends, see Suzanne April Brenner, *The Domestication of Desire: Women, Wealth, and Modernity in Java* (Princeton: Princeton University Press, 1998); Chantal Vuldy, *Pekalongan: Batik et Islam dans une ville du Nord de Java* (Paris: Ecole des Hautes Etudes en Sciences Sociales, 1987); and Gretch G. Weix, "Following the Family/Firm: Patronage and Piecework in a Kudus Cigarette Factory" (Ph.D. diss., Cornell University, 1990).

4. Brenner, *Domestication of Desire,* 121.

5. See John MacDougall, "Patterns of Military Control in the Indonesian Higher Central Bureaucracy," *Indonesia* 33 (April 1982), 89–121.

6. Ben Anderson, "Current Data on the Indonesian Military Elite," *Indonesia* 40 (October 1985), 136.

7. Hotman M. Siahaan and Tjahjo Purnomo W., *Pamong Mengabdi Desa: Biografi Mohammad Noer* (Surabaya: Yayasan Keluarga Bhakti dan Surabaya Post, 1997); Burhan Ma-

genda, "The Surviving Aristocracy in Indonesia: Politics in Three Provinces of the Outer Islands" (Ph.D. diss., Cornell University, 1989).

8. On the position of Catholics in Indonesian society during the early Suharto years, see *Ichtisar Statistik Tentang Geredja Katolik di Indonesia: 1949–1967* (Bogor: Lembaga Penelitian dan Pembangunan Sosial, 1968).

9. Richard Tanter, "Intelligence Agencies and Third World Militarization: A Case Study of Indonesia, 1966–1989" (Ph.D. diss., Monash University, 1991), 321–325, 430–432.

10. Donald Hindley, "Alirans and the Fall of the Old Order," *Indonesia* 9 (April 1970), 23–66.

11. Herbert Feith, *The Decline of Constitutional Democracy in Indonesia* (Ithaca: Cornell University Press, 1962), 129–131; Rudolf Mrazek, *Sjahrir: Politics and Exile in Indonesia* (Ithaca: Cornell University Southeast Asia Program, 1994), 403–457.

12. See Subroto, "Recollections of My Career," *Bulletin of Indonesian Economic Studies* 34, no. 2 (August 1998), 67–92, especially 70–76.

13. See the exhaustive account in François Raillon, *Les Etudiants indonésiens et l'Ordre Nouveau: Politique et idéologie du Mahasiswa Indonesia (1966–1974)* (Paris: Editions de la Maison des Sciences de L'Homme, 1984).

14. See, for example, the highly tendentious account of PSI history and activities in Marzuki Arifin S.E., *Fakta, Analisa Lengkap dan Latar Belakang Peristiwa 15 Januari 1974* (Jakarta: Publishing House Indonesia, 1974), especially 21–75.

15. See Andrée Feillard, *Islam et armée dans l'Indonésie contemporaine* (Paris: L'Harmattan, 1995), 3–138; Agus Sunyoto, *Banser Berjihad Menumpas PKI* (Tulungagung: Thorqoh Agung, 1996); and Hermawan Sulistyo, "The Forgotten Years: The Missing History of Indonesia's Mass Slaughter (Jombang-Kediri, 1965–1966)" (Ph.D. diss., Arizona State University, 1997).

16. Ken Ward, *The 1971 Election in Indonesia: An East Java Case Study* (Clayton, Victoria: Monash Papers on Southeast Asia, 1974), 90–113, 157–178.

17. Feillard, *Islam et armée*, pp. 125–127, 143–156.

18. Mohammad Kamal Hassan, *Muslim Intellectual Responses to "New Order" Modernization in Indonesia* (Kuala Lumpur: Dewan Bahasa dan Pustaka Kementerian Pelajaran Malaysia, 1980), 78–141.

19. Arifin, *Fakta*, 21–75.

20. On the repression of Islamic activists and organizations in the 1980s, see Human Rights Watch, *Human Rights in Indonesia and East Timor* (New York: Human Rights Watch, 1989), 76–85.

21. See, for example, Avery Willis Jr., *Indonesian Revival: Why Two Million Came to Christ* (South Pasadena, Calif.: William Carey Library, 1977); and Robert W. Hefner, "Islamizing Java? Religion and Politics in Rural East Java," *Journal of Asian Studies* 46, no. 3 (August 1987), 533–554.

22. See, for example, Hyung-Jun Kim, "Unto You Your Religion and unto Me My Religion: Muslim-Christian Relations in a Javanese Village," *Sojourn* 13, no. 1 (April 1989), 62–85.

23. Hefner, "Islamizing Java?" 545–546. The study translated and cited by Hefner is Pierre Labrousse and Farida Soemargono, "De l'Islam comme morale du developpement: L'Action des bureaux de propagation de la foi (Lembaga Dakwah) vue de Surabaya," *Archipel* 30 (1985), 224.

24. For a very sensitive and illuminating account of the religious practices and milieu of the new urban poor in Bandung, for example, see Martin van Bruinessen, *Rakyat Kecil, Islam dan Politik* (Yogyakarta: Yayasan Bentang Budaya, 1998).

25. See Departemen Agama Republik Indonesia, *Data Potensi Pondok Pesantren Seluruh Indonesia* (Jakarta: Dirjen Pembinaan Kelembagaan Agama Islam, Direktorat Pembinaan

Perguruan Agama Islam, Departemen Agama Republik Indonesia, 1997), cited in Julia Day Howell, "Sufism and the Indonesian Islamic Revival," *Journal of Asian Studies* 60, no. 3 (August 2001), 701–729.

26. "Islam Sebagai Baju Zirah di Kalangan Muda," *Tempo,* May 13 1989, 74–78; and Nurhayati Djamas, "Gerakan Kebangkitan Islam Kaum Muda," in Abdul Aziz, ed., *Gerakan Islam Kontemporer di Indonesia* (Jakarta: Pustaka Firdaus, 1989), 207–287.

27. Asna Hasin, "Philosophical and Sociological Aspects of Da'wah: A Study of Dewan Dakwah Islamiyah Indonesia" (Ph.D. diss., Columbia University, 1998), 318–319.

28. Moeslim Abdurrahman, "On Hajj Tourism: In Search of Piety and Identity in The New Order Indonesia" (Ph.D. diss., University of Illinois at Urbana-Champaign, 2000).

29. Howell, "Sufism and the Indonesian Islamic Revival," 718–722.

30. On the rise of "pop Islam," see François Raillon, "L'Ordre Nouveau et l'Islam ou l'imbroglio de la foi et de la politique," *Archipel* 30 (1985), 229–261.

31. "Satria Berdakwah, Raja dari Bawah," *Tempo,* June 20, 1984, 27–30.

32. "Saya Ustad, Bukan Artis," *Tempo,* April 28, 1990, 74–78; "Dai-Dai baru Bak Matahari Terbit," *Tempo,* April 11, 1992, 14–20.

33. Gregory Starrett, *Putting Islam to Work: Education, Politics, and Religious Transformation in Egypt* (Berkeley: University of California Press, 1998), 9–10 (emphasis added).

34. Olivier Roy, *The Failure of Political Islam* (Cambridge: Harvard University Press, 1994), 97–98.

35. See "Huru-Hara di Tanjung Priok," *Tempo,* September 22, 1984, 12–15; H. A. M. Fatwa, *Demokrasi dan Keyakinan Beragama Diadili: Pembelaan Drs. H. AM. Fatwa didepan Pengadilan Negeri Jakarta Pusat Desember 1985* (Jakarta: Yayasan Lembaga Bantuan Hukum Indonesia, 1989); Nurhayati Djamas, "Behind the Tanjung Priok Incident, 1984: The Problem of Political Participation in Indonesia" (M.A. thesis, Cornell University, 1991); and *Tanjung Priok Berdarah: Tanggung Jawab Siapa? Kumpulan Fakta dan Data* (Jakarta: Gema Insani, 1998).

36. Stanley, *Seputar Kedung Ombo* (Jakarta: Lembaga Studi dan Advokasi Masyarakat, 1994); Muthmainnah, *Jembatan Suramadu: Respon Ulama terhadap Industrialisasi* (Yogyakarta: LKPSM, 1998).

37. See John T. Sidel, "Riots, Church Burnings, Conspiracies: The Moral Economy of the Indonesian Crowd in the Late Twentieth Century," in Ingrid Wessel and Georgia Wimhofer, eds., *Violence in Indonesia* (Hamburg: Abera Verlag Markus Voss, 2001), 47–63.

38. See Masashi Nishihara, *Golkar and the Indonesian Elections of 1971* (Ithaca: Cornell Modern Indonesia Project, 1972); and Ward, *1971 Election in Indonesia.*

39. Syamsuddin Haris, *PPP dan Politik Orde Baru* (Jakarta: Gramedia, 1991), 113.

40. John Pemberton, "Notes on the 1982 General Election in Solo," *Indonesia* 41 (April 1986), 10.

41. See R. William Liddle, "The 1977 Indonesian Election and New Order Legitimacy," in *Southeast Asian Affairs 1978* (Singapore: Institute for Southeast Asian Studies, 1978), 122–138.

42. For contrasting accounts of these developments, see Haris, *PPP dan Politik Orde Baru;* and Feillard, *Islam et armée.*

43. "Ini Partai, Bukannya Komplotan," *Tempo,* August 25, 1984, 15 (my translation).

44. Haris, *PPP dan Politik Orde Baru,* 112–113.

45. James T. Siegel, *A New Criminal Type in Jakarta: Counter-Revolution Today* (Durham, N.C.: Duke University Press, 1998), 9.

46. Ruth McVey, *Redesigning the Cosmos: Belief Systems and State Power in Indonesia* (Copenhagen: Nordic Institute of Asian Studies, 1993), 21.

47. On HMI during this period, see, for example, "Dulu HMI Lahirkan Kader Intelektual Islam dan Bangsa, Kini . . . ?," *Surabaya Post,* March 3, 1989; "Dibutuhkan 'Gus Dur' di

HMI," *Surabaya Post,* November 29, 1992; and "M.Yahya Zaini, S.H., Ketua Umum PB HMI: HMI Beda dengan ICMI," *Surabaya Post,* January 15, 1995.

48. Darul Aqsha, Dick van der Meij, and Johan Hendrik Meuleman, *Islam in Indonesia: A Survey of Events and Developments from 1988 to March 1993* (Jakarta: Indonesia-Netherlands Cooperation in Islamic Studies, 1995), 263–276.

49. See Feillard, *Islam et armée,* chap. 12.

50. See Chris Manning, *Indonesian Labour in Transition: An East Asian Success Story?* (Cambridge: Cambridge University Press, 1998), 177–188.

51. Siegel, *New Criminal Type in Jakarta.*

52. Karen Brooks, "The Rustle of Ghosts: Bung Karno in the New Order," *Indonesia* 60 (February 1996), 61–100.

53. Howard Dick, *Surabaya, City of Work: A Socioeconomic History, 1900–2000* (Athens: Ohio University Center for International Studies, 2002), 471.

54. Brenner, *Domestication of Desire,* 91.

55. Erawati Nurrhamah dan Nur Samsi, eds., *Politik Ala Mudrik: "Politisi Kampung Mendobrak"* (Surakarta: PT Pabelan, 1998); and M. Hari Mulyadi, Soedarmono, Abraham Setiyadi, Hari D. Utomo, Rohadi Didiek Wahyudiono, Tatang Badru Tamam, and M. Amin, *Runtuhnya Kekuasaan "Kraton Alit": Studi Radikalisasi Sosial "Wong Sala" dan Kerusuhan Mei 1998 di Surakarta* (Solo: Lembaga Pengembangan Teknologi Pedesaan, 1999).

Chapter 4. Buildings on Fire

1. See, for example, M. Amien Rais, *Demi Kepentingan Bangsa* (Yogyakarta: Pustaka Pelajar, 1997); and M. Amien Rais, *Refleksi Amien Rais: Dari Persoalan Semut Sampai Gajah* (Jakarta: Gema Insani Press, 1997).

2. Basofi Soedirman, Soetandyo Wignoyoseobroto, et al., *Bonek: Berani Karena Bersama* (Surabaya: Hipotesa, 1997).

3. See "Amuk Massal Warga Sumberanyar," *Tiras,* February 9, 1995, 52–53; "Berebut Tanah Warisan Jepang," *Tiras,* November 2, 1995, 71–72; and "Aksi Massa Berkedok Lingkungan," *Sinar,* December 2, 1995, 27.

4. On the events in Medan, see Human Rights Watch, *The Medan Demonstrations and Beyond* (New York: Human Rights Watch, 1994); "Kasus Buruh Medan: Memandang Dari Sisi Lain," *Bergerak,* July 24, 1994, 18–26; Arief Djati, "Pemogokan Umum Kaum Buruh Medan 14–15 April 1994: Melawan Dengan Kekuatan, Dihadang Dengan Pengadilan" (unpublished manuscript, Surabaya, 1995); and Muchtar Pakpahan, *Lima Tahun Memimpin SBSI: Pilihan Atau Panggilan* (Jakarta: Pustaka Forum Adil Sejahtera, 1997).

5. Santoso, Lukas Luwarso, Gibran Ajidarma, and Irawan Saptono, *Peristiwa 27 Juli* (Jakarta: Aliansi Jurnalis Independen/Institut Studi Arus Informasi, 1997).

6. Aswab Mahasin, "The Santri Middle Class: An Insider's View," in Richard Tanter and Kenneth Young, eds., *The Politics of Middle Class Indonesia* (Clayton, Victoria: Monash University Centre of Southeast Asian Studies, 1990), 142.

7. Howard W. Dick, *Surabaya, City of Work: A Socioeconomic History, 1900–2000* (Athens: Ohio University Center for International Studies, 2002), 412–413.

8. See Darul Aqsha, Dick van der Meij, and Johan Hendrik Meuleman, *Islam in Indonesia: A Survey of Events and Developments from 1988 to March 1993* (Jakarta: INIS, 1995), 479–486.

9. See "Kronologi Perusakan Gereja di Surabaya Tanggal 9 Juni 1996," in Paul Tahalele and Thomas Santoso, eds., *Beginikah Kemerdekaan Kita?* (Surabaya: Forum Komunikasi Kristiani Indonesia, 1997), 155–156.

10. For a sense of Christian churches, congregations, and schools in Surabaya, for exam-

ple, see "Kawula Muda Tindukan Gereja," *Surabaya Post,* May 12, 1991; "Gereja Surabaya Mandi Cahaya Natal," *Surabaya Post,* December 26, 1991; and "Giliran Sekolah Swasta Rebut Favorit," *Surabaya Post,* June 1, 1994.

11. On these events, see the lucid and thoughtful treatment in Jacques Bertrand, *Nationalism and Ethnic Conflict in Indonesia* (Cambridge: Cambridge University Press, 2004), 94–100.

12. "Ratusan Pemuda dan Pelajar di Purwakarta Mengamuk," *Merdeka,* November 2, 1995; "Purwakarta Mengamuk," *Forum Keadilan,* November 20, 1995, 28–29.

13. See Hiroko Horikoshi, "A Traditional Leader in a Time of Change: The Kijaji and Ulama in West Java" (Ph.D. diss., University of Illinois at Urbana-Champaign, 1976).

14. "Warga Purwakarta Serbu Toserba Nusantara," *Republika,* November 3, 1995.

15. "Aksi Perusakan Masih Terus Berlangsung di Purwakarta," *Merdeka,* November 3, 1995.

16. Chantal Vuldy, *Pekalongan: Batik et Islam dans une ville du Nord de Java* (Paris: Ecole des Hautes Etudes en Sciences Sociales, 1987), 18.

17. "Kobaran SARA Menjalar di Pantura," *Forum Keadilan,* December 18, 1995, 12–15.

18. Andrée Feillard, *Islam et armée dans l'Indonésie contemporaine* (Paris: L'Harmattan, 1995), 331–332.

19. "Santri Lora Kholil Mayoritas Anak-anak," *Surabaya Post,* November 30, 1996, 16.

20. See, for example, "Potret Situbondo, Tempat Kerusuhan itu," *Republika,* October 15, 1996; and "Situbondo, Dik, Kota Santri," *Kompas,* October 22, 1996.

21. On Madura and Madurese areas of East Java, see Laurence Husson, *La Migration Maduraise vers l'Est de Java: "Manger le Vent ou Gratter la Terre"* (Paris: L'Harmattan, 1995), especially 213–32; and A. Mansurnoor, *Islam in an Indonesian World: Ulamas in Madura* (Yogyakarta: Gadjah Mada University Press, 1990).

22. Quoted in Ahmad Suaedy, Th. Sumartana, Elga Sarapung, and Lutfi Rahman, *Draft Laporan Survai Peristiwa Situbondo 10 Oktober 1996* (Yogyakarta: Institut Dialog Antar Iman di Indonesia (Institut DIAN/Interfidei), 1996), 15.

23. On the Naqsyabandiyah and other Sufi *tarekat* in Indonesia, see Martin van Bruinessen, *Tarekat Naqsyabandiyah di Indonesia* (Bandung: Mizan, 1992); Mahmud Sujuthi, *Politik Tarekat: Qadiriyah wa Naqsyabandiyah Jombang* (Yogyakarta: Galang Press, 2001); and Julia Day Howell, "Sufism and the Indonesian Islamic Revival," *Journal of Asian Studies* 60, no. 3 (August 2001), 701–729.

24. "Si Pendiam Bikin Perkara," *Gatra,* October 19, 1996; "Kisah Murid Mudarso," *Tiras,* October 24, 1996, 15.

25. "Pelecehan Ulama' dan Agama," undated letter of K.H. Zaini Abd. Aziz to Polsek Kapongan, Situbondo; "Semua Bermula Dari Saleh," *Aula,* November 1996, 27.

26. Suaedy et al., *Draft Laporan,* 22.

27. See Tim Pencari Fakta GP Ansor Jatim, *Fakta dan Kesaksian Tragedi Situbondo* (Surabaya, 1997): "Ti-hati, Ini Kota Santri," *Aula,* November 1996, 14; and uaedy et al., *Draft Laporan,* 26–30.

28. "Ti-hati, Ini Kota Santri," 15–17; Tim Pencari Fakta GP Ansor Jatim *Fakta dan Kesaksian,* 31–38; Suaedy et al., *Draft Laporan,* 30–34.

29. "Tersangka 'Kasus Situbondo' Meninggal di RSUD," *Surabaya Post,* December 9, 1996 , 16.

30. "Di Balik Kerusuhan Tasikmalaya (1): Menimbun Sekam di atas Bara," *Republika,* January 7, 1997; Bupati Kepala Daerah Tingkat II Tasikmalaya, *Rencana Rehabilitasi Kotip Tasikmalaya dan Sekitarnya Akibat Kerusuhan Massa Pada Tanggal 26 Desember 1996* (Tasikmalaya, 1997).

31. On Islamic schools in Tasik in general, and K.H. Ruchyat's Pondok Pesantren Cipaasung in particular, see "Hajat Desa Sambut 8.000 Tamu," *Surabaya Post,* October 19, 1994.

32. See, for example, Julia Day Howell, M. A. Subandi, and Peter L. Nelson, "New Faces of Indonesian Sufism: A Demographic Profile of Tarekat Qodiriyyah-Naqsyabandiyyah, Pesantren Suryalaya, in the 1990s," *Review of Indonesian and Malaysian Affairs* 35, no. 2 (Summer 2001), 33–59; "90 Tahun Pondok Pesantren Suryalaya: 'Berilah Aku Kemampuan untuk MencintaiMu,'" *Surabaya Post,* September 6, 1995.

33. Loekman Soetrisno, ed., *Perilaku Kekerasan Kolektif: Kondisi dan Pemicu* (Yogyakarta: Pusat Penelitian Pembangunan Pedesaan dan Kawasan, Universitas Gadjah Mada, 1997), 87–89.

34. "Takut Timbulkan Keresahan, Pembangunan Plaza Mewah Distop," *Merdeka,* February 7, 1997.

35. On accusations of Christian proselytization efforts in Tasikmalaya, see "Kristenisasi di Tasikmalaya dan Bekasi," *Media Dakwah,* March 1997, 48–49.

36. For a brief description of this school, see "Pimpinan Pondok Pesantren Condong: Kami Terguncang dan Tersinggung," *Kompas,* December 30, 1996.

37. See Toriq Hadad, ed., *Amarah Tasikmalaya: Konflik di Basis Islam* (Jakarta: Institut Studi Arus Informasi, 1998), 11–19, 55–63; "Kronologi Kasus Tasikmalaya," *Republika,* December 30, 1996; "Draft Buku Putih Tasikmalaya" (undated, unpublished paper in the possession of the author), 7–10; and Soetrisno, *Perilaku Kekerasan Kolektif,* 112–123.

38. "Sembilan Polisi Aniaya Tiga Pengasuh Pesantren," *Republika,* December 26, 1996.

39. On the series of events that unfolded on December 24–26, see Hadad *Amarah Tasikmalaya,* 17–29; "Draft Buku Putih Tasikmalaya," 9–18; "Kerusuhan Landa Tasikmalaya," *Kompas,* December 27, 1996; and "Tujuh Jam, Massa Kacau Tasikmalaya," *Merdeka,* December 27, 1996.

40. "Di Balik Kerusuhan Tasikmalaya (2–Habis): Siapa Penyulut Emosi Massa?" *Republika,* January 8, 1997; Soetrisno, *Perilaku Kekerasan Kolektif,* 131–133.

41. "Pangdam Siliwangi: Brutal, Bukan Sikap Warga Tasik," *Republika,* December 28, 1996; "Perusuh di Tasik Kebanyakan Maling, Sopir dan Copet," *Merdeka,* January 13, 1997.

42. "Agustiana Divonis 8 Tahun Penjara," *Kompas,* December 19, 1997; also Hadad, *Amarah Tasikmalaya,* 68–86; and court documents in the possession of the author titled "Sampul Berkas Perkara Reister Nomor PDS-04: Fps. 1/01/1997," Kejaksaan Negeri Tasikmalaya.

43. Andreas Harsono, Benny Subianto, Lukas Luwarso, and Prasetyohadi, *Huru-Hara Rengasdengklok* (Jakarta: Institut Studi Arus Informasi, 1997), 89–103.

44. On these trends, see "Bupati Karawang: Ada yang Membuat Massa Bergerak," *Republika,* January 31, 1997; "Buntut Kerusuhan: Ramai-ramai Menyudutkan Islam" *Media Dakwah,* March 1997, 45–47; and "Bom Waktu di Rengasdengklok," *Media Dakwah,* March 1997, 53–57; and Harsono et al. *Huru-Hara Rengasdengklok,* 57–76.

45. For accounts of the riot's inception, see "Kerusuhan Rengasdengklok Teratasi," *Republika,* January 31, 1997; "Encik Gioh Sempat Panggil Polisi," *Republika,* February 1, 1997; "Pemicu 'Rengadengklok' Dituntut 4 Tahun," *Media Indonesia,* April 7, 1997; "Pemicu Kerusuhan Rengasdengklok Dihukum 3 Tahun 6 Bulan Penjara," *Kompas,* April 8, 1997; and Harsono et al., *Huru-Hara Rengasdengklok,* 5–11, 27–39.

46. On the rapid spread and subsequent exhaustion of the rioting, see "Kota Sejarah Rengasdengklok Rusuh," *Media Indonesia,* January 31, 1997; "Kami nggak Tahu, Para Pemuda itu Datang dari Mana," *Republika,* January 31, 1997; and Harsono et al., *Huru-Hara Rengasdengklok,* 12–26.

47. For a lucid and well-informed account, see Indraneel Datta, "Parliamentary Politics in Soeharto's New Order, 1987–1998" (Ph.D. diss., University of London, 2003).

48. Erawati Nurrahmah and Nur Samsi, eds., *Politik Ala Mudrick: "Politisi Kampung Mendobrak"* (Surakarta: PT Pabelan Jayakarta, 1998).

49. Ibid., 39–41.

50. "Gus Dur-Mbak Tutut Gelar Rapat Akbar," *Surabaya Post,* February 7, 1997; "Gus Dur dan Mbak Tutut Hadiri Istigosah Kubro," *Surabaya Post,* March 29, 1997; "Gus Dur: Mbak Tutut Tokoh Masa Depan," *Surabaya Post,* April 3, 1997.

51. See "Kerusuhan di Jateng lukai 3 Orang, Buntut Bentrokan Pemuda," *Bisnis Indonesia,* February 14, 1997; "Bupati: Tidak Ada Kaitan dengan Politik," *Republika,* February 14, 1997; "Sebanyak 12 Sepeda Motor Rusak Dalam Perkelahian Pemuda," *Suara Karya,* February 14, 1997.

52. "Rabu Dinihari Pekalongan Rusuh Lagi," *Republika,* March 27, 1997.

53. "Pekalongan Pulih, Lima 'Dalang' Diburu," *Media Indonesia,* March 29, 1997.

54. On these accusations, see "KH Afifudin Bantah Picu Kerusuhan Pekalongan," *Republika,* April 1, 1997.

55. "Kerusuhan Kembali Terjadi di Pekalongan," *Merdeka,* April 7, 1997.

56. On the disturbances that marred the twenty-fourth anniversary of the founding of PPP, for example, see "Kerusuhan di Wonosobo dan Banjarnegara," *Kompas,* April 10, 1997; "Wonosobo-Banjarnegara Dilanda Keributan," *Republika,* April 10, 1997; "Kerusuhan Nyaris Terulang lagi di Pekalongan," *Republika,* April 10, 1997; and "Aksi Brutal Landa Wonosobo," *Suara Karya,* April 10, 1997. On subsequent clashes in Pekalongan, see "Perusakan di Pekalongan dan Insiden Kecil di Solo," *Suara Pembaruan,* April 21, 1997; "Kerusuhan Kembali Guncang Pekalongan," *Suara Karya,* April 24, 1997; and "Massa Rusak Rumah Ketua Pantarlih Kodya Pekalongan," *Republika,* April 24, 1997.

57. Soetrisno, *Perilaku Kekerasan Kolektif,* 140–150; Hairus Salim and Andi Achdian, *Amuk Banjarmasin* (Jakarta: Yayasan Lembaga Bantuan Hukum Indonesia, 1997), 17–40.

58. Salim and Achdian, *Amuk Banjarmasin,* 41–56; Soetrisno, *Perilaku Kekerasan Kolektif,* 150–154.

59. Salim and Achdian, *Amuk Banjarmasin,* 53.

60. Soetrisno, *Perilaku Kekerasan Kolektif,* 154–156; Salim and Achdian, *Amuk Banjarmasin,* 61–98.

61. See, for example, "Sampang Bergolak, Kantor Golkar Dibakar," *Surabaya Post,* May 30, 1997; "Panas di Tapal Kuda," *Sinar,* July 5, 1997, 62–63.

62. On Kalla, see François Raillon, "How to Become a National Entrepreneur: The Rise of Indonesian Capitalists," *Archipel* 41 (1991), 106. In late 2004, Kalla was elected first as Indonesia's vice president and subsequently as the chairman of Golkar, the strongest party in the parliament.

63. See Heru Hendratmoko, Sukriansyah S. Latif, and Tomi Lebang, *Amuk Makassar* (Jakarta: Institut Studi Arus Informasi, 1998), 82; A. Muis, "Akar Kerusuhan Ujungpandang," *Adil,* September 24–30, 1997, 11; and A. Muis, "Biang Peristiwa 15 September," *Forum Keadilan,* October 6, 1997, 27.

64. Hendratmoko, Latif, and Lebang, *Amuk Makassar,* 83–84.

65. Ibid., 35–103; "Mencari Sebab Amuk Meledak," *Forum Keadilan,* October 6, 1997, 19–20.

66. "Anni Dibunuh, Ujungpandang Terpanggang," *Forum Keadilan,* October 6, 1997, 12–16.

67. "Jubaedi Saleh: 'Saya Tidak Benci Orang Cina,'" *Forum Keadilan,* October 6, 1997, 17; Hendratmoko, Latif, and Lebang, *Amuk Makassar,* 30–33.

68. "Kerusuhan Ujungpandang Sudah Teratasi," *Suara Karya,* September 17, 1997; "Musnahnya Kelenteng Ibu Agung Bahari," *Adil,* September 24–30, 1997; "Seusai Api Membakar Kota Daeng," *Ummat,* September 29, 1997; "Catatan dari Ujungpandang (Bagian Pertama): Riak Sebuah proses Marjinalisasi," *Republika,* October 15, 1997.

69. "Mengapa Ujungpandang Meradang?" *Adil,* September 24–30, 1997, 8–9; Hendratmoko, Latif, and Lebang, *Amuk Makassar,* 8–25.

70. Takashi Shiraishi, "Anti-Sinicism in Java's New Order," in Daniel Chirot and Anthony

Reid, eds., *Essential Outsiders: Chinese and Jews in the Modern Transformation of Southeast Asia and Central Europe* (Seattle: University of Washington Press, 1997), 190.

71. Takashi Shiraishi, *An Age in Motion: Popular Radicalism in Java, 1912–1926* (Ithaca: Cornell University Press, 1990).

72. The Siauw Giap, "Group Conflict in a Plural Society," *Revue du Sud-Est Asiatique* 1–2 (1966), 1–31, 185–217.

73. See J. A. C. Mackie, "Anti-Chinese Outbreaks in Indonesia, 1959–68," in J. A. C. Mackie, ed., *The Chinese in Indonesia: Five Essays* (Honolulu: University Press of Hawaii, 1976), 77–138.

74. Herbert Feith, "The Dynamics of Guided Democracy," in Ruth McVey, ed., *Indonesia* (New Haven, Conn.: HRAF Press, 1963), 349.

75. On the riots, see Selo Soemardjan, ed., *Gerakan 10 Mei 1963 di Sukabumi* (Bandung: P. T. Eresco, 1963). On the national-level political backdrop, see Mackie, "Anti-Chinese Outbreaks," 82–110.

76. On this speech, see David Jenkins, *Suharto and His Generals: Indonesian Military Politics, 1975–1983* (Ithaca: Cornell Modern Indonesia Project, 1984); and C. van Dijk, "Major Developments in Indonesia in the First Half of 1980: The General Elections Act and Two Speeches by Suharto," *Review of Indonesian and Malaysian Affairs* 14, no. 2 (December 1980), 125–152, especially 125–143.

77. On the Petisi Limapuluh group, see Jenkins, *Suharto and His Generals*, especially 162–170.

78. On the rioting in Makassar (then known as Ujungpandang), see, for example, "Karena Masih Terjadi Pengrusakan: Jam-Malam Berlaku di Ujungpandang," *Pedoman Rakyat,* April 12, 1980; "Dengan Terjadinya Aksi-2 Pengrusakan: Di Ujung Pandang jam malam," *Harian Tegas,* April 12, 1980; "Diperiksa, Sekelompok Orang di Ujungpandang," *Merdeka,* April 14, 1980; and "An Anti-Chinese Rampage," *Far Eastern Economic Review,* May 2, 1990, 24–25.

79. On the riots in Solo, Semarang, and other towns in Java, see, for example, "Murid SGO Solo Merusak Toko-toko," *Merdeka,* November 21, 1980; "Keadaan Jawa Tengah dapat dikuasai," *Surabaya Post,* December 4, 1980; "Small Fight with Big Results," *Far Eastern Economic Review,* December 5, 1980, 10–12; "Jawa Tengah, Normal Kembali," *Tempo,* December 6, 1980, 12–14; "Tidak Ada Lagi Jam Malam," *Tempo,* December 13, 1980, 12–14; "Dari Pasar Klewer ke Pasar Ya'ik," *Tempo,* December 13, 1980, 54–56; "Sala setelah peristiwa itu," *Surabaya Post,* January 26, 1981; P. Bambang Siswoyo, *Huru Hara Solo Semarang* (Surakarta: BP Bhakti Pertiwi, 1981); and C. van Dijk, "Survey of Major Political Developments in Indonesia in the Second Half of 1980: Crime Prevention, Anti-Chinese Riots, and the PDI Party Congress," *Review of Indonesian and Malaysian Affairs* 15, no. 1 (1981), 93–125, especially 97–101.

80. See C. van Dijk, *Rebellion under the Banner of Islam: The Darul Islam in Indonesia* (The Hague: Martinus Nijhoff, 1981).

81. For the machinations of a much despised *konglomerat lokal* in Rengasdengklok, for example, see Benny Subianto, "Potret Konglomerat Lokal," in Harsono et al., *Huru-Hara Rengasdengklok,* 92–108.

82. For a taste of the publicity surrounding the dropping of the ban on the *jilbab,* see "Penerapan Jilbab Tunggu SK Dirjen," *Surabaya Post,* February 18, 1991; and "Aini, Arti, Nurul, dan Widy: Bersyukur Meski Harus Tergusur," *Surabaya Post,* February 24, 1991.

83. For two very different treatments of the significance of the *jilbab* and the veil, see Suzanne Brenner, "Reconstructing Self and Society: Javanese Muslim Women and 'The Veil,'" *American Ethnologist* 23, no. 4 (November 1996), 673–697; and Anne-Emmanuelle Berger, "The Newly Veiled Woman: Irigaray, Specularity, and the Islamic Veil," *Diacritics* 28, no. 1 (Spring 1998), 93–119.

84. Paul R. Brass, *Theft of an Idol: Text and Context in the Representation of Collective Violence* (Princeton: Princeton University Press, 1997), 16.

85. On focalization and transvaluation, see Stanley J. Tambiah, *Leveling Crowds: Ethnonationalist Conflicts and Collective Violence in South Asia* (Berkeley: University of California Press, 1996), 81.

86. See Clark McPhail and David Miller, "The Assembling Process: A Theoretical and Empirical Examination," *American Sociological Review* 38 (December 1973), 721–735.

87. See Elias Canetti, *Crowds and Power* (New York: Noonday Press, 1984), 73–75.

88. See James T. Siegel, "Early Thoughts on the Violence of May 13 and 14, 1998, in Jakarta," *Indonesia* 66 (October 1998), 75–108.

89. James T. Siegel, *Solo in the New Order: Language and Hierarchy in an Indonesian City* (Princeton: Princeton University Press, 1986), 246.

Chapter 5. Crisis, Conspiracy, Conflagration

1. "Demonstrasi: Impala Udin Versus VW," *Tempo*, August 11, 1973, 6.

2. See "DPR: RUU 9 Titik Api," *Tempo*, August 18, 1973, 6–7; "RUU Perkawinan: Sumpah Para Ulama," *Tempo*, 1 September 1973, 10; "RUU Perkawinan, Aksi Dan Reaksi," *Tempo*, September 8, 1973, 6–9; "Beberapa Pasal Masalah," *Tempo*, September 8, 1973, 9–10; and Donald K. Emmerson, *Indonesia's Elite: Political Culture and Cultural Politics* (Ithaca: Cornell University Press, 1976), 229–245.

3. See, for example, "DPR: Suara Khatib dan Ancaman Gregorius, *Tempo*, August 25, 1973, 6; "RUU Perkawinan: Mencabut & Merubah," *Tempo*, September 22, 1973, 8–9; "RUU Perkawinan: Tanggapan & Keluhan," *Tempo*, September 29, 1973, 6–7; Emmerson, *Indonesia's Elite*, 230–235.

4. Michael Sean Malley, "A Political Biography of Major General Soedjono Hoemardani, 1918–1986" (M.A. thesis, Cornell University, 1990).

5. See Richard Tanter, "Intelligence Agencies and Third World Militarization: A Case Study of Indonesia, 1966–1989" (Ph.D. diss., Monash University, 1991), especially 321–325, 430–432.

6. On this backdrop, see, for example, Heru Cahyono, *Peranan Ulama Dalam Golkar, 1971–1980: Dari Pemilu Sampai Malari* (Jakarta: Pustaka Sinar Harapan, 1992), 143–170.

7. "Mahasiswa: Katakanlah Dengan Senyum," *Tempo*, January 19, 1974, 5–6; "Demonstrasi: Tri Tura Baru 1974," *Tempo*, January 19, 1974, 6–7; Emmerson, *Indonesia's Elite*, 245–247.

8. "Musibah Bagi Golongan Menengah & Bawah," *Tempo*, January 26, 1974, 5–9.

9. Jeffrey A. Winters, *Power in Motion: Capital Mobility and the Indonesian State* (Ithaca: Cornell University Press, 1996).

10. See Heru Cahyono, *Pangkopkamtib Jenderal Soemitro dan Peristiwa 15 Januari '74* (Jakarta: Pustaka Sinar Harapan, 1998), especially 182–239; and Marzuki Arifin *Peristiwa 15 Januari 1974* (Jakarta: Publishing House Indonesia, 1985).

11. International Monetary Fund, "Indonesia—Memorandum of Economic and Financial Policies," January 15, 1998. Copy in possession of the author.

12. On the unfolding economic crisis, see Ross H. McLeod, "Postscript to the Survey of Recent Developments: On Causes and Cures for the Rupiah Crisis," *Bulletin of Indonesian Economic Studies* 33, no. 3 (December 1997), 35–52; Hadi Soesastro and M. Chatib Basri, "Survey of Recent Developments," *Bulletin of Indonesian Economic Studies* 34, no. 1 (April 1998), 3–54.

13. See, for example, "Bambang Tri Gugat Menkeu ke PTUN: Ini Menyangkut Kredibilitas Saya," *Surabaya Post*, November 4, 1997; "Bambang dan Probo PTUN-kan Pemerintah:

Penutupan Bank Andromeda Sangat Ironis," *Jawa Pos,* November 4, 1997; "Langkah Misterius di Balik Likuidasi," *Forum Keadilan,* November 17, 1997; and "Di Balik Skenario Likuidasi 16 Bank," *Infobank,* November 1997, 2–5.

14. "Inflasi Surabaya 21,21 persen," *Surya,* March 5, 1998.

15. See, for example, "Isu Kudeta, Pasar Diserbu," *Surya,* January 9, 1998; and John McBeth, "Ground Zero," *Far Eastern Economic Review,* January 22, 1998, 14–17.

16. "Mereka Bicara tentang Sofyan dll," *D & R,* February 21, 1998, 29–33.

17. See, for example, Wanandi's comments as quoted in "CSIS: Konglomerat bisa kabur," *Surya,* January 18, 1998.

18. See also "Kontroversi Sofyan Wanandi Setelah Ledakan," *Forum Keadilan,* February 23, 1998, 12–21.

19. See, for example, "Lebih Jauh Dengan Mayjen TNI Sjafrie Sjamsoeddin," *Kompas,* March 1, 1998.

20. On this case, see, for example, the following magazine cover stories: "Bom untuk Konglomerat," *D&R,* February 7, 1998, 24–27; "Sofjan Wanandi dan CSIS," *Gatra,* February 14, 1998, 23–32; "Dituduh Apa Lagi Sofyan Wanandi?" *D&R,* February 14, 1998, 20–21.

21. See Panglima ABRI Telepon 13 Konglomerat," *Kompas,* January 15, 1998; "ABRI imbau nonpri jual dolar," *Surya,* January 15, 1998.

22. "Syarwan: Mereka Penghkianat," *Republika,* January 24, 1998; "'Ada Yang Sengaja Goyang Indonesia," *Jawa Pos,* February 12, 1998.

23. For vivid photographs of this affair, see "Buka Puasa Kopassus," *Kompas,* January 24, 1998; "Prabowo Dan Ulama," *Republika,* January 24, 1998; and "Buka Puasa Bersama di Mako Kopassus Cijantung," *Media Dakwah,* February 1998. On KISDI and DDII more generally, see chapter 7.

24. See, for example, the articles in *Media Dakwah,* February 1998, 41–59.

25. "Ketua Kisdi: Sofyan Wanandi Pengkhianat," *Memorandum,* February 9, 1998.

26. I attended a meeting at the Surabaya office of the newspaper *Republika,* for example, where Hussein Umar spoke about CSIS and the Wanandi brothers, the economic crisis, and Habibie's candidacy for the vice presidential post.

27. On the MUI call for a jihad, see, for example, "Seruan Jihad untuk Siapa?," *D & R,* February 21, 1998, 72–73; Masdar F. Mas'udi, "Call for Jihad 'May Have Caused Riots,'" *Jakarta Post,* February 20, 1998; and Rosdiansyah, "Seruan jihad MUI penyebab kerusuhan?" *Surya,* March 5, 1998.

28. "PPP desak Matahari Solo turunkan harga," *Surya,* February 20, 1998.

29. See, for example, "Operasi Sembako, Dua Spekulan Diperiksa," *Jawa Pos,* January 16, 1998; "Diperiksa, Tiga Gudang Penyimpanan Sembako," *Jawa Pos,* January 18, 1998; "Cari dan Temukan Para Penimbun," *Republika,* February 15, 1998; "Penimbun Sembako di Padang Resmi Jadi Tersangka," *Republika,* February 18, 1998; "Pengusaha Giling Padi Trauma, Dituduh Menimbun," *Kompas,* February 21, 1998; and "13 Penimbun Sembako Jadi Tersangka," *Republika,* 24 Februari 1998.

30. See, for example, "Walikota Bangga, Warganya Gelar Pasar Murah Sembako," *Surabaya Post,* February 27, 1998; "Bagi-bagi Sembako," *Surabaya Post,* February 28, 1998.

31. See, for example, "Ponpes Jatim Jadi Distributor Sembako," *Republika,* February 19, 1998; "Pesantren, Distributor Sembako?" *Jawa Pos,* February 25, 1998.

32. See, for example, "Dari Resah ke Rusuh," *D & R,* January 24, 1998, 28–29; "Jember: Sembako Membawa Rusuh," *Ummat,* January 26, 1998, 20.

33. Indonesian and magazines featured hundreds of articles about the riots in January and February 1998. For an English-language summary, see Human Rights Watch, *Indonesia Alert: Economic Crisis Leads to Scapegoating of Ethnic Chinese* (New York: Human Rights Watch, 1998), especially 8–15.

34. "Bila Masyarakat Rentan Isu," *D & R,* February 21, 1998, 52.

35. *The Number of Churches Closed, Destroyed, or Burnt Down Every Month in Period 1998* (Surabaya: ICCF, 1998).

36. John McBeth and Salil Tripathi, "Playing with Ire," *Far Eastern Economic Review,* March 5, 1998, 18–19; "Kerusuhan di Cirebon Diduga Melibatkan Perusuh Bayaran," *Republika,* February 17, 1998.

37. See, for example, Michael Richardson, "U.S. Commander Sounds Alert on Indonesia Unrest," *International Herald Tribune,* February 7–8, 1998, 1, 4.

38. On the sense of disappointment with the cabinet in ICMI circles, see "Staf Ahli Wapres, Kompensasi bagi ICMI?"; "Habibie Selesai, Mereka Juga"; and "Karena Wapres Bukan Ban Serep," all in *Jawa Pos,* April 4, 1998.

39. See, for example, John McBeth, "The Twilight Zone," *Far Eastern Economic Review,* April 16, 1998, 18–20.

40. International Monetary Fund, "Indonesia—Supplementary Memorandum of Economic and Financial Policies," 10 April 1998. Copy in possession of the author.

41. "Jangan Sebarkan Sentimen SARA," *Kompas,* February 10, 1998; "KSAD Jenderal TNI Wiranto: Hasutan Pihak Tertentu Jadi Pemicu Kerusuhan," *Republika,* February 16, 1998.

42. "Karlina Leksono: 'Kita Sudah Terlalu Lama Diam,'" *D & R,* March 14, 1998, 34–37.

43. See "Sebuah Ikhtiar di Tengah Kemustahilan," *D & R,* February 28, 1998, 20; and "Emil Salim: 'Ini Pertarungan Antar-Ide,'" *D & R,* February 28, 1998, 21–23.

44. For a thoroughly researched and carefully documented study of the student movement, see Frank Feulner, "At the Forefront of Reform: Student Protests and Regime Transition in Indonesia" (Ph.D. diss., University of London, 2001).

45. "1998: The Nationwide Student Protest Movement and the Opening to Democratic Reform," in Human Rights Watch/Asia, *Academic Freedom in Indonesia: Dismantling Soeharto-Era Barriers* (New York: Human Rights Watch/Asia, 1998).

46. See, for example, "Prof. Dr. Ichlasul Amal M.A.: 'Mahasiswa-lah yang Sekarang Punya Power . . . ,'" *D & R,* April 4, 1998, 20–21.

47. "Agar Menjadi people Power?," *D & R,* May 2, 1998, 67–68; "Membangun Basis Perjuangan Rakyat," *D & R,* May 2, 1998, 69–70; "'Intifadah Campus Meluas," *D & R,* May 2, 1998, 71.

48. "Dialog Sebagai Salah Satu Cara," *D & R,* April 25, 1998, 48–49.

49. "Membentuk Tim, Mencari Penculik," *Forum Keadilan,* May 4, 1998; "Mayjen TNI (Purn.) Samsudin: 'Apa Mungkin Seorang Jenderal Bisa Melakukan Perbuatan Itu?'" *Forum Keadilan,* May 4, 1998.

50. "Sudah Jatuh, Tertimpa Tangga Pula," *D & R,* May 9, 1998.

51. See "IMF Executive Board Completes First Review of Indonesia's Economic Program," International Monetary Fund News Brief No. 98/11, May 4, 1998; and "International Monetary Fund Press Briefing on First Review of Indonesia's Economic Program by Stanley Fischer and Hubert Neiss," May 4, 1998. Copies in possession of the author.

52. See "Percik Bara Seantero Nusantara," *Forum Keadilan,* June 1, 1998, 18–20.

53. See, for example, "Kantor gubernur dan DPRD dijaga ketat," *Surya,* May 9, 1998.

54. "Habibie clarifies ICMI's views," *Jakarta Post,* May 10, 1998.

55. See "Di Ujung Aksi Damai," *Forum Keadilan,* June 1, 1998, 10–16.

56. See, for example, "Si Pelaku Bisa Diketahui Dari Komandanna," *Forum Keadilan,* June 1, 1998, 74–78; "Misteri, Keanehan, Campur Aduk Dalam Trisakti Berdarah," *Gatra,* June 13, 1998; "Sidang Penembakan Mahasiswa Trisakti: Keberadaan Pasukan Lain Dipertanyakan," *Kompas,* June 16, 1998; "Danpomdam Jaya, Kolonel Hendardji: 'Ada Pihak yang Mau Menututup-nutupi Kasus Ini,'" *Forum Keadilan,* June 16, 1998; "Sidang Penembakan Mahasiswa Trisakti: Perintah Tembak Hanya Ada pada Pangdam," *Kompas,* June 17, 1998; and "Sidang Kasus Trisakti: Ada Tembakan dari Arah Citraland," *Kompas,* June 25, 1998.

57. See Anggit Noegroho and Bambang Harsri Irawan, *Rekaman Lensa Peristiwa Mei 1998 Di Solo* (Solo: Aksara Solopos, 1998).

58. See, for example, "Jakarta Dilanda Kerusuhan Massa," *Kompas,* May 14, 1998; "Perusuh Menjarah," *Kompas,* May 15, 1998; and "Kerusuhan Makin Hebat: 7 Tewas, ratusan mobil dibakar, toko2 hancur," *Pos Kota,* May 15, 1998.

59. See Tim Relawan Untuk Kemanusiaan, *Sujud di Hadapan Korban: Tragedi Jakarta Mei 1998* (Jakarta: Divisi Data Tim Relawan, 1998).

60. See Tim Pemburu Fakta, *Puncak Kebiadaban Bangsa: Pemerkosaan Etnik Tionghoa 13–14 Mei '98* (Jakarta: Yayasan Karyawan Matra, 1998).

61. "Over 150,000 Flee Abroad During Riots: Ministry," *Jakarta Post,* June 9, 1998.

62. Tim Relawan Untuk Kemanusiaan, *Dokumentasi Awal No. 1: Pola Kerusuhan di Jakarta dan Sekitarnya* (Jakarta: Tim Relawan Untuk Kemanusiaan, 1998); Tim Relawan Untuk Kemanusiaan, *Dokumentasi Awal No. 2: Status Penjarahan dalam Kerusuhan* (Jakarta: Tim Relawan Untuk Kemanusiaan, 1998).

63. See, for example, "Ketika Itu Saya di Australia," *Tajuk,* September 3, 1998, 20–21.

64. See "Saksi-Saksi Setelah 100 Hari," *Tajuk,* September 3, 1998, 16–19; and "TGPF Temukan Indikasi Kopassus Terlibat Kerusuhan," *SiaR,* September 30, 1998.

65. See, in particular, Tim Gabungan Pencari Fakta, *Laporan Akhir Peristiwa Kerusuhan Tanggal 13–15 Mei Jakarta, Solo, Palembang, Lampung, Surabaya, dan Medan* (Jakarta: TGPF, October 1998), "Seri 2: Data-Data Kerusuhan," 25–80, and "Seri 6: Verifikasi," 322–364.

66. Fakta, *Laporan Akhir,* "Ringkasan Eksekutif," 9.

67. See Tim Relawan Untuk Kemanusiaan, *Dokumentasi Awal No. 3: Perkosaan Massal dalam Rentetan Kerusuhan* (Jakarta: Tim Relawan Untuk Kemanusiaan, 1998); Fakta, *Puncak Kebiadaban Bangsa;* Human Rights Watch, *Indonesia: The Damaging Debate on Rapes of Ethnic Chinese Women* (New York: Human Rights Watch, 1998); and Human Rights Watch, *Better Protection of Rapes Investigators Needed* (New York: Human Rights Watch, October 12, 1998).

68. See Fakta, *Laporan Akhir,* "Seri 2: Data-Data Kerusuhan," 130–132; and M. Hari Mulyadi, Soedarmono et al. *Runtuhnya Kekuasaan "Kraton Alit" (Studi Radikalisasi Sosial "Wong Sala" dan Kerusuhan Mei 1998 di Surakarta* (Solo: Lembaga Pengembangan Teknologi Pedesaan, 1999), 467–558.

69. Other research has also confirmed the broad contours of this pattern. See, for example, Agus Budi Purnomo and Dadan U.D., "Analisa Keruangan Kerusuhan Mei 1998 di DKI Jakarta" (Jakarta: Pusat Penelitian Perkotaan Lembaga Penelitian Universitas Trisakti, 1998), cited in Rene L. Pattiradjawane, "Peristiwa Mei 1998 di Jakarta: Titik Terendah Sejarah Orang Etnis Cina di Indonesia," in I. Wibowo, ed., *Harga yang Harus Dibayar: Sketsa Pergulatan Etnis Cina di Indonesia* (Jakarta: Gramedia Pustaka Utama, 2000), 220–226. See also: "Peta Amuk di Kota Hantu," *Tempo,* May 25, 2003, 164–166.

70. I served as an expert witness in a legal dispute in London involving insurance claims for damaged Ramayana department stores and provided guidance and assistance to private investigators hired to examine and document the events of May 13–15, 1998 at various Ramayana outlets in the greater Jakarta area. Aside from my own involvement in the case and in visiting the sites of various Ramayana stores in and around Jakarta, in my possession is extensive documentation from the case, including copies of signed affidavits by eyewitnesses present during the rioting.

71. See, for example, "Menhamkam/Pangab: Situasi Jakarta Sudah Normal," *Kompas,* May 17, 1998; and "Merevisi Dua Keppres Berumur Sebelas Hari," *Forum Keadilan,* June 1, 1998, 80–85.

72. "Presiden Segera 'Reshuffle' Kabinet," *Kompas,* May 17, 1998.

73. "Para Tokoh Bentuk Majelis Amanat Rakyat," *Kompas,* May 15, 1998.

74. "Pimpinan DPR: Sebaiknya Pak Harto Mundur," *Kompas,* May 19, 1998; "Pimpinan DPR: Demi Persatuan, Presiden Sebaiknya Mundur," *Republika,* May 19, 1998; "Presiden Diminta Mundur," *Media Indonesia,* May 19, 1998.

75. Keith B. Richburg, "Seven Days That Toppled a Titan: Back-Room Intrigue Led to Suharto's Fall," *Washington Post,* May 24, 1998.

76. For summaries of the events leading up to Suharto's resignation, see, for example, "Detik-Detik Menjelang Pak Harto Berhenti," *Forum Keadilan,* June 17, 1998; "Detik-Detik Soeharto Berhenti Versi Habibie," *Kompas,* June 7, 1998; and S. Sinansari ecip, *Kronologi Situasi Penggulingan Soeharto Reportase Jurnalistik 72 Jam Yang Menegangkan* (Jakarta: Mizan Pustaka, 1998).

77. Robin Madrid, "Islamic Students in the Indonesian Student Movement, 1998–1999: Forces for Moderation," *Bulletin for Concerned Asian Scholars* 31, no. 3 (July–September 1999), 17–32.

78. See, for example, "Misteri Romo Sandy," *Panji Masyarakat,* November 18, 1998, 70–72; "Isu Perkosaan Massal: Polisi Menyidik Romo Sandyawan," *Media Dakwah,* September 1998, 15–16; and "Wawancara dengan Fadli Zon SS: Konspirasi Menghancurkan Prabowo," *Media Dakwah,* January 1999, 14–16.

79. See, for example, "Pernyataan Sikap Soal Prabowo dan Dewan Kehormatan Perwira," *Media Dakwah,* September 1998, 14; "Mengapa Prabowo Mendekat," *Sabili,* September 2, 1998, 10–14; "Mengapa Prabowo Disingkirkan," *Sabili,* September 2, 1999, 15–19; "Fitnah Keji Buat Prabowo," *Media Dakwah,* January 1999, 13–14; and "Memburu Prabowo," *Media Dakwah,* January 1999, 17–18.

80. Lieutenant General Johny Lumintang, a Menadonese Protestant, was formally named to replace Prabowo as Kostrad commander but served less than a day before he was replaced by Lieutenant General Djamari Chaniago. Major General Luhut Pandjaitan, another Christian, was reportedly Wiranto's choice to replace Muchdi as commander of Kopassus, but at the last minute Major General Syahrir was named to the post in his stead. Both Lumintang and Pandjaitan were widely known to have been at odds with Prabowo over the previous years.

81. On this series of events, see Geoffrey Forrester, "A Jakarta Diary, May 1998," in Geoffrey Forrester and R. J. May, eds., *The Fall of Soeharto* (London: C. Hurst, 1998), especially 58–60.

82. See James T. Siegel, "Early Thoughts on the Violence of May 13 and 14, 1998 in Jakarta," *Indonesia* 66 (October 1998), 75–108.

83. Arief W. Djati, personal communication.

Chapter 6. From Lynchings to Communal Violence

1. See, for example, the comments of Ahmad Sumargono, a leading light of KISDI, the Indonesian Committee for Solidarity with the Muslim World, and Partai Bulan Bintang, the Crescent and Stars Party, in "Ahmad Sumargono: 'Kalau Status Quo ini Menguntungkan Islam, Mengapa Tidak?'" *Tempo,* November 23, 1998, 32–35.

2. See, for example, the articles in the October 1998 issue of *Media Dakwah,* a monthly magazine published by DDII.

3. See, for example, "Sebagian WNI Etnis Tionghoa di Jatim Masih Galau," *Suara Pembaruan,* June 29, 1998.

4. Akhmad Fikri AF, *Laporan Investigasi "Amuk Massa Purworejo": Dari pengobongan Ngebong hingga pengrusakan rumah-rumah ibadat* (Yogyakarta: Tim Relawan Yogyakarta, 1998).

5. See, for example, Paul Tahalele, *The Church and Human Rights in Indonesia* (Surabaya: Indonesia Christian Communication Forum, 1998), 17–19.

6. On these events, see, for example, "Gara-gara Onderdil, Beras, dan Acung," *Forum Keadilan,* October 5, 1998, 20–21.

7. See, for example, "Kisah Peduli Dari Kota Karawang," *Tajuk,* March 4, 1999, 12–17. Also in my possession is an unpublished report by the human rights group Yayasan Lembaga Bantuan Hukum Indonesia titled "Amok di Karawang," which provides a detailed account of these events.

8. See, for example, "Meredam Penjarah dan Penadah," *Forum Keadilan,* August 10, 1998, 10–12; and "Tren Baru: Menjarah Komoditas Unggulan," *Forum Keadilan,* August 10, 1998, 16–17.

9. See, for example, "Berjihad Mendukun Sidang," *Tempo,* November 30, 1998, 48.

10. "MUI Serukan Aparat Ambil Alih Pengamanan SI MPR," *Republika,* November 12, 1998.

11. "Di Mana Ada Forkot di Situ Ada Furkon," *Tempo,* November 23, 1998, 30–31.

12. See, for example, "Pam Swakarsa: Aktor atau Korban?," *Tempo,* November 30, 1998, 42–44; and "Sidang Berakhir, Darah Mengalir," *Forum Keadilan,* November 30, 1998, 12–16.

13. On the Front Pembela Islam's Ramadan activities in 1999 and 2000, see *Indonesia: Violence and Radical Muslims* (Jakarta: International Crisis Group, October 10, 2001), 7–8.

14. On the Front Pembela Islam, see, for example, the three articles on December 1, 2000, on "Operasi Jeda Maksiat ala FPI," by the *Detik* website (http://www.detik.com,) as well as the two brief pieces put out on February 23, 2000, by TNI Watch! on the SiaR News Service website (http://apchr.murdoch.edu.au/minihub/siarlist/maillist.html): "Mengenal Laskar Pembela Islam (LPI) dan Front Pembela Islam (FPI)," and "Struktur Organisasi Front Pembela Islam (FPI)."

15. On this point, see Henk Schulte Nordholt, "Renegotiating boundaries: Access, Agency and Identity in Post-Soeharto Indonesia," *Bijdragen tot de Taal-, Land- en Volkenkunde* 159, no. 4 (2003), 550–589.

16. Kees van Dijk, "The Good, the Bad and the Ugly: Explaining the Unexplainable: Amuk Massa in Indonesia"; and Freek Colombijn, "Maling, Maling! The Lynching of Petty Criminals," both in Freek Colombijn and J. Thomas Lindblad, eds., *Roots of Violence in Indonesia: Contemporary Violence in Historical Perspective* (Leiden: KITLV Press, 2002), 277–297, 299–329.

17. Careful and thoughtful treatments of this incident are David Mitchell, "Tragedy in Sumba," *Inside Indonesia* 58 (April-June 1999); and Jacqueline A. C. Vel, "Tribal Battle in a Remote Island: Crisis and Violence in Sumba (Eastern Indonesia)," *Indonesia* 72 (October 2001), 141–158.

18. On these events, see *Communal Violence in Indonesia: Lessons From Kalimantan* (Jakarta/Brussels: International Crisis Group, 27 June 2001).

19. Edward Peake, "Tradition, Christianity, and the State in Understandings of Sickness and Healing in South Nias, Indonesia" (Ph.D. diss., University of London, 2000).

20. These events are described in a brief unpublished account that I obtained: Tim Advokasi PC PMII Tasikmalaya, "Rusuh di Kampung Hanja" (July 2000).

21. See, for example, "Korban Pembantaian 'Dukun Santet' Jatim 163 Orang," *Jawa Pos,* October 8, 1998.

22. Police officials in Ciamis registered thirty-seven victims of such killings in 1999. See "Anyir Darah di 'Sungai Manis,'" *Tempo,* May 11–17, 1999.

23. Clifford Geertz, *The Religion of Java* (Chicago: University of Chicago Press, 1960), 110.

24. See, for example, "Memberlakukan KUHP Majapahit?" *Tempo,* December 31, 1983, 64–65; and Ronny Nitibaskara, "Observations on the Practice of Sorcery in Java," in C. W. Watson and Roy Ellen, eds., *Understanding Witchcraft and Sorcery in Southeast Asia* (Honolulu: University of Hawaii Press, 1993), 129–130.

25. See, for example, "Kepala, badan dan kaki dikubur tepisah," *Surya,* November 25, 1997; "Dieksekusi kawanan ala ninja," *Surya,* November 26, 1997; "Tiga 'dukun' dibakar hidup-hidup," *Surya,* November 26, 1997; "Pembantaian para dukun santet mengarah hukum rimba," *Surya,* November 27, 1997; "Santet Lagi, Kali Ini Lolos," *Jawa Pos,* November 29, 1997; "Kambuh Lagi, Gerombolan Pembasmi 'Dukun Santet,'" *D & R,* December 13, 1997, 98–99.

26. "Pro dan Kontra Pasal Santet," *D & R,* February 14, 1998, 33–34.

27. "Pinggiran Bondowoso rusuh," *Surya,* January 5, 1998; "Pemicu diselidiki, aparat siaga," *Surya,* January 5, 1998; and Yudi Burhan, "Laporan Kegiatan" (Surabaya: Lembaga Bantuan Hukum Surabaya, February 18–20, 1998).

28. See, for example, "Tidak Benar Saya Halalkan Darah Warga NU," *Oposisi,* October-November 28, 1998, 16–17; "NU Tercabik-cabik Lagi?" *Memo Minggu,* August 1998, 6.

29. See, for example, Robert W. Hefner, "Islamizing Java? Religion and Politics in Rural East Java," *Journal of Asian Studies* 46, no. 3 (August 1987), 533–554.

30. See the brief account titled "Balambangan's Einde (1767–1777)," in H. J. de Graaf, *Geschiedenis van Indonesie* (Bandung: W. Van Hoeve, 1949), 272–275.

31. Laurence Husson, *La Migration Madurese vers l'Est de Java* (Paris: L'Harmattan, 1995), 145–158.

32. Graeme J. Hugo, "Population movements in Indonesia during the colonial period," in James J. Fox, ed., *Indonesia: The Making of a Culture* (Canberra: Australian National University Research School of Pacific Studies, 1980), 106, cited in Andrew Beatty, *Varieties of Javanese Religion: An Anthropological Account* (Cambridge: Cambridge University Press, 1999), 17.

33. Aris Ananta, Evid Nurvidya Arifin, and Leo Suryadinata, *Indonesian Electoral Behaviour: A Statistical Perspective* (Singapore: Institute of Southeast Asian Studies, 2004), 78–79.

34. Beatty, *Varieties of Javanese Religion,* 1–2.

35. See, for example, Centre for Village Studies, Gadjah Mada University, "Rural Violence in Klaten and Banyuwangi," and "Additional Data on Counter-Revolutionary Cruelties in Indonesia, Especially in East Java," both in Robert Cribb, ed., *The Indonesian Killings of 1965–1966: Studies from Java and Bali* (Clayton, Victoria: Monash University Centre of Southeast Asian Studies, 1990), especially 150, 154–157, and 174–176.

36. Beatty, *Varieties of Javanese Religion,* 123.

37. For an ethnographic account of ongoing religious change in Malang in the 1990s, see Sven Cederroth, "New Order Modernization and Islam: Village Officials and Religious Teachers," in Hans Antlov and Sven Cederroth, eds., *Leadership on Java: Gentle Hints, Authoritarian Rule* (Richmond, Surrey: Curzon Press, 1994), 137–162. For a broader portrait of the major religious and cultural zones of East Java, see Ron Hatley, "Mapping Cultural Regions of Java," in Ron Hatley, Jim Schiller, Anton Lucas, and Barbara Martin-Schiller, *Other Javas Away from the Kraton* (Clayton, Victoria: Monash University Centre of Southeast Asian Studies, 1984), 1–32.

38. On the religious landscape of West Java, see Hiroko Horikoshi, "A Traditional Leader in a Time of Change: The Kijaji and Ulama in West Java" (Ph.D. diss., University of Illinois at Urbana-Champaign, 1976). On Ciamis in particular, see the three detailed articles in *Tempo,* May 11–17, 1999: "Ciamis di Abad Kegelapan," "Ketika Teluh Menebar Maut," and "Tragedi Pesisir Laut Selatan."

39. Ben White, *Agroindustry and Contract Farmers in Upland West Java,* Working Paper Series no. 234 (The Hague: Institute of Social Studies, November 1996), 11–12.

40. Robert W. Hefner, *The Political Economy of Mountain Java: An Interpretive History* (Berkeley: University of California Press, 1990), 9.

41. Lakpesdam-NU Jombang, "Hasil Penelitian Pelanggaran Hak-Hak Asasi Manusia di Jawa Timur: Studi Kasus: Identifikasi Faktor-faktor Penyebab Pembantaian berdalih 'dukun santet' dan Isu Ninja di Banyuwangi dan Jember" (undated, unpublished report), 17–20.

42. Ibid., 17–20.

43. Ibid., 20.

44. Ibid., 21.

45. This pattern corresponds to the one sketched in James T. Siegel, "Suharto, Witches," *Indonesia* 71 (April 2000), 27–78. This article, and subsequent discussions with Siegel, greatly shaped my understanding of the killings.

46. Abdul Manan, Imam Sumaatmadja, and Veven Sp Wardhana, *Geger Santet Banyuwangi* (Jakarta: Institut Studi Arus Informasi, 2001), 81–104.

47. Ibid., 15–16.

48. See George J. Aditjondro, "Ninjas, Nanggalas, Monuments, and Mossad Manuals: An Anthropology of Indonesian State Terror in East Timor," in Jeffrey A. Sluka, ed., *Death Squad: The Anthropology of State Terror* (Philadelphia: University of Pennsylvania Press, 2000), 158–188; and Fadjar J. Thufail, "Ninjas in Narratives of Local and National Violence in Post-Suharto Indonesia," in Mary Zurbuchen, ed., *Beginning to Remember: The Past in the Indonesian Present* (Seattle: University of Washington Press, 2005), 150–167.

49. See, for example, "Gus Dur: Dalang Kerusuhan di Kabinet," *Jawa Pos,* October 18, 1998.

50. See, for example, "Kisah Desertir Kopassus dan Ninja-Ninja Banyuwangi," and "Kasus Banyuwangi: Kongsi Baru Hartono-Prabowo?," *Detak,* November 3–9, 1998, 6, 21.

51. See, for example, "Di Balik Aksi Teror," *Aula,* November 1998, 12–33, especially 28–33. *Aula* is the official monthly magazine of Nahdlatul Ulama (NU).

52. See, for example, "Ada Selebaran, Ada yang Dibayar Rp 9.000," *Jawa Pos,* October 3, 1998; and Manan, Sumaatmadja, and Wardhana, *Geger Santet Banyuwangi,* 52, 56–57. On similar developments in the 1999 *dukun santet* killings in southern Malang and Ciamis, see: "Pelaku Kasus Santet di Malang Dibayar Rp 3 Juta," *Jawa Pos,* 26 Desember 1999; and "Pembunuhan Berantai: Membetot Sayap Komplotan Elang Ciamis," *Gamma* 26 April 1999.

53. See, for example, "Nasib Tragis 'Ninja' Gila," *Detak,* 3–9 November 1998, 20; and Manan, Sumaatmadja, and Wardhana, *Geger Santet Banyuwangi,* 73–79.

54. Manan, Sumaatmadja, and Wardhana, *Geger Santet Banyuwangi,* 31–32.

55. "Melawan Santet dengan Sumpah Pocong," *D&R,* 7 November 1998, 38–39; Manan, Sumaatmadja, and Wardhana, *Geger Santet Banyuwangi,* 58–65. See also, for example, "Dituduh Dukun Santet, 7 Orang Sumpah Alquran Disaksikan Muspida, Kiai, dan Masyarakat Pasuruan," *Jawa Pos,* 2 November 1998.

56. Manan, Sumaatmadja, and Wardhana, *Geger Santet Banyuwangi,* 61–62.

57. See, for example, Manan, Sumaatmadja, and Wardhana, *Geger Santet Banyuwangi,* 33–36.

58. "NU Antisipasi Aksi Pembantaian 'Dukun Santet' Malang," *Jawa Pos,* December 28, 1999; "NU Bantah Malang Selatan Basis NU Sekaligus PKI," *Jawa Pos,* January 7, 2000.

59. See Albert Schrauwers, *Colonial "Reformation" in the Highlands of Central Sulawesi, Indonesia, 1892–1995* (Toronto: University of Toronto Press, 2000).

60. Lorraine V. Aragon, *Fields of the Lord: Animism, Christian Minorities, and State Development in Indonesia* (Honolulu: University of Hawaii Press, 2000), 24.

61. Albert Schrauwers, "Through a Glass Darkly: Charity, Conspiracy, and Power in New Order Indonesia," in Harry G. West and Todd Sanders, eds., *Transparency and Conspiracy: Ethnographies of Suspicion in the New World Order* (Durham, N.C.: Duke University Press, 2003), 136–139.

62. On Bugis migratory patterns and their consequences in Central Sulawesi, see Greg Acciaioli, "Principles and Strategies of Bugis Migration: Some Contextual Factors Relating to Ethnic Conflict," *Masyarakat Indonesia* 25, no. 2 (1999), 239–268.

63. On the effects of the cocoa boom on Central Sulawesi, see Tania Murray Li, "Two Tales and Three Silences: Critical Reflections on Indonesian Violence," paper presented at the Con-

ference on Violence in Eastern Indonesia: Causes and Consequences, University of Hawai'i and East-West Center, Honolulu, May 16–18, 2003. I am grateful to Professor Li for sharing a draft of this paper.

64. See Arianto Sangaji, "Segregasi Masyarakat Poso," *Seputar Rakyat,* December 2003–January 2004, 16–17; and George J. Aditjondro, "Kerusuhan Poso dan Morowali, Akar Permasalahan dan Jalan Keluarnya" (paper presented at a Propatria seminar, "Penerapan Keadaan Darurat di Aceh, Papua dan Poso?" in Jakarta on January 7, 2004), 14–15.

65. Lorraine V. Aragon, "Communal Violence in Poso, Central Sulawesi: Where People Eat Fish and Fish Eat People," *Indonesia* 72 (October 2001), 56.

66. Hasan, Darwis, Syakir Mahid, Haliadi, *Sejarah Poso* (Yogyakarta: Penerbit Tiara Wacana Yogya, 2004), 266.

67. Schrauwers, "Through a Glass Darkly," 129–132.

68. Megawati's PDIP was especially popular in Bali, Central Java, and among Javanese communities in the Outer Islands as well, thus raising the specter of a strong showing for the party among Balinese transmigrants and in the sizable pockets of—overwhelmingly Muslim—Javanese migration in Poso.

69. The creation of the Morowali regency appears to have reduced the Muslim percentage of the population of Poso regency from 63 percent in 1997 to 56 percent in 2000, with the Protestant percentage rising from 34 percent in 1997 to 40 percent in 2000. The remaining 3–4 percent of the population consisted of Catholics, whether of Chinese or Flores origin, and Hindu transmigrants from Bali. Compare M. Hamdan Basyar, "Sketsa Kabupaten Poso," in M. Hamdan Basyar, ed., *Konflik Poso: Pemetaan dan Pencarian Pola-Pola Alternatif Penyelesaiannya* (Jakarta: P2P-LIPI, 2003), 18–19; and Leo Suryadinata, Evi Burvidya Arifin, and Aris Ananta, *Indonesia's Population: Ethnicity and Religion in a Changing Political Landscape* (Singapore: Institute of Southeast Asian Studies, 2003), 172–175.

70. For a sketch of settlement patterns within Poso regency, see Sangaji, "Segregasi Masyarakat Poso," 13–17.

71. Aragon, "Communal Violence in Poso," 57–58. The 2000 census indicated that some 20 percent of the Poso population was Javanese, many of these found in rural concentrations of transmigrants outside the city.

72. On this brotherhood, see Martin van Bruinessen, "The Tariqa Khalwatiyya in South Celebes," in Harry A. Poeze and Pim Schoorl, eds., *Excursies in Celebes: Een bundel bijdragen bij het afscheid van J. Noorduyn* (Leiden: KITLV Uitgeverij, 1991), 251–269.

73. On the diversity of religious practices and beliefs in South Sulawesi, for example, see Thomas Gibson, "Islam and the Spirit Cults in New Order Indonesia: Global Flows vs. Local Knowledge," *Indonesia* 69 (April 2000), 41–70.

74. On the two-term entrenchment of the *bupati* of Poso in the 1990s, his ICMI affiliation and other Islamic associational links, his nepotistic personnel practices, and his patronage of local Muslim construction contractors and other businessmen, see Aditjondro, "Kerusuhan Poso dan Morowali," 23–26, and, on his treatment of a prominent Muslim plantation owner and cattle baron in a rural area now part of Morowali regency, 32–33.

75. Aragon, *Fields of the Lord,* 315–316.

76. For different accounts of this first episode of violence in Poso, see Aragon, "Communal Violence in Poso," 60–62; M. Hamdan Basyar and Bayu Setiawan, "Rangkaian Peristiwa Kekerasan di Poso," in Basyar, *Konflik Poso,* 30–32; and S. Sinasari ecip, *Rusuh Poso Rujuk Malino* (Jakarta: Cahaya Timur, 2002), 8–10. For a very careful and thoughtful treatment of media coverage of the violence, see also Lorraine V. Aragon, "Mass Media Fragmentation and Narratives of Violent Action in Sulawesi's Poso Conflict," *Indonesia* 79 (October 2005), 1–55.

77. Aragon, "Communal Violence in Poso," 60–64.

78. See "Poso Bakal Rusuh Kembali," *Mercusuar,* April 15, 2001, cited in "Pernyataan

Sikap Crisis Center GKST Mengenai Kerusuhan (Sulawesi Tengah)," *Eskol-Net,* June 18, 2000, and in the sources given in the note 79.

79. Aragon, "Communal Violence in Poso," pp. 64–66; Basyar and Setiawan, "Rangkaian," 32–38; Sinasari, *Rusuh Poso,* 12–20.

80. On the paramilitary training camp, see "Jika 'Perdamaian' Terasa Membosankan," *Suara Hidayatullah,* October 2000; and "Poso Rioters Got Supply of Guns," *Jakarta Post,* January 30, 2001.

81. On this incident, which received wide national and international coverage, see "Poso Menangis, Ratusan Nyawa Melayang di Pesantren Wali Songo," *Kompas,* June 13, 2000, which cites figures of two hundred killed, including sixty victims whose corpses were found in a nearby river. For an eyewitness account, see "Kisah Pengasuh Ponpes Wali Songo Poso Yang Selamat Diikat dan Disiksa, Lolos Lewat Sungai," *Riau Pos,* June 14, 2000. For English-language accounts, see "Bloodbath," *Far Eastern Economic Review,* July 6, 2000; and *Crisis in Poso: A Rapid Response Media Assessment in Central Sulawesi* (Jakarta: Alliance of Independent Journalists and Internews Indonesia, 28 July 2000).

82. On the violence from late May through July 2000, see Aragon, "Communal Violence in Poso," 66–70; Basyar and Setiawan, "Rangkaian," 38–45; Sinasari, *Rusuh Poso,* 20–33; and "Tragedi Poso, Duka Kita Bersama," *Tempo,* June 18, 2000, 20–22.

83. For impressionistic mid-2001 reportage from Poso, see "Poso, Bara yang Belum Padam," *Kompas,* June 13, 2001.

84. Basyar and Setiawan, "Rangkaian," pp. 45–48; Sinasari, *Rusuh Poso,* pp. 33–34; and Brad Adams, Mike Jendrzecjzyk, Malcolm Smart, Joseph Saunders, and Aaron Brenner, *Breakdown: Four Years of Communal Violence in Central Sulawesi* (New York: Human Rights Watch, December 2002), 21–23.

85. On the violence of October–December 2001, and the role of Laskar Jihad and other such Muslim militias therein, see Bashar and Setiawan, "Rangkaian," 48–49; Sinasari, *Rusuh Poso,* 44–61; Adams et al., *Breakdown,* 20–29; and *Indonesia Backgrounder: Jihad in Central Sulawesi* (Jakarta/Brussels: International Crisis Group, 3 February 2004), 11–14. For Laskar Jihad's own account of its activities in Poso during these months, see Dewan Pimpinan Pusat Forum Komunikasi Ahlus Sunnah Wal Jamaah, "Kronologi Poso Membara (October 15–December 4, 2001)" (http://www.laskarjihad.or.id), December 5, 2001.

86. For such broad-brush estimates, see M. Hamdan Basyar and Dhurorudin Mashad, "Pendahuluan," in Basyar, *Konflik Poso,* 1–14.

87. Arianto Sangaji, "Pasukan Terlatih dan Perubahan Pola Kekerasan di Poso?" *Kompas,* October 17, 2003.

88. On the broad pattern of violence in 2002, see Adams et al., *Breakdown,* 34–38. On the events of August 2002, see, for example, "Warga Matako dan Malitu di Poso Mengungsi," *Republika,* August 10, 2002; "Deklarasi Malino Belum Efektif," *Kompas,* August 12, 2002; "Christian Delegates Shun Poso Peace Talks," *Jakarta Post,* August 14, 2002; "Five Killed in Fresh Violence in Poso," *Jakarta Post,* August 14, 2002; "Kapolri: Penyerang Dari Luar," *Tempo Interaktif,* August 14, 2002; "Poso Tense as Six Killed in Christian Village," *Jakarta Post,* August 14, 2002; "Situasi Poso Kian Mencekam," *Tempo Interaktif,* Agustus 14, 2002; and "Truk dan Bus Tak Berani Lewat," *Tempo Interaktif,* August 14, 2002.

89. "Kekerasan Tak Kunjung Padam," *Seputar Rakyat,* Desember 2003–Januari 2004, 3–5.

90. Eight predominantly Muslim coastal subdistricts (*kecamatan*) were hived off to become the new regency of Tojo Una-Una, leaving Poso with a population of 150,000 and reconfiguring its electoral districts to guarantee Christian dominance of its DPRD. See "Undang-Undang Republik Indonesia *Nomor* 32 Tahun 2003 tentang Pementukan Kabupaten Tojo Una-Una Di Provinsi Sulawesi Tengah," signed into law by the then president (and PDIP chairwoman) Megawati Soekarnoputri on 18 December 2003.

91. For reports of these attacks, see "Kelompok Bersenjata Serang Poso, 8 Tewas," *Kompas,* October 13, 2003; "Poso Calm as More Troops Arrive," *Jakarta Post,* October 14, 2003; "Polisi Masih Mengejar Pelaku," *Kompas,* October 14, 2003; and "Teror Masih Berlanjut di Poso; Lima Orang Ditangkap," *Kompas,* October 18, 2003.

92. See "Tension Engulfs Poso after Reverend Shot Dead," *Jakarta Post,* March 31, 2004; "Poso PAN chairman detained in arms case," *Jakarta Post,* April 7, 2004; and "Hunt on for Killer of Poso Village Chief," *Jakarta Post,* November 7, 2004. On the apparent victory of the PDIP-PDS coalition in Poso, see "Konflik Poso, Tak Kunjung Sudah," *Info Masyarakat,* November 18, 2004.

93. See, for example, the figures cited in Basyar and Mashad, "Pendahuluan," 1–14.

94. See, for example, Arianto Sangaji, "Memangkas Peredaran Senjata Api di Poso," *Seputar Rakyat,* December 2003–January 2004, 18–23.

95. On the avoidance of violent conflict elsewhere in Central Sulawesi, see Greg Acciaioli, "Grounds of Conflict, Idioms of Harmony: Custom, Religion, and Nationalism in Violence Avoidance at the Lindu Plain, Central Sulawesi," *Indonesia* 72 (October 2001), 81–114. On the possibility of violent interreligious conflict in South Sulawesi, moreover, see *Indonesia: Managing Decentralisation and Conflict in South Sulawesi* (Jakarta/Brussels: International Crisis Group, 18 July 2003); and such articles as "Sulawesi, Maluku Jilid II?" in the October 2000 issue of the Jakarta-based Islamic magazine *Suara Hidayatullah.*

96. Ananta, Arifin, and Suryadinata, *Indonesian Electoral Behaviour,* 53.

97. Even today, the coastal municipality of Ternate in Cavite province, just south of Manila Bay, bears witness to the extent of this influence.

98. Leonard Y. Andaya, *The World of Maluku: Eastern Indonesia in the Early Modern Period* (Honolulu: University of Hawai'i Press, 1993).

99. Richard Chauvel, *Nationalists, Soldiers, and Separatists: The Ambonese Islands from Colonialism to Revolt, 1880–1950* (Leiden: KITLV Press, 1990), 25–35.

100. Ibid., 52.

101. Ibid., 37–38.

102. James T. Collins, *Ambonese Malay and Creolization Theory* (Kuala Lumpur: Dewan Bahasa dan Pustaka Kementerian Pelajaran Malaysia, 1980), 13.

103. See Richard Chauvel, "Ambon's Other Half: Some Preliminary Observations on Ambonese Moslem Society and History," *Review of Indonesian and Malayan Affairs* 14, no. 1 (1980), 40–80.

104. Collins, *Ambonese Malay,* 11.

105. Christian Kiem, "Re-Islamization among Muslim Youth in Ternate Town, Eastern Indonesia," *Sojourn* 8, no. 1 (February 1993), 92–127.

106. Tamrin Amal Tomagola, "Ambon Terbakar," *Tempo,* February 1, 1999, 24–25; and Riwanto Tirtosudarmo, "The Impact of Migration in Eastern Indonesia," *Jakarta Post,* April 6, 1999.

107. Jacques Bertrand, "Legacies of the Authoritarian Past: Religious Violence in Indonesia's Moluccan Islands," *Pacific Affairs* 75, no. 1 (Spring 2002), 67.

108. S. Sinansari ecip, *Menyulut Ambon—Kronologi Merambatnya Berbagai Kerusuhan Lintas Wilayah di Indonesia* (Bandung: Mizan, November 1999), 68–70.

109. Bertrand, "Legacies of the Authoritarian Past," 69–71. See also John Pieris, *Tragedi Maluku: Sebuah Krisis Peradaban* (Jakarta: Yayasan Obor Indonesia, 2004), 222–230.

110. Dieter Bartels, "Guarding the Invisible Mountain: Intervillage Alliances, Religious Syncretism, and Ethnic Identity among Ambonese Christians and Moslems in the Moluccas" (Ph.D. diss., Cornell University, 1977).

111. Paschalis Maria Laksono, "Wuut Ainmehe Nifun, Manut Ainmehe Tilor (Eggs from One Fish and One Bird): A Study of the Maintenance of Social Boundaries in the Kei Islands" (Ph.D. diss., Cornell University, 1990), 123–124.

112. David Mearns, "Urban Kampongs in Ambon: Whose Domain? Whose Desa?" *Australian Journal of Anthropology* 10, no. 1 (April 1999), 15–33.

113. In this vein, see, in particular, Bartels, "Guarding the Invisible Mountain"; and Tri Ratnawati, "Interactions between Adat and Religious Institutions and the New Order State: A Case Study of Two Islamic and Christian Villages in Central Moluccas," *Masyarakat Indonesia* 29, no. 1 (2003), 1–22.

114. On Muslims and Protestants in North Maluku, for example, see Kiem, "Re-Islamization among Muslim Youth in Ternate" Nils Ole Bubandt, "Warriors of the Hornbili, Victims of the Mantis: History and Embodied Morality among the Buli of Central Halmahera" (Ph.D. thesis, Australian National University, 1995); Christopher R. Duncan, "Ethnic Identity, Christian Conversion, and Resettlement among the Forest Tobelo of Northeastern Halmahera, Indonesia" (Ph.D. diss., Yale University, 1998). On Catholics in Southeast Maluku, see Laksono, "Wuut Ainmehe Nifun," especially 87–166, 171–178.

115. See, for example, Franz von Benda-Beckmann and Tanja Taale, "Land, Trees, and Houses: Changing (Un)certainties in Property Relationships on Ambon," in David Mearns and Chris Healey, eds., *Remaking Maluku: Social Transformation in Eastern Indonesia* (Darwin: Northern Territory University Centre for Southeast Asian Studies, 1996), 39–63; and Mearns, "Urban Kampongs in Ambon, 15–33.

116. Gerry van Klinken, "Small Town Wars: Post-Authoritarian Communal Violence in Indonesia" (unpublished manuscript), 46. Many thanks to the author for making his important forthcoming book available and for granting me permission to quote this passage.

117. On the establishment of the GPM, see Chauvel, *Nationalists, Soldiers, and Separatists,* 156–160; Theodor Muller-Kruger, *Sejarah Gereja di Indonesia* (Jakarta: Badan Penerbitan Kristen, 1966), 83–97; and Th. van den End, *Ragi Carita: Sejarah Gereja di Indonesia* (Jakarta: BPK Gunung Mulia, 2001), 158–168.

118. Dieter Bartels, "Your God Is No Longer Mine: Moslem-Christian Fratricide in the Central Moluccas (Indonesia) after a Half-Millennium of Tolerant Co-Existence and Ethnic Unity" (unpublished paper, 2000), 8.

119. Karel Steenbrink, "Interpretations of Christian-Muslim Violence in the Moluccas," *Studies in Interreligious Dialogue* 11, no. 1 (2001), 87.

120. For a map of the U.S.-based evangelical New Tribes Mission stations in Maluku in the 1990s, for example, see Duncan, "Ethnic Identity, Christian Conversion, and Resettlement," 106.

121. Bartels, "Your God Is No Longer Mine," 9. See also Keebet von Benda-Beckmann, "The Practice of Care: Social Security in Moslem Ambonese Society," in Mearns and Healey, *Remaking Maluku,* 121–139.

122. Chauvel, "Ambon's Other Half," 79.

123. Bartels, "Guarding the Invisible Mountain," 326.

124. Collins, *Ambonese Malay,* 13.

125. See, for example, the account of embittered old men in a Muslim coastal village on the island of Seram, in Juliet Patricia Lee, "Out of Order: The Politics of Modernity in Indonesia" (Ph.D. diss., University of Virginia, 1999), 83–118.

126. On Ambon Plaza, see ibid., 207–259.

127. See "Jaringan Provokator Kerusuhan Ambon," *Tajuk,* April 1, 1999, 19–23.

128. "7 Gereja dan 11 Mobil Dibakar," *Detik,* November 23, 1998; "Mayat-mayat Jadi 14 Orang," *Detik,* November 23, 1998; "Preman-Warga Bentrok, 6 Tewas," *Jawa Pos,* November 23, 1998; "Bentrokan diKetapang, Jakbar, 7 Tewas," *Republika,* November 23, 1998; and "Kerusuhan di Jakarta Enam Orang Tewas," *Kompas,* November 23, 1998.

129. For a detailed account of the backdrop to and process of the rioting in Kupang, see Riza Sihbudi and Moch. Nurhasim, *Kerusuhan Sosial di Indonesia: Studi Kasus Kupang, Mataram, dan Sambas* (Jakarta: Grasindo, 2001), 42–100.

130. On this dimension of the local scene, see Gerry van Klinken, "The Maluku Wars: Bringing Society Back In," *Indonesia* 71 (April 2001), 1–26: "Jaringan Provokator," and "Opek Merebut Birokrasi, Coker Menghunus Parang," *Tempo,* March 15, 1999, 22–23.

131. Fighting between Protestant and Muslim youths in the Southeastern Maluku island district's capital town of Dobo (supplemented by forces drawn from nearby villages) on January 15–17, 1999, had left eight casualties (all but one of which were Muslim) and damage to dozens of homes and shops. But it remains unclear to what extent knowledge of these events was circulating—and contributing to interreligious tensions—in Ambon when violence began there a few days later.

132. Human Rights Watch, *Indonesia: The Violence in Ambon* (New York: Human Rights Watch, March 1999), 10–20.

133. For contrasting accounts of the violence, see Yayasan Sala Waku Maluku/Yayasan Lembaga Bantuan Hukum Indonesia, *Laporan Hasil Investigasi Kasus Kerusuhan di Maluku* (Ambon: Yayasan Sala Waku Maluku, 1999); Tim Penyusun al-Mukmin, *Tragedi Ambon* (Jakarta: Yayasan Al-Mukmin, 1999); and Sinansari, *Menyulut Ambon,* 96–126.

134. "Ambon Mencari Juru Damai," *Tempo,* March 8, 1999, 26.

135. For a detailed (if not disinterested) account of this process in one neighborhood in Ambon City, see Yayasan Sala Waku Maluku, *Laporan Hasil Investigasi,* 41–42.

136. Margaretha Margawati and Tony Aryanto, "Konflik Antaragama atau Politisasi Agama?" *Jurnal Antropologi Indonesia* 63 (2000), 124.

137. Even high-ranking security officials in Jakarta conceded the case. See "Batalyon Terakhir Tiba di Ambon: Suaidi: Kami Akan Tegas dan Netral," *Detik,* March 9, 1999; "Tiga LSM Bertemu Jenderal Wiranto: Diakui Ada Aparat Tak Netral," *Detik,* March 9, 1999; "Pangab Akui Aparat di Ambon tak Adil," *Republika,* March 10, 1999.

138. "Organic" referring to those stationed locally as part of the permanent territorial command structure. For a somewhat more conspiratorial view, see George Junus Aditjondro, "Guns, Pamphlets, and Handie-Talkies: How the Military Exploited Local Ethno-Religious Tensions in Maluku to Preserve Their Political and Economic Privileges," in Ingrid Wessel and Georgia Wimhofer, eds., *Violence in Indonesia* (Hamburg: Abera Verlag, 2001), 100–128.

139. See, for example, "Pemuda Islam Ancam Lakukan Jihad di Ambon," *Detik,* March 2, 1999; "Jihad untuk Ambon di UI Salemba," *Detik,* March 4, 1999; "Setelah Subuh Berdarah Menyuarakan Kemarahan Umat," *Tempo,* March 15, 1999; "Intervensi RMS-Amerika," *Obyektif,* March 18–24, 1999; "Ambon: The Land of Jihad?" and "Di Mana Batas Jihad?" *D & R,* March 22–27, 1999, 50–53, 56–57.

140. On the 1999 election results in Maluku, see Ananta, Arifin, and Suryadinata, *Indonesian Electoral Behaviour,* 362–363; and Sri Yanuarti, Yusuf, Josephine Maria, and Mardyanto Wahyu Triatmoko, *Konflik di Maluku Tengah: Penyebab, Karakteristik, dan Penyelesaian Jangka Panjang* (Jakarta: Lembaga Ilmu Pengetahuan Indonesia, 2003), 38.

141. On this point, see Laksono, "Wuut Ainmehe Nifun," 31–33.

142. The creation of the new province was allegedly designed to claim more seats and votes for Golkar and President Habibie in the October 1999 session to elect the new president.

143. See Patricia Spyer, "Fire without Smoke and Other Phantoms of Ambon's Violence: Media Effects, Agency, and the Work of Imagination," *Indonesia* 74 (October 2002), 21–36.

144. Phillip Winn, "Banda Burns," *Inside Indonesia* 61 (January–March 2000).

145. By the end of 2000, as many as 140,000 IDPs were estimated to be seeking refuge from the violence within the province of Maluku, with tens of additional thousands fleeing to safe havens elsewhere in Indonesia. Government of the Republic of Indonesia and International Agencies, *The Maluku Crisis: Report of The Joint Assessment Mission* (Jakarta: 6 February 2000), 7–8.

146. For accounts of violence in Ambon and elsewhere in Central Maluku in the latter half of 1999, see, for example, "Ambon Berdarah-Darah Lagi!" *Aliansi Keadilan,* July 28, 1999;

"Keadaan di Ambon Masih Mencekam," *Republika,* August 13, 1999; "Kerusuhan Ambon Masih Menyala," *Tempo,* August 8, 1999; "Sembilan Aparat Tertembak di Ambon," *Kompas,* November 29, 1999; "31 Tewas Dalam Kerusuhan di Seram Barat," *Kompas,* December 4, 1999; and "Pertikaian Maluku Terus Berlanjut," *Kompas,* December 6, 1999.

147. On the backdrop to the formation of the new district of Malifut, and on the subsequent pattern of violence in North Maluku in August-December 1999, see Tamrin Amal Tomagola, "Tragedi Maluku Utara," *Masyarakat Indonesia* 25, no. 2 (1999), 289–302; Chris Wilson, "The Ethnic Origins of Religious Conflict in North Maluku Province, Indonesia, 1999–2000," *Indonesia* 79 (April 2005), 69–91; and Christopher R. Duncan, "The Other Maluku: Chronologies of Conflict in North Maluku," *Indonesia* 80 (October 2005), 53–80. The paragraphs below draw heavily on these accounts.

148. On the Gereja Masehi Injili Halmahera (GMIH) and the New Tribes Mission in Tobelo, see Duncan, "Ethnic Identity, Christian Conversion, and Resettlement."

149. Tomagola, "Tragedi Maluku Utara," 291–292. See also Smith Alhadar, "The Forgotten War in North Maluku," *Inside Indonesia* 63 (July–September 2000).

150. On "cascading" violence, see Nils Ole Bubandt, "Malukan Apocalypse: Themes in the Dynamics of Violence in Eastern Indonesia," in Wessel and Wimhofer, *Violence in Indonesia,* 228–253.

151. A copy of the forged letter has been reproduced in Henry H. Sitohang, Hidayaturohman, M. Dian Nafi', Moehamad Ramdhan, and Sabar Subekti, *Menuju Rekonsiliasi di Halmahera* (Jakarta: Pusat Pemberdayaan untuk Rekonsiliasi dan Perdamaian, 2003), 175–178.

152. On the massacre in Tobelo and Galela, see "Kepolisian Benarkan 216 Transmigran Dibantai di Masjid Maluku Utara," *Republika,* January 17, 2000; "Perang Satu Keluarga Dua Agama," *Tempo,* January 23, 2000, 26–27; "Berlindung di Hutan, Kondisinya Memprihatinkan: Tak Diketahui, Nasib Ribuan Muslim Tobelo," *Pikiran Rakyat,* January 30, 2000.

153. "Suara Kecewa dari Maluku," *Tempo,* February 6, 2000, 23.

154. On these events, see "Kerusuhan Ambon: Api Masih Berkobar di Hari Suci," *Tempo,* January 9, 2000, 24–25.

155. On the events of December 29, 1999–January 5, 2000, in Masohi, see Majelis Ulama Indonesia Kabupaten Maluku Tengah, "Laporan Khusus Kerusuhan di Masohi dan sekitarnya," Masohi, January 7, 2000. The accusations contained in this report were faithfully reported in "Pertikaian Masih Terjadi di Maluku; Bupati, Dandim, dan Kapolres Diduga Terlibat Penyerangan," *Republika,* January 13, 2000.

156. Eggi Sudjana had been well known as an Islamic activist since the 1980s, when he led a splinter group of the modernist Muslim university students' association HMI, which refused to recognize Pancasila as its founding principles. See Achmad Fachruddin, *Jihad Sang Demonstran: Pergulatan Politik dan Ideologi Eggi Sudjana dari era Soeharto hingga era Gus Dur* (Jakarta: Raja Grafindo Persada, 2000).

157. On these events, see Sihbudi and Nurhasim, *Kerusuhan Sosial di Indonesia,* 106–122; and "Ketika 'Iblis' Berkuasa," *Tempo,* January 30, 2000, 26–28.

158. On this pattern, see *Indonesia: Overcoming Murder and Chaos in Maluku* (Jakarta/Brussels: International Crisis Group, 19 December 2000), 9.

159. For pessimistic early assessments of the imposition of civil emergency status on Maluku, see "Darurat Sipil Maluku, Lalu Apa?" *Tempo,* July 9, 2000, 20–23; "Meredam Maluku dengan Pasal Karet," *Tempo,* July 9, 2000, 24–25; and "Maluku Darurat, Maluku Kian Gawat," *Tempo,* July 16, 2000, 32–33.

160. *Indonesia: The Search for Peace in Maluku* (Jakarta/Brussels: International Crisis Group, 8 February 2002), 9–10.

161. See, for example, the illuminating religiously coded maps appended to Yanuarti et al., *Konflik di Maluku Tengah,* 151–153.

162. *Indonesia: The Search for Peace in Maluku,* 11–13.

163. "Dari Pertemuan 'Malino II': Dua Pihak Dambakan Penghentian Konflik," *Kompas,* February 12, 2002; "Pertemuan Dua Pihak Maluku: Disepakati untuk Mengakhiri Konflik," *Kompas,* February 13, 2002.

164. "Kristen dan Muslim di Ambon Berbaur Lagi," *Kompas,* March 2, 2002; "Pasar Kaget Ambon: Kawasan Damai Tanpa Rekayasa," *Kompas,* March 5, 2002.

165. "Warga Maluku Utara Sambut Baik Rencana Pencabutan Darsi," *Republika,* August 2, 2002.

166. "Panglima Laskar Jihad Ja'far Umar ditangkap," *Media Indonesia,* May 4, 2002.

167. See, for example, "Warga Kristen Kudamati serahkan senjata," *Republika,* June 30, 2002; and "Sweeping tetap dilaksanakan," *Jawa Pos,* July 2, 2002.

168. "Ambon Mencekam, 11 Orang Tewas," *Surabaya Post,* April 28, 2002; "Rusuh di Ambon, 12 Orang Tewas," *Suara Merdeka,* April 29, 2001.

169. "Jurus Baru Membabat Para Desertir," *Tempo,* June 10–16, 2002.

170. See, for example, "Upaya Perdamaian di Maluku Diwarnai Empat Ledakan di Ambon," *Kompas,* February 14, 2002; "Maluku Utara diguncang bom," *Jawa Pos,* July 12, 2002; and "Ambon Calm after Major Bomb Blast Injures 53," *Jakarta Post,* July 28, 2002.

171. On this upsurge of violence, see Muhammad Najib Azca, "Membaca Konflik (Baru) Ambon," *Koran Tempo,* May 9, 2004; and *Indonesia: Violence Erupts Again in Ambon* (Jakarta/Brussels: International Crisis Group, 17 May 2004).

172. Siegel, "Suharto, Witches," 36.

173. Ibid., 36–37.

174. See Pipit Rochijat, "Am I PKI or Non-PKI?" *Indonesia* 40 (October 1985), 37–52, translated by Benedict Anderson (who provides a brief but thoughtful afterword, 53–56).

175. For accounts of different faiths in different areas of Indonesia, see Hefner, "Islamizing Java?"; Peake, "Tradition, Christianity, and the State"; R. A. F. Paul Webb, "The Sickle and the Cross: Christians and Communists in Bali, Flores, Sumba, and Timor, 1965–67," *Journal of Southeast Asian Studies* 17, no. 1 (1986), 94–112; and Avery Willis Jr., *Indonesian Revival: Why Two Million Came to Christ* (South Pasadena, Calif.: William Carey Library, 1977).

176. See Patricia Spyer, "Serial Conversion/Conversion to Seriality: Religion, State, and Number in Aru, Eastern Indonesia," in Peter van der Veer, ed., *Conversion to Modernities: The Globalization of Christianity* (London: Routledge, 1996), 171–198, especially 171.

177. Ibid., 191. On the logics of seriality, see also Ian Hacking, *The Taming of Chance* (Cambridge: Cambridge University Press, 1990); and Benedict Anderson, "Nationalism, Identity, and the World-in-Motion: On The Logics of Seriality," in Pheng Cheah and Bruce Robbins, eds., *Cosmopolitics: Thinking and Feeling beyond the Nation* (Minneapolis: University of Minnesota Press, 1998), 117–133.

178. Ananta, Arifin, and Suryadinata, *Indonesian Electoral Behaviour,* 24, 53. Central Kalimantan and West Kalimantan, the sites of violent "ethnic cleansing" of immigrant Madurese communities in 1997, 1999, and 2001, were 74 percent and 58 percent Muslim, respectively. The other provinces within this band of provinces were Jakarta (DKI), East Kalimantan, and North Sumatra, all of which merit further treatment as counterfactual cases of nonoccurrence of communal violence during this period.

179. Ibid., 345–346.

180. P. M. Laksono, "We Are All One: How Custom Overcame Religious Rivalry in Southeast Maluku," *Inside Indonesia,* April—June 2002. This argument was articulated earlier and elaborated in greater detail in Laksono, "Wuut Ainmehe Nifun," 39, 75–84.

181. Aragon, "Communal Violence in Poso," 47.

182. Gerry van Klinken, "What Caused the Ambon Violence?" *Inside Indonesia* 60 (October–December 1999).

183. Siegel, "Suharto, Witches," 52.

184. On the alleged prominence of recent Christian converts from among the upland On-dae and the forest-based Tobelo in the anti-Muslim pogroms in Poso and North Maluku, re-spectively, see Aditjondro, "Kerusuhan Poso dan Morowali," 4; and Christopher R. Duncan, "Savage Imagery: (Mis)representations of the Forest Tobelo of Indonesia," *Asia Pacific Journal of Anthropology* 2, no. 1 (May 2001), 45–62. Duncan casts doubt on reports blaming the Forest Tobelo's supposed primitive savagery for the pogroms of December 1999–January 2000 in North Halmahera. In his earlier work, however, he also noted: "As their attitudes to-wards Christianity have changed since conversion, their attitudes about Islam have solidified. Instead of seeing Islam in terms of pork taboos and funny prayer positions, they now view it as the wrong choice made by misguided people who have not been informed about Jesus Christ" (Duncan, "Ethnic Identity, Christian Conversion and Resettlement," 170).

185. Allen Feldman, *Formations of Violence: The Narrative of the Body and Political Terror in Northern Ireland* (Chicago: University of Chicago Press, 1991), 17–45, at 35.

186. On the shift from "hardmen" to "gunmen" in Belfast, for example, see ibid., 46–84.

Chapter 7. Jihad and Religious Violence

1. On tensions and incidents of small-scale violence in the West Sulawesi regency of Ma-masa, however, see *Decentralisation and Conflict in Indonesia: The Mamasa Case* (Jakarta/Brussels: International Crisis Group, May 2005).

2. The explosion of two bombs in the Protestant town of Tentena in Poso regency killed at least twenty people and wounded more than fifty others in late May 2005, on the eve of the campaign for a new *bupati* under the new system of direct elections of local executives. On the bombings, see "Bom Dahsyat Guncang Tentena, 20 Orang Tewas, 53 Terluka," *Kompas*, May 29, 2005; "Dikhawatirkan Poso Makin Rawan Jelang Pilkada," *Kompas*, May 30, 2005; "Ka-sus Bom Poso: Dua Orang Terus Diburu, 13 Sudah Ditangkap," *Kompas*, June 2, 2005.

3. For a sympathetic account of Laskar Jihad's role in Maluku, see Mohammad Shoelhi, *Laskar Jihad: Kambing Hitam Konflik Maluku* (Jakarta: Puzam, 2002).

4. *Indonesia: Overcoming Murder and Chaos in Maluku* (Jakarta/Brussels: International Crisis Group, December 2000), 8–14.

5. *Indonesia: The Search for Peace in Maluku* (Jakarta/Brussels: International Crisis Group, February 2002), 13–14.

6. See Dewan Pimpinan Pusat Forum Komunikasi Ahlus Sunnah wal Jamaah, "Kro-nologi Poso Membara (15 Oktober–4 Desember 2001)," December 5, 2001 (http://www.laskarjihad.or.id); *Breakdown: Four Years of Communal Violence in Central Sulawesi* (New York: Human Rights Watch, December 2002); and *Indonesia Backgrounder: Jihad in Central Sulawesi* (Jakarta/Brussels: International Crisis Group, February 2004).

7. On this series of events in Ngawi, see "Ngawi Mencekam, Kader PDI-P Diculik," *Kompas*, December 2, 2001; "Ngawi Kondusif, Polisi Tahan 80 Orang Lagi," *Kompas*, De-cember 3, 2001; and Ustadz Ja'far Umar Thalib, "Pernyataan Pers: Kasus Ngawi, Jawa Timur: Umat Islam Perang Melawan Para Preman," December 3, 2001 http://www.laskarjihad.or.id). See also the series of articles in the Surabaya-based newspaper *Jawa Pos* on these events.

8. "Setelah Bang Haji Dikecewakan Mega," *Tempo*, May 19, 2002, 24–26; "Jaringan Luas Sang Ustad," *Tempo*, May 19, 2002, 28–29; "Repotnya Menarik Laskar Kopiah Putih," *Tempo*, May 19, 2002, 30–31.

9. For a fine early overview of the rise and fall of Laskar Jihad, see Michael Davis, "Laskar Jihad and the Political Position of Conservative Islam in Indonesia," *Contemporary Southeast Asia* 24, no. 1 (April 2002), 12–32. For the subsequent definitive account of Laskar

Jihad, see Noorhaidi Hasan, "Laskar Jihad: Islam, Militancy and the Quest for Identity in Post–New Order Indonesia" (Ph.D. thesis, Utrecht University, 2005).

10. For a useful chronology of bomb attacks in Indonesia, see "Teror Bom di Indonesia (Beberapa di Luar Negeri) dari Waktu ke Waktu," *Tempo Interaktif,* April 17, 2004; and "193 Ledakan Bom Selama Tahun 1999–2003," *Suara Merdeka,* September 10, 2004.

11. See the articles published under the rubric "Siapa Sebenarnya Pembom Istiqlal?" *Tempo,* May 3, 1999, 22–29.

12. See the series of articles published in the investigative report "Cerita dari Mosaik Bom Natal," *Tempo,* February 25, 2001, 60–80.

13. See Hermawan Sulistyo, ed., *Bom Bali: Buku Putih tidak resmi Investigasi Teror Bom Bali* (Jakarta: Pensil 324, 2002); and "Setahun Bom Bali," *Tempo,* October 19, 2003, 28–83.

14. "Ledakan di Hotel JW Marriott Mirip Ledakan Bom Bali," *Kompas,* August 6, 2003; "Terrorists Strike Again," *Jakarta Post,* August 6, 2003; "Bom Diledakkan Melalui Telepon Seluler," *Kompas,* August 7, 2003.

15. "Satu Jejak Bom Kuningan," *Tempo,* October 3, 2004.

16. See "Dari Martapura Untuk Bali," *Tempo,* October 9, 2005, 26–27; and the series of related articles headed "Bali Kembali Dilanda Teror," *Tempo,* October 16, 2005, 26–42.

17. Noorhaidi Hasan, "Faith and Politics: The Rise of the Laskar Jihad in the Era of Transition in Indonesia," *Indonesia* 73 (April 2002), 145–169.

18. See, for example, "Al-Qaidah 'made in Madiun'?" *Tempo,* February 3, 2002, 20–22; "Al Islam, Ba'asyir, Zakaria, dan Amrozi," *Kompas,* November 8, 2002; "Muhammad Zakaria 'Diinvestigasi Tajam,'" *Kompas,* November 10, 2002; "Dari Kiai Sinori hingga Amrozi," *Kompas,* November 13, 2002; Eriyanto dan Agus Sudibyo, "Amrozi, Terorisme, dan Desa Tenggulun," *Pantau,* January 2003, 12–20; and "Asmar Graduated from Ngruki School," *Jakarta Post,* August 11, 2003. For broad overviews, see Es. Soepriyadi, *Ngruki dan Jaringan Terorisme: Melacak Jejak Abu Bakar Ba'asyir dan Jaringannya dari Ngruki sampai Bom Bali* (Jakarta: Al-Mawardi Prima, 2003).

19. For materials from the founding congress of MMI, see Irfan Suryahardi Awwas, ed., *Risalah Kongres Mujahidin I dan Penegakan Syari'ah Islam* (Yogyakarta: Wihdah Press, 2001).

20. See, for example, *White Paper: The Jemaah Islamiyah Arrests and the Threat of Terrorism* (Singapore: Ministry of Home Affairs, 2003).

21. For sympathetic treatments of Ba'asyir's personal history and his persecution at the hands of the Indonesian authorities (and their American and Australian sponsors), see Fauzan Al-Anshari, *Saya Teroris? (Sebuah "Pledoi")* (Jakarta: Penerbit Republika, 2002); Irfan Suryahardi Awwas, *Dakwah dan Jihad Abu Bakar Ba'asyir* (Yogyakarta: Wihdah Press, 2003); Irfan Suryahardi Awwas, *Pengadilan Teroris: Klarifikasi Fakta dan Dusta yang Terungkap di Persidangan* (Yogyakarta: Wihdah Press, 2004).

22. See, for example, Stephen C. Headley, *Durga's Mosque: Cosmology, Conversion, and Community in Central Javanese Islam* (Singapore: Institute of Southeast Asian Studies, 2004); and Mark R. Woodward, *Islam in Java: Normative Piety and Mysticism in the Sultanate of Yogyakarta* (Tempe: University of Arizona Press, 1989).

23. On Solo, for example, see Suzanne April Brenner, *The Domestication of Desire: Women, Wealth, and Modernity in Java* (Princeton: Princeton University Press, 1998); John Pemberton, *On the Subject of "Java"* (Ithaca: Cornell University Press, 1994); James T. Siegel, *Solo in the New Order: Language and Hierarchy in an Indonesian City* (Princeton: Princeton University Press, 1986).

24. On the 1912 founding of Muhammadiyah in Yogyakarta and Sarekat Islam in Solo, respectively, see Mitsuo Nakamura, "The Crescent Arises over the Banyan Tree: A Study of

Reformist Muslim Movement in a Central Javanese Town" (Ph.D. diss., Cornell University, 1975); and Takashi Shiraishi, *An Age in Motion: Popular Radicalism in Java, 1912–1926* (Ithaca: Cornell University Press, 1990).

25. Hasan, "Laskar Jihad," 161–193.

26. See Farha Abdul Kadir Assegaff, "Peran Perempuan Islam (Penelitian di Pondok Pesantren Al Mukmin, Sukoharjo, Jawa Tengah" (BA Honors Thesis, Sociological Studies Program, Faculty of Social Sciences, Gadjah Mada University, 1995), 60–70; and Zuly Qodir, *Ada Apa Dengan Pondok Pesantren Ngruki* (Bantul: Pondok Edukasi, 2003).

27. For an excellent broad overview, see Martin van Bruinessen, "Genealogies of Islamic Radicalism in Post-Suharto Indonesia," *South East Asia Research* 10, no. 2 (March 2003), 117–154.

28. On Persis and Al-Irsyad, see Howard M. Federspiel, *Islam and Ideology in the Emerging Indonesian State: The Persatuan Islam (PERSIS), 1923 to 1957* (Leiden: Brill, 2001); Natalie Mobini-Kesheh, *The Hadrami Awakening: Community and Identity in the Netherlands East Indies, 1900–1942* (Ithaca: Cornell University Southeast Asia Program, 1999), especially 71–90.

29. Federspiel, *Islam and Ideology*, 88–89.

30. Mobini-Kesheh, *Hadrami Awakening*, 83.

31. Asna Husin, "Philosophical and Sociological Aspects of Da'wah: A Study of Dewan Dakwah Islamiyah Indonesia" (Ph.D. diss., Columbia University, 1998), 147–176; "Bermula dari Masjid Salman," *Tempo*, May 13, 1989, 79–81; Abdul Aziz, Imam Tholkhah, and Soetarman, eds., *Gerakan Islam Kontemporer di Indonesia* (Jakarta: Pustaka Firdaus, 1989).

32. On the prominence of wealthy Hadhramis in Jakarta's elite circles, see Mona Abaza, "Markets of Faith: Jakartan Da'wa and Islamic Gentrification," *Archipel* 67 (2004), 173–202; and "The Past Catches Up," *Far Eastern Economic Review*, November 14, 2002.

33. See, for example, Martin van Bruinessen, *Rakyat Kecil, Islam dan Politik* (Yogyakarta: Bentang, 1998), 47–107, on a community in Bandung mostly populated by migrants from areas of West Java known for their involvement in the Darul Islam rebellion.

34. On *Media Dakwah*, see R. William Liddle, "Media Dakwah Scripturalism: One Form of Islamic Political Thought and Action in New Order Indonesia," in Mark R. Woodward, ed., *Toward a New Paradigm: Recent Developments in Indonesian Islamic Thought* (Tempe: Arizona State University Program for Southeast Asian Studies, 1996), 323–355; and Robert W. Hefner, "Print Islam: Mass Media and Ideological Rivalries among Indonesian Muslims," *Indonesia* 64 (October 1997), 77–103.

35. *Indonesia Backgrounder: Jihad in Central Sulawesi* (Jakarta/Brussels: International Crisis Group, February 2004).

36. On Sayyaf, see Barnett R. Rubin, *The Fragmentation of Afghanistan: State Formation and Collapse in the International System* (New Haven: Yale University, 2002), 83, 220–221, 197–199; and Olivier Roy, *Islam and Resistance in Afghanistan* (Cambridge: Cambridge University Press, 1990), 135–136.

37. On the relationship between Sayyaf and bin Laden, see, for example, Peter L. Bergen, *Holy War, Inc.: Inside the Secret World of Osama bin Laden* (New York: Free Press, 2001), 50–60.

38. For example, Imam Samudra, a key figure in the Christmas Eve 2000 church bombings and the October 2002 Bali bombing, grew up in a strict Islamic milieu in Banten, West Java; he was drawn into the orbit of a local Persatuan Islam school and recruited to join a *jihadi* training camp in Afghanistan while attending a sermon at a Jakarta mosque closely affiliated with DDII. See Imam Samudra, *Aku Melawan Teroris!* (Solo: Jazera, 2004), 21–43. On his role in the bombings, see "Otak Bom Bali Ditangkap," *Jawa Pos*, November 22, 2002; "Imam Samudra Akui Terlibat Peledakan di Batam," *Kompas*, November 28, 2002; and "Imam Akui Terlibat Peledakan Atrium Senen," *Kompas*, December 2, 2002.

39. See, for example, Divisi Penerangan DPP FKAWJ, "Laskar Jihad Menjawab: Manhaj Usamah bin Laden," found under the rubric "Laskar Jihad Tidak Terkait Usamah bin Laden—Oktober 2, 2001—Q&A," at http://www.laskarjihad.or.id/service/qa/qa01okt/qa011002.htm. Here bin Laden was labeled with the Arabic epithet of khawarij for his—illegitimate—call for rebellion against the Saudi Arabian government, whose Muslim leadership and implementation of Islamic law defined it as a legitimate authority. For a broader analysis of Ja'far Umar Thalib's public pronouncements on bin Laden and the use of the term *Khawarij*, see Muhammad Sirozi, "The Intellectual Roots of Islamic Radicalism in Indonesia: Ja'far Umar Thalib of Laskar Jihad (Jihad Fighters) and His Educational Background," *The Muslim World* 95 (January 2005), 81–120, especially 87–88.

40. See, for example, *Al-Qaeda in Southeast Asia: The Case of the "Ngruki Network" in Indonesia* (Jakarta/Brussels: International Crisis Group, August 2002), 5–6. On the same point but with reference to Al-Qaeda, see Jason Burke, *Al-Qaeda: The True Story of Radical Islam* (London: Penguin Books, 2003), especially 1–21.

41. See *Recycling Militants in Indonesia: Darul Islam and the Australian Embassy Bombing* (Jakarta/Brussels: International Crisis Group, February 2005). On Abdul Wahid Kadungga, son-in-law of Kahar Muzakkar, the leader of the Darul Islam–affiliated rebellion in South Sulawesi in the 1950s, see "Bom Bali: Penghubung atau Juru Dakwah?" *Tempo*, January 12, 2002; and "Abdul Wahid Kadungga: Aktivis Internasional," *Suara Hidayatullah*, October 2000.

42. *Indonesia Backgrounder: How the Jemaah Islamiyah Terrorist Network Operates* (Jakarta/Brussels: International Crisis Group, December 2002), i.

43. On the experiences of alleged Jemaah Islamiyah activists in training camps in Afghanistan and the southern Philippines, see *Jemaah Islamiyah in South East Asia: Damaged but Still Dangerous* (Jakarta/Brussels: International Crisis Group, August 2003), 2–18; and Nasir Abas, *Membongkar Jamaah Islamiyah: Pengakuan Mantan Anggota JI* (Jakarta: Grafindo, 2005), 19–167.

44. See, for example, "Investigasi: Seorang Imam dalam Dua Wajah," *Tempo*, July 14, 2000, 60–78; Al Chaidar, *Sepak Terjang KW9 Abu Toto Menyelewengkan NKA-NII pasca S.M. Kartosoewirjo* (Jakarta: Madani Press, 2000); "Al Chaidar, DI/NII, dan Teror Bom," *Detikcom*, November 23, 2001; Umar Abduh, *Pesantren Al-Zaytun Sesat? Investigasi Mega Proyek Dalam Gerakan NII* (Jakarta: Darul Falah, 2001); Umar Abduh, *Membongkar Gerakan Sesat NII di Balik Pesantren Mewah Al-Zaytun* (Jakarta: Lembaga Penelitian dan Pengkajian Islam, 2001).

45. See, for example, David Jenkins, *Suharto and His Generals: Indonesian Military Politics, 1975–1983* (Ithaca: Cornell Modern Indonesia Project, 1984), 53–56; Heru Cahyono, *Peranan Ulama Dalam Golkar, 1971–1980: Dari Pemilu sampai Malari* (Jakarta: Pustaka Sinar Harapan, 1992), 70–93; Heru Cahyono, *Pangkopkamtib Jenderal Soemitro dan Peristiwa, 15 Januari '74* (Jakarta: Pustaka Sinar Harapan, 1998), 70–73, 92–94, 182–204; and Ken Conboy, *Intel: Inside Indonesia's Intelligence Service* (Jakarta: Equinox, 2004), 140–142.

46. Assegaff, "Peran Perempuan Islam," 50–51.

47. See Al Chaidar, *Lampung Bersimbah Darah: Menelusuri Kejahatan "Negara Intelijen" Orde Baru Dalam Peristiwa Jama'ah Warsidi* (Jakarta: Madani Press, 2000); and Abdul Syukur, *Gerakan Usroh Di Indonesia: Peristiwa Lampung 1989* (Yogyakarta: Ombak, 2003).

48. See, for example, Irfan S. Awwas, *Trauma Lampung Berdarah: Di Balik Manuver Hendro Priyono* (Yogyakarta: Wihdah Press, 2000).

49. See, for example, "Nur Dituding, Hidayat Mengelak," *Tempo*, February 25, 2001, 68; "Bom di Jalur Kontak GAM-TNI," *Tempo*, February 25, 2001, 71–72; "Tamu Misterius Biara Fransiskan," *Tempo*, February 25, 2001, 76; "'Nyanyian' Pengebom Medan," *Tempo*, February 25, 2001, 78–79; "Kol. Inf. Dasiri Musnar: 'Buktikan Saya Terlibat,'" *Tempo*, February 25, 2001, 80; "Telepon Sjafrie di Saku Sang 'Cuak,'" *Tempo*, January 5, 2002.

50. *Indonesia Backgrounder: Why Salafism and Terrorism Mostly Don't Mix* (Southeast Asia/Brussels: International Crisis Group, September 2004).

51. Of the 153 members of the PDIP elected to the DPR in 1999, only ninety-six (63 percent) were registered as Muslims, with at least thirty-six Protestants (23 percent), twelve Catholics, and seven Hindus among the remaining MPs. See *Wajah Dewan Perwakilan Rakyat Republik Indonesia Pemilihan Umum 1999* (Jakarta: Kompas, 2000), 3–155.

52. For a broad overview of the first year of the Wahid administration, see Kees van Dijk, *A Country in Despair: Indonesia between 1997 and 2000* (Leiden: KITLV Press, 2001), 431–534.

53. See, for example, comments on Wahid by the chairman of Persatuan Islam at the time in "KH Shiddiq Amien, Ketua Umum Persis: Kemusyrikan Dibiarkan, Syariat Malah Ditolak," *Suara Hidayatullah*, Oktober 2000.

54. For a recent overview of some of these trends, see Julia Day Howell, "Muslims, the New Age, and Marginal Religions in Indonesia: Changing Meanings of Religious Pluralism," *Social Compass* 52, no. 4 (December 2005), 473–493.

55. See, for example, the series of articles and photographs depicting the January 2000 massacre of Muslim villagers in Galela, North Maluku, under the cover story rubric "Detik-detik Terakhir Muslim Galela," Sabili, March 8, 2000, 20–44, esp. 25 for detailed tabulation of Muslim casualties (said to number 3,567) and IDPs (said to number 91,509) in North Maluku.

56. On the broader pattern of co-optation and accommodation of political parties in post-Suharto Indonesia, see Dan Slater, "Indonesia's Accountability Trap: Party Cartels and Presidential Power after Democratic Transition," *Indonesia* 78 (October 2004), 61–92.

57. For a broad overview of the full spectrum of Islamic political parties in Indonesia since 2001, see Anies Rasyid Baswedan, "Political Islam in Indonesia: Present and Future Trajectory," *Asian Survey* 44, no. 5 (2004), 269–290.

58. On the background and aftermath of this episode, see *ManilaGate: Kontroversi Penangkapan Tamsil Linrung* (Jakarta: Merah Putih, 2003). See also "Tamsil Linrung: 'Ini Perbuatan Politisi dan Intel Busuk,'" *Tempo*, April 7, 2002, 36; "Siapa Tersengat Rekayasa Manila?" *Tempo*, April 14, 2002, 24–25; and "Target: Agus Dwikarna," *Tempo*, April 14, 2002, 27. On Agus Dwikarna, see Dias Pradadimara and Burhaman Junedding, "Who Is Calling for Islamic Law? The Struggle to Implement Islamic Law in South Sulawesi," *Inside Indonesia* (October–December 2002). For early snapshots of KOMPAK's activities, see the four-page supplement titled "KOMPAK: Komite Penanggulangan Krisis" in *Media Dakwah*, September 1998.

59. On the arrest of Fathur Rahman Al-Ghozi, a Pesantren Ngruki graduate and son of a PBB regional assemblyman (and former accused Komando Jihad member), in Manila, for example, see "Al-Qaidah 'made in Madiun'?" *Tempo*, February 3, 2002, 20–22; "Muhammad Zainuri, Ayah Fathur: 'Anak Saya Lahir di Indonesia,'" *Tempo*, February 3, 2002, 23; "Catatan Perjalanan Seorang 'Teroris,'" *Tempo*, February 24, 2002, 23. On the arrest in Malaysia and Singapore of activists also linked to Ba'asyir, see "Tim Jibril, Al-Qaidah Dari Solo?" *Tempo*, February 24, 2002, 20–22; "Setelah Intel Melayu Bersatu," *Tempo*, February 24, 2002, 24–26; "Sapu Bersih Gaya Dr. M," *Tempo*, February 24, 2002, 30.

60. "Of Missiles and Terrorism," *Far Eastern Economic Review*, November 9, 2001, 22–23. See also "Wawancara Paul Wolfowitz: 'Aksi Teror di Indonesia Disusupi Al-Qaidah,'" *Tempo Interaktif*, November 19, 2001.

61. See Pinardi, *Sekarmadji Maridjan Kartosuwirjo* (Jakarta: Aryaguna, 1964); Hiroko Horikoshi, "The Dar Ul-Islam Movement in West Java (1948–62): An Experience in the Historical Process," *Indonesia* 20 (October 1975), 59–86; C. van Dijk, *Rebellion under the Banner of Islam: The Darul Islam in Indonesia* (The Hague: Martinus Nijhoff, 1981); S. Soebardi, "Kartosuwiryo and the Darul Islam Rebellion in Indonesia," *Journal of Southeast Asian Studies*, March 1983, 109–133.

62. See *Indonesia: Muslims On Trial* (London: Tapol, 1987), especially 71–87.

63. See John T. Sidel, "Other Schools, Other Pilgrimages, Other Dreams: The Making and Unmaking of 'Jihad' in Southeast Asia," in James Siegel and Audrey Kahin, eds., *Southeast Asia over Three Generations: Essays Presented to Benedict R. O'G. Anderson* (Ithaca: Cornell University Southeast Asia Program, 2003), 347–382.

64. See Aurel Croissant, "Unrest in South Thailand: Contours, Causes, and Consequences since 2001," *Contemporary Southeast Asia*, 27, no. 1 (April 2005), 21–43, especially 1–35; and *Southern Thailand: Insurgency, Not Jihad* (Singapore/Brussels: International Crisis Group, May 2005), especially 33–36.

65. See Farish Noor, "Blood, Sweat, and Jihad: The Radicalization of the Political Discourse of the Pan-Malaysian Islamic Party (PAS) from 1982 Onwards," *Contemporary Southeast Asia* 25, no. 2 (August 2003), 200–232; and Zabidi Mohamed, *Rahsia dalam Rahsia Maunah: Kebenaran yang Sebenar* (Kuala Lumpur: Zabidi, 2003).

66. Olivier Roy, *The Failure of Political Islam* (Cambridge: Harvard University Press, 1994).

67. Mohammed M. Hafez, *Why Muslims Rebel: Repression and Resistance in the Islamic World* (Boulder, Colo.: Lynne Rienner, 2003).

68. Roy, *Failure of Political Islam*, ix.

69. See, in particular, "Impasses of Islamist Ideology," in ibid., 60–74.

70. For this argument, see Gilles Kepel, *Jihad: The Trail of Political Islam* (London: I. B. Tauris, 2002).

71. See Gilles Kepel et Yann Richard, eds., *Intellectuels et Militants de l'Islam Contemporain* (Paris: Editions du Seuil, 1990); Dale Eickelman and James Piscatori, *Muslim Politics* (Princeton: Princeton University Press, 1996); Gregory Starrett, *Putting Islam to Work: Education, Politics, and Religious Transformation in Egypt* (Berkeley: University of California Press, 1998); and Dale Eickelman and Jon Anderson, eds., *New Media in the Muslim World: The Emerging Public Sphere* (Bloomington: Indiana University Press, 2003).

72. For arguments along these lines, see Olivier Roy, *Globalised Islam: The Search for a New Ummah* (London: Hurst, 2004).

73. For the best available account of the emergence and transformation of Al-Qaeda along these lines, see Fawaz A. Gerges, *The Far Enemy: Why Jihad Went Global* (Cambridge: Cambridge University Press, 2005).

74. See, in particular, Carrie Rosefsky Wickham, *Mobilizing Islam: Religion, Activism, and Political Change in Egypt* (New York: Columbia University Press, 2002); Quintan Wiktorowicz, ed., *Islamic Activism: A Social Movement Theory Approach* (Bloomington: Indiana University Press, 2004); Quintan Wiktorowicz, "Framing Jihad: Intramovement Framing Contests and al-Qaeda's Struggle for Sacred Authority," *International Review of Social History* 49, suppl. (2004), 159–177; and David Leheny, "Terrorism, Social Movements, and International Security: How Al Qaeda Affects Southeast Asia," *Japanese Journal of Political Science* 6, no. 1 (2005), 87–109.

75. On the broadening of social movements theory to encompass the wider realm of "contentious politics," see Doug McAdam, Sidney Tarrow, and Charles Tilly, *Dynamics of Contention* (Cambridge: Cambridge University Press, 2001).

76. Sidney Tarrow, *Power in Movement: Social Movements and Contentious Politics* (Cambridge: Cambridge University Press, 1998).

77. On the dangers of conflating interreligious violence with interreligious intolerance, see David Nirenberg, *Communities of Violence: Persecution of Minorities in the Middle Ages* (Princeton: Princeton University Press, 1996).

Glossary

Indonesian Terms

abangan	impious, syncretic, or Javanist in Islamic practices and beliefs
adat	custom, customary law
agama	state-recognized religion(s) .
aksi sepihak	unilateral land seizures
aliran	stream, current
bahaya laten komunis	"latent communist threat"
bai'at	oath of loyalty (Arabic: *bai'a*)
belum beragama	not yet having a religion
bupati	regent
camat	subdistrict heads
da'i	Islamic missionary, preacher, propagator of the faith
dangdut	popular music
dakwah	Islamic missionary activity, proselytization (Arabic: *da'wa*)
desa	village
dukun santet	sorcerer, witch, practitioner of black magic
Golongan Karya	Functional Groups (political party)
gotong-royong	community practices of reciprocity and mutual aid
hansip	police-trained civilian neighborhood security guards

263

jaringan	network
jemaah	religious congregation or 'flock' (Arabic: *jama'ah*)
jihad nasional	national jihad
jilbab	head scarf worn by Muslim women
kabupaten	regency
kampung	neighborhood (also *kampong*)
kecamatan	district
kelas bawah	underclass
kepala desa	village headman
kerusuhan	disturbance, riot
kesenjangan sosial	"social gap"
khotbah	Muslim Friday sermon (Arabic: *kutba*)
klenteng	Chinese temple (also *kelenteng*)
konglomerat	business mogul or tycoon
kongsi	mutual-help organization
konvoi	election campaign motorcade
kotamadya	cities
kyai	traditional Islamic teacher, especially on Java (also *kiyayi*)
langgar	Islamic prayer house
madrasah	modernist Islamic school
main hakim sendiri	"taking the law into one's hands," mob justice, lynching
masjid	mosque
massa	mob, crowd
modin	village-level Muslim religious leaders
muballigh	Islamic preacher
musholla	Islamic prayer house
musyawarah	rule by consensus
mutasi	rotations within the military command structure
oknum	"rogue element"
pasar murah	distribution centers for "nine basic goods"
pasisir	coastal area
pela	inter-village alliance (on Ambon)
pembangunan	"development"
pemekaran	redistricting, creation of new districts or regencies

pemuda	youth
pengajian	Islamic study class
penyambung lidah rakyat	"extension of the tongue of the people"
peranakan	native-born (but of at least partial immigrant ancestry)
pergerakan	social movement
pesantren	traditional Islamic boarding school, especially on Java
pilkades	elections for village headmen
PorosTengah	"Central Axis" of Islamic parties
posko	local command/communications post
preman	gangster, thug
pribumi	"indigenous"
priyayi	Javanese aristocracy
propinsi	provinces
provokator	agent provocateur or instigator
putra	son
putri	daughter
Rakyat	The People
ronda	neighborhood watch
santri	pupil at Islamic boarding school; devout Muslim
sekwilda	regional secretary
siskamling	"security environment system"
slametan	communal feasting rituals
solat ied	annual mass prayer service held the first morning after fast
suksesi	succession
surat kaleng	anonymous letters
tabligh akbar	Islamic public sermon or rally
tanah bengkok	communal lands awarded to village officials
tarekat	Sufi brotherhood (Arabic: *tariqa*)
totok	foreign-born, or of pure immigrant ancestry
ulama	Islamic scholar (Arabic: *'alim;* pl. *'ulama*)
Ummat	the Islamic community (Arabic: *'ummah*)

ustadz	junior instructor at traditional Islamic school
vihara	Buddhist temple
walikota	mayor
wong cilik	"little people"
wong desa	"villagers"

Indonesian Initialisms and Abbreviated Forms

BAKIN	National Intelligence Coordinating Agency
BIN	National Intelligence Agency
Brimob	Riot Police Brigade
CIDES	Center for Information and Development Studies
CSIS	Center for Strategic and International Studies
DDII	Indonesian Islamic Propagation Council
DPR	People's Representative Assembly
DPRD	Regional People's Representative Assembly
FKAWJ	Communications Forum for the Sunni Faithful
FPI	Front for the Defenders of Islam
Furkon	Forum of Muslim Believers for Justice and the Constitution
GKST	Central Sulawesi Protestant Church
GMIH	Halmahera Evangelical Church
GPM	Maluku Protestant Church
HMI	Islamic Students' Association
IAIN	State Institute for the Study of Islam
ICMI	All-Indonesian Association of Islamic Intellectuals
IDP	internally displaced persons
ISAI	Institut Studi Arus Informasi
KISDI	Indonesian Committee for World Muslim Solidarity
KOPASSUS	Special Forces Command
KOPKAMTIB	Command for the Restoration of Security and Order

KOSTRAD	Army Strategic Reserve Command
KTP	Kartu Tanda Pengenalan, or national identity cards
MMI	Council of Indonesian Mujahidin
MPR	People's Consultative Assembly
MUI	Council of Indonesian Islamic Scholars
NU	Nahdlatul Ulama
Pam Swakarsa	Voluntary Security Units
PAN	National Mandate Party
PBB	Crescent Star Party
PDI	Indonesian Democratic Party
PDIP	Indonesian Democratic Party of Struggle
PDS	Partai Damai Sejahtera, or Prosperous Peace Party
Persis	(Persatuan Islam) Union of Islam
PK	Justice Party
PKB	National Awakening Party
PKI	Indonesian Communist Party
PKS	Justice and Prosperity Party
PMII	Indonesian Islamic Students' Movement
PNI	Indonesian Nationalist Party
PPP	United Development Party
PRD	Partai Rakyat Demokrasi or People's Democratic Party
PSI	Indonesian Socialist Party
RMS	Republik Maluku Selatan, or Republic of South Maluku
SBSI	Indonesian Prosperous Workers' Union
THHK	Tiong Hoa Hwee Koan
TNI	Indonesian Armed Forces
YLBHI	Yayasan Lembaga Bantuan Hukum Indonesia, or Indonesian Legal Aid Society

Index